Caste and Class in a Southern Town

John Dollard was born in Wisconsin in 1900. He received his A.B. from the University of Wisconsin in 1922, and his A.M. (1930) and Ph.D. (1931) from the University of Chicago. He is now Professor of Psychology at Yale University, where he did research work from 1932 to 1952 in the Institute of Human Relations.

Other Books by the Same Author

Criteria for the Life History

Frustration and Aggression
(*with L. W. Doob, N. E. Miller, O. H. Mowrer, and R. R. Sears*)

Children of Bondage
(*with Allison Davis*)

Social Learning and Imitation
(*with Neal E. Miller*)

Victory Over Fear

Fear in Battle

Personality and Psychotherapy
(*with Neal E. Miller*)

Steps in Psychotherapy
(*with Frank Auld, Jr. and Alice Marsden White*)

Caste and Class in a Southern Town

JOHN DOLLARD, PH.D.

Professor of Psychology
Yale University

THIRD EDITION

DOUBLEDAY ANCHOR BOOKS

Doubleday & Company, Inc., Garden City, New York

To
Victorine Day Dollard

Caste and Class in a Southern Town was originally published by Yale University Press in 1937. The Second Edition was published by Harper & Brothers in 1949. The
Third Edition was published by Anchor Books in 1957.

COVER BY ELLEN RASKIN
TYPOGRAPHY BY EDWARD GOREY

CONTENTS

PREFACE—1957

I expected to lose my friends in Southerntown when this
book was published. Candid analysis cannot be combined
with friendship either in life or social studies. Still it was
painful when the matter turned out as I had expected. There
were no letters either in praise or protest. As far as I could
tell from second-hand contacts, publication had little effect
on town or people. The name of the town was not revealed
nor is there any record of individuals feeling exposed or
damaged by the account. Apparently sources and identities
were fairly well scrambled.

Having no new information about Southerntown, I have
not altered the book from the first printing. Neither have I
attempted to bring it "up to date." Since 1937 my research
interests have taken a swing away from problems of the
community and have increasingly centered in the psychological field. I am therefore no longer up on Negro problems.
If the book is worth reprinting it is because of what I saw
in Southerntown in 1935–36. I am not any less interested in
sociological matters for having become more interested in
the psychological branch of social science, but I am less well
informed.

I had already been interested in psychological problems
as a graduate student, and this interest was greatly increased
through the Yale seminar on the "Impact of Culture on
Personality" which I ran with the unforgettable Edward
Sapir. This seminar taught me how exceeding blowzy our
notions about personality were. It was thought at the time
that psychologists especially needed to have cultural perspectives added to their methods of perception. While this
was true, it turned out, for me at least, that the culture
scientists had rather the better of the bargain. Their systematic concepts seemed to me superior to the status of personality theory. I headed therefore for this open country.

At the same time, by identification by Neal E. Miller,

Carl I. Hovland, Samuel A. Stouffer and others, I came under pressure of the experimentalists on methodological grounds. I had to amplify my mathematical and statistical background. I had to learn something of psycho-physical methods as applied to scaling and rating, and hence to test and scale construction. The importance of reliable and valid data was greatly raised up in my mind.

I should like to be able to testify that were I to do this study of Southerntown over, now that I have better tools, I could do it much better. I am not so sure. The significant, the truly explanatory, data on the South is hidden behind great sets of defensive habits. Much of the relevant material can appear only in intimate relations where fear is reduced. The relation of friendship is such a one; the psychoanalytic relation, another. Where friendships must be formed or patients acquired in order to sample adequately, the difficulties are grave indeed. Not every *n*th person can be a friend. One cannot find people willing to accept the psychoanalytic condition of free association by routine picking from the city directory. We know the defects of such a study as mine much better than the remedies.

However, despite methodological lacks no unprejudiced person who deeply knew the Southerntown situation or similar situations seemed to quarrel about the facts. Nothing has happened since 1936 which has served to unconvince me about what I saw. It seems as real now as then. We are all still in the hot water of conflict between our democratic ideals and our personal acceptance of caste status for the Negro. We are still deliberately or unwittingly profiting by, defending, concealing or ignoring the caste system.

I would not have the reader think that I believe this book to be a good example of scientific work in its best and terminal form. I see it rather as part of the exploratory work of science, of the fumbling and fiddling out of which more authoritative descriptions of reality will emerge. I wish I could be certain that we would have time for a final scientific description of our society before we shall be called to account for its disastrous imperfections.

There are two changes, however, which I know I would

make if I were trying to do this job over. I would unscramble the caste and class picture after the manner of W. L. Warner and his group. In this study I omitted the rôle of white upper class, neglected relations between groups in lower class, and failed to clarify the relations between parallel classes in the two castes. My study also omits consideration of the important rôle of social cliques in organizing societal life. The pattern study here is *Deep South*[1] by Davis and the Gardners.

I would not wish, nevertheless, to lack the skills and perspectives my own life has imposed on me. I see man also as Freud saw him. If Warner, like Durkheim, sees man poised and timeless in the frieze of structure, Freud sees him the ambitious beast, shivering in the high wind of culture. Seen close, he smokes.

Nowadays I would also insist on an analysis of individual habit and learning. As Miller and I have said in our *Social Learning and Imitation*,[2] to understand man, one must know the *principles* on which he learns as well as the *conditions* under which he learns. In this connection, I still feel it useful to speak of "gains" and privations attached to class membership as is done in this book. I think it worthwhile to consider the nature of class frustrations and the fate of the aggressions they produce (an idea later intensively developed by a group of us at the Institute of Human Relations).

As Sumner saw, a social class breaks down into persons with habits. The study of the history of individual habit is important wherever the problem of change appears, for social change means individual habit change. For example, the cost to the individual of social mobility can be finally evaluated only in habit terms. Were I doing Southerntown over again, I would try to see the life of the people as a set of habits motivated by drive and learned under conditions of reinforcement. This imaginary Southerntown would therefore be a more unified book. The conditions-principles idea

[1] Davis, Allison, and Gardner, G. and M., *Deep South*, University of Chicago Press, 1941.
[2] Miller, N. E., and Dollard, John, *Social Learning and Imitation*, Yale University Press, 1941.

must be represented with the same unity in behavior science as it is in the life we observe.

However swift the pace may seem to participants, social systems change slowly. There have been only three major changes in American structure since colonial times. The first was the abolition of hereditary titles at the time of the Revolutionary War. This change made our aristocracy less conspicuous and our social structure less rigid. The second change was the abolition of slavery. Emancipation made a caste out of Negroes, reduced some handicaps but maintained many of their crippling disabilities. The greatest gains of Emancipation were that it gave the Negroes freedom to move and enabled them to organize the fundamental unit of the family along conventional lines. Finally, white society itself has been "middle-classified" by the movement of large numbers of white people from lower to middle class. This movement apparently coincides with the rise of urban civilization and the service industries.

The Negroes, however, as Davis and Gardner have shown, have tended to lag here. There are still disproportionate numbers of them in lower class. In Negro society middle class is still a population spike on a broad base instead of a large section of a true pyramid, as one finds it in white society. The *evolutionary* change which can now occur, and be furthered by human resolution, is to move larger and larger numbers of Negroes into the middle class of their caste. Economic factors seem at the present time to favor this change. Continued pressure to equalize educational opportunities as between Negroes and whites can also aid. Similarly, the effort to make our Government, at least, evenhanded and neutral in its treatment of Negro citizens should be pressed vigorously by all those who realize that change is inevitable but wish to bring it about in an orderly manner.

If white men can solve the color problem, the United States is in an excellent position to do it. We have the most amenable color problem which faces any modern nation. The Negro is thoroughly American. He is the brown man with the most thorough indoctrination in Western culture. He is much more a modern man than are, for instance, the brown-skinned populations of South America. American Negroes have no independent culture groupings, such as those faced by white society in South Africa. There are no important religious differences between whites and Negroes such as the British confronted in India. There is much existing admixture in white society. We have a history of workable accommodation with Negro people. Negro leaders are amenable and are still deeply involved in the processes and devoted to the goals of our American society. If the white man can ever live on equal and peaceable terms with the Negro in the frame of a democratic society it should be here.

Let us show that it can be done. At this moment revolutionary ways of solving the problem do not look good. They solve the Negro problem, like the "white" problem, by a scorching tyranny.

The American Negro, at least, has an idea of a goal worth standing in line for. In the American evolutionary scheme, every ethnic group has had to stand in line, to endure the cruel paring of beloved culture habits, to work and wait for assimilation. In one sense, therefore, the Negro has met the same fate as every other ethnic group which has been introduced to the society. It may also be that the Negro "line" moves more slowly than that of the truly ethnic groups, but this is not the important issue. The fact of caste, however, is not in doubt and the caste system would relegate the Negro *forever* to an inferior position in the society. It is the caste device for placing Negroes which must be abandoned. The Negro may have to wait, but he must know that he has a future in American society and that he *can* attain the same goal of dignified participation which is held out to other Americans.

But we must keep the pressure up. If, internationally, we must defend our society as a whole—root and branch, good and bad—we must keep molding and changing it locally and internally. Change is occurring and must increasingly occur in economic, educational and political fields. Through these changes we shall gradually reduce the cultural and moral stigmata which are the last reasons and rationalizations by which many justify caste.

I believe that Americans instinctively hate the caste system and will not too long abide it. Even those whose regional culture imposes on them a double standard of value dislike the caste system and wish basically to be rid of it. The distress produced by this contradictory state of affairs is greatly increased since our social system has come under the world's eye. As defenders of an alternate mode of life to that proposed by the Communists we are under additional compulsion to make our mode one which can integrate men of every color and culture.

Formerly we could afford to suppose that the Negro problem was local. If our national moral ideas were at odds with our local practices toward Negroes, the pain was ours alone. But two world wars, the emergence of a powerful Communist state, the modern plane and atomic fission have radically changed the situation. Our social system is under world inspection and is literally being looked at by several billion people or their competent agents. We cannot without deadly inconsistency lead a campaign in the name of freedom when we tolerate at home a system which is only a good long jump from slavery as far as Negroes are concerned. At present we cannot offer our system as one on which the world can model itself because no group which has colored citizens could copy it. Since world government must be self-government by white and colored people, we cannot convert anyone to our system unless we solve this problem.

Perhaps by force and the actions of uneasy physicists, we can maintain the status quo for a while longer, but only for a while. Two billion people can't be wrong—not permanently. The accidents of culture which have led to white dominance for the last seven hundred years will be washed out. We shall go about solving the color problem ourselves, cost what it may, or it will be solved for us in ways not to our liking.

JOHN DOLLARD

Caste and Class in a Southern Town

CHAPTER I

The Research Site

〰〰〰〰〰〰〰〰〰〰〰〰〰〰〰〰〰〰〰〰〰〰〰

The researcher cannot always be sure that the book he starts to write is the one it will be given him to finish. My original plan was to study the personality of Negroes in the South, to get a few life histories, and to learn something about the manner in which the Negro person grows up. It was far from my wish to make a study of a community, to consider the intricate problem of the cultural heritage of the Negro, or to deal with the emotional structure of a specific small town in the deep South. I was compelled, however, to study the community, for the individual life is rooted in it.

Only a few days of five months in Southerntown[1] had passed before I realized that whites and whiteness form an inseparable part of the mental life of the Negro. He has a white employer, often white ancestors, sometimes white playmates, and he lives by a set of rules which are imposed by white society. The lives of white and Negro people are so dynamically joined and fixed in one system that neither can be understood without the other. This insight put an end to the plan of collecting Negro life histories in a social void.

Negro life histories refer at every point to a total situation, i.e., to Southerntown itself, the surrounding county, the southeastern culture area, and in a strict sense the whole region which is bound to American cotton economy. This observation came as a very unwelcome perception, since it necessitated getting a perspective on the community and the county, and informing myself incidentally on many appar-

[1] I acknowledge with pleasure my debt of analogy to the Lynds. See Robert S. and Helen M. Lynd, *Middletown* (New York, 1929). The name "Southerntown" is fictitious and the research does not refer to any real town of this name.

ently remote matters. Study of the social context of the lives
of Negroes has crowded out the original objective of the
research, at least so far as the publication of specific life
histories is concerned; but the material has been invaluable
even though it is not presented in full. It serves to characterize the structure of the caste and class relationships in
the town itself, rather than to show the linear development
of any one life. From the initial purpose of the research
there has remained one insistent emphasis. It is the attempt
to see the social situation as a means of patterning the
affects of white and Negro people, as a mold for love,
hatred, jealousy, deference, submissiveness, and fear. Only
in the individual life can one see these emotional forces
surging against the barriers and outlets of the governing
social order.

In order to share the shock of contact with a strange
situation, I should like to wipe my vision clean of the effect
of wont and habit and to see Southerntown again afresh as
I first visited it.[2] It is a small town, just about large enough
to qualify under the census as an urban area.[3] It is flat as a
tennis court but with a bit of a tilt, the white people living
on the upper half. Should floods come, the Negro quarter
would be first under water. Southerntown is bisected by a
railroad, and its tracks divide people according to color, the
whites living on one side and the Negroes on the other.
Some exceptions to this rule occur; there are a few Negro
cabins behind the homes of the white persons for whom
they work, and there are two Negro families with houses
boldly fronting on a respectable street on the white side.
A yellow bayou filled with turtlebacks curls through the
town and separates the business and residential districts
on the white side.

On the white side of the town the houses are, in general,

[2] The use of the first person singular occurs with some frequency in the earlier chapters of the book. It is used reluctantly but with the following hope: first, that it will show the
researcher as separated from his data, and second, that it will
give the reader a more vivid sense of the research experience.
The repetition of the alternatives, "you," "one," or "we," seems
much less desirable than the occasional use of "I."

[3] I.e., over 2500 people.

commodious, well painted, shrubbed, and neat. Fans buzz in them during the summer months. They are screened and as cool as they can be in this climate. There seem to be few houses of poorer grade on the white side, and one does not in fact see many unkempt white people in the town. The streets are paved in the white area and telephone wires run through the trees. There is a cleared play-space for children around most of the houses.

The other side of the tracks, sometimes called "nigger town," yields a different picture. Here the houses are small and cheap. Walking along the street, one sees the flash of a big white bed in most of the rooms and comes later to realize that it is not from choice but from necessity that most rooms must do duty as bedrooms in addition to some other function. A well-cropped lawn is a rarity, as is a well-built house. At night one sees kerosene lamps gleaming through the windows; in a few of the houses, electric bulbs. Only two paved streets traverse this area where fifteen hundred people live. In the evening groups of people sit on their front porches to keep cool, lacking the fans and electric refrigeration which are so useful in combatting summer heat. Behind the houses the frequent privies testify to the fact that these people are not wholly included in our modern technology, as are those on the other side of the railroad tracks.

Another feature of life on the two sides of the tracks is immediately striking. In general the white side is quieter, especially at night; there are fewer people moving on the streets, although the number of whites and Negroes in town is about the same. A sense of discipline and order is more apparent. People are more likely to move about in cars. There is less walking, loitering, and laughing than on the Negro side. It is not true by any means that the Negroes are riotous in their behavior, but they seem to be more on foot, more in motion, and a carefree tone pervades their laughing and joking.

The slum of the town is on the Negro side, a particularly dark and dingy street, where the night life of the place is concentrated. The white people say, "You ought to see the flats on Saturday night, and then you will know what the niggers are really like." Gamblers, prostitutes, and bootleggers all congregate there, although, to be sure, the slum is but little slummier than the rest of the Negro district.

The small industrial section devoted to ginning cotton and pressing cotton seed is isolated at one end of the town more or less in the Negro quarter. A square block of buildings and the four streets around it make up the business district. One street has six or seven department stores, owned and run almost exclusively by Jews. The thirsty traveler may stop and honk before one of the three drugstores and receive courteous curb service, although the polite northerner is frequently a little abashed at delivering a vulgar toot to a southern white man. He gets used to it, however, and is glad to feel the cool shock of a "coke" in the throat while still sitting in his automobile. There is a small and very hot hotel with an adjoining restaurant. The number of lawyers in Southerntown is amazing until one remembers the important rôle of the lawyer-politician. One of the streets is lined with stores serving Negroes, though very few are owned by Negroes. A single floor of one building is reserved for the few Negro professional persons in the town.

Adjacent to the business block a domed courthouse is set in a little park-like space, a spigot for administrative services to the county, for Southerntown is the county seat. On the cool side of the building, on a summer's afternoon, a few white men lounge and talk.

Downtown of an evening, one of the streets is densely lined with cars. The center of this activity is the movie theater, white downstairs and colored in the gallery, with separate entrances. People are great movie-goers and discussers in this town. "Bank Night" in particular is memorable with the excitement of the drawing and a very bad picture to identify it. On Saturday the movie is invariably a Western picture, for then, we are told, the rural people come to town and they like "Westerns."

Saturday is by all odds the big day of the week. In the summer the stores are open all afternoon and evening (though closed on Thursday afternoons). The country Negroes mill through the streets and talk excitedly, buying, and enjoying the stimulation of the town crowds. The country whites are paler and less vivacious; there are not so many of them, but still a considerable number. "Rednecks" they are called, and their necks, it is true, are red, due to open shirts and daily exposure to the sun.

Sunday is a quiet day on the white side. Through open church windows one hears organ and choir music. The Negroes take Sunday solemnly, too, but there seems a little more activity on their side of the town.

The other days of the week are much alike during the summer; but in September the high-sided cotton wagons begin to rumble into the gin, drawn usually by poor and wiry mules. On the average day, between six and seven in the morning, a little tide of traffic laps from the Negro to the white side of town. The Negro women are going to work as maids and cooks in white houses. An hour later the white businessmen go to work, and still later their wives go out to do their shopping. The men usually come home for dinner at noon, and it is a big meal. Between two and three o'clock, in the dead heat of the afternoon, the black tide reverses itself, and the Negro women go home to get the main meal of the day for their own families. They return around five and go back home again at dusk after the whites have finished supper and the dishes are done.

If the summer is hot, expectant, and marked by steady work for both whites and Negroes, the fall is the season of intense activity. It is the time of the settlement on the plantations when the Negro cropper becomes an independent buyer. During the three fall months Southerntown does most of its retail business and lives its most exciting life. During January and February comes the dullest season, when people work in anticipation of the next cotton crop, whose cultivation polarizes all activity in this area. Then again the hopeful spring, the summer of steady work, and the exhilaration of money to spend and good business in the fall.

Summer days seem long, still, and intensely hot. Well-to-do white people—they are but few—leave for the coast, the North, or the Carolina mountains. Occasionally thunderheads appear in the great bowl of sky above the sweeping flat lands and a sudden passionate shower falls through the bright sunlight; or a tumultuous storm lashes the sky with lightning, bends the trees, and fills the lower roads ankle-deep with water. Winter is the season of heavy rains and it does occasionally snow. The rainfall is fairly heavy, forty to fifty inches; and the growing season is long, over two hundred and ten days.[4]

Stretching out from the town in various directions are gravel roads. Now and then, surprisingly, a few miles of concrete will appear and disappear without seeming reason unless one knows where county lines begin. Through the car windows one sees flat cotton fields, an occasional puff of woodland against the horizon, rain-blackened Negro cabins in great numbers along the road and, in the fields, the cotton crop in some stage of its growth or decay. Huddled store buildings and gas stations appear every few miles, and here and there, but less frequently than the sentimental northerner would imagine, a plantation mansion. On a summer night after rainless weeks a mantle of dust hangs over the gravel roads, choking the driver and discouraging speed. If one feels the lure of more concentrated town life, there are cities thirty or forty miles away. If a car owner, one frequently drives there for a cold drink, a movie, or just for the ride.

The following incidents may serve to illustrate the initial appearance of strangeness. I took my laundry one day to a Negro laundress (the newcomer is quickly and competitively solicited for the privilege of doing his wash) and asked her when it would be ready. She said, "Oh, tomorrow evening." After supper the next day I went back. She reproached me on the ground that it had been done for five or six hours and I could have had it earlier: "I expected you to come around about two o'clock this evening." Morning is from when you get up until around two, and evening is from then on. At first I thought that only Negroes used the word in this way, but later found that white people do too.

Courteous white friends with cars will say, "Can I carry you home?" and the phrase always brought to mind the im-

[4] Howard W. Odum, *Southern Regions of the United States* (Chapel Hill, 1936).

age of picking something up in one's arms and carrying it, because this is the way we would use the word in the North; but it merely means "give you a ride." The past participle of "do" is used in an unfamiliar way; people say, "I done took it home with me," or "I thought he had done gone but he had not." Of rhythm, inflection, and accent in speech I can say nothing that is technically descriptive, but merely remark that it is a strange world for northern ears. The strangeness, of course, is reciprocal; for example, the burring middle-western "r" sounds harsh and crude to Southern-towners. One linguistic sin they do not admit, namely the use of "you-all" in addressing a single person; it always implies plurality even though only one person may be physically visible.

Another type of incident will define the dilemma of the researcher more aptly. One morning a Negro friend came to my boarding house and knocked on the *front* door. It was a crisis for him, for the family, and for me. Perhaps he felt a sense of his own dignity as a middle-class Negro, perhaps he felt that the house had become extraterritorial to southern society because I was living there. He was left standing on the porch and the family member who called me seemed unhappy and reproachful. I had unwittingly aided in im-posing a humiliation on my hosts. The interview on the front porch was constrained on both sides. Small towns have eyes and ears, and Southerntown is strict in its policing of newcomers. My Negro friend brought still another Negro up on the porch to meet me. Should we shake hands? Would he be insulted if I did not, or would he accept the situation? I kept hands in pockets and did not do it, a device that was often useful in resolving such a situation. My Negro friend must have noticed this, but with genuine politeness he gave no sign and even later seemed not to hold it against me. In point of fact, we were fortunate. He might have been sent away rudely, or told to go to the back door, or I might have been severely condemned. Still there was a strain in the social atmosphere of the house thereafter, a strain which informed me that Negroes might not change their behavior toward this house and its occupants because I was a resident there. As a researcher in Southerntown one lives always with a sense of spiritual torsion, willing but unable to conform to the conflicting elements in the social pattern.

Southerntown is, the Negroes say, a "good town" for Negroes and is known as such in the country round about. Sturdevant, ten miles away, is known as a "bad town"; race contacts there are shot through with a tenser feeling, and there have been more incidents. The Negroes in Southerntown were formerly much better off than they are now, owned more land, even ran business institutions in the town, and took especial pride in their bank. The depression, they say, has largely wiped them out. But even in a good town, say Negro informants, both they and I must be careful, and add, "When in Rome do as the Romans do." They tell me in this way that they are excusing me from according them the type of treatment they would expect if we were on northern ground. They know also that they, rather than I, may be blamed for indiscretions, since "they ought to know better" in the eyes of the local white people. Before I went to Southerntown, I wondered if the Negroes would talk to me and how freely; after I got there I wondered why they talked as they did. There is no doubt that they feel emotionally allied with the North and northerners as against the southern white system, just as the white South suspects, and with good historical reason, the existence of such feelings of alliance. Middle-class Negroes who have northern conceptions of personal rights hope for sympathy and support from northerners.

One reason why the Negroes talk appeared rather clearly early in my stay. They feel that they have little opportunity to work directly on southern social structure, in order to advance their interests. Negroes are not in a position to demand what they want, by reason of their exclusion from political life and the limitations on other social participation. It is a devious route, but they hope to influence the white South by arousing public opinion in the North, to which southerners are much more responsive than we ordinarily think. The Negroes picture the northern man going back and writing a book in defense of their interests; such a book, they vaguely feel, might result in a minim of force in northern public opinion which might tend to shame or coerce southern white people into making concessions. The collective sense of guilt of the white caste for the effect of the social system on the Negroes is no small factor in improving Negro opportunities such as those along educational lines. Perhaps the Negro feels also some personal relief in talking to the northern observer. Resentments which cannot be effectively expressed in the local situation can be communicated to him. The northern researcher is often also a person of more objectivity on cultural matters than the Negro has ever met or would ordinarily meet, even in the North, and he may find this objective reception a refreshing experience and one calculated to raise his self-esteem which is so sadly battered in daily life.

The nature of my reception by the white people will also aid in identifying the social situation in the town. They displayed an immediate courtesy unfamiliar to a northerner. They seemed to talk more freely about themselves and their concerns, to fall easily into conversation, and to show an agreeable interest in the stranger. They seemed as "solid" in cordiality as in politics. This reception was, of course, an aid to the research, where the crucial problem was to objectify the life of Southerntown by participating and reacting in it. A number of white friends came forward early and remained loyal throughout the study, sometimes in trying circumstances. They tried immediately to instruct me in the etiquette of the situation and to protect me against foolish mistakes. The local people admitted quite early, while I was still sparring for orientation, that they were suspicious of students from the North and tended to think of them as investigators bent upon fomenting trouble and upsetting the situation. There have been such persons and they have left a bad taste, sometimes repaying with ill-humored misrepresentations the courtesy of their southern hosts. It would be all right, I was told, if I were not interested in the economic situation, in social equality for Negroes, or in propaganda. Even at that, some of the educated people might understand what I was doing, but the majority would not. Early I heard the rumor that I was an organizer of Negro labor and in explanation was told that, when white people did not know what a northern white man was doing in the town, they suspected him of being an organizer. A white woman friend told me that I was being criticized for studying the Negro and was suspected of coming primarily to stir up trouble and make the Negroes unmanageable. She defended me, however, and refused to hear any critical remarks. She said she thought the Negroes ought to be studied and that intelligent people would understand this. She stated that she, too, was a friend of the Negro and said that Almighty God had made them out of the same dust from which He created the rest of us.

I put into immediate circulation an exact account of what I wished to do, namely, to get some life-history material from Negroes, explaining that we know very little about how Negro persons mature, in contrast to our knowledge concerning white people. I added that I was acting in the situation as a scientist and not merely as a member of white society, and that my contacts with local Negroes would always be based on my scientific interest. Obviously I would not have come all this distance to fraternize with Negroes when I could do so quite as well in my home town. I let it be known also that I was not accustomed to the southern way of treating Negroes, that my ways were different, and that I did not expect people to be altogether satisfied with my actions. I asked on this score, however, the indulgence usually accorded to the stranger. This explanation seemed to satisfy people during the initiation of my research, and the plan really worked out quite well. All in all, the white people showed me exceptional tolerance and good will. Their liberality can be appreciated best when the emotional values centering around the caste situation are understood.

Everyone was interested in the question of what I would do with the material. I said that I was not certain, which was true at that time; perhaps a couple of scientific papers, I said, possibly a book. One white informant tried to discourage the latter, saying she did not see how I could write a book in so short a time, that the study of the Negro ought to be made by someone who had grown up with him, used him as a servant, and so on. Sometimes in such discussions I would counter with the objection that, granted it is an advantage to grow up with the Negro, there may also be disadvantages, such as the bias of the person who cannot question the rightness of his customary life. On this score there were many long arguments. I had the constant sense of arousing some emotion and much comment, and a feeling that beyond the fringe of my immediate friends and acquaintances I was viewed with suspicion. Some people took another tack and said they were glad to see me getting things straight, since a great number of northerners do not see the problem right at all. They often ridiculed those fly-by-night travelers from Yankee-land who spend a few protected days in the South and then go home as experts on the Negro problem. Behind the query whether I was writing a book, I often sensed the suspicion: Are you going to put what I say in it? Dare I trust myself to deal with you informally? Other white people in response to the same suspicion would talk obviously for publication with the implication: "You can put this down in your book and put my name to it too, for all that." Often in these first discussions I took the bull by the horns and said that no twenty books I could write would make such an impression in the North as the news that one Negro had been tied to the back of a car and dragged about the streets until dead.[5] And as for the South, I said, the situation seemed quite stable. If the Civil War could not change it, how could I hope to do so, even if I wanted to? This sometimes brought amusement and relief. There were other informants who were fully in accord with my objectives, who were willing to have the situation studied and to have anything come out of it that was honest. The major fact, however, seemed to be that my presence raised a note of apprehension and fear. Let sleeping dogs lie. It is likely that the situation is so tense and painfully contradictory that the truth about it is not welcome, for even the sympathetic truth disturbs the situation and raises new problems before which any given individual is helpless.

My inner feeling was that of being tolerated by the white people, of living in an ill-defined but ever-present atmosphere of hostility, and of suffering a degree of isolation as a

[5] Reported as of another town in this state by an informant who had witnessed it.

penalty for my research interest in the Negro. With some people my status as a university researcher was an important fact. Many others would talk to me so long as I suppressed completely any dissenting or objective comment on the situation. Still others genuinely strove to show me fairly how they looked at the problem. Some tried to indoctrinate me thoroughly with the white caste attitudes at the outset and severed relationships as soon as it became clear that, while I was interested in knowing what these attitudes were, I could not readily absorb them into my own character and behavior.

It will orient the research to give a few familiar facts about the state, county, and town. The state is in the southeastern region, as Odum[6] defines it, and is in the deep South. The general impression gained about it from reading the statistical tables, as in Odum,[7] is that you can usually find it near the bottom of any list of states graded on a national scale of cultural and economic values. In general, one may say that it is Democratic, dry, Protestant, agrar-

[6] Odum, *op. cit.* In this, as in other cases of statistical or census material, I shall not give page citations but shall ask the reader to believe that I have them and have no motive for withholding them except to preserve the anonymity of the town and of my informants. It seems one of the unavoidable limitations of this type of research that such anonymity must be maintained. After all, one is interested in this town and its people as a specimen of a small southern community and not as a means of purveying gossip, of exposing individuals, or of developing a journalistic type of report. My work has been unusually facilitated by the concrete and valuable report of Odum, cited above. It might also be stated, once and for all, that there is much statistical material on this region and even on the town that cannot be integrated in any way with my study. Such "objective" data I have omitted to report on the ground that objectivity is a lesser consideration than relevancy. For example, I cannot find any good reason, except that of this illustration, for telling the reader that the number of beef cattle in this county has decreased between 1920 and 1929. One might say that it tends to reveal an increasing attention to the staple crop and a decreasing attention to other forms of agriculture. But to give such an historical account is not the object of my research. Data similar in their lack of pertinence are therefore omitted.

[7] *Ibid.*

ian. It voted against resubmission of the prohibition amendment,[8] though people say that the voters vote dry even if they have to stagger to the polls to do it. It is among the states with the lowest percentage of urban population; so the politician is the friend of the farmer. It is among the states with the highest percentage of population living on farms,[9] and among those with the highest percentage of Negro population. Ninety-eight percent of the white population are American born. One gets a striking impression of the fact that one is dealing with an indigenous white American population by going into a third- or fourth-grade classroom and seeing the number of blond, red, and brown-haired children. Other indications about the state will be given in their appropriate place in this volume.

Any study of the town inevitably involves the surrounding rural plantation region because the town itself is a depot for goods and services to the mass of the surrounding population. Its function is to provide mercantile, legal, medical, administrative, educational, communicative, and other services. It has no independent industrial relationship to the outside world, such as the presence of manufacturing industries might give it. The county was settled in the latter part of the expansionist movement of the cotton economy, a movement which introduced the first planters and their slaves about a hundred years ago. It is now densely populated as compared with the rest of the state. Of its approximately 75,000 people, about 70 percent are Negroes, a most important fact from the standpoint of race contacts; this means that there are about 240 Negroes per 100 white persons in the county.[10] The white people of the county are almost exclusively of native stock, the foreign-born being a mere handful.[11] They have, therefore, been exposed to the full course of historical circumstances out of which the present-day social structure and attitudes toward the

[8] *Ibid.*

[9] *Ibid.*

[10] *Negroes in the United States*, U. S. Dept. of Commerce, Bureau of the Census. Here again the exact citation will not be given for the reasons advanced above.

[11] *Fifteenth Census of the United States* (1930), Population, Vol. III, Part I.

Negro have evolved. The median white family includes one full person more than the median Negro family in the county, although the Negro birth rate per 1000 population is seven persons higher than for the white.[12] Outside Southerntown, which is its only urban area, the county has about 3500 people who are listed as "rural non-farm," evidently the dwellers in the villages and crossroads hamlets which one sees from the automobile.

Four fifths of the land of the county is tilled, most of it undoubtedly in cotton. The town has a slight excess of females over males, and of Negroes over whites. Apparently, too, it includes most of the foreign-born of the county. These, observation indicates, are probably mainly Italians and Jews, with a very few Chinese. The median size of both white and Negro families is smaller in the town than in the county, but the white family remains about a full person larger than the Negro. Slightly more than 90 percent of the houses are one-family dwellings, and one cannot be sure that those with two or more families are not the overcrowded Negro cabins.

Since the researcher, of course, is not interested in this town as an esoteric item in American civilization, the question arises as to whether it is typical, and in particular, of what it is typical. In answer one may say that it is probably an average small town in a rural county devoted to a staple crop and characterized by a black belt history and psychology. We know that 70.2 percent of the southeastern region is rural and that of the 29.8 percent of the population classed as urban, 15.2 percent lies outside of the metropolitan districts. It is in this latter group that our town falls. In type of economy it is certainly not typical of the whole south or even perhaps of the statistical mode in the southeastern region. It is rather more likely to represent an extreme of a general tendency, in some degree a relic of a bygone plantation and black belt culture. Attitudes here would certainly be different from those in towns and counties with smaller percentages of Negroes. They would likewise differ somewhat from social attitudes in metropolitan

[12] *Fifteenth Census of the United States* (1930), Population, Vol. III, Part I.

centers. They would certainly deviate from those in the industrial areas and the mill villages.[13] An authority[14] states that this region is as typical of the old agrarian South as any now existing. Differences between metropolitan attitudes and those in our town were exemplified by a visitor from a large town in the South. Conversation turned upon the use of the word "nigger." A local girl commented on the way northerners pronounce it, like "nig-gurr" instead of "niggah." The city girl intervened at this point to state that in her city the white people say "colored girl" and not "nigger." The local girl then remembered how she had said "nigger" before her sister's cook in this same big town and her sister had hastily made reference to a "colored girl," adding afterwards that the cook was too good to lose by insulting her. In the larger town the white people had accommodated themselves to the changed claims of the Negroes and had begun to avoid the word offensive to them.

It must be clear that we are not attempting to judge the relationships of whites and Negroes or to pronounce a verdict on the social situation from any point of supposed superiority. It seems very likely that the emotional situation described herein could be re-created in any part of the country, if ample time were given and if the numbers of the two races were comparable to those in Southerntown. The advantages of the situation for research of this type lie in the sharply marked nature of the caste and class system, the encysted local and regional development, and the freedom from confusion of cultural influences characteristic of the larger cities.

In the attempt to grasp in a single perspective the emotional structure of this community I am painfully conscious of limitations of ability and time, and the need of aid from other specialists. It has seemed, however, worthwhile to attempt to give a unified picture of the emotional underpinning which vitalizes social relationships in Southerntown.

[13] Broadus Mitchell and George Sinclair Mitchell, *The Industrial Revolution in the South* (Baltimore, 1930), pp. 127-128.
[14] Purposely nameless.

CHAPTER II

Research Method

The method of this research is of necessity adapted to the nature of the material. The aim of the study is to grasp and describe the emotional structure which runs parallel to the formal social structure in the community. Method must conform to material and not vice versa. For example, the census taker has also worked in Southerntown; his method is good for his purposes, but it would not work for mine. We do not yet know how to set up the schedule which would make it possible for him to get the kind of material our study envisages, if indeed such a research could be made a part of a government project. The latter seems very doubtful, for could a republican government concede the existence of social classes and would it dare to enumerate individuals on this basis? Could the government make a census of white and Negro individuals who live in relationships of concubinage? Could the government admit and classify the amount of hostility across race lines which actually exists? Even if any of these questions were to be answered in the affirmative, we should still lack the pattern which would give meaning to the individual items. It is this emotional pattern of life which must first be sensed and described. As an item in sociological research the attempt is made here to demonstrate an affect-conscious social science at work with a particular problem, i.e., the nature of a small town community in the deep South.

Many times during the conduct of the research and the arrangement of the materials I have had a bad conscience on the score of method. Should the researcher expect to be believed if he cannot hook his findings into the number system and present them in the manner conventional in the physical sciences? So far I have managed to stave off this pressure by such consolations as these: the first loyalty of a scientist is to his material; he must seek it where it can be found and grasp it as it permits. If he does not do this, he is likely to find himself an aimless imitator of others, of better methods not applicable to his field. He does well to watch his tendency to imitate the methods of other fields, being sure that if he does this he will be imitating the type of material controlled as well as the method by which it is controlled.

Through the study runs the assumption that the adult man will tend to develop the feelings appropriate to his reality situation and, as a corollary, that all men in the same situation will tend to develop essentially the same feelings; if adult personalities do not possess the expected uniform responses, explanation must first be sought in the life history of the individual for variant circumstances which might produce unique attitudes. Beyond the life history still is the biological set or "way of experiencing"[1] as an explanatory factor. The development of attitudes appropriate to a changed reality is nicely illustrated by the behavior of white outsiders who come into Southerntown and become permanent residents. They soon take over, it is said, the attitudes proper to their caste and class toward the Negro. My own observation tends to bear out this statement. If an outsider does not thus adjust his conduct, he is not really living in the community; such is the case, for example, if he happens to be there as a social researcher, seeing the situation in the objective terms of the outsider. Apart from such situations, however, we expect a person to respond according to the demands of his concrete social position. According to this hypothesis, all slaves in the South had a recognizable common psychology. All middle-class white people will show common emotional responses. All white people who feel the pressure of Negro competi-

[1] Kahn's concept of the biological factors as a manner of taking on social experience may prove a fertile one in the social science field. Biological variables so defined seem to anticipate social experience and thus to become "socially relevant." See Eugen Kahn and Louis H. Cohen, "The Way of Experiencing as a Psychiatric Concept," *Psychol. Monographs* (1936), Vol. 47, Whole No. 212, pp. 381-389.

tion in various spheres will tend to react in similar ways. The research which follows has served to suggest and sustain this hypothesis, and much of our problem will be to indicate what the marks of various common social rôles are and what the occupants of such "social rôles" experience.

The basic method used in the study was that of participation in the social life of Southerntown. This social sharing was of two degrees and involved two rôles; there was first the casual participation possible as a "Yankee down here studying Negroes," and second the more intensive participation and the more specific rôle of the life-history taker. The casual rôle will be described first. If people in Southerntown watched me carefully, as they did, I also watched them, listened, thought about and participated in the common life then going on. The primary research instrument would seem to be the observing human intelligence trying to make sense out of the experience; and the experience was full of problems and uncertainty in fact. Perhaps it does not compare well with more objective-seeming instruments, such as a previously prepared set of questions, but as to this question the reader can judge for himself. It has the value of offering to perception the actual, natural human contact with all of the real feelings present and unguarded. In this connection the proper sensitization of the observer must be of importance. Some may be very good at this sort of thing and others not. Perception of social events based on participation is difficult to standardize; yet I believe that my experience can be repeated, that others can be trained to see what I have seen, and more, and that the construct has predictive value.

Of course, both whites and Negroes are protective of their culture. They aim to put the best face on it, and to appear as rational as possible in the eyes of the observer. White people have had good reason to mistrust northern witnesses of their social experience and to expect a disguised, if not overt, hostility from them. The researcher learns by living and observing in the actual situation, by keeping away from emotional consolidation with the society, by fleeting empathy which is followed by reflection and distance. He can use a good ear for the overtones in a social situation; for the little clues and contradictions in the statements and behavior of others; for jokes made at his expense; and for the implicit boundaries which guide his relationships to others, and which oftentimes are not visible until he has transgressed them. People may not tell him directly what he wants to know, perhaps may not know how to, and they will certainly not be able to give him a theory of their culture. What they will do is illustrate it for him, act it out, and in the best case be their true selves before his eyes.

In general two kinds of observation were made, first as to what people said, and second as to what they did and seemed to feel. The first type is easily understood in terms of many conversations with Negro and white people about particular problems, conversations in parlors, loafing at the hotel, in automobiles, in business places, and the like. Observation without discussion was at least equally important. One could notice at what point in a conversation people became excited and what they did; one could see the sequence of behavior at a Negro picnic or revival meeting, or note the reception of a Yankee in a social group of white people. In the struggle for clarity one should constantly record the material as it comes, make hypotheses, and reject or modify them; the observer must make active, formative use of his data.

Practically none of the material was gained by direct interrogation and none of it by set questions. Beyond the fact of my general announced objective I did not appear in the rôle of a questioner, but rather settled into the life of the community and was variously defined as a boarder, a friend, a buyer of gasoline, a person with hay fever, and so on. For this reason informants did not square off and get deliberately set to answer questions. There was no cross-examination of the anthropological or psychiatric type. We have seen in psychoanalysis all too well how the subject's defenses are raised by the device of ruthless questioning. This does not mean, of course, that no bias was present in the responses of my informants, but it does mean that this bias was less aroused. The material is all set in a natural context, it is implicative, it points before and after, and it has in every case a concrete setting. I was able to enter into the flow of events in Southerntown pretty much as they were naturally set to occur, since, in the course of time, my presence became less conspicuous and disturbing.

An important aspect of the method is to watch the feeling tone of the statements people make and the acts they do. This is often more definitive than the words uttered or the external character of the act. People can say *no,* for example, in such a way that it means *yes,* and vice versa. The feeling tone indicated in giving a permission may indicate that if it is acted on, the recipient can count on terminating his effective contact with the grantor.

It is of the utmost importance to watch one's own mental life, fantasies, and responses in contact with the new culture. This sometimes passes by the name of meditation or reflection. One should certainly indulge in it liberally in order that the new experiences may not pass into one's field notebook without passing through one's integrating mental life. New impressions should be painstakingly and immediately recorded in writing because they soon cool off and the sensitive edge of one's reacting mental surface is dulled by repetition. The object of study is, of course, precisely the emotional reactions of oneself and one's associates in the concrete social situation. These reactions, which are registered in good part in one's own uncensored vagaries of thought and feeling, may often give the clue to understanding the overt behavior of others and oneself.

The researcher should be a good listener, and preferably should find it easy to make social contacts. This is equivalent to saying that his social fear should be low. If he genuinely participates in the social life, every other member becomes in some manner an informant, and he can never be certain when he will learn the most important things. To do this type of research he must pay the price of intense awareness of self and others and must constantly attempt to define relationships which are ordinarily taken for granted.

One methodological caution at this point. We should remark how the bizarre is likely to stand out in experience and how selective our perception is, how we tend to see what makes us comfortable or wards off painful feelings. Odd people and those under pressure do and say the conspicuous things, and we must beware of judging the whole situation by them. Comfortable people talk less and come forward less readily to the newcomer. The researcher must watch also for systematic bias on the part of the informant, and here his knowledge of the social structure comes to his aid. The danger in a biased person exists only when the researcher does not know he is biased or how he is biased. Out of these catch-as-catch-can contacts with various persons, white and Negro, one slowly generates a picture of the total social situation and of the attitude structures accompanying and charging it.

The more intensive method used in the field was the systematic gathering of life-history materials, especially from Negro people. At first sight this might not appear to be a technique suited to studying a community, and it was one of the surprises of the research that it proved to be so. Although it views the community through the eyes of a very few informants, it nevertheless sees their reactions to the community in all their depths and contradictions.[2] The point could be dramatically illustrated by presenting data on a single life, but this is not possible at the present time. Excerpts from the life-history materials have been used, however, in describing the community. In the daily interviewing which provides life-history material one can visualize the flow of events, casual and important, in the town. Reactions to these events are observable in the dreams and fantasies of the informants. One receives a mi-

[2] Actually this should be nothing new; every psychoanalysis is a study of an acculturated human being who plays a social rôle in a community and whose personality is to some degree a function of the systematic social life in which he participates. It should be the case, therefore, that any analysis can be utilized as an instrument of study of a community. Very likely this is not done because of the necessity of concentrating on the therapeutic problem which has been so continuously to the fore in the history of the use of the analytic method. Perhaps when those competent to practice this method have the leisure to study the material of an analysis from the community angle, they may be able to derive much that is of value to social theory.

nute account of their daily actions, a picture, not attainable in any other way, of the actual functioning of the person in his life situation. If the subject happens to be an important unit in the social life of the community, one may find all the crucial issues represented in a single personality. Some observations on the life history as a linear description of a personality will be made later;[3] it is to be stressed as one window looking out on the collective life.

The initial plan in the research was to gather accounts of the social and emotional growth of Negroes, and with this objective the psychoanalytical interviewing method was adapted to the exigencies of the situation. In ordinary analysis the subject is conscious of life difficulties and comes for help. This consideration differentiates my activity from psychoanalysis. None of my subjects were aware of personality difficulties of any considerable importance to them. This fact made advisable a different method of interesting them in the work. I let it be known that insight into one's own personality might be gained through the interviews, and that such insight could be useful in various life situations, such as those, for example, of parent or teacher. Several informants were thus induced to coöperate. It was further stated that an important research issue was involved, namely that of illuminating the inner life of the Negro person and showing his successes and tribulations. It was pointed out that many people do not attribute a complex mental life to the Negro, that I felt this to be an untruth, and that I planned to test my conviction by gathering life-history materials. This was a strong motive with a number of my informants. In the end more or less intensive work was carried on with nine Negro people, three women and six men. For those among the group who were teachers I managed to get school credit in one of the Negro colleges as an additional reward for their intensive work, averaging four hours a week, with me.

The next problem was finding a place to work. Here the researcher meets the race problem in a tangible form. My first thought was to use the house in which I was rooming,

[3] In the Appendix.

but I never put this question up to my hosts; I knew by then that it would be unbearably awkward all around. I could hardly expect to get the type of rapport with my Negro informants necessary for life-history work and still treat them as southern white people do; they would hardly maintain the contact if they had to come to the back door of my house, be called by their first names, or risk still other humiliations. For a time I thought of trying to evade the front-door issue by pretending that my room was an office, having a big sign made with my name on it and posting it on the front of my residence, if I could get permission to do this; but I abandoned this idea as bizarre. A second thought was the house of the informant. This, however, would have forced me to run from place to place during most of the day. Furthermore, the poorer informants did not have a room which could be isolated for an hour a day. A third thought, and this seemed for a while an inspiration, was that one of the public schools might serve as a meeting place; but some objections appeared to this. In the first place, the white principal of the city schools was out of town and his permission had to be secured. Even if it were given, I was not sure that the Negroes would be at ease in the environment of the white school. This objection applied also, of course, to my house. If we tried the Negro school, we faced the following difficulties: it was on the outskirts of town and would be a considerable walk; it was isolated; I would be alone there with women informants, which might not look well in the eyes of the community; and, finally, if we had a serious rain, the building might easily be marooned. A fourth thought was the courthouse, but this seemed out of the question for lack of space, since the building is intensively used. A fifth idea, a true inspiration,[4] proved to be the solution. I rented an office in one of the buildings where professional people were housed. Since it was a business building, Negroes could come and go by the front door like anyone else, and no unusual attention was paid to their movements. It was at one and

[4] One of my white friends made this suggestion and rented me the office. I wish I were free to mention his name in appreciation.

the same time isolated and public. It had a certain professional atmosphere which was proper to my work and did not raise the question of social equality any more than it did in the case of the physician or lawyer working there. Furthermore, I let it be known that, while my doors were closed, they were not locked, and that if anyone, white or colored, felt impelled to know what was going on inside at any time, he or she could come in without knocking. Of course, no one ever did this, but it probably served to settle much suspicion of what I was doing. That I had Negro women informants was an important point. Since white men are suspected when they have secret contacts with Negro women, I had to take every means of stressing that the object here was truly professional.[5]

With the aid of another white friend I secured some office furniture, two rocking chairs, and a table. My informant sat beside the table in one of these chairs and I in the other, so that we could turn our heads and converse but did not have to look steadily at one another. By this means we were both freed of the strain of constant face-to-face conversation, a freedom especially valuable when something embarrassing had to be said. The informant was invited to talk about his life in his own way, beginning where he chose and saying what he chose. It was stressed that the researcher would use the material in no way to the detriment of the informant and that communication of more than ordinary freedom would be appropriate. I explained that I would not ask set questions because I could not know

[5] Northern men are not beyond suspicion on this point either by southern whites or Negroes. This suspicion is frequently shown at the present time in jokes about Yankees who timidly but obviously take up the subject of Negro women with southern men. An historical indication that northern men are not immune to the attraction of Negro women is provided by Reuter, though, to be sure, the onus of responsibility is put on the Negro women. He says, "Wherever the Union armies went in the South, they were besieged by an army of Negro women," and implies that venereal diseases, previously little known among Negroes, followed in the wake of the Union armies. E. B. Reuter, *The Mulatto in the United States* (Boston, 1918), p. 161; quoted by permission of Richard G. Badger.

in advance what questions would bring out the important information about the informant; surely that was something which only he could know, and I might spoil his chance to give an account of himself if I intruded with inappropriate questions. A further modification of the technical analytical method was that I made as few comments as possible and did not press for material from the unconscious level, although unintentionally I sometimes got it. It seemed unethical for me to raise problems that could not be settled in the time at my disposal, which was far short of that required for a thorough analysis. Informants were specifically told that they were not undergoing analysis, although they might incidentally learn some things which psychoanalytic research has made available to us.[6]

The material and point of view presented in the following pages is in considerable degree derived from these life histories, although none of it is set into the individual life context. It would be necessary to get corresponding life histories from white people to present the results with technical adequacy, although we can already anticipate much about these histories in view of our knowledge of Negroes.

Since memory is so fallible, especially after months, I made immediate notes on all of my material while it was fresh in my mind, whether it concerned life-history interviews or my less formalized participation in community life. Skill can be developed in recalling the weavings of a conversation, the statements of others, and one's own responses and actions. It is a form of skill in which I have had much practice[7] and which is indispensable in this type of field work. While not beyond the suspicion of error, it is better than any other device we have for freehand interviewing. Its use leaves the social situation intact and natural, and

[6] It is necessary to know how to carry out an analysis in full in order to come short of this goal intelligently. My "modification" is really this and not a surface imitation of the technique.

[7] For five years I have been recording daily materials from analytic interviews, mental hospital cases, and from sociological field subjects.

does not put the informant on the grid with the suspicion that everything he says may be used against him. This "remembering in context," incidentally, is exhausting work; it takes about as much time as the actual interviewing and demands much patience in recounting matters that at the time may seem trivial or out of context.

Of course, one cannot gather many life histories even in a long period of research, let alone record them. Comparison of detailed histories suggests another hypothesis. It is that in the field of the mores and collective life, any person is a good sample of his culture. In every life history of a Negro will be found the dilemmas typical of his class and caste position. Though psychological type may differ in marked ways from case to case, the class or caste rôle is steadily observable as a conditioning factor. Differences, for example, between compulsive and hysterical Negroes may not be important when compared with their likenesses as members of the Negro caste upon whom a definite social rôle is forced. In the latter sense any Negro informant can represent the system sufficiently adequately to permit a description of the caste rôle of the Negro. Experience tended first to suggest and later to confirm this assumption. It is exactly the function of any culture to pattern its objects characteristically and to leave on every single individual the mark of the mores. This conception will be illustrated when we point out the systematic differences in character structure between middle-class and lower-class Negroes.

The first objective in the research is to perceive and state the master forms of social and emotional relations in Southerntown. Only at a few points can the data be presented in statistical form. The method is, however, implicitly quantitative in that judgments are made in terms of more or less.[8] It is not through lack of intent that the study fails to be more exact, but rather because it has not been possible to do more than establish the general pattern in this study and to indicate possible units for more detailed study. My belief is that if researchers use the conceptions later to be pre-

[8] *See* George Lundberg, "Quantitative Methods in Social Psychology," *Amer. Sociol. Rev.* (1936), Vol. I, No. 1, pp. 43-46.

sented, they can identify the main emotional forces in Southerntown and effectively understand and predict behavior. The important research act has been exposure and reaction to the social milieu, and a constant attempt to verbalize and organize the ensuing experience. In many cases, as will be shown, the facts used are matters of common agreement in the community and among researchers on the problem of race relations. What has been added here in these cases is a psychological perspective and organization of these "facts." Many who concede the factual nature of the material do not see fully its implications and interrelations. For example, I make much of the statement of southern white people that the Negroes are "like children." Examination has revealed truth in this statement, but it needs to be qualified in various ways, i.e., it is especially true of lower-class but not middle-class Negroes, it is overstressed by the whites as a defense, and it represents the patriarchal white-caste attitude toward lower-caste Negroes.

Not a few challenges concerning my method were raised by white informants in Southerntown. They said repeatedly that the Negroes would give me selected information, that, being subtle psychologists, they could read my mind and thus anticipate what I wanted to hear. Although phrased as a methodological caution, this was often really an objection to my working with Negroes at all. To one very intelligent objector I retorted that the most incredible types of misinformation came from white people and asked him if he did not think the whites were on the whole less trustworthy informants than the Negroes. He agreed that this might be true. In other cases I stated that I expected biased information from both whites and Negroes, that the systematic biases of the informant were just what I wanted most to know about, and that I was on the watch for evidences of them. In still other instances I pointed out how exceedingly hard it is to lie successfully in the face of the interviewing technique here used. One can lie on the witness stand after being carefully coached on questions anticipated by one's attorney, but it is almost impossible to lie systematically with consistent inventiveness day after day. By "lie" is meant, of course, *consciously* to misrepresent experience. Still such accusations of unreliability of Negroes urged caution and careful checking, and the constant watching of informants for bias. To be biased, of course, means, among other things, to be socially typed, to have a social perspective from which it is necessary to view experience. Many comments came to me from white people tending to discredit Negroes as informants. For example, one friend told me that I had been criticized for sitting on a porch with "niggers." He said that the very Negroes with whom I sat had reported the fact to their white employers, and he implied that anything one said or did with them was certain to get back to the white people. Naturally, he implied that Negroes would not be frank with me if they knew they would later report our conversation to their white patrons. I told him that I did not remember sitting on any porch with Negroes and reminded him that I was certain to be criticized no matter how carefully I acted. Here also was the implication that I was under constant surveillance by the white group, even though through the eyes of my supposedly treacherous Negro informants.

No attempt has been made to reproduce speech peculiarities of either whites or Negroes. Paraphrases have had to suffice, since I did not take notes at the time and was not trained to record dialect correctly. It is possible to remember the idea sequence when the exact words cannot be recalled.

In sociological reporting what is easily printed is often not the most valuable material, while what is most revealing is sometimes not so easily printed. Community researchers commonly lament the materials they have to leave out in presenting their findings. The reason is, I suppose, that one can never be really ruthless in reporting human experience. In order to get the knowledge in the first place, one must participate significantly in the collective life. This means that one must come into human contact with people and this in turn means intimacy, sharing, and mutual identification. Since most intimacies carry an explicit or implicit confidential sign and are to be revealed by the researcher only with due care for the effect on the informant, he is limited in all manner of subtle ways in respect to using specific bits of material. One cannot disregard these obligations without guilt, or without arousing hate against the betrayer. This dilemma of research has been long familiar in the study of the individual; it is not so well known, but equally valid, in studying a community. It is a great limitation to genuine objectivity and adequacy of social science reporting. What can one say of a social theory which must omit the presentation of some of its most valuable facts? People seem to feel also that objectivity is equivalent to hostility and that one is either for them or against them. Since the researcher cannot always agree with his informants, he cannot please them by his report, no matter how fair, in the eyes of an outsider, he is able to be; the informants do not want him to be fair, but rather actively partisan on their side.

It is at a great sacrifice, for example, that I do not identify the state and town. To do so, of course, would be to identify my informants. These I should have liked to place at the front of the book in a cast of characters, with a psychological description after each name. In this way the reader could have judged each item of material in the light of the character structure and social position of the informant. It would be most useful to be able to evaluate each item of information in this way. The book could indeed be rewritten from this standpoint since all my notes are labeled and the necessary knowledge about the individuals is available. But to do so would be an intolerable breach of trust and in certain cases might endanger my informants. For example, a Negro told me of a white man, a former resident of the town, who had been notorious for pursuing Negro girls. He hastily warned me not to indicate him as the source of the datum, since he did not want to get "into trouble." Actually he was afraid of tattling on the whites and of exposing a white man to the hostile criticism of the local community and the outside world; retribution of some kind would have been certain, as he knew. White informants who reveal the intimacies of life in Southerntown also imperil themselves. They do not wish to be known as renegades to their caste and local community.[9]

No person in Southerntown or outside it will be able to identify the source of any information given to me; my disguises of the material have made anonymity certain. Some of my informants were well-known people, others obscure and socially inconsequential. With some I had formal relationships, such as the interviews with the life-history group, and with others my contacts were informal and casual. All told I had fifty or sixty informants, that is, persons with whom I had at least three or four conversations of some length; with perhaps another hundred and fifty persons I had still briefer acquaintance. In some cases, of course, my contacts extended over a hundred hours with given informants. In reporting particular incidents the sex of the person giving a bit of information has been changed when this change was not important; marriage status and number of children and relatives have frequently been altered, always with care to preserve the correct impression. Places and names have been almost entirely omitted. Some of my information came from persons with whom my contact was so oblique or casual that no one in Southertown, either white or Negro, knew that I was acquainted with them. It is certain that every informant will recognize the protective precaution which runs through all the recorded incidents.

Despite the concealment of identities, I must affirm emphatically that every bit of information used has a specific social context which is identifiable, that the person giving it was known to me, and that the type of rapport or hostility characteristic of our relationship was under study. None of this material is the result of vague general impressions. The blame must fall upon our social life and not upon me that I am unable to transmit the facts with full verisimilitude.

A minor feature of the research has been that my canvass of the literature on race followed, rather than preceded, my

---

[9] Note the care with which Herskovits has disguised names of places and persons in dealing with a primitive community, where, it would seem, the need for such disguise is much less than in my case. *See* Melville J. Herskovits, *Rebel Destiny* (New York, 1934), p. xiii.

field experience. It seemed advisable to try for the advantage which lies in naïveté and a freshened perception of the local scene at the risk of repeating the well-documented findings of others. No attempt will be made to buttress this report by masses of citations. My wish is to give the reader as deep a sense of participation as may be in what I have heard, seen, and sensed.

As stated, the object is to reveal the main structure of white-Negro adjustment in Southerntown from the standpoint of emotional factors. Of course, no classifying system works perfectly for manifold reality; my own comes partly out of knowledge and theory brought to the research scene and partly out of the exigencies of the material, with the resulting interplay between the two. If I could, I would show the reader the situation as it must appear to the eyes of a Negro or white child who is being added to the group and who comes gradually to feel the pressure of the main collective structure on his own emotional life. If the experience of a person under the strain of acculturating forces could be clearly sensed and recorded, we would have a dynamic picture of the social organization of Southerntown. The researcher's brief social participation is some approximation, likely a very inadequate one, of this experience.

CHAPTER III

Bias

In speaking of bias we are still talking about research method. Often the most significant aspect of an investigator's method is his bias, unacknowledged but having tremendous force in directing research perception. For example, anyone familiar with the literature on American race problems will have noticed how neatly it cleaves into two groups on the basis of sectional bias, northern or southern.

In the present state of social science knowledge most of our techniques seem biased when considered by themselves. Since there is no unified sociological concept system to direct perception, I shall discuss my various instruments separately and classify them as actual or possible forms of bias. Mentioned here as biases of the observer are sectional, personal, sociological, and psychological forms of perception. If it were insisted at the outset, for example, that such a research as this should get results only in tabular form, this insistence would seem a marked type of bias, although the effort to quantify is not ordinarily regarded as biased. The task of an exploratory study is to pick out the crude outlines of the object later to be more exactly defined. In this exploration the examination of the observer's bias can be of great aid.

It had never occurred to me to consider my own bias until I got into the field. Here, however, one harsh experience brought it sharply to mind. One hot morning I made bold to present a letter of introduction to a well-known southern writer. He met me on his porch and, after an exchange of formalities, inquired what I was doing. I told him briefly. He responded at once that I had little chance of learning anything about the personality of Negroes; he had lived among them for years and had not learned much; so what hope could there be for me? Since I had heard this before, I did not take it too seriously. Then he said something, however, which made me angry but which eventually I took very seriously. I had the idea in the back of my mind, he told me, that he was prejudiced and untrustworthy, and I came prepared not to believe what he had to say. I assumed unconsciously that he was blinded by race prejudice, as it is called in the North. I must feel this way, he said, because all northerners come south with this idea, no matter what their formal protestations may be. At this point, I decided that he had taught me enough and went my way, but I marveled at his candor and his insight. He had not been in essence discourteous, merely uncomfortably frank.

Returning to my research, I examined the material I had already collected and found abundant evidence of the attitude attributed to me—an attitude which had safely survived my sociological graduate training. An example from my notes written before this meeting will demonstrate the point.

These white people down here are very charming and really exert themselves to do friendly things once you are accepted, but they seem very much like the psychotics one sometimes meets in a mental hospital. They are sane and charming except on one point, and on this point they are quite unreliable. One has exactly the sense of a whole society with a psychotic spot, an irrational, heavily protected sore through which all manner of venomous hatreds and irrational lusts may pour, and—you are eternally striking against this spot.

This excerpt reveals an obvious bias in the form of an invidious comparison of southern white people with psychotics, and it further indicates disbelief in what they say, exactly as my informant asserted.

The shock of this experience sufficed to bring about a serious reconsideration of the subject of bias and a conscious awareness of it which persisted during the entire data-gathering period. The example just cited illustrates clearly the sectional bias on the part of northerners of which southern white people are so conscious. There has been a long history of bitter and aggressive men going into the

South from the northeast, and the newcomer is appropri-
ately classified at once, especially when his avowed motive
is "to study the Negro." One attempt to escape such a classification is to refer to oneself as a "student of society" and
imply thereby a lack of bias. Actually, however, there was
no escaping the fact that I was a northerner making a study
of the South. At first I wanted to escape it; I preferred to
hold up an image of myself as without affect and objective.
This illusion could not be maintained and for the reason
above alleged, namely, that southerners did not believe it
and that it was not true. Northern readers and students need
to be reminded of their sectional bias and of the necessity
of reckoning with it in all dealings with the South or southerners. Most of us still take pride in the fact that "we" saved
the Union and freed the slaves and rebuked properly the
arrogance of South Carolina and the rest. Many of us can
recall our schoolroom thrills in singing "Tenting Tonight,"
"John Brown's Body," and other Civil War songs. Many of
us can experience vicariously the anxiety of four long years
of war and the relief at knowing that "the right" was upheld even at such a price. Many, too, vaguely remember
stories of ancestors who died or were wounded in the War.
Behind the romantic legend which now conceals the realities of the conflict, considerable antisouthern sentiment can
still be mobilized today. We inherit an abolitionist tradition,
which has soaked into our frame of social perception. The
visitor is brought up short when he first hears of the "War
between the States," a name which stresses the independence and autonomy once claimed by the individual southern states. Southern writers and scientists have not been
lacking in appreciation of northern regional bias. The schol-
arly A. H. Stone[1] has made the point clearly, as Thomas N.

---

[1] "And it is an intensely practical matter. The child who
was born in Boston in 1860 grew to manhood amidst surroundings and influences which through no conscious purpose of his
own shaped and determined his attitude toward the American
race problem in 1890. The man of the same age in Charleston
was merely looking at the same problem in the light of a different environment." A. H. Stone, *Studies in the American
Race Problem* (New York, 1908), p. x; quoted by permission
of Doubleday, Doran & Co.

Page[2] had done even earlier, and more recently Howard W. Odum[3] has referred to the "emotional set" of northern intellectuals.

The only possible conclusion from this experience was that I had the typical sectional bias to be expected of a northerner, and I thereupon set out to isolate and discount it. For one thing, I began to pay serious attention to what southern white people told me about the interracial situation, and although I did not always agree with them, I always learned from them. The persistence of an unacknowledged and unresisted sectional bias might have barred me from much indispensable information. The discovery of sectional bias had another advantage, namely, that I realized I was irrevocably a northerner and ended my attempts to pass for anything else. This was a healthier rôle and permitted a much more honest interaction with southern white people. The shock of being a "Yankee," instead of a sociologist, soon wore off and compensatory advantages were revealed.

A second form of bias which cannot be ignored is personal bias. A notion that there might be such in my case dawned upon me when I realized that people were forever

[2] "No statement of any Southern white person, however pure in life, lofty in morals, high-minded in principle he might be, was accepted. His experience, his position, his character, counted for nothing. He was assumed to be so designing or so prejudiced that his counsel was valueless.

"It is a phase of the case which has not yet wholly disappeared, and even now we have presented to us in a large section of the country the singular spectacle of evidence being weighed rather by a man's geographical position than by his character and his opportunity for knowledge." Thomas N. Page, *The Negro: The Southerner's Problem* (New York, 1904), pp. 36-37; quoted by permission of Charles Scribner's Sons.

[3] "The South judged the North unfavorably for its tendency to promiscuous judgments of everything 'down there,' 'down South in Dixie,' as being peculiar to southern temperament or temper. . . . It was surprised to note the emotional set of the intellectuals and to find so many of them usurping the purported southern dogmatism. It was tired of being solicited for funds to be added to the national surplus to be used in remaking the South." Howard W. Odum, *An American Epoch* (New York, 1930), p. 100; quoted by permission of Henry Holt & Co.

asking overtly or by implication: "What is this particular Yankee sociologist among all possible Yankee sociologists doing down here studying niggers?" On several occasions this question was directly and impolitely asked, more often indirectly and courteously, but it seemed to be in everyone's mind. It finally occurred to me to ask myself: What *was* I doing down there? Sectional bias supplied part of the answer. I was there on the old northern errand of showing up the evils of the southern system in its treatment of the Negro, and the suspicion could not be avoided that I wanted to make my research come out that way. The personal aspect of my interest, however, derived from another source, not necessarily a discreditable one, but still a bias. It was what might be called a strong feeling for the underdog, a feeling grounded in my own life history and to some extent previously revealed in self-examination. This resulted recognizably in a tendency to feel with Negroes, to be specially accessible to unusual incidents recording oppressive treatment of them, and to stand with them against the dominance of the white caste. Whatever may be the advantage of such a tendency to the social reformer, it is out of place in the researcher, whose business is to see clearly and report correctly. A pro-Negro bias generates disbelief in the statements of southern white people and supports the wish to pillory and humiliate them. From this form of bias, no doubt, came the abolitionists' idealization of Negroes and the lack of realism in their social action with reference to Negroes.

There is another form of personal bias and it pulls in quite another direction. The fact of being a socially mobile person and a member of a middle-class university group inevitably creates a bias tending to make one's research come out in such a way as to be acceptable to members of one's social class; the possible penalty is rejection or isolation by them. The words we use and the thoughts we think, even in research, are likely to label us as loyal or disloyal members of our own class. Further, the middle-class researcher could easily make the mistake of assuming that all Negroes are disciplined middle-class persons like himself, undoubtedly an immortal error in northern perception of the Negro. He might attribute to all Negroes his own restless urges toward mobility and postulate on their behalf an unhappiness which they do not feel in their lot. He will certainly exaggerate the desirability of his own class position and underestimate the frustrations and sacrifices entailed by it. The best chance of avoiding these erroneous forms of perception is to have a clear understanding of one's own class position, past and present. Undoubtedly many researchers who have gone south unaware of this bias have been seduced by the hospitality of the middle- and upper-class southern white people, have formed agreeable ties with them, and have thereupon been pulled into the southern mode of perception of the racial problem. This is to some extent unavoidable since southern white people are often courteous hosts and one inevitably identifies with them. One feels the implied stipulation: "If you like me, think as I do." Unconsciously the researcher wants to please those who have displayed cordiality and generosity by seeing eye-to-eye with them at all points. He is in like danger of being influenced by friendly relations with cultivated Negroes. In referring to the race question Stone[4] has specifically stressed the necessity of examining one's own bias.

In talking with informants I noticed constantly the different manner in which we viewed various daily incidents, such as a suicide, a divorce, or a dream. This difference can be attributed to a psychological mode of perception resulting from my psychoanalytic training.[5] Psychological obser-

---

[4] "I know of no graver responsibility which a teacher can assume than that which devolves upon him when he essays to lecture on any phase of this general question, for he should know not only his subject, but himself as well." Stone, *op. cit.*, p. 12; quoted by permission of Doubleday, Doran & Co.

[5] The major unit of this training has been gained through contact with the Freudian psychoanalytic movement. Direct personal training has been received from Doctors Hanns Sachs, H. D. Lasswell, A. Kardiner, and Karen Horney. A training year was spent attending the course of instruction in the Berlin Psychoanalytic Institute. Control analyses have been conducted with the latter two analysts named above. The writings and views of Freud have become so thoroughly worked through my thinking that I had rather ascribe to him a major orientation of my thought than cite him as frequently as I would otherwise have to.

vation deserves to be classed as a bias, because its utility is not generally conceded in the social science field. The analyst is concerned with individual meanings, with the affect which accompanies any act, with the position of an item of observed behavior in the character and life history of the informant. In particular he is trained to watch for the reservations with which people carry out formally defined social actions, the repression required by social conformity, and, in general, to see, behind the surface of a smooth social façade, the often unknown and usually unacknowledged emotional forces which drive and support social action. This point of view gives a solid sense of man as an animal and tends to stress the biological driving forces of human action. Culture is seen as a device for modeling and remodeling a recalcitrant animal and as performing the remarkable feat of his socialization. We learn from this view, for example, that while animals may be made docile in social life by reducing drive forces (i.e., by actual castration), men are made tractable by culture (i.e., by internalizing social prohibitions). Psychological perception or bias makes the problem more complex but permits explanations which are impossible on the institutional-historical level of perception; it fosters a tendency to watch details of behavior, to ponder on them, and to try to make systematic sense of whatever fragments of the individual life one can get hold of.

A fourth attitude, the sociological, perhaps deserves least of all to be called a bias; yet from the standpoint of Southerntown it was definitely regarded as such, and it is still far from widespread enough to have the agreement necessary for a tested method. First and foremost, it involves distance from the object of study, an intellectual distance provided by the many comparisons one is able to make with any given community. It challenges the sense of absoluteness and rightness with which all culture bearers view their social habits. One sees the community comparatively and historically, and in this perspective it seems historically determined and relative. By using this view also one sees not a mere forest of individuals, but rather a collectivity interacting—something more than an aggregate of individual animals. When we speak of a "society," we refer to the central object of study. Conceptualization takes place in terms of groups and group relations and not in terms of a specious isolation of individuals. As one of my teachers expressed it, one sees the individual as a specimen of a group rather than as one of a mere aggregate of individuals.[6]

Another feature of the sociological bias is its insistence upon fully utilizing the social heritage in explaining human action before having recourse to biological factors. Taken by itself this frequently leads to a kind of sociologism which excludes the biological life altogether. It is probably a truly biased view if used apart from a valid mode of psychological perception. Southerntowners certainly found the sociological point of view very irritating when it was occasionally brought to the fore; as, for example, in denying the categorical inferiority of Negroes and explaining their present status in terms of historical circumstances.

By reciting these various forms of bias I do not by any means imply that I have freed myself completely from them; I claim only that some control is possible where insight is present. The essential view here is that the rational self of the observer may turn its perceptual engine not only at the "outside" world which affects the sensory apparatus, but just as profitably at the inside world of unacknowledged and unverbalized attitudes which often guide uncritical vision of outside events. This rational self is the only instrument in human problem-solving; thinking of it positionally, we may guess that it receives impulse stimulation from the inside and sense data from outside the body envelope. Since this self or ego is formed by a society it is obviously impossible to liberate it totally from the biased view of the world transmitted by that society, but is it not at least a small gain to urge that the possibiliy of emotional and conventional inner bias be guarded against? The "self" warned of this possibility may exercise a valuable criticism on its own operations.

Doubtless my report will reflect bias of which I am not aware and which therefore cannot be discussed here. It

[6] Professor E. W. Burgess made this point forcefully in one of his courses and I do not remember his having published it.

should be remembered, also, that these formulations as to bias are the result of my research and did not exist prior to the field work. They were by no means underfoot in an obstructive way while the data were being gathered, since one might become so sensitized to the danger of bias that he could do nothing at all. Nevertheless, if the researcher asks others to accept his "intelligence in contact with the data" as a useful instrument of research, he should make every legitimate effort to criticize and sharpen it. Since for the moment mechanical controls of perception seem to be out of reach in this field, there is good reason for turning about and questioning the mental instrument which is used in their stead. Evidences of bias may undoubtedly be discovered in other researches in the field of race relations, but we will not try to convict anyone else on this score; rather it is for every researcher to examine his own equipment and indicate his alertness to this possibility in himself.

CHAPTER IV

Attitudes toward the North and Their History

≈≈≈≈≈≈≈≈≈≈≈≈≈≈≈≈≈≈≈≈≈≈≈≈≈≈≈≈≈≈

A white man with whom I had a certain amount of friendly rivalry once asked me a question. We were discussing the Ethiopian situation, which was in the foreground of the news at that time, and he asked if many Negroes from Southerntown were planning to go over and fight on the Ethiopian side. I said I did not think local Negroes took the idea seriously and added that I often told the Negroes that Ethiopia is one of the few places in the world where human slavery still exists. He asked, "Well, are you northerners going to do anything about it?" I responded that I did not think we would have to act in this case because Mussolini seemed likely to take care of the matter. It was banter, of course, but I was conscious, nevertheless, of the edge to his voice and the implication that we northerners were a lot of busybodies who had a tendency toward idealistic crusades which tangled us up in other people's business.

Over and over again the past loomed up in these attitudes toward me as a northern researcher. Sometimes I felt like the last of the carpet-baggers, like a lone raider following in the wake of the Union armies. This feeling was accentuated when I was being introduced in the town. Some friend who had accepted the idea of my research whould take me around to see a white person of importance. The new man was unfailingly cordial and would politely inquire about my business in Southerntown. When he heard that I was down there "studying the nigger problem," the social atmosphere grew chilly and I felt at best on probation and suspect. It seemed that people had attitudes of hostility prepared for the Negro researcher. It was so exactly what a Yankee *would* be doing down there.

In this case my social inheritance and sectional membership defined me in a more or less unwelcome manner. Was it, they seemed to ask, another case of a critic posing as a friend but actually inspired by a theoretical and impractical bias? This raised the question very strongly of the nature of the attitude set toward northerners and of the history of these attitudes. It is out of the question to attempt to write a history of the Negro or of the South; the following views give only a context which is necessary for this research.

There was abundant evidence of suspicion and antagonism in local attitudes and my rôle as student of the Negro was such as to bring it into action with full force. In explanation of the coolness of some people toward my plans, a white friend told me that the North-South rivalry is by no means ended. When he was in the army, he related, the boys from the North and South took "emotional" sides whenever an issue came up between representatives of the two groups, especially any racial issue. The feeling was more intense just after the World War. The southerners expected trouble when they got home because they had seen Negro boys sitting on porches with white people in France, and sometimes, in the cabarets, with French women. Many southern boys mailed home their army pistols "to shoot niggers with," they said. But, in fact, the postwar situation had not been as bad as anticipated and the Negro had again accepted his well-defined place. It was clear that I fell into the category of those who permitted or approved of Negro boys being in cabarets with French women, and that the appearance of a northerner raises images of this type. Another man, well-known as a liberal, stressed the difference between his practical interest in the Negro problem and my purely theoretical interest in it. He insisted that northern theorists who criticize the South endanger the work of small groups of liberal southerners who are trying to bring about some kind of justice. Every time a critical article appears in a northern journal the southerners feel that they do not receive credit for their actual good works, such as, for example, the lynchings they prevent. Another thing irritating to southerners is that we "think we know niggers," whereas actually we do not, and judge the whole group by the few cultivated people we may happen to know. A white informant said I probably had this notion, but that I would not have it after remaining in the South for several years. She added that many Negroes have bed bugs and warned me to be careful about who laundered my clothes lest bed bugs be brought into the house.[1] She referred also to the offensive odors of Negroes. Most southern informants agreed that northerners are quite settled in the belief that they know the Negro and therefore do not take the trouble to study local conditions.

I heard many criticisms of the way northern politicians have fraternized with Negroes, and repeated mention of the visit of a Republican president who got off his train in a town and shook hands with various Negroes, calling them Mr. and Mrs., but neglected to have any dealings with the white people. This sort of thing exasperates the white group because it tends to upset the racial adjustment and cause trouble.[2]

A white woman who had recently come to Southerntown reported only one complaint against me: I had addressed a certain Negro woman as Mrs. My rôle in this case was clear. I had called up all the unfavorable stereotypes with regard to northerners. It was useless to explain that the woman was a high-class Negro, that I could not help saying it because "no other words would come out of my mouth." Frequently in such circumstances I would add that I *was* a northerner and was not trying to be anything else, that I was as polite

[1] In this sentence I have reported in paraphrase what an informant said to me. I will follow the custom throughout the book of putting such quotations in the "historical present" tense. This tense indicates, then, a paraphrased statement, believed by an informant to be true, and having still whatever truth it possessed when uttered. We have no very convenient way of dealing with such a type of quotation in the writing of English; in German it would be put into the subjunctive. The repetitious use of quotation marks would be boring. Very often the reader will find slangy phrases in the material in the "historical present" tense; these are used as direct quotations from or the most effective paraphrases of the informant's speech.

[2] This informant showed no understanding of the nature of this behavior as a symbolic act with vote-getting possibilities in the North, both among whites and among Negroes.

as possible and tried to follow the customs as far as I could.

Many rumors circulate in Southerntown about the queer and obnoxious attitudes of northern people. A southern girl told me that Yankees usually think southern whites are lazy and get the Negroes to do everything for them. She believes that there is much misunderstanding and hostility toward the South in the North. For example, she mentioned Robert E. Lee and added that of course we, of the North, do not feel the same way about him as they do down there; a proposal to build a monument to him in the national cemetery at Arlington was protested by a group of northern women, she said, on the ground that he was not a citizen of the United States. She felt that northerners do not recognize southerners as belonging to the United States even now.

A plantation owner told me that northerners usually think of southerners as lazy and mean to Negroes. He pointed out how hard he works and gave an instance of how his wife took care of a certain Negro on his plantation. The doctor told her that the Negro was sick with heart trouble and was going to die, and added that only good food and rest could save him. The wife took responsibility for the Negro herself from that time on and fed him out of her own kitchen with special soups, meats, and vegetables. The Negro said that she saved his life. The man asked me if I thought there was a Yankee in the North who would do that for a Negro. I replied that we do not have plantations and so it would be hard to say. The point was, of course, my theoretical idealism versus his practical kindness in respect to Negroes.

There are professional southerners, too, just as there are chauvinists in any society. One of them said it was good I was coming to Southerntown, since northerners have peculiar ideas about the South and should actually become familiar with the situation instead of acting on theoretical presuppositions. It made his blood boil, he said, when he went North, to see Negroes riding in streetcars side by side with whites, to see them eating in the same restaurants, to see Negro men and white women together. It would have the same effect, he added, on any southerner.

The story was told of a southern woman who moved to Chicago and was called upon by a Negro woman from a few blocks away, a social call, mind you! The woman said, "I am from the South and in my country niggers come to the back door when they come, and they don't come to call. Good day." The informant was fascinated and scandalized by such an improbable event but evidently accepted it as the sort of thing that could easily happen in the North. A number of people think of the North as cold, both in climate and emotions. A student stated that he had never been up north and thought of it as remote and inhospitable. At his southern college every student spoke to every other student without the formality of introduction. He believed he would miss this sort of thing in the North, where people are reserved, hurried, and somewhat suspicious of one another.

Particular hostility to northern intellectuals appeared in a number of cases. One man apparently read *The Nation, The American Mercury,* and other journals that took a radical attitude on the matter of race inequality just to irritate himself. He was a "stand-patter" on the race question. He believed that college newspapers in particular should not indulge in theoretical "radicalism" because he sensed danger to the caste system in the South. "Many students not dry behind the ears yet" reflect the subversive views of their southern university professors.

In some cases there is quite active fear of northern interference. It was reported that in this county a number of planters refused to accept Rosenwald money to aid in building schools because they feared the money would be followed by attempts at outside influence or domination of their schools. In many cases these same planters built new schools or aided their tenants to do so. This attitude, of course, can hardly be characteristic in view of the amount of money the Rosenwald Fund has dispensed for this purpose.

Epithets have great emotional value and we must sense the full force of such words. These epithets frequently define the central issues in a society. "Nigger-lover" is a phrase used in Southerntown and not infrequently applied to northerners. It is evidently no light thing to call a southerner this and to do so would lead to physical violence in most cases. To be a "nigger-lover" suggests that the person is a traitor to his caste, the white caste, and that his fondness for Negroes is headlong and impractical. One cannot help thinking of the antonym: Are persons loyal to the white caste necessarily "nigger-haters"? Does it mean that if you "love niggers," you thereby put yourself in the class of hating southern whites? My white friends uniformly denied hating Negroes.

Then there is the term "nigger." How is it used and what are the variants of it? One day a college student asked me about my work, and then hazarded a guess, "Studying nigruhs?" I answered experimentally, "Yes, I am studying personality among the niggers." He said, "I am glad to hear you say 'nigger,' I see you understand about that. I don't mind hearing people say 'nigruh,' but I hate to hear them say 'knee-grow' the way they do up North. I had a girl from Michigan once who said it that way." Evidently the southern white men say "nigger" as standard practice, "nigruh," a slightly more respectful form, when talking to a northerner (from whom they expect criticism on the score of treatment of Negroes), but never Negro; that is the hallmark of a northerner and a caste-enemy.[3]

There is also the matter of the term "Yankee." I had always thought of myself as a middle westerner and of "Yankee" as an obsolete designation for people from New England. The term, however, was in quite lively use in Southerntown and I soon learned that I was one. Various people gave me their ideas of what Yankees are. At first I thought they were the descendants of people from the states which had fought against the South, and this is the case in the main. Minnesota men, as well as Massachusetts men, would be Yankees. In other cases people were not so clear as to whether or not a man from Idaho might not be a Yankee, or even one from California. Some thought that in the case of persons from states which had fought for the Union they used the term, "damn Yankees." My judgment in the end was that anybody can be a "Yankee" who does not share the attitudes of the white caste on the race ques-

---

[3] This was suspected by Professor E. Sapir, who in a conversation before this investigation outlined the case substantially as above.

tion. An Oklahoma man is definitely not a Yankee, nor is a Texan. The term indicates an "out-grouper," a potentially critical or hostile person, and the use of the word has the psychological effect of making the newcomer feel strange and isolated and on his best behavior in order not to be disliked. It is from Yankees that unfavorable opinions in regard to the South are expected. It is Yankees who "love niggers" and Yankees who have impractical and theoretical ideas on questions of social equality. It is Yankees also who have an incurable tendency to meddle with other people's social arrangements.

On the other hand, one is assured that Yankees can change. When they come down South and have real experience with the racial problem to replace their book learning, they usually accept the social arrangements and become loyal white-caste members. A number of cases of this were pointed out, especially those of northerners who had come to do business in the South. One man told me that he had changed his views about "niggers" since he had been in Southerntown and had come to feel much as southern people do. It seemed clear, to me at least, why he had drawn new inferences from this experience, and had changed his attitudes to those of the white caste. It seemed very likely that he had to accept southern views because his social contacts and those of his wife and family were with whites; he could not stand out against the tremendous pressure of white sentiment; and further, he could advance his economic interests only by coöperating with the dominant group. A social or economic boycott would quickly end any attempt to remain a Yankee.

Only one kind of person could retain his northern attitudes intact, one so situated that he would not mind the boycott. There is such a man living near Southerntown, a well-to-do person who has been a planter for many years. He is said to have defied southern custom at many points. He would do the unheard-of thing, for example, of taking Negroes in at the front door of his house, seating them in the parlor, and offering them refreshments. He would visit the house of a Negro, when he had the mind to, and if he came at meal time, would insist on having a plate put on for him. It was further reported that he disliked southern white people and would have nothing to do with them, even to the point of buying his supplies from Sears Roebuck so that he would not have to go to town. He did not even want his manager to buy in Southerntown. Because of his wealth he has been able to isolate himself from the pressure of southern sentiment and to remain a Yankee, a meddling Yankee of the type southerners do not like. Still, he is tolerated in the community.

Sometimes southern people are amused, as well as pleased, at the speed with which Yankees take over their attitudes. There was the case of a northerner who came down and stayed two years in the community. At the end of this time someone criticized the South in his presence. The two-year-old southerner defended, "We southerners don't actually do things that way."

Southerntown is a vertible Cheka in its vigilance on caste matters. There are constant and potent pressures to compel every white person to act his caste rôle correctly. Once I was walking to a Negro home, one of the few on the white side of Southerntown, and had to ask for directions. A white woman on one of the porches told me and then said, "You know that niggers live there, don't you?" She was at once expressing surprise and defining the situation so that I would be sure to behave correctly.

It is undoubtedly true that I drew the full force of these pressures toward conformity because of my interest in the Negro problem. If I had come as a medical researcher, my being a northerner might have been much less conspicuous, or if I had been explicitly studying white social organization or personality to the exclusion of the Negro problem. In either case accommodative attitudes with northerners would have functioned which would have tended to heal over the Civil War wounds and to offer a basis of pleasant relations. There are many of these accommodative attitudes; for example, people expressed the opinion that they are glad slavery is gone and that perhaps even having such a terrible war was not too big a price to pay. In a friendly mood informants would say, "The War is over and there is no sense in perpetuating old differences; all that is past and gone." Commercial relationships between North and South with their reciprocal service have built up a basis of accord and the common cultural ties have been powerfully restored. A northern businessman would be much less conscious of the old antagonisms. It is only when the differing views on the Negro and his status are brought sharply forward that the older attitudes toward the North are reinstated. The vitality of these different views is still a major fact of American society and exists beside and behind the commercial and cultural bindings.

The force of historical influence as a present fact struck me once when I attended a meeting of a Rotary Club. I had known in a general way of the occupation and federal military administration of the South after the Civil War, but had never understood it emotionally. Perhaps this is always the case when one's own ox is not gored. At any rate, the Rotary speaker referred to the "ravages of the War between the States and the even more terrible ravages of the carpet-bagger days which followed it." This was the first time I had heard "War between the States," but this was not all. The carpet-bagger days were evidently the brief period of Negro supremacy supported by northern force and this was felt to be, by this man at least, a more terrible humiliation than defeat in war. Later I raised with various friends the question whether most white southerners know the history of the Civil War, the humiliations of reconstruction days, "carpet-baggism," and Negro rule. They felt that this knowledge is general and has not dimmed with time. The possible recurrence of Negro supremacy is an ever-present threat and a dominating consideration in southern social life. Southern society is no less active than ours in transmitting its version of history.[4]

It is worthwhile to formulate very briefly some historical views on the nature of the racial problem in America, especially since it seems clear that the mores of America have

---

[4] "It is a well known fact that textbook publishers publish two different textbooks concerning Civil War histories—one for the North and the other for the South." W. J. Robertson, *The Changing South* (New York, 1927), p. 144; quoted by permission of Liveright Publishing Corp.

been in conflict from the outset on the treatment of Negroes. A consideration of some importance is that in earliest times there seems to have been a common area of culture influence in Europe and Africa. Herskovits[5] has referred to an "Old World culture province of which Africa is but a part," and indicated a number of common traits in this area, such as the use of iron and the spread of proverbs. Although the cultures in Europe and Africa were certainly identifiably different at the time slave exportation to the Americas began, they were not as radically differentiated as some have supposed. Native Africans had good title to being human from the outset, in the same sense that we assert our own claims to humanity. Herskovits gives a number of facts which offer a new perspective on the nature of the slave trade and the types of Negro that were brought here; he shows that the American slaves came from the West Coast area instead of being gathered from all Central Africa, as was sometimes supposed; that they were probably drawn from all social classes in their African societies and not merely from slave classes; that the institution of plantation slavery existed in their societies and that they were therefore familiar with it before they came to America; that large numbers came to the United States from intermediate points, mainly the islands of the West Indies where some degree of familiarity with Western customs had been gained during "seasoning"; and finally, since opportunities for assimilating Western European culture were uniquely good in the United States, that the Negroes attained here the greatest difference from their native African culture types.[6] We must think of them as landing in the United States with a personality structure keyed to effective action in one of their own societies, and not as mere animals unaccustomed to participation in a complex social life. It is a part of our social vanity to overestimate the value of our own ways and habits, though our technical superiority over the Africans must be affirmed; the proof of

[5] M. J. Herskovits, "Social History of the Negro." In *Handbook of Social Psychology*, edited by C. Murchison (Clark University Press, 1935), p. 212.

[6] Herskovits, *op. cit.*, pp. 237-253.

this is that it is we who enslaved the Africans and not they us.

It is well known that the Greek and Roman societies utilized human slaves, and it seems that the practice had never completely faded out in Western Europe, especially in the southern countries. So far as white Europeans were concerned, however, slavery had long been replaced by serfdom at the opening of the era of discovery of the new world; the difference between these two systems was perhaps not so great as it has since come to seem. Undoubtedly the influence of Christian ideology with its equalitarian concept had a share in changing the lot of the average man from the slave to the serf status; this same Christian ideal of the equality of souls in the sight of God had, perhaps inadvertently, prepared the way for the commercial and technological developments which were to offer a new social rôle to the simplest citizen, i.e., freedom to advance his status according to his social usefulness. Important for us is the idea that Christianity offered a new notion of human dignity to the masses of white people who had occupied a servile status in the aristocratic class system of Western Europe. It was actually only in the eighteenth and nineteenth centuries that these equalitarian concepts were translated into social and political institutions. The situation of black people from another society, however, was different from that of white Europeans. At the beginning of the Colonial era they might still be enslaved; the protection of Christian notions of human worth and value did not yet apply to them; but even in their case it was not possible to enslave them without suitable rationalizations. The excuse used was to stress the importance of saving African souls by enslaving and converting them;[7] actually, of course, the motive was the wish to profit from the trade itself and from the labor of the slaves in a plantation system.

The slow passing of the feudal order in Europe, however, left its ideational heritage and also the possibility of recreating in a new land that which had vanished at home. Rising

[7] William G. Sumner, *Folkways* (Boston, 1906), p. 299.

against and finally destroying the slave-feudal organization of society in Europe was the free, competitive, individualistic tradition represented first in commerce and later
in industrial organization. Perhaps one may say that in the
United States these two traditions were continued in the
aristocratic order of the plantation economy in the South
on the one hand, and in the small farms and commercial
and industrial activity of the North on the other.[8] Geographic differences probably acted selectively on these two
currents in the European mores, made small farmers and
merchants of the men of the North and planters and feu-
dalists of the ruling group in the South. A plantation
economy is particularly suited to a staple crop, to the absolute control of masses of labor, and to a fixed social order
in which individuals remain in the places where they are
born.

Geographic conditions in the North, on the contrary,
seemed to lead to the small farm, the factory, and to a
varied and steadily more industrialized economy. Here
social advancement of humble individuals was not only tolerated but was of the essence of the system. At least the
participants in such a competitive system must believe that
social advancement is possible or they will not work as they
must if the system is to survive. There is no doubt that in
the past hard work has frequently been rewarded by movement to higher social and economic position. Differences in
the two areas persist to this day. They are well represented
in the aristocratic, agrarian tradition in the South[9] and in
the equalitarian ideology of the North which has become
the master pattern of the American mores.

Besides these two conceptions of a social order it should
be noted that the American colonists brought with them
and established in America their patriarchal family form.
The establishment of this monogamous family as the Amer-

---

[8] A. G. Keller, *Colonization—A Study of the Founding of
New Societies* (Boston, 1908), p. 14.
[9] Twelve Southerners, *I Take My Stand* (New York, 1930).
Here is admirably expressed the faith in the agricultural mode
of life as a human value and the corresponding antagonism to
an industrial civilization.

ican ideal has been of no little importance so far as the Negro is concerned. This family form was relatively impervious to dissolution. It tolerated only one legitimate sexual object. It permitted no bacchanalian interludes when the monogamous taboos were lifted. All women were tabooed by an extension of the incest barrier, except the legitimate wife. It seems possible that these restrictions were experienced as a severe limitation by individuals growing up in this family form and that as a result there was generated continuous pressure in these individuals to escape from the frustrating situation. The use of Negro slaves as sexual objects may have been a welcome outlet from these harassing limitations, an outlet which was taken, be it noted, with the usual patriarchal stipulation, that the white women were still reserved to the master caste. The widespread fact of miscegenation is more easily understandable on the basis of this assumption, since it would seem that miscegenation would not occur if monogamous marriage took care of the sexual needs of individuals. There were always, of course, unmarried individuals to whom these considerations would not apply.

The recent history of Western European nations seems to confirm our supposition that already in the first two hundred years of the settlement of North America there was a trend in the Western European mores leading to individualism and democracy and guaranteeing social opportunity to the masses of common men. If this be true, we may look upon slavery as an institution which appeared in America in full strength while it was being rejected by the emerging new patterns in Western Europe. Slavery stands against our technical trends which demand a mobile, replaceable labor supply and which generate useful energy in individuals by offering them hope of advancement. Machines cannot tell whether the hands that tend them are white or black. The fastening of this outmoded institution on American society has engendered social and regional differences of great significance. The dilemma can be studied today in the personality records of middle-class Negro people; and it is equally evident in the struggles of southern white people to adjust themselves to two different trends in their treatment of Negroes. One of these trends is the feudal one which would keep the Negro in his "place"; the other is the democratic one which would permit him unrestricted opportunity for personal advancement.

There was conflict on this point in the drafting of the constitution itself, a constitution which finally indirectly recognized slavery by taxing Negroes as "imports."[10] The issue might have lapsed and the importation of slaves have become unprofitable, had not the cotton gin been invented in 1793 and the hope of profit in the plantation system indefinitely increased. The issue never thereafter lost its commanding character in the American political and social scene.[11] The Negroes have been and for the moment, at least, still are the "bottom rail" of the southern economic and social system.

The period from 1800 to 1860 showed the driving power of the plantation economy and witnessed its steady expansion south and west. Parallel developments in the North carried the northern type of economy westward into ever new lands. These antagonistic developments were reflected in a steady series of unsatisfactory compromises in the political field. Two competing modes of life were set up and the conflict in the American mores was made concrete in rival states and regions, in different political philosophies, and finally in armies in the field.

After the thirties there was a marked growth in abolitionist sentiment in the North. Persistent agitation by small groups of intellectuals, the stressing of religious ideals of hu-

[10] Theodore D. Jervey, *The Slave Trade* (Columbia, S. C., 1935), p. 16.

[11] "From a consideration of the wisdom, propriety and morality of importing African slaves as an article of commerce in 1787, the Negro Question in the United States had progressed to the wisdom and propriety of preventing any extension of the institution of slavery beyond those limits in which it existed in 1820, and from this, with repeated agitations, fairly shaking the Union to its foundation, followed by compromises satisfactory to none, there had flared up a consideration of the reopening of the Slave Trade in 1856, swiftly followed by Secession and war in 1860, and Emancipation, as a war measure, in 1863, directed against the eleven Confederate States." Jervey, *op. cit.*, p. 124; quoted by permission of The State Co.

man dignity, regional resistance from the South, all had finally resulted in a strong mass movement against slavery. In this agitation the equalitarian ideal, originally Christian, became a political dogma and played a major rôle. It amounted to a campaign against the status order in the South, in addition to its formal object of freeing the slaves.[12] The successful stirring of the northern masses can, it seems, only be explained by the tremendous conviction of rightness of their own democratic mores. Undoubtedly they idealized the Negro whom they were striving to liberate. Undoubtedly also they followed the common psychological device of making a beast and devil out of the antagonist, the southern planter class. It seems clear from expressions of the period that northerners identified themselves with the Negro and defended his rights, as if their own were challenged at the same time. Perhaps the common northerner sensed the danger to his personal status and hopes of social advancement in the existence of such a bad example as was provided by the enslavement of the Negro in the South. He may have felt that his own personal gain in status was too recent and too shaky to be secure against the continued force of such an example. The eventual power of the abolitionist folk movement can be best explained in this way which is, after all, only another way of saying that the conflict over slavery was a conflict in the mores in respect to personal dignity, freedom, and opportunity for social advancement. Additional force is given to this idea by the realization that in 1861 there were about four million foreign-born persons in the nineteen million inhabitants of the North, a majority of them relatively recent immigrants, many coming as a result of extrusion from their home lands after struggles against a still-feudal social order.[13] One cannot omit to notice that the North may have wasted on antislavery much of the energy that might have been spent on local and sectional types of social reorganization. Undoubtedly the growth of the labor movement was

[12] Perspective on this period has been gained by consultation with a social historian, Dr. Robert A. Warner, of the Institute of Human Relations.

[13] Robertson, *op. cit.*, p. 23.

impeded by the fact of the Civil War, thereby giving to American capitalism a long heyday when social attention was focused on other issues. Still the abolitionists may have been wise in directing their fury at the intolerable presence of human slavery in libertarian America.

Above and beyond abolition, there is much that is mysterious about the Civil War, as about all wars; symbols of sectional and national difference seem to be unexpectedly welcome to humans. People like to define themselves off against others, to receive social legitimation for their hatreds, and to bloat out egotistically their own self-ideal. Once the issue is joined all manner of irrelevant passions, foolish and noble, liberate themselves in war. And these symbols of difference between nations and regions seem to be carefully preserved and to be hauled out again when needed as the targets for personal discontent. After the Civil War the southern states were reassimilated into the Union by a policy marked in its vengefulness. The victory of the North seemed to be accepted by northerners as a warrant for the destruction of the southern social system. The immediate enfranchisement and full social participation guaranteed to the Negro by the reconstruction Congress completely upset former social relationships in the South. Northern force in southern areas could not be maintained for long, and northern vengeance and bitterness, sufficient to maintain military rule, disappeared fairly rapidly. The result was a continuation of the War on a different field. The folk sense of the South, habituated to the subordination of the Negro, reacted to reconstruction by intensified pressure for his subordination. This pressure is often explained as a reaction to the carpet-bag regimes and to indiscretion in government.[14] It does not matter much how it is phrased; the southern conception of the Negro and his place would have been reëstablished no matter how tactful or sensible the reconstruction measures might have been. Nothing short of extirpation of the middle- and upper-class whites could have changed the result greatly. The solid South emerged from the War, but

[14] Paul Lewinson, *Race, Class and Party* (New York, 1932), p. 42.

we should not forget that it had been even more solid before the War.[15]

Emancipation gave the Negro for the first time a means of protest against undesirable conditions, viz., migration. Whatever else may be said, we must remember that in the slave status the worker was bound to the land at the will of his master and, if he changed his residence, he did not do so at his own wish. This is the ultimate in diminished freedom from the standpoint of our social system. Forcing a Negro to leave his home when he did not wish to, on the other hand, was a constant threat to the security of personal ties, in particular those of family and neighborhood; however infrequently this may have happened in fact in slavery days, the legal possibility of sale of a person must have been a constant barrier to the development of a stable family institution. This weak family structure in turn reacted on individual character at every point; in particular it operated against the formation of stable, active, independent characters of the American frontier type. It may be that simple northern people were led in the end to perceive the slave system as a threat to such fundamental social values; this would help to explain the power of the final reaction against the southern institutions. At any rate, it was the threat of physically fixing the Negro to the land by vagrancy statutes that evoked the most vigorous of the reconstruction measures. Fundamental to all "freedom" in our system is free disposition of one's own person, and the right to move where advantage seems to lead. With this freedom, and with the educational opportunities made available to Negroes at first through northern zeal, some Negroes have risen to middle-class status since Civil War. The Negro is still discriminated against in the race for economic power and status, but his gains over the slave rôle are by no means inconsequential.

The aristocratic domination of southern politics was destroyed by the Civil War, and during reconstruction the poorer white people were increasingly admitted to political participation and power; otherwise they might have com-

[15] Robertson, *op. cit.*, p. 51.

bined with similarly disadvantaged Negroes. In this sense the white South did indeed become more "solid," in that more white men achieved a formal stake in the operation of the political system. Whites were needed at first to outweigh Negro votes, and later an ideology of the superiority of whiteness captured their allegiance. To some extent the traditional rivalry of these poorer white people with Negroes became conventionalized as the total white attitude.[16] It is still observable, although in Southerntown it does not play the rôle popularly assigned to it. As will be indicated, the poorer whites show less than the predicted resentment of Negroes and the middle-class whites much more.

The Ku Klux Klan and other more powerful secret orders were folk movements for the intimidation of Negroes and for the reëstablishment of the social distance that formerly existed between whites and Negroes. Although the work of such orders differed in different regions, this function was invariable.[17] The Klan was outmoded when its objectives—such as political and social subordination of Negroes—were legalized and when arrangements tending to consolidate the older positions of the races were complete. In place of the slave system, as a method by which the two racial groups lived together, appeared a caste system, a much less secure system, to be sure, from the standpoint of the white group, but nevertheless workable, as has been proved. These then are the results of northern interference in the South: solidarity based on whiteness, the emergence into the political sun of the lower-class whites, and the caste system with its elaborate social code replacing the slavery system of earlier days.

It has frequently been observed that there was a rise in race hostility following the War and it is certainly true that lynchings increased. It is important to see that slavery was a method of subordinating Negroes which, once established, did not require continuous, active white pressure for its maintenance, but tended to fall into routine and to permit

---

[16] Charles S. Johnson, *The Negro in American Civilization* (New York, 1930), pp. 12-13.

[17] Lewinson, *op. cit.*, pp. 50-51.

accommodative adjustments to arise between the races. There was policing in the plantation areas, but much more conspicuous was the stable and peaceable adjustment of the two races. The caste system, on the other hand, is a less secure method of subordinating Negroes, and, at least while it is being imposed, requires quite active aggression against them. From this standpoint it appears that the relative infrequency of lynchings under slavery was evidence of the fixity of the subordinate rôle of the Negro.

It frequently happens that, if a person cannot hate the one who causes an injustice, he will turn his hatred to someone else only indirectly related to the hated object. It may be that after the bloody Civil War the defeated South turned its spent and fruitless hostility for the North to the Negroes who were in part the cause of the conflict. Southerners could not avenge themselves directly against the North, but could and did take action against the Negroes for whom the North had fought. To punish the Negroes would be a kind of deflected expression of hostility toward the victors who might have won the actual war but who could not win the struggle for emancipation of the Negro. Such a sentiment would also reënforce the wish to reëstablish social relations as nearly as possible on the prewar basis. It is certainly true today that Negroes and Yankees tend to be associated in the mind of the white southerner; and it is frequently alleged that northern attempts to alter the situation of the Negro are followed by increased pressure on him rather than by melioration of his lot.

Slavery was a means of keeping the peace between the races from one point of view, but it had to be maintained ultimately by force, as indeed all societies do. The use of force was most apparent when counteraggression on the part of those coerced was most obvious, in the case, for example, of slave revolt. It was true that force could be kept in the background and even greatly diminished, once the underdogs had acquired the habit of suppressing protest against the slave system and aggression had become blunted within the slave personality. This acceptance of frustrating circumstances without open resistance we call "accommodation." But when protest became open, forceful measures had to be, and were, used.

The purpose of these brief historical references is to show that there is a conflict between the dominant American mores, which are expressed formally in the Declaration of Independence, and the regional mores of the South which have had to deal with the Negroes. Two different and contradictory conceptions of human worth are operating in one social field. The resulting conflict has done more than any other to wrack the American constitutional system, and it is still one of the major sources of unbalance in our social life. The present-day continuation of this dilemma is plainly visible in Southerntown and is an aspect of the personal lives of all its people.

CHAPTER V

Caste and Class in Southerntown

〜〜〜〜〜〜〜〜〜〜〜〜〜〜〜〜〜〜〜〜〜〜〜

A discussion of caste and class in Southerntown may well begin with a classic story on race relations. A Negro was found by the conductor sitting in the white car of a southern train. He was challenged and told to go to the Jim Crow car. He objected, said he belonged in the white car, and gave as his reason, "Boss, I'se resigned from de colored race." This story is a play on the most serious issue in Southerntown; and it illustrates how futile it would be to pretend that one can study Negro personality without reference to white society. The incredulous white conductor is quite as necessary to the anecdote as the ingenuous Negro. Every fact about Negroes is likely to have an obverse side with meanings for the whites.

Description of social life in Southerntown inevitably involves a discussion of the nature of caste and class.[1] Caste and class distinctions are ways of dividing people according to the behavior expected of them in the society. Caste and class show the relations in which people stand to one another in Southerntown; they organize local life securely and make social coöperation possible. They deserve a detailed discussion in order that the emotional patterns appropriate to them may come into clear outline. We do not have here any racial soul or genius defending its heritage, as is often alleged; what we see is a moral and status order in operation, whose operators safeguard and perpetuate their positions in it.

[1] The views of Professor W. L. Warner, of the University of Chicago, have made the conception of social division by class a working tool in this research. See W. Lloyd Warner, "American Caste and Class," *Amer. J. Sociol.* (1936), Vol. 42, No. 2, pp. 234-237.

Caste has replaced slavery as a means of maintaining the essence of the old status order in the South.[2] By means of it racial animosity is held at a minimum.[3] Caste is often seen as a barrier to social contact or, at least, to some forms of social contact. It defines a superior and inferior group and regulates the behavior of the members of each group. In essence the caste idea seems to be a barrier to legitimate descent. A union of members of the two castes may not have a legitimate child. All such children are members of the lower caste and cannot be legitimated into the upper caste by the fact that they have an upper-caste father or mother. Caste in Southerntown is also a categorical barrier to sexual congress between upper-caste women and lower-caste men, within or without the married state. It does not result in such a barrier between upper-caste men and lower-caste women. In this it seems to be modeled on the patriarchal family with its possessive prerogatives of the male; it has a double standard of the same type. Nothing else seems absolute about the caste barrier. It does not totally exclude social contact and seems to have no other mark so distinctive as the marriage and sexual prohibition.

It is necessary to remind ourselves that American democratic mores are set in quite another current. They do not recognize barriers to legitimate descent or preferential rights to sex relationships. Democratic society guarantees equal opportunity to enjoy whatever goods and services society has to offer; there are no arbitrary limitations based on race or color. This is the sense in which northerners seem theoretical to southerners when the Negro is discussed. Northerners look at the Negro through the constitutional window; southerners look at him through the caste window. In the train of the barriers to legitimate descent and sexual contact come other limitations. The caste line works out also as an automatic block to social advancement for the Negro and this means that the highest prestige prizes are not accessible to him. For example, we bring millions

[2] W. A. Dunning, "The Undoing of Reconstruction," *Atlantic Monthly* (1901), Vol. 88, p. 449; also W. E. B. Du Bois, *The Negro* (New York, 1915), p. 149.

[3] James E. Cutler, *Lynch-law* (New York, 1905), p. 218.

of boys into the world who are in training as future presidents of the United States; no one expects, however, that Negro boys are really included. Their caste membership silently excludes them from such high hopes.

American caste is pinned not to cultural but to biological features—to color, features, hair form, and the like. This badge is categorical regardless of the social value of the individual. It is in this sense that caste is "undemocratic" since it accepts an arbitrary token as a means of barring Negroes from equal opportunity and equal recognition of social merit.[4] Negroid body form was at one time a mark of a Negro culture and is still to some degree a mark of an inferior assimilation of white culture; but both of these differentiating marks of Negroes are rapidly diminishing and in the course of time the physical stigmata may be left isolated as the only warrant of caste difference. The cultural stigmata of the past seem likely to disappear altogether.

Inferior caste results in a degree of social isolation for the individuals concerned. It tends to limit the personal development of members so that it is more difficult for them to compete for the highest social rewards and position. American policy is somewhat contradictory on this score, since we really do not keep the caste barrier fixed by the most effective methods. Slavery in this sense is much superior as a method of holding a population as a subject group. The upper caste would be more secure if the inferior caste were to have a separate language, or at least if its acquisition of our speech were limited. It would be safer also if lower-caste members were not able to read, if there were no social or religious sharing, and if the group were geographically immobile and extremely limited in social participation. The leaven of our dominant democratic mores has, however, made such a firm adjustment impossible; war broke up the southern approximation of it and we have a system of subjugation which is, for all its seeming firmness, shaky and contradictory.

Caste members tend to develop a distinctive psychology. This is no less true of the white caste than of the Negro, and

[4] Donald Young, *American Minority Peoples* (New York, 1932), pp. 580-581.

we must never forget that we have two castes in the South and not just one. Southern white solidarity is caste solidarity. Nor should we overlook the fact that most of us, in the North as well as South, are members of the white caste, that we do, in practice, define the Negro as something categorically inferior and demand special privileges for ourselves and fellow whites. Our sympathy also tends to run along caste lines, even if it is not so acute in the North by virtue of the absence of the problem in a crucial form; northern Negroes are not numerous enough to be designated as out-groups in most northern communities.

The slogans of the white caste are among the most common expressions in Southerntown: "Niggers are all right in their place." "Would you want your sister to marry a nigger?" "Whenever whites have come in contact with blacks the world over, they have always been the dominant race," etc. Here is certainly a situation in which prediction is possible in the social sciences because these beliefs may be elicited at will from high and low in the southern white caste. Their repetition can in fact become tedious, and one is surprised at the sense of originality which those who repeat them often seem to feel. These expressions are always heavily supported from the emotional side and are impressive in the actual situation. White-caste members exhibit an appropriate pride in the achievements of their caste and like to stress its superiority in management and social responsibility.[5] In the Negro caste also a distinctive emotional set tends to develop, a psychology which is an accurate response to the caste position of the Negro.

The solidarity of the white caste on sexual and social issues has been widely noticed. When southern white people tell a northerner that after a few years in the South he will feel about Negroes just as southerners do, they are making the point that he joins the white caste. The solicitation is extremely active, though informal, and one must stand by one's caste to survive. Negroes, of course, know the power of white solidarity better than any one else. A Negro put it this way: Although white men often appear

[5] A. H. Stone, *Studies in the American Race Problem* (New York, 1908), p. 87.

to be good friends to Negroes, if a Negro commits a crime against a white man, the white friend will invariably turn against him; whereas if a white man has any little trouble, all his white friends flock to him and defend him. He says it is different with Negro friends: they stick by you better. Raper[6] has cited the case of a white infantryman who actually used a bayonet in defending a Negro charged with rape. This white man was never able to keep a position in his town thereafter; his white fellow workers forced him to leave for one reason or another.

A feature of white solidarity, as has been noted, is the harsh term that brands the caste traitor—"nigger-lover." Such a man enjoys the benefits of white solidarity, but does not stand by his caste. In the epithet there is an implication of inferiority and perhaps a threat of being classed with the scorned Negro.

To the Negro, of course, the caste barrier is an ever-present solid fact. His education is incomplete until he has learned to make some adjustment to it, usually the one preferred by the white caste.[7] Since our democratic society is built on equal opportunity to achieve the highest social distinction, highest class position, and highest financial rewards, the caste barrier is obviously in contradiction with it. The Negro must haul down his social expectations and resign himself to a relative immobility in contrast to the dominant spirit of our society. This dominant spirit is well expressed by the notion of "beginning at the bottom and

[6] Arthur F. Raper, *The Tragedy of Lynching* (Chapel Hill, 1933), p. 244.

[7] "The question of the child's future is a serious dilemma for Negro parents. Awaiting each colored boy and girl are cramping limitations and buttressed obstacles, in addition to those that must be met by youth in general; and this dilemma approaches suffering in proportion to the parents' knowledge of and the child's innocence of those conditions. Some parents up to the last moment strive to spare the child the bitter knowledge; the child of less sensitive parents is likely to have this knowledge driven in upon him from infancy. And no Negro parent can definitely say which is the wiser course, for either of them may lead to spiritual disaster for the child." J. W. Johnson, *Along This Way* (New York, 1933), p. 56; quoted by permission of the Viking Press.

working to the top." Moton[8] has pointed out that the Negro may begin at the bottom but, on the average, he may expect to stay there, or pretty close to it.

There was no lack of appreciation of this fact among my informants. A Negro plantation manager, a very rare specimen, said that the Negroes on his plantation tend to improve faster under a Negro manager. They say to themselves that what he can do, they can do; whereas with a white boss they feel that the gulf is too great and make no effort to improve. My informant believed that white men cultivate this sense of intrinsic superiority of the whites and use it to keep the Negroes in their places, as the whites see them. A woman Negro informant said that white people do not like to see Negroes get along well. For example, her mother has a very pleasant house with flowers in the yard and pretty decorations in and around it. A white man who came there to bring her some laundry saw how attractive the place was, and then went to a miserable Negro cabin next door and called her mother over there. The informant said that he was so mean he did not like to go to a Negro house that was nice. She had to add in all truthfulness that white people have come to the house, have gone through it, and complimented her mother on it. A third Negro explained that he had been talking with a white man that morning; they had leaned over the fence and gossiped for about an hour. The white man discussed political candidates, asked the Negro his opinion of this one and that one. The informant felt this was all well and good, but rather ironical since he could not vote. He thought the white people in America have their minds pretty well made up about

[8] "One subtle and serious result of this condition is that Negro youths are deprived of many of the incentives that stimulate ambition. There is comparatively little in American industry which spurs the Negro to do his best. In the majority of places where Negroes serve, there is no such thing as 'beginning at the bottom and working to the top.' A porter or messenger in a bank has little or no prospect of being anything more than a porter or messenger to the end of his days." R. R. Moton, *What the Negro Thinks* (Garden City, N. Y., 1932), p. 201; quoted by permission of Doubleday, Doran & Co.

the Negro; they are determined not to let him get anywhere. By "getting anywhere" he meant they will not let the Negro have full opportunity for social advancement and do not expect of him the efforts appropriate to it.

On the other hand, Negroes, like other Americans, pursue the goals and ideals which are characteristic of America and cannot in these days ignorantly accept their "place" as once they could. The Negro shares inevitably the values of the dominant group and aspires to full participation in it. Many Negroes also have white blood which gives them another type of claim to social consideration.

Since our social values are best represented by white persons, the Negro aspires also to whiteness. As Reuter[9] says, the "center of gravity of the hybrid group is outside itself." This presents a difficulty, however, because, while white culture may be assimilated, whiteness itself cannot be imitated. For Negroes there is a definite pull toward all of the identifying marks of the white caste, cultural and physical. It is not believed that Negroes want to be "white" in any abstract sense; what they want is to be indistinguishably full participants in American society. For the present, to be white seems to be the best guarantee of this complete human status. Such a discussion as the following brings out the issue clearly.

A Negro schoolteacher remarked that Negro babies often change their color after they are born, and asked me what changes white babies undergo. I answered that their hair and eyes often change color, the nose form changes, and the ratio of the head to the body becomes smaller as they grow. Informant said regretfully that Negro babies frequently become darker as they grow and the hair changes

[9] "The desire of the mixed-blood man is always and everywhere to be a white man; to be classed with and become a part of the superior race. The ideal—the center of gravity—of the hybrid group is outside itself. The ideal of beauty, of success, of all that is good and desirable is typified by the superior race. The ambition of the man of mixed-blood is to be identified with the superior group, to share its life, its work and its civilization." E. B. Reuter, *The Mulatto in the United States* (Boston, 1918), p. 315; quoted by permission of Richard G. Badger.

texture. Colored babies' hair is likely to be very fluffy. If the baby has a lot of thick hair when small, it will probably turn out later to be bad; but if it has thin hair or none at all, it is more likely to be good. By "bad" and "good" she meant farther from or nearer to the straight hair of the white type. The above is enlightening in that it indicates the anxiety which exists about the future caste marks of the child.

The same woman also commented upon one of her students who is very sullen and mean, but whose older brother has a much better disposition. She thought the younger one sensitive because his lips are heavy and he is so much darker than his brother, and she felt the boys' mother might be at fault, since she is said to show open favoritism toward the lighter brother. It is impossible to know how much of a rôle this sensitivity to caste characteristics plays, but it must be very great in a Negro family since the fact of good or bad caste marks plays such an important part in the future success of the child.

Another of my informants was discussing with his wife the question of children they might have. He told her he supposed that one of their children would be dark (that is, much darker than they were—his wife is also brown-skinned and a bit darker than he). The idea that one of their children should be dark infuriated the wife and she became much upset over it. He thinks the reason is that her mother was very dark and that she is afraid his prediction is all too true.

First caste awareness apparently occurs very early. One Negro said he used to hear his parents and their guests talking; the conversation would always be about the bad treatment received by the Negroes, their hard lot, etc. Still another source of racial awareness occurred in the family because his brothers and sisters were of different shades. The darker ones would assume that the lighter ones wanted to be white and, if they showed any arrogance in behavior, it was said of them that they were trying to act like whites; in fact the lighter children did not have to be nearly as bold as the darker ones to draw this reproach.

Another informant was taught by his mother to prefer

"brighter" Negro girls. He is fairly light himself. When he thought of marrying, he could not consider any real dark girls. He said his mother felt like this because the brighter people are treated more like men and women and get more concessions from the whites; it was obvious, too, that this informant wished to advance his own status by marrying a light woman.

The principle here seems very simple. Whiteness represents full personal dignity and full participation in American society. Blackness or darkness represents limitation and inferiority; and sometimes even animal character is imputed to it. The Negroes share sufficiently in American society to want to be fully human in the American sense and to this end they prefer to be as light as possible, since the white caste seems to grant some recognition, informally of course, to the lighter colors. Consciousness of color and accurate discrimination between shades is a well-developed Negro caste mark in Southerntown; whites, of course, are not nearly so skilful in distinguishing and naming various shades.

The question of color comes up constantly in reference to marriage within the Negro group. A woman informant said her mother objected to her marriage to a very dark man. Informant did not know the reason at the time and the mother did not press her objections. Later, however, it became clear that the mother did not like the fact that the husband was so dark. She was extraordinarily sensitive to color and preferred the lighter people. The same informant stated that light Negro men frequently like darker women, whereas very dark men like lighter women. She says this belief is widely held by colored people. A professional man in particular likes to have a very light wife. It is believed that, if a man is very dark and his wife very light, he is likely to be madly in love with her.

There is, of course, no absolute rule on this score. Personal qualities undoubtedly interfere with the tendency to "marry light." Since the marriage choice remains so often with the man in our society, it usually follows that the woman is lighter than the man, since he has the chance to choose. Class considerations, however, enter here also. A man may marry a darker woman because she is of a better class than he; she may have, for example, some exceptional skill or talent, like being a nurse, a teacher, a singer, a caterer, or what not. Another informant said that her mother was quite dark, much darker than her father. She added that this always seemed to be a sore point with the mother. She never seemed to be able to forgive the father for being a light-skinned man, and wanted the girls to marry light men. The mother eventually divorced the father, the informant thought because of their difference in color. It seemed possible in this case that the lighter husband had superior social advantages which humiliated his wife or made her jealous.

A Negro man said that his father, who was very light and could almost pass for a white man, was often used as a peacemaker between the races because of his light color. His mother and his mother's side of the family were dark, but she always preferred light people. She thought they received much better treatment than dark Negroes: "The black man always gets the worst of it." The whites like Negroes with white features or skin color and tend to trust them more than dark Negroes. He said that white employers have a tendency to separate the light from the dark Negroes, as, for example, when a foreman will assign all the darker Negroes to work in a cluster and will separate out the lighter ones in the same way. I asked him how it was that a man as light as his father married a woman as dark as his mother, since I had been told that men usually marry lighter women. He said that this was not always the case and that sometimes lighter people preferred darker people; but he himself seemed puzzled on this point. The same informant stated that mulatto families in his childhood community were always at a social premium. For instance, the light-colored men had many more sexual opportunities than darker men would have, that is, opportunities with Negro women. His father, he said, was so light that he was constantly mistaken for a white man; this was embarrassing to him and was one of the reasons he stayed away from church, since when he went to church, people would begin to show him the courtesies accorded to white people.

This emphasis on whiteness as a means to achieve full human dignity has been repeatedly noted. Delusions of being white in color are quite common in Negro psychotics and have been noted by many researchers.[10]

As an hypothesis it might be worth saying that the whites may prefer on a straight narcissistic basis those Negroes who look most white. He who looks most like me is most entitled to my love and confidence; he who is strange is more likely to be dangerous. The presence of "white" hair and features is a kind of guarantee of good relations between the white and the Negro.

As a result of caste pressure, there is a sort of passive solidarity within the Negro caste. This is illustrated by a complaint often made by the police in Southerntown. They say that Negroes will not testify against other Negroes; that often, for example, those who have been right at the scene of a murder will not talk and will pretend to know nothing about it. Then the police have to use third-degree methods to get the truth out of them. The Negroes have a reputation with whites of shielding, hiding, and aiding criminal members of their race. The degree of solidarity is disappointingly small, though, from the standpoint of middle-class

[10] "Among those of the grandiose type who show a pathological transformation of the personality and entertain ideas of an exalted position, the writer finds it a very common delusion entertained by the colored women that they are white; that they are the mothers of the white nurses and physicians; each one will claim that she is the only white person among these patients and that all the others are 'niggers.' This is symptomatic of definite types of maladjustment, for it must be assumed that an individual who realizes that she has a proportion of white blood in her veins would naturally have aspirations and wishes that she might be white; that the excess of white blood might dominate. This wish fulfillment characterizes the delusional solution of existing difficulties as a harbor into which the sore mentality of the patient can retreat. The women rarely aspire to anything higher than to be a preacher, but some believe they are prophets and possess divine power." Mary O'Malley, "Psychoses in the Colored Race," *Amer. J. Insan.* (1914), Vol. 71, p. 325.

Negroes. One of my informants stated that a certain prominent Negro scholar was a talented man, but that many Negroes were disappointed in him because he did not take a stronger attitude of leadership for the "group." She said that one of the constant disappointments with Negro leaders is that they work for their own selfish interests and forget the group which they represent.

Another Southerntown Negro showed how membership in the Negro caste is forced on the Negro, not chosen by him. He illustrated this statement by referring to the contrary behavior of the Negroes in the North. On one occasion in Ohio he was riding on a bus in which were two white people and a Negro girl. The white people sat up in front, as did the informant, but the girl went to the back of the bus. He felt this was somewhat characteristic of northern Negroes; they do not want to cluster with other Negroes. He later found out that she came from an Ohio town where there were only eight or nine Negro families. These families all go to different churches and live in different parts of the town; they do not want to be grouped together by the whites. The dispersion is explained by the fact that, if they cluster by their own wish, then the whites will make them cluster legally. They had best stay apart and view themselves as individuals and not as members of a group. In the South, on the contrary, Negroes have no choice; an appearance of solidarity is forced on them by segregation but it does not result in sentiments of being bound together.

It is frequently alleged, and with truth, that the social arrangement of having two castes in the South is a means of limiting conflict between the races, a conflict which is always potential whenever the races use the same schools, trains, amusement facilities, etc. There is another and less desirable feature of the caste arrangement: It limits the possibility of sympathetic contact. Middle-class Negroes are especially sensitive to their isolation and feel the lack of a forum in Southerntown where problems of the two races could be discussed. It is often something of a discovery when white people learn that there are Negro people of refined feeling and noteworthy talent, because they stand in such sharp contrast to the white-caste stereotype of the Negro.[11]

Caste as a barrier to social equality between the races will be discussed in another connection. The word "social" is here used in the narrow sense of polite social participation and not in the sociological sense of any traditionally guided contact. Negroes are not admitted on equal terms to the amusements and entertainments of the whites. How completely this is understood by the Negroes is illustrated by the following sinister story. A Southerntown white girl of exceptional warmth and sensibility had a Negro friend of whom she was very fond, and often said that she wished this Negro woman were white. Once she asked her friend whether she might bring a man she knew to her house and whether the Negro woman would have some of her good fruit cake for them. The latter said "Gladly," and as she was leaving asked, "Do you want me to put clean sheets on the bed?" The girl, somewhat startled, said "No." When they got there, the Negro woman took them into her own room, a combination bedroom and sitting room with a radio. After a while she left them there alone. The girl was appalled to notice on a tray near the bed an outfit of contraceptive materials. After an hour or two the Negro woman came back, knocked on the door, and served them a light supper. The behavior of the white girl in this case was certainly unconventional, but the Negro woman's interpreta-

---

[11] "This discovery of the educated colored woman is of deep significance. It is she who must lift her people, but she can do so little without our help! The experience of one club woman is typical here. . . .

" 'I had such a sense of adventure when I first began to get acquainted with those women here. You know we couldn't even get the poorer Negroes to clean up except through these educated ones. The first time I went to talk to them about it you can't think how rattled I was. I'd been speaking in public for years, and never thought about being embarrassed. But they looked so different from any Negroes I'd known. I didn't know what their thoughts were like, or how to get at them. I've done some mental gymnastics since, and I trust I'm a broader woman for it.' " L. H. Hammond, "Southern Women and Racial Adjustment," The Trustees of the John F. Slater Fund, Occasional Papers (1917), No. 19, pp. 18-19.

tion was ruthlessly according to the code; the only way she could understand it was to think that the white couple had made an excuse to use her house for a rendezvous.

The full implications of the caste concept will be worked out steadily throughout the study. It is important now to discuss the classes within each of the castes, white and Negro,[12] classes which are so obvious a feature of life in Southerntown.

The existence of social classes in the South has been noted by many observers despite the convention that social class is not a feature of our American democratic society. We are not accustomed to think in these terms and, to be sure, the class hierarchy is not so clearly marked in the northern states. At least three classes may be noticed which we designate briefly as lower, middle, and upper. The existence of these classes was quite clear in the South even before the War.[13] It may be that this picture is clearer to Negroes than to others; at least, an astute Negro writer has commented on the class problem and asserted that Negroes have characteristic attitudes toward each one of the classes in the white group.[14]

---

[12] "It is theoretically possible to have castes without classes, classes without castes, or classes within castes. The latter possibility represents the actual conditions in the United States today." Young, *op. cit.*, p. 581; quoted by permission of Harper & Bros.

[13] "The whole system, therefore, stratified Southern society. At the bottom was the slave, a chattel rather than a person; at the top, the plantation-owner and slave-holder. Ground between these two millstones were the proletarian 'poor whites,' 'hill billies,' 'red necks,' and 'clay-eaters,' and a middle class, mostly agricultural, of small farmers and town dwellers, who,— as is usual with middle classes—to some degree looked up with veneration and emulative pride to the aristocrats of the system, to some degree bitterly opposed them." Paul Lewinson, *Race, Class and Party* (New York, 1932), p. 7; quoted by permission of the Oxford University Press.

[14] "But Negroes of every type recognize at least three distinct types of white people: first, the upper stratum of white society recognized as the better class of white people, variously styled as 'quality folks' or 'first class people' or 'real white folks'—in the vernacular, 'sho nuff 'ristocrats'; at the other extremity are the 'poor white trash' including 'crackers,' 'red

The existence of the lower-class whites or poor white group has been one of the continuous features of southern social organization.[15] One might say of them that they have neither capital, talent, nor ancestry to give them preferential claims on income or prestige. From the standpoint of social usefulness, they have arms and legs and minimum skills, usually of the agricultural type. Biologically they are old Americans. In the area surrounding Southerntown they seem to have a certain amount of diffuse resentment against upper-class white people and some resentment against Negroes, especially the middle-class Negroes. They seem to face the greatest difficulties in gaining status because they do not have the capital to begin making any kind of advance, nor do they have the resolute and tormented determination of some of the immigrant groups. Since their chances of social advancement are relatively low, they have little to lose in status or economic reward by lax behavior and in general they do not maintain the personal standards of the middle-class whites. Apparently in some areas they play an unusual rôle in forceful demonstration against the Negro.[16] If it is said that the Negroes do not have social equality in the South, it is equally true that this class of white people does not have it either, unless it be at infrequent political picnics and barbecues. In an economic sense their competitors are the lower-class Negroes and, since the whites have the political instrument to work with, they are

---

necks,' or 'sagers,' according to the particular region considered. Between these is a third class recognized as 'half strainers,' that aspiring element risen from the lower class who, with some effort, affect the ways of the upper classes; who are at the same time the most aggressive in setting up racial discrimination. Toward each group the Negro maintains a definite and characteristic attitude." Moton, *op. cit.*, p. 18; quoted by permission of Doubleday, Doran & Co.

[15] Frederick L. Olmsted, *A Journey in the Seaboard Slave States* (New York, 1904), II, 42.

[16] "Furthermore, to lessen crime and eradicate lynching, the controlling group of white people will need also to prepare the voteless, propertyless, unattached whites—over half of the Southern white population—for an intelligent participation in citizenship." Raper, *op. cit.*, pp. 38-39; quoted by permission of the University of North Carolina Press.

enabled to gain some advantages over their rivals; on the other hand they face economic disadvantages in the form of the alliance between the field Negroes and the white owners which tends to exclude them from plantation work. A shred of statistical information on this issue indicates that the lower-class people, white and Negro, are numerous in this state since it is one in which fewest families have radios and telephones,[17] perhaps a mark of middle-class status.

In contrast to the lower-class white people, and distinct from them, is the middle-class group. In general, middle-class members have risen from the lower class rather than fallen from the upper. Their class membership is based on small capital holdings, or on the possession of social skill, managerial or professional, which enables them to make a claim on a larger income and gives them a higher position in the eyes of others. One feels their spirit to be energetic and acquisitive. In the main they intend to make their way by their exertions and personal contributions to the welfare of the community. Their personal standards of behavior, on questions of drinking, divorce, and profanity, seem to be more rigorous than those of the classes above or below them. They seem to be religious and are in fact faithful churchgoers. These people are the best demonstrations of the "equal chances" offered by American society. Their class position itself is a way station to still higher prestige levels. Usually some degree of education is combined with capital when the latter is present; if not, the capital may be invested in the education of the children and thus win for the family line a secure middle-class position. It should be noted that there is a limit to our democratic possibility of social advancement for any and every individual; this limit is reached when previous acquisition and use of capital by others constitute a barrier to the advancement of new group members.

Middle-class white people in Southerntown seem to have a great deal of contempt for the lower-class whites, and this contempt often flares into open animosity. They also

[17] Howard W. Odum, *Southern Regions of the United States* (Chapel Hill, 1936).

have vigorous hostile attitudes toward the Negroes and are seldom found in the ranks of those who take the friendly attitude toward the Negro evinced by the white aristocracy. They hold that the main tormentors of the Negro are the lower-class whites, a statement which the Negroes tend to confute. Negroes, especially the most vocal of the middle-class Negroes, say that their real antagonists are not the whites of the highest or the lowest status; the former have too much to be jealous and the latter get from the upper-class whites the same treatment as the Negroes. A number of informants believed, on the contrary, that the lower-class whites sympathized with the Negroes. The Negroes have a name for the middle-class white group which corresponds remarkably well with their position in the eyes of the sociological analyst; they call them "strainers," those who are pressing forward and straining to get on in the world. Middle-class people must stress sharply the differences between themselves and the lower-class whites and Negroes because they are none too sure that the differences are very important or permanent.

Often in the face of economic reverses middle-class families will cling bitterly to their class standards, one of which is education for their children. They will endure great hardships and humiliation to make this education possible rather than risk demoting the family line to a lower-class position. They will struggle to maintain their children in the same class, to see that they marry appropriate persons, that the daughter has the right kind of a wedding, and so on.

Most of the businessmen in Southerntown fall in the group of middle-class people. The following note on a Rotary Club meeting will give an idea of what they hear on such an occasion:

Attended Rotary Club luncheon today; the speaker talked about how much bigger profits one can make if one takes a human attitude toward one's employees, considers them not as automatons but as persons. We should have work for our hands to do, clean thoughts for our minds, love in our hearts, etc. Much emotion on part of speaker, fluent speech full of clichés and quotations from inspirational sources. The chairman said in his speech of thanks, and in justification

of Rotary, that it was only in a Rotary Club that one
hear such a speech.

There seems to be, on the whole, a much better
plining of members within the middle-class group th
the case with the other two classes. As "strainers" the
on the march to higher status position and, like an
on the march, they are provident, industrious, vigilan
determined. For example, the professional wing h
maintain careful personal standards in order not to
in public estimation. Teachers must "watch their
since they have a certain idealized rôle before the y
There seems to be in this group a sense of insecurity
acts as a goad to abstemious behavior and close cont
impulse.

A person who has fallen from his class position i
sorry state.[18] One of the middle-class families was v
sympathized with because it had such a member. Thi
could not be made to work consistently and all class
sure (shame) put on him to do so was ineffectua
drank a great deal, more than was tolerated or pe
possible to a middle-class man. Finally he comp
dropped his claims on middle-class and upper-caste
sideration by living more or less *openly* with a Negre
cubine. He has finally become a dependent individua
is supported by his relatives, is socially disgraced, ar
no claims on the esteem accorded to other members
middle-class family.

This is not to say that all middle-class members
are able to conform to the strictest standards. The p
presented here is the one which middle-class indiv
strive toward and which most of them manage to ap
imate. Disordered personalities exist in this class,
drinkers will be found, sex delinquencies are not unk
although there is usually the attempt to keep them
In considering the "strains" of modern life in refere

[18] "Social classes, on the other hand, are less rigid, and
dividual may gain or lose class status, for it is based o
transitory qualities as personal wealth, education, n
rank, political preferment, and individual achievement."
op. cit., p. 580; quoted by permission of Harper & Bros.

nervous and mental disorder, one might well note those imposed on individuals in this class where the pressure toward individual achievement and advancement, which require exceptional impulse renunciation, is so great.

So powerful is the strain toward a democratic uniformity in our society that the emerging lower and middle classes have tended to replace the old aristocratic upper class in social significance; but it will still be worth while to identify this class group. It is the remains of the ruling group against which the Civil War was fought, a group whose claims to precedence were heavily discredited by defeat in the War. Since it is but little represented in Southerntown, we will try to characterize it for the culture area of the South as a whole. Although it has lost its actual grip on the social machine to a very great extent, it has maintained the momentum of its social prestige and assimilation into it is still a great value[19] in the South.

To be an upper-class person is to have a certain kind of memory of the past and to hold a certain rôle in the eyes of others with similar memories. If, on meeting a southern person, the stranger could by chance open a history book and ask him to thumb through it, and if the southerner stopped now and then to say, "Oh, yes, that is Governor So-and-so; he was my grandmother's brother," or "General Blank married a second cousin of my mother, she was of the South Carolina Blanks, you know," he would be dealing with an upper-class person. Originally, no doubt, membership in this class was based on a strong position in the economic system[20] and entry to it was often secured by possession of special social skills and money. Like all aristocratic traits, however, class membership tends to be socially inherited and does not continually need the underpinning of actual economic pre-eminence. In its day this was a functioning class leading in statecraft and agriculture, and disciplining its individuals for leadership. Nowadays it

[19] For discussion of social values, *see* W. I. Thomas and Florian Znaniecki, *The Polish Peasant in Europe and America* (New York, 1927), II, 1831 ff.

[20] U. B. Phillips, *American Negro Slavery* (New York, 1918), p. 180.

seems to be based largely on memories of interrelationship
with other leading families of the past, rather than on current achievement. It still differentiates sufficiently the behavior of those who are born into it so that it is a formative
force in the culture.

The immediately striking thing at a dinner party of upper-class people is the astonishing degree of interrelationship of the members. There are echoes of old transactions,
such as whose relative sold what house and piece of land
to whose grandfather, and there is amazing knowledge of
the tangled genealogies of all the leading families. One is
much impressed by the poise and social readiness of the
group, their ease in conversation, and the grace and certainty with which they receive a stranger. They know that
they are placed indefinitely in the social world by the strings
which bind them to their ancestors and that they have a
form of personal security which cannot be taken away by
economic disaster or by anything short of death or destruction to those who remain. The ancestors are potentially
present every time an upper-class group gathers; even
though in the case of the younger members of this class
there is less frequent trading of memories and old associations.

With this class, which is sure of itself socially, a freer
measure of impulse expression is possible than with the
stressful middle-class group. There is a more tolerant attitude toward religion and drinking and a less intensive sense
of scandal about personal delinquencies.

A number of times in seeking Negro informants I was advised by upper-class white people to consult this or that
aristocratic planter who had lived with the Negroes all his
life and knew them well; he would refer me to several intelligent Negroes on his place who could tell me the situation. I did indeed avail myself of these sources of information, but realized too that I was being passed on from one
class member to another and it was presumed to be guaranteed that by these means I would get "safe" information
from this class standpoint. As a matter of fact, the information was, for the most part, extremely good and realistic

in the sense that it checked with other observations, but it tended to have an inevitable class bias.

Here is a note made on a visit with a young southern man whom I met on a train:

Met a young man on the train last night and fell into conversation. Apparently he comes of a well-known family here. Says grandfather told him about having been a courier for General Hood in the Civil War. Says when they say "war" down here, they mean the Civil War, not the World War. Says northern people feel that southerners are mean toward Negroes; says this is not so, his family have always had Negro slaves and servants and have loved them. Gives example of personal services to Negroes. Feels people have not gotten over the Civil War. He wanted me to learn about the "real South," says southern hospitality is not a myth but exists in the small upper group. Wishes I could see it as he knows it from his own home. Said that he wished that his family were still prosperous so that he could take me to his home and show me the real thing. Despaired of communicating the real South to me by word.

My friend above commented on the affection of his family for Negroes, undoubtedly correctly. One finds this quite regularly as an upper-class mark, this tolerant, poised affection. But the Negroes have to be the right kind, the "old-timy" ones who draw out this friendliness in the class to which they were once related as slaves. Still, in all cases the upper-class attitudes toward Negroes seem mild and there is no sense of being challenged or threatened by them. An upper-class woman in Southerntown commented on the hostility of certain middle-class whites, whom she named, for the Negroes, and said that she came from the upper group who like Negroes. In actual life, she was known to be rather foolish and indulgent in her treatment of them, at least according to prevailing standards in Southerntown. This lenient attitude is undoubtedly an historical resultant in the upper class who have had long accommodative relations with Negroes as master to slave, have many personal memories of them, and have been freed from the competition which middle- and lower-class people have experienced. Raper[21] has noted this cordial relationship between

21 Raper, *op. cit.*, p. 202.

Negroes and the wealthiest whites, a relationship which is very important to understand since it can be transferred also to the white factory owner or employer in the North. The indulgent upper-class attitude toward Negroes is shown by many of the stories written about them since the War. Chesnutt[22] has captured the spirit very well, as has also Judge Moore.[23] Page[24] refers to this love of old-timy Negroes, a love which was indeed well deserved in view of the rôle which the Negroes had to play in serving the upper-class white people of the South.

The lower- and middle-class whites are indeed in some ways not so near to upper-class white people as the Negroes, perhaps again for the reason that class antagonism separated the white groups in earlier days and some relics of it still exist despite present-day solidarity against the Negro caste. The mammy tradition is frequently thought of as a criterion of upper-class membership; it is a point which whites like to remember and Negroes like to forget.[25]

It seemed, from my small contact, that the upper-class group, on the whole, is less bound by the southern mores and folkways than the other classes. They are, of course, likely to be more traveled, better read, and even acquainted with some social movements which it would be almost a scandal to know about in the other classes. My experience is too limited to make the following statement as a con-

[22] Charles W. Chesnutt, *The Conjure Woman* (Boston, 1899).

[23] *See*, among other works, John T. Moore, *Ole Mistis* (Nashville, 1897).

[24] T. N. Page, *The Negro: The Southerner's Problem* (New York, 1904), p. 195.

[25] "I know the temptation for them to do so is very strong, because the honor point on the escutcheon of Southern aristocracy, the *sine qua non* of a background of family, of good breeding and social prestige, in the South is the Black Mammy. Of course, many of the white people who boast of having had black mammies are romancing. Naturally, Negroes had black mammies, but black mammies for white people were expensive luxuries, and comparatively few white people had them." Johnson, *op. cit.*, pp. 9-10; quoted by permission of the Viking Press.

firmed impression, but the only protestors against white solidarity and the current treatment of the Negro whom I encountered were upper-class people.

As already observed, we have a situation in Southerntown where there are not only castes, but classes within the two castes. It seems reasonable also to posit three classes within the Negro group, although only two of them will be discussed here. There was no chance for me to examine the criteria for the upper-class Negroes, although undoubtedly such a designation is worth making in view of what is known of Negroes in Philadelphia, Washington, Charleston, New Orleans, and other cities. Here we will discuss only the lower- and middle-class Negro groups as they are actually represented in Southerntown.

The Negro lower class is the same "arms and legs" group with the simplest of agricultural skills and personalities adapted to continue peaceably a subordinate rôle in the plantation economy. It is at the bottom of the economic and social system and forms a broad base on which society in this area rests, a fact by no means true for the whole South. Attention would be called to the class, in the first place, by the type of observation made by one of my Negro informants who was a teacher. This man told me that his disciplinary problems are much more severe with children who come from tenant homes; the children who come from Negro landowning families submit more easily to school routine. An example from the tenant group is the case of a little girl of twelve who became very hostile toward a ten-year-old girl. The father of the twelve-year-old girl was at the State Prison farm. Saying, "Well, I want to see my father anyway, so I am going to kill you and get sent up there," she chased the ten-year-old with a pair of scissors, and when the child got safely away she threatened to kill her the next day. Presumably the landowning Negroes are in or on the edge of the middle class and have acquired the refinements of behavior and personal repressions characteristic of that class. It is this lower class whom southerners hold up to northerners as the reality of the problem with which the South has to deal in contrast with the northerners' idealized picture of the Negro.[26] This peasant class of Negroes has been very well described by Johnson[27] who observes among them also a pressure to escape the limitations of their class status by means of educating their children. Reuter[28] also posits among them a wish to cross the caste barrier, at least in the sense of arranging life so that they will be as much in contact with lighter people as possible and have lighter children. It is in this class also that the presence of the mother-centered family has been noticed by Frazier.[29] It is apparently more difficult to stay alive in this group of Negroes because we learn that in this state the rural Negro death rate is markedly higher than the rural white death rate, and the infant mortality per thousand live births for rural Negroes is almost twice as high as for rural white.[30] The behavior of middle-class Negroes is differentiated from that of the lower-class group; when a southerner says "Negro" he refers invariably to his stereotype of the lower-class Negro. It is this group which

[26] Very likely this ideal was achieved in the following way: the northerner identified himself with the Negro and assumed incorrectly that the lower-class Negro was like himself. Whenever he talked about the scandalous disadvantages suffered by the Negro he was thinking how he would feel in a similar situation and attributing his own indignation to the Negro. Possibly this was not altogether incorrect since humans tend to react similarly in the same situations. But it was probably a great exaggeration of the actual reaction of the Negro. The southerner, on the contrary, with the real lower-class Negro before him, reacted sharply against such an identification and stressed all possible points of difference to justify his superior caste position.

[27] Charles S. Johnson, *Shadow of the Plantation* (Chicago, 1934), p. 133.

[28] *Op. cit.*, p. 181.

[29] Frazier says, "There is, first, the tradition of female dominance with a corresponding maternal family pattern, which appears in its purest and most primitive form on the remnants of the old plantations of the South. However, the maternal family flourishes to a larger extent in the cities and small towns. It seems to diminish in importance as Negro men find a place in industry." E. Franklin Frazier, "Traditions and Patterns of Negro Family Life in the United States," *Pub. of the Amer. Sociol. Soc.* (1934), Vol. 28, pp. 125-126.

[30] Odum, *op. cit.*

draws and seems to deserve the low opinion of the whites.

The class grouping, as we shall see, tends to be similar in the two castes, with the crucial exception that the hope of social advancement in the Negro middle class is emphatically limited by the caste barrier. Another differentiation is that social advancement in the Negro middle class seems more often due to developed talent or skill than to capital accumulation. Not infrequently, too, Negroes are aware of a family lineage and family tradition, although there is also a wide spread consciousness of plantation cabin background. Frequently awareness of white blood and corresponding lightness of color play a rôle among the middle group of Negroes.

The impression one gets from Southerntown is that the Negro middle-class people are mostly teachers and ministers of the gospel, apparently a characteristic finding.[31] There are two physicians, no lawyers, and a few businessmen including only two people who control a considerable acreage of land.

The attempt of the middle class to mark itself off from the pilloried lower-class Negroes seems constant. For example, the wife of a professional man said that she recently started her four-year-old son off to kindergarten in the Negro school. One day he came home from school and said, "Me wants something to eat." She told him that he had never learned that at home and he would not get it if he asked for it that way. She deplores the fact that she must send her son to school with children of illiterate families who get him into such ways of talking, but there is nothing else to do.

---

[31] "That the number of Negro ministers is comparatively high is not surprising when the fact is considered that for decades the Negro has been highly restricted professionally, and that for quite a long while the ministry and teaching were the principal professions open to Negroes. Even today these two professions claim the larger number; and, with the exception of teaching, far more Negroes are found in the ministry than in any other profession. According to the 1930 census, there were 54,439 Negro teachers and 25,034 Negro clergymen." B. E. Mays and J. W. Nicholson, *The Negro's Church* (New York, 1933), p. 39; quoted by permission of Harper & Bros.

She is a woman of college grade. It may be that historically the Negro middle (and upper) classes are derived for the most part from the house servants[32] and the free Negroes who formed one-ninth of the total Negro population in 1860.[33] Undoubtedly, too, this class contains more mixed blood than the lower-class Negroes.[34] The bi-racial arrangement has probably provided a social rôle for the middle-class Negro which he would not have if he were exposed to the direct competition of the white middle-class group.[35] It is easy, in Southerntown at least, to observe the presence of persons of mixed blood in the middle class by talking to a group of county teachers or taking the frequently offered opportunity to "say a few words" at a rural Negro church. The teacher group is markedly more Caucasoid in its characteristics.

Middle-class Negroes follow, at least as an ideal, the highest standards of sexual morality. It is not certain that they measure up to them any better than do the whites, but it is certain that they appreciate them. One of my informants said, for example, that her stern conscience probably came from her mother and father; she mentioned her father in particular in this connection, saying that he had never done anything low or mean and never had any illegitimate

---

[32] Ophelia Settle, "Social Attitudes During the Slave Regime: Household Servants versus Field Hands," *Pub. of the Amer. Sociol. Soc.* (May, 1934), Vol. 28, No. 2, pp. 95-96.

[33] Benjamin Brawley, *A Short History of the American Negro* (New York, 1931), p. 102.

[34] "Thus by association, education, and tradition, the mulattoes came to be superior men. They had white blood and because of their white blood they had superior advantages. The white man considered them superior and, as a consequence of this, they considered themselves superior. This gave them a confidence in themselves that the black Negroes did not have. They felt more important. Among the Negro group they enjoyed a prestige because of their mixed blood, and this reacted to further inflate the mulattoes' idea of themselves. So, entirely aside from any question of racial superiority, the mulatto is and always has been the superior man." Reuter, *op. cit.*, pp. 181-182; quoted by permission of Richard G. Badger.

[35] Reuter, *op. cit.*, p. 359.

children. He always took pride in the fact that, although the family had little in the way of possessions, they had integrity and were persons of high standards. As a bad example, she cited a man in the community who had formerly been a peasant Negro but had become well-to-do. He was known to have had a number of illegitimate children by different mothers and was judged to be not really of the middle class for this reason.

Another Negro woman refused a man who proposed to her several times because she did not like his family. He had a sister who was "very careless in her social relationships" and lived with a number of men successively without marrying them or getting support from any of them; meanwhile her brother supported her. He disapproved what his sister did but continued to support her; and the informant felt his sister would always come first, that is, his allegiance would remain fixed to lower-class standards. This same conflict was represented several times in Negro middle-class families, one of the partners holding to middle-class standards and fearing that the other would drag down the family status by behavior appropriate to the lower class.

Education is, of course, a passion with the middle-class Negroes, as has been frequently noted.[36] The most extraordinary sacrifices may be made by parents to give their children opportunities for status advancement through education.

There is a good deal of shame among middle-class Negroes over the caste marks which whites take to be typical of all Negroes. Resentment of the mammy tradition has already been indicated. One of my woman informants told me of a Negro woman who made candy in a southern town and who put a dummy of herself outside her store as an advertisement. The dummy showed a very dark woman with a bandana around her head. The Negroes resented this fiercely and my informant thought the reason was that it reminded them of the mammy stereotype of the whites which they so much resent. For herself, she did not see why the resentment was so great, because she thought if the

[36] C. S. Johnson, *op. cit.*, p. 66.

woman could make candy better than anyone else, it was all to the credit of the race. Again, there seems to be antagonism to spirituals since they are reminders of the slave situation. The same informant said that she thought it was foolish for her group to be ashamed of the spirituals; they ought to be proud of anything they could do better than anyone else. Middle-class Negro churches tend to be more sedate than the lower-class churches.[37] The reason probably is that the emotionalism of the lower-class churches has become associated in white minds with primitive and animal behavior, and the middle-class Negroes wish to deny such a trait in themselves. It is often irritating to the spiritual-loving northerner to go to a concert in Southerntown. He wants spirituals and still more of them. All he will get will be a small group, usually beautifully sung. And he has to bear with a soprano soloist who sings "Trees" in a sentimental manner, various other vocal solos of indifferent quality, and a lot of piano playing, some good and some bad. This is probably what he might find in any small town; but after all, most small towns do not have and cannot sing spirituals. The fact seems to be that the classical part of the entertainment is stressed to show what the group can do and that it is not deficient in appreciation of "the best" in music.

The better discipline of the middle-class group in respect to aggression is another feature by which it is differentiated from the lower class. It is a point of pride that no one has been in jail or arrested.[38]

Observation indicates also that middle-class Negro men take pride in the fact that their wives do not work outside the home. In this, of course, they follow the valuations of their class, white or colored. Women at home are much better protected against sexual temptation than those who work out, which in turn is probably effective in helping to consolidate the middle-class family.[39]

It is the Negro middle class which feels most bitterly

[37] N. N. Puckett, *Folk Beliefs of the Southern Negro* (Chapel Hill, 1926), p. 543.

[38] C. S. Johnson, *op. cit.*, pp. 84-85.

[39] Stone, *op. cit.*, p. 187.

the pressure of the caste barrier with its damaging effect on individual self-esteem; this barrier sets the Negro outside the possibility of achieving personal dignity in the fullest American sense. It seems likely that this fact, rather than a desire to be white in any physical sense, is at the bottom of the distress of so many people with mixed blood. Their sense of injustice is all the more keen since the personal achievement characteristic of middle-class Negro people is categorically superior to the large lower-class white group and to some of the middle-class whites.[40]

Be it noted that a blank appears in the description of the Negro class pattern where the upper class ought to be. I will not attempt to fill this in from memory or imagination, but will leave it to better informed researchers. Very likely it can be made a useful concept. One detects in some Negroes in Southerntown a stress on lineage similar to that found among upper-class white people. Family connections appeared frequently in one such conversation, "my grandfather's grandfather," "my granduncle," etc. On the other hand, among Negroes, there must be a strong tendency against remembering ancestry. It tends to remind Negroes of slavery days, a remembrance which is bound to be painful while the pattern of Negro subordination persists as it does today. Let us remember the negative value often placed on the beautiful spirituals—"slave songs." And while some Negroes may count their own light color as an asset, they cannot escape the bitterness of our social judgment on bastardy which inevitably accompanies the memory of a white ancestor. No such ancestor can, of course, be legitimate. In one or two cases recourse was taken to memories, legendary or factual, of descent from African princes who never did work, who were brought over to boss other Negroes. In another case the ancestor was a Seminole chieftain

[40] "A glance at the next diagram, remembering that the number of classes and their relative size are purely imaginary, immediately establishes the obvious but neglected fact that there are Negroes whose class status, within their caste, is superior to the class status of any number of white people." Young, *op. cit.*, pp. 582-583; quoted by permission of Harper & Bros.

and the Negro stressed that he had free blood in his veins. The problem of ancestry, however, is bound to be a complex and painful one for Negroes when they become fully aware of the dominant American moral standards.

The advantage of outlining clearly a scheme of caste and class distinctions is that it enables one to place people and to have some systematic expectations of them. Let us practice a little by reminding ourselves that the "poor whites" are upper caste but lower class, that the researcher is upper caste but middle class, that my best Negro informant was middle class but lower caste, and so on. It is within such a frame of reference that personality differences achieve their right perspective. Comparisons of psychological facts are only truly effective when the subjects are similar as to caste and class. A murder done by a lower-class Negro is a different kind of fact from a similar act by the president of the Rotary Club, who is, of course, upper caste and middle class; and in real life the two acts are treated differently by the group itself. Strain on the individual personality undoubtedly differs as between the castes and classes. An hypothesis, which needs to be tested, is that it is greatest in the middle-class Negro group for the reason that severe impulse restriction is enjoined without appropriate compensation from the status side. The more clearly the necessity of making out the systematic form of the social life comes home, the more one sees how qualified must be any social psychology which is developed by members of a single class.

One useful result of clarifying the class and caste picture is to learn that white middle-class people show some loyalty for their Negro classmates across the caste line. Observations to this effect come from both white and Negro sides. This loyalty really should be described as an ambivalent relationship: hostility along caste lines, loyalty along class lines. A Negro informant says that educated colored people get much better treatment than uneducated ones. White people tend to be more respectful and friendly. This is the positive side of class loyalty. Still and all, she says, they seem to resent seeing a colored person dressed up and looking nice. She often feels criticized by white eyes when she goes out in a tastefully designed dress. This is the negative side of caste hostility.

A grandson of a Negro, highly placed in an economic sense, reported the civilities that his grandfather had received in contrast to other Negroes. He was said to have had good white friends in Southerntown. Three or four of these friends had his picture on their office walls and in their offices they somewhat relaxed the severity of caste conventions in talking to him. The grandson thinks that white people in the town show him deference because of his family and economic background. On the other hand, the grandfather had still to submit to galling restrictions, was addressed by his first name, and could not share in civic enterprises on equal terms.

It has sometimes seemed, in explanation of this ambivalence, that the class conflict centers around economic position and advantage, whereas the caste conflict centers around social, and ultimately sexual, contact. The white man can have a certain loyalty to members of his class in the Negro group providing the barriers against more intimate contact are maintained. The argument against "marrying a nigger" would come up as quickly against a middle-class as against a lower-class Negro.

The explanation of the class loyalty does not seem far to seek. After all, the middle-class Negro buys more gas, better groceries, more insurance, more medical services, sees the lawyer oftener, and is in general a good customer. Since there is competition among white people in performing these services, some deference tends to be doled out to the middle-class Negroes as a bid for their business. It is important, furthermore that Negro employers should follow the customs of white landowners, and it is worth something in the way of respect to keep the Negro landowners in line. One Negro owner says that the whites put pressure on him to treat his tenants as they do theirs; otherwise it would create discontent because tenants would come to the whites and talk about the especially good treatment they receive at a Negro's place. Since the informant conforms and does not set a bad example to Negro tenants, the white people are very nice to him.

In another case also the reason for the superior rapport between the middle classes was clear. A Negro informant told me that he had consolidated himself with the whites in the following way. A number of Negroes were killed by a railroad train. Through his influence they did not sue the railroad, and it might have been a costly suit. In return for this favor informant received special protection of various types, for example, police protection. Once, he had hit a car driven by a white woman who chanced also to be pregnant, an especially unfavorable detail; the chief of police declared it a mere accident and let him go, whereas the officer on the spot had been abusive and was about to take him to jail.

A young middle-class Negro man told me what it felt like to come back to Southerntown from a northern city. He got into the Jim Crow car at Chicago instead of at Cairo, Illinois, where the Jim Crow line begins. The accommodations were as good for Negroes as for whites. When he passed out of Cairo he wished he could turn back north. He had a gloomy anticipation of his stay in Southerntown and resolved to keep out of contact with the white people when possible. Contrary to expectation, he has been rather flattered by the reception he has received. The whites have taken a friendly interest in him and have gone out of their way to lead him into conversation. He has not minded being here and is not especially anxious to return North in the fall. He agrees that the good treatment is probably due to high-class status.

Another Negro man says he found little difficulty in getting along with white people once he got a bit of money together and made a start. He thinks they did try to prevent him from getting a start, but after he got it, they encouraged him. This implies simply a generalized middle-class resistance against competition from lower-class Negroes, but a recognition of similarity once middle-class status is achieved.

In accounting for the alliance between the middle classes in the two castes one should not overlook the cultural and personality similarities which they share. As already noted, southern white people are occasionally surprised when they have their first real contact with a middle-class Negro person. The surprise is evidence of their recognition of similarity in culture, if not in color.

Another question of interest that arises from this classification is the way in which lower-class white people in the North differ from lower-class Negroes in the South. Since I have not studied the class question in the North I can offer only a guess. In so far as the lower class in the North has been recruited steadily for a century from foreign immigrants, it differs greatly from Negroes for obvious reasons. Whereas the Negroes have little hope of highest status because of the caste barrier, the immigrants have every hope of it, have come here expressly to strive for personal advancement and constantly see members of their own groups winning recognition. This hope of advancement tends to middle-class-ify all of northern society. The immigrants, further, were not all in the same class position in their home lands. Undoubtedly many of them already had middle-class standards and left their home lands under middle-class pressures toward advancement. Once in the northern status structure, they show the energy and drive characteristic of a mobile class. The immigrants are, in one manner of speaking, our "Negroes," but they are temporary Negroes.

A comparison of the lower-class whites in the South and the lower-class Negroes is also important. One can say that the whites are much like the Negroes in respect to economic position, but have superior social status. They are able to affect the operations of the state by their votes and get a kind of noisy, if ineffectual, political representation. They are not categorically debarred from rising in the white-status scale, as are the Negroes.[41] It is an impression, which should be checked, that direct sexual and aggressive expression, though freer among lower-class whites than in the upper classes, is still less common than with the Negroes. This aspect of the problem must be definitively studied.

The hostility between the middle-class and lower-class

[41] Bi-racialism is after all a comparatively feeble structure which, as at present developed or likely to develop, would hardly take care of a Negro middle class in numbers proportionate to that of the white.

whites is striking around Southerntown. Informant after informant from the middle-class group came forward with derogatory opinions relating to the poorer whites. A landowner told how mean his white tenants are, how spiteful and gossipy they are toward one another, how they always complain and demand things of him. He is going to replace them next year with Negroes. Another said that the white tenants are mean and disagreeable and contrasted them unfavorably with the Negroes who "know their place." Another said that the white tenants are not tractable at all, as are the Negroes, and that planters much prefer Negroes. A result is that there are many more poor whites than Negroes on the federal relief budget. This informant felt that the federal relief people are too easy, that there should be some hard-headed men in the relief office instead of softhearted women. He said the poor whites are a very mean class; they will come into a store, order something, and say, "Charge it to Tom Smith"; they will not even have enough respect for their boss to say "Mr. Smith." He said that the poor whites around Southerntown are the worst class he knows of, worse than in other sections of the South. They do not even dress up on Sunday, have no respect for others' property, and will curse a man going by in a car just because he has something and they have not.

Often these attitudes toward the lower-class whites will come out in the gossip which circulates at the time of a political campaign. A middle-class informant referred to one of the candidates as a "redneck" and a "peckerwood." He said that the candidate was just trash and he was not going to vote for him; and added scornfully that the candidate's father was still a tenant just outside of town. The man had been disloyal to his friends and benefactors and was in general an ungracious upstart. These attitudes are obviously intended to resist the emergence of the candidate in question from his class and they show the ordinarily strong class antagonism in lurid exaggeration.

Another informant referred to two classes of white tenants, the "sorry" white tenants and the others. He thinks the sorry ones are mainly poor whites with a long lower-class tradition; the others are probably persons who have been pressed down through misfortune to the level of the tenant farmer. The latter have more orderly habits of work and some "culture." Here middle-class loyalty extends to those who have lost class status but still conform more nearly to middle-class standards.

Something should be said in detail about class structure in Southerntown. The white population is composed largely of middle-class persons. The Negro population is divided between a great mass of lower-class Negroes and a film of middle-class people. There seem to be very few upper- or lower-class whites in Southerntown, although probably more of the latter than of the former. This was expressed by a white informant who claimed that the white people in this town are *nouveau riche* or climbers, and not the real old southern type. The Southerntown area has not been settled as long as older regions of the South and still has a trace of the frontier social structure. It has been so prosperous at various times within recent years that a man who could get hold of land, even rent it, could make himself more or less independent with a very few crops. The result has been the advancement to middle-class status of considerable numbers of people, formerly less secure. In this sense "white superiority" in Southerntown really turns out to be the superiority of the white middle class which is automatically protected against competition from the Negroes by the caste barrier. It is difficult to make out from the statistics on gainful occupations for the county just how people may be divided by classes. There are only a few such data for Southerntown. One cannot tell how many Negro landowners there are, but they must be few; the number of Negro farm managers and foremen is negligible. Negroes comprise 80 percent of the farm laborers. The number of Negroes in skilled trades is also negligible. Only one out of forty persons in the postal service is a Negro. Activities connected with telephone and telegraph companies are a white monopoly. One out of twenty persons in banking and brokerage is a Negro, one out of five in insurance and real estate, and one out of seven in wholesale and retail trade; and it seems likely that in these cases the Negroes do the roustabout work. One out of ten of the employees in public service is a Negro, but 97 per-cent of the women listed under "domestic and personal service" are Negro women.[42] In a county where about three quarters of the people are Negroes it can be seen that they are decisively underrepresented in occupations which might lead to inclusion within middle-class status. This accords absolutely with personal observation and opinions of informants, white and Negro. It tends to justify the conclusion that we are dealing in Southerntown with a white middle-class group and a Negro group largely of the lower class.[43] This conclusion is quite important for the sake of the logical structure of the research and should be carefully noted. It is, however, asserted to be true only of Southerntown.

[42] All statistics in this paragraph are taken from the *Fifteenth Census of the United States*, 1930.

[43] A reader of the manuscript has asked for the numbers of persons in the castes and classes in Southerntown itself. The only certain statement that can be made is the following: The number in the two castes is about equal. Only guesses can be made about numbers in the social classes within the castes. The guesses are: practically all the white people in Southern-town are middle-class people. There are few upper- and lower-class whites. Probably eight out of ten Negroes are lower class; the remainder are middle class and there are few or no upper-class Negroes.

In the county there are 2.4 Negroes to every white man. Nothing more certain can be said about class division than that the lower-class white people must heavily outnumber their middle class, and the lower-class Negroes still more heavily preponderate over the middle class of their caste. There are a few upper-class white people in the county, but probably still fewer or no upper-class Negroes.

CHAPTER VI

Gains of the White Middle Class: Economic

〜〜〜〜〜〜〜〜〜〜〜〜〜〜〜〜〜〜〜〜〜〜〜〜〜〜〜〜〜〜

We now know that the middle-class white people "run the society" in Southerntown. The Negro caste in town and county is the greater part of the group. Managing the affairs of Southerntown is no easy task and so it will hardly be done out of sheer altruism; it is legitimate on good American principles to ask what the managers get out of it. Or we may ask, in other words, how does the social system operate? What rewards are available to the caste rulers and what renunciations are required of them?

There is an answer to this question which is often proposed by sociology. It runs like this. What we have in the Southerntown area is a social machine with its members interacting on one another in historically defined ways. This machine has inertia and goes on working according to its traditionally prescribed pattern. The societal unit continues to function until it is in some manner disorganized; it then goes through a cycle from disorganization to reorganization, and orderly social life continues.[1] This description is tenable, but it does not satisfy the researcher approaching the scene who is biased in the manner that I have described. "Social inertia" or "momentum of culture patterns" is not detailed or dynamic. We should like to know something not only about the class structure but also about the differential advantages and disadvantages of membership in any particular caste or class; and, in particular, we wish to state these advantages and disadvantages from the standpoint of the types of direct personal, ultimately organic,

[1] William I. Thomas and Florian Znaniecki, *The Polish Peasant in Europe and America* (New York, 1927), II, 1117-1123.

gratification derived. Here, however, the researcher feels acutely the lack of a psychology which is keyed to our social science knowledge.[2]

An attempt, admittedly crude, will be made to state the advantages of the white middle class by listing three gains. Nor will it be maintained that the middle-class people are in every sense gainers; there are also disadvantages to this class position. In using the concept of "gains" we are not leaving the "social" plane of perception; we will merely turn the picture around and look for a moment at the individuals rather than at the society,[3] at middle-class persons rather than at the middle class. After all, individual wishes and attitudes are mobilized in real situations with genuine clashes of interest. People do not act out a class rôle with listless impersonality. We want to know what middle-class whites want and will fight for, and to get some sense of the complex emotional reënforcements of the formal social rôle.

Three gains are seen as accruing to the middle-class white group; they are the economic, sexual, and prestige gains. The white middle class is so placed that it makes all of these gains from the Negroes and some of them from the lower-class whites. The whites are little discussed since the writer has not had direct contact with them, but much that can be said of the lower-class Negro can also be said of them.[4]

Class structure being taken as it is, let us see what the middle-class whites gain in an economic way. For one thing, they avoid the manual work and the more monotonous types of work. It seems to be true (in our society) that people avoid heavy manual labor as a career when they can. This is one of the pressures that tends to squeeze people out of lower-class groups. Such work is perceived as onerous and the aversion to it is perhaps related to some

---

[2] John Dollard, *Criteria for the Life History* (New Haven, 1935), pp. 270-288.

[3] Charles H. Cooley, *Human Nature and the Social Order* (New York, 1902), pp. 1-3.

[4] In the Appendix, by Dr. L. W. Doob, this question is discussed.

primitive indolence characteristic of the organism itself.[5] This tendency is believed to exist apart from the negative value which manual work has in our society and the higher prestige accorded to the white-collar job. In the main, middle-class people do not mow their own lawns, cook their own meals, clean up their own houses, not to speak of farming their own land. In the second place the hardest, or at least the most avoided, kind of work, namely manual labor, is also cheapest. Relatively, middle-class people get much higher returns for their work than do the lower-class groups who perform the more laborious tasks. In practice this second advantage means that the middle group has a larger share of the goods and services which flow from the common operation of the socio-industrial machine in Southerntown and county. They have better houses and lawns, more fans, electric iceboxes, radios, screens, better food, newer cars and clothes, more movies, books and travel, and more efficient schools and colleges accessible to their children.

To make the matter concrete, it is observed that middle-class whites pick very little of the cotton. Cotton picking is a backbreaking job; most professional pickers go along on their knees and have a kind of knee-pad, like football pads. A good part of the picking is done in the hottest season of the year and the hours are long. Further, one must requisition the whole family for the task and keep the children out of school until the picking is done. It is both an urgent type of activity, since one always picks against the danger of bad weather, and a monotonous one. The picture should not be made too doleful since there are undoubtedly positive values associated with cotton picking, such as the collective talking and singing with which it may be interspersed, the joy of physical effort, the optimism created by the prospect of getting money in hand, and so on. Still, it seems to take a good deal of social pressure to get people to do this work; there is a danger that they will slide over on public relief rather than do it;

---

[5] Doubtless this tendency is based on the pleasure-pain balance as described by Freud; *see* Sigmund Freud, *Introductory Lectures on Psychoanalysis* (London, 1922), pp. 298-299.

and machines which take over such work are always greeted with public acclaim.

If the reader would get a vivid sense of this gain, let him remember the last time that he had a ten- or twelve-hour stretch of monotonous and low-paid physical work to do, such as engine wiping, strawberry picking, or pushing a wheelbarrow. It will help to bring the realization that the wish for status advancement is not only a prestige suction from above; there is also the squeeze of disagreeable work from below to urge him toward managerial, intellectual activities.

A few facts provided about the economic life of the state[6] will aid in understanding our smaller area. It is a poor state for both castes and all social classes. The system so operates that the lower caste and the lower classes in both castes come off worst from an economic standpoint. The state is, for example, in the group of states with lowest per capita personal income for farm population, lowest average federal income tax, and lowest per capita estimated true wealth. It is a state in which the ratio of total taxes to private income is relatively very high, a pressure which falls overtly on the middle- and upper-class groups but which is suitably passed on to the lower classes. Although the state ranks high in percentage of population who are farmers and in the percentage of income derived from farming, it is a poor agricultural state, since the gross income per individual farmer is low. The farm power used is largely man and animal power, since less than 10 percent of the farmers have tractors.

In order to make the implications of class and caste truly clear from an economic standpoint, one should know what the members of the various classes actually own and what their income is. The census volumes do not give us this information, and it seems to be one of the features of the American conception of privacy to keep it secret. Without it, it is difficult to make the class-gain point as convincingly as one would like. The census, however, does give some indirect indications which must serve in its stead. Here

[6] By Howard W. Odum, *Southern Regions of the United States* (Chapel Hill, 1936).

we will treat of the county, urging again that Southern-town is, to a great extent, a depot for goods and services to the surrounding area. Although the state as a whole is poor, this is a comparatively prosperous county within the state, as is shown by the high value of products sold per farm. This is probably to be accounted for by the concentration on cotton as a staple crop. One cannot be sure from the census figures, but it seems that about 90 percent of the crop value of the county comes from cotton. Three fourths of the families in the county are Negro and one quarter are white. One fifth of the white families own their own homes, whereas 7 percent of the Negro families own their own homes. It will be seen from this that there is a great group of lower-class white people, but that they are outnumbered more than three to one by the lower-class Negroes. White home-owners are about double the number of the Negro home-owners, despite the differences in population of whites and Negroes. The typical farm holding is small, somewhere around twenty-five acres. The piece of land which a tenant holds from his landlord is here considered a "farm" and this acreage represents about what the average tenant does actually farm. There are, of course, very few apartment houses or multiple family dwellings, and it appears from the census that 95 percent of all the dwellings in the county are one-family dwellings, obviously largely Negro cabins. Cabin and town house are equated in this form of counting, just as a twenty-five-acre farm and a thousand-acre plantation may be. About one family in twenty-five in this county has a radio. This is much below the American farm average, let alone the urban average for families. One American farm family in five has a radio. In the state of Wisconsin approximately two families out of five have radios. Doubtless the scarcity of radios can be correlated with the large number of Negro and white tenants, that is, lower-class people, in this county. As a matter of record it may be said that the Negro death rates for 1930 and 1931 were more than twice as high as those for whites. No stress is laid on this figure because it is difficult to make the necessary qualifications. It may be, for example, that the low death rate among whites is conditioned by the fact that this has been an active area for white migration and that the younger white people have recently come in, i.e., those least likely to die; whereas it is an area from which there has been active Negro emigration in recent years, in which case the young people are most likely to go and leave the old behind, i.e., those most likely to die. Apart from this there is evidence that Negroes do not have adequate medical service available. The foregoing statistics for the county of course include Southerntown. The figures seem to be quite typical of Southerntown, in so far as the Negroes are concerned; but they are probably not typical for the whites, since, as we know, they are largely middle-class people. One cannot tell for certain from the urban figures how many Negroes own homes because the census material is not worked up to show this fact.

Although an argument can be made from the above data as to the economic gains of the white middle-class people, the picture of the town itself is more convincing than the scattered figures. One hesitates always to trust unchecked impressions, but it is too plain to be doubted that the lower-class people, white and Negro, have the more laborious and monotonous work and for it get a proportionately smaller share of the purchasing power of the community. The contrast between the personal appearance of the Negroes and whites, the sections of town that they live in, the kinds of jobs they do are too obvious to permit any other conclusion. The Negroes seem to inherit the castoff clothes, automobiles, food and social customs of the whites, and are marked off by a general sort of secondhandedness. In one case this is a real danger to life and property. All too frequently at night one comes on "one-eyed" cars on the road, or cars without tail lights, or cars without any lights at all which are stalled or changing tires. This is one of the greatest traffic hazards in this county and white people say it is one of the sources of frequent accidents during night driving.

The mass of Negro homes in the town seem bare and poorly furnished, if one can judge by sample visits. The middle-class Negro homes are much better, but even there the limitations of income and taste are plain. Bathrooms in the houses seem to be very unusual, as is indoor plumbing. The worst cabins are miserably plain and poor; they are very hot in summer and hard to keep warm in winter. Rural Negro homes seem to be monotonously the same plain and crowded cabins as are occupied by the lower-class group in Southerntown, perhaps on the whole a little worse. They have been well described in another but more or less similar area.[7] At times a personal observation would lead to new information. One day I saw an old Negro watering the lawn in front of the house; his clothes were tattered and his shoes broken out, almost ruined. Being new in Southerntown I wondered if he wore such patched and worn shoes through choice or sloth and mentioned this to one of my Negro informants. He explained that men here could not afford to buy shoes very often, that average wages for unskilled men in Southerntown are from seventy-five cents to a dollar and a quarter per day. On these wages one has to wear clothes and shoes until they are utterly useless and sometimes even afterward. Informant said he saw women walking barefoot on Main Street in December and January last winter when it was very cold. The same informant told of a Negro cropper, now a preacher, who in eleven years of cropping got a cash income only three times. Then he added that the Negroes are shiftless because they have no incentive to improve their farms and

[7] "As to toilet facilities, 310 used open privies near by the house, 296 had no sewage disposal. Two hundred and fifty-eight used open wells for their water supply, 243 used well-pumps, 32 used springs, and 81 families had no water on the place at all.

"Such dwellings and surroundings constitute a dreary setting for families and their children. One reaction to this is the constant wandering-about in search of something better, with respect to both housing and labor terms. The crowding-together of families in these small rooms destroys all privacy, dulls the desire for neatness and cleanliness, and renders virtually impossible the development of any sense of beauty. It is a cheerless condition of life with but few avenues of escape even for those who keep alive a flickering desire for something better." C. S. Johnson, *Shadow of the Plantation* (Chicago, 1934), p. 100; quoted by permission of the University of Chicago Press.

homes; they do not get anywhere at the end anyway and the improvements go to the white man. Evidence contrary to this statement will be presented later.

Another indication of the low Negro standard of living is the presence of pellagra. Recorded cases per 10,000 are high in this county. This again is a complex issue since the Negroes could, though apparently they do not, raise the garden truck which would cut down the incidence of this deficiency disease. Apparently instead they take what the "boss man" gives them. Evidence of a caste difference in the standard of living are the facts about delivery of infants. The census shows that about 90 percent of the white children are delivered by physicians, only 10 percent by midwives; on the contrary, 15 percent of the colored children are delivered by physicians, 85 percent by midwives. Informants say that the training of the midwife is usually slight. She knows how to care for a normal delivery and knows some of the signs presaging a difficult birth, in which case she calls a doctor. It is said locally that Negro women have babies easier than white women do. Since midwives do not give anæsthetics one concludes that nature has shown a kind and exceptional foresight. Hospital delivered babies seem confined, by report at least, to middle-class white and occasional Negro women. Whether or not the fact demonstrates the advantage of having a doctor over a midwife, it is certain that for 1930 and 1931 the infant mortality among the colored in the county was three times as great as it was among the whites.

Another incident will illuminate the economic level of the Negro. At supper one day a guest asked where the fire had been that afternoon. A girl replied, "Oh, down in nigger town." Another remarked on the flippant phrase, "Oh, down in nigger town"; probably the fire had burned everything the "poor nigger" had. The hostess commented that the Negro would probably come around begging tomorrow, saying he had lost everything. Middle-class white people have commonly this experience of being begged from by Negroes; in this case it would seem that the begging is a substitute for fire insurance and is an appeal to the benevolence which middle- and upper-class people used to have, and still have to some degree, toward Negroes.

Lower-class Negro informants make it quite clear how pinched they feel by the situation. One, a high-school girl, with tastes developed by her education, told how hard her mother had to struggle to get a little extra for them to eat. Her stepfather would be satisfied with meat, bread, and syrup three times a day, which they have, but she and her mother need something more. The stepfather pays $3.50 a month rent for the house. He gets $3.00 a month from his church by being secretary of it. He has owned a little land but is losing it through inability to pay the taxes; he is still trying to pay them but always getting more behind.

Another informant asked to come and talk to me about some of her "problems." I anticipated a discussion of the difficulties which middle-class girls sometimes have with their mothers, such as not being able to go to parties, and the like. But this was not the case. She said her worst problem is that they are so poor; she is ashamed of her mother's having only one dress, which she keeps clean but has to wear everywhere. They have nothing in the house for amusement, no piano, no radio, no books, no newspapers. She is having a hard time to get to school and her father does not give her money now. Her mother earns a little money by taking in washing. They work very hard and just manage to get by. For example, she went to summer school this summer; her mother had to borrow $19.25 to send her and she "washed it out" for a white lady at the rate of one dollar a week. She says her mother is very loyal to her and tries to push her ahead, that they are more like sisters than mother and daughter.

Both materials gained from interviews and such statistical data as we have point to the fact of the economic gain which the middle-class white people make over the lower-class Negroes and whites. We must stress in this connection that it is not out of meanness that they make it; rather that is the way the system works and the middle-class people do just what the lower-class people would like to be in a position to do. The system is so set up that a great favorable differential exists for the white middle-class group. It is quite possible that better distribution of the existing income would serve rather to impoverish the middle-class whites than to benefit very much the lower-class Negroes or whites. We could then infer that the system as it operates does not utilize land and labor to its maximum advantage. In this case only a greater total return, as well as a more equitable distribution, would help.[8]

In speaking of landownership one need not always assume that the land is owned by those middle-class southern whites who operate it. Oftentimes the southerners are agents for northern capitalists, particularly banks and insurance companies that have taken over the land on which they held mortgages. But northern culture is not imposed with northern money. Imported capital is used southern style, as it must be, although the returns from the system are frequently exported to the northern owner. No northerner should point with scorn at the bad state of the Negroes in this area; he cannot be too sure that a part of his income is not derived from their work. It is to be affirmed, therefore, that although in respect to the Negroes the middle-class whites who operate the local system do make a gain, they are often not the only gainers, since frequently they do not own the land which they administer. Without the actual figures on landownership, it is impossible to clarify the situation further.

The economic gain seems quite as clear in the case of women, so many of whom, as we know, do household work in the white homes. There is no census material on their wages, but reports from the white and Negro people place the amounts as very low. A case was instanced of a colored woman who cooked at a white house. This woman had five children, from whom she was separated most of the day, and received for her work three dollars a week. The case was aired when an appeal was made on her behalf to the local relief station for aid in caring for the children.

A sixteen-year-old colored girl from the high school was acting as children's nurse in the house of a white profes-

[8] I owe this suggestion to Dr. Erich Fromm who brought it forward in a conversation. It is viewed, of course, as a query or proposition rather than as a matter of fact.

sional man during the summer months. She got there at six in the morning and worked until seven at night for $1.50 a week. She says that they pay the colored women very poorly here. She is trying to get a job as a maid for $1.50 or $2.00 a week.

A remarkable exploitive spirit was encountered in one middle-class informant, a vulgar and atypical person, to be sure. She was telling about her maid and said she loved to be able to reach up to the bell above her bed at three in the morning, ring, and have the girl come scrambling in with a pitcher of ice water. She said that was why she "loved" Negroes. She paid her maid very well, though, with a cabin on her land, food, and $2.50 a week. Recently the girl had asked for a twenty-five cent a week raise and her employer told her "You go to hell" and laughed. She paid her maid less per week in cash than the cost of having her laundry done outside; in addition the girl did all the cooking, and besides stayed seven nights a week with informant's young son. The story, though not typical, illustrates what a mean person can do in a situation like this, and there are always some such mean people in every social group.

But cheap help is not always good help. Middle-class people seem generally to make use of Negro house servants, cooks, chambermaids, nurses for children, and houseboys. From them one hears frequent complaints about the lack of efficiency of these servants and many examples are given. Frequently the visitor is asked if we would stand for such behavior from servants in the North and he has to admit that the Negroes are often trying.

This report will give something of the atmosphere. A white housewife told the story of her cook, Opal. Opal came one day and borrowed a party dress and three dollars; the white woman gave the favors reluctantly because she had learned from experience not to extend credit to Negroes. Instead of paying back they are likely to run away. This was the case with Opal who did not return for several days. Her mistress finally set out to look for her and learned from another Negro that Opal did not intend to come back. Word was sent to her that, if she did not return the dress and the three dollars immediately, she would be arrested for obtaining money under false pretenses. By the next morning the dress had been secretly returned and hung up in the closet and the three dollars came back with it. Opal was discharged and another cook hired. Three weeks later Opal returned one morning about six o'clock and said she was going to work again. She started working around the kitchen, wanted to oust the other cook, and insisted she would stay even without pay. But the mistress refused to discharge the new cook and finally Opal left again, this time for good.

A new light was cast on this situation, however, by the husband of the white informant. It appeared that the mistress herself was soft-hearted, fixed on Opal, and uncertain in dealing with her. The husband disapproved of the way his wife acted and thought the reason Opal was so unaccountable was that his wife humored her and was foolish in dealing with her. For example, Opal was repeatedly taken back after being fired under the most tempestuous circumstances and money was loaned to her when it was unlikely that she would return it. It seemed that the white woman had presented as a peculiarity of the Negro what was, at least in part, a character defect of her own, namely, her fond generosity and her loving to play the forgiving rôle.

There is constant report of the unreliability and instability of Negro servants, how they stay away from work for unaccountable reasons, and how mysterious their mental processes are. Just by chance, however, I heard a woman from Washington consoling a local housewife who complained on this score. The Washingtonian said that actually in the South the Negroes worked for almost nothing, but in Washington they demanded five to ten dollars a week, two half-days off, free at seven o'clock at night or overtime. Further, she said that when they first come from the South to Washington they are all right, but are spoiled rapidly by the servants there and learn to make the same extravagant demands. It may be that the economic gain is less in Washington.

The question of the relation of the tenant farmer to the

planter bears on the issue of the economic gain. The arrangements governing planter-tenant relations are the traditional half-and-half sharing which replaced the slavery adjustment. Whether the long-run advantages of emancipation anticipated by Lewinson[9] have actually occurred is a moot question still. Certainly the status of the Negro has been bettered. His mobility makes him free to seek work elsewhere, an important lever in bettering his status at home. From the standpoint of the planters, however, the situation is much more vexatious than might seem from the knowledge of their class position. Difficulties in fixing the labor supply, spendthrift habits in prosperity, and the vagaries of the world cotton market make planting a risky business.

The cycle of the year in Southerntown and county follows the natural cycle of the cotton growth. Local people picture it in the following way. The cotton year begins in March at planting time. To tenants the owner usually advances about ten dollars a month from this time on, for the five or six months until the crop is made and the cotton ginned. The cropper must cut old stalks, plow, plant, harrow, chop (with a hoe between the rows), pick cotton, and haul it into Southerntown to be ginned. He then re-

[9] "As Stephens rightly indicated, the whole complex of Southern institutions depended on the economic, social, and political subordination of the Negro. Of this subordination, slavery had been the basis. When slavery was destroyed the labor system on which the whole Southern community depended was destroyed with it; and more: the vested rights of the slave-holders were attacked, and the position of the poorer whites as laborers and free peasants menaced. However uneconomical the system had been for the community as a whole, however heavy a charge on the large plantation owners, however great a handicap to the poorer whites, its destruction promised advantages only in the long run. The difficulties, the disturbance of equities, involved in bridging the gap was one of the factors which aborted any early desires in the South for emancipation, whether these arose from statesmanlike vision, or from the enlightened self-interest of either slave-owners or the lower orders." Paul Lewinson, *Race, Class and Party* (New York, 1932), pp. 27-28; quoted by permission of the Oxford University Press.

ceives (even the dishonest planters allow) the money for the pressed seed ($32 per ton this year). The tenant gets credit also for his half of the price of the cotton bale ($37.50 at present prices) to apply on what he owes the owner. As soon as his debt is paid off, he can keep the proceeds as the cotton is sold, bale by bale. In addition to the fifty dollars or so which may have been advanced for food, the owner may have paid for medical services. It is expected that a cropper will have enough left at the end of the season to carry him to the following March when he may expect another month's "furnish." In the fall discreet tenants look about for a new "sitshashun" (one white informant used this word with the superior laughter of the middle-class southerner at the naïveté of the Negro). In most cases the contracts for the following year are made by Christmas. Planters usually give an allowance of Christmas money to their expected tenants for the next year, which is, of course, deducted the following fall. Many planters charge 25 percent interest on their advances to the tenant, whatever the length of time they are made for; some charge 20 percent, others as low as 15. In explanation one informant stressed the high prices planters have to pay for their money (but the highest quoted was 12 percent— the government land banks loan for 6 percent but make other charges that run up the rate). The fact is stressed that planters have to take risks after giving croppers early season advances; no labor has yet been done and the tenant may leave. Some planters give their tenants no money loans as "furnish," but instead credit slips on local merchants. Informant said defensively, needing approval, that he makes a profit on what he sells to his tenants (tenants are not partners but business rivals to be treated as such). For example, he made a lucky buy on corn in the fall at sixty cents a bushel. In the spring he sold it to his tenants for ninety cents. Again, he bought "duck," to make the bags into which the pickers put the cotton, at ninety-nine cents a bag and sold the bags to the tenants for a dollar and a quarter. "Business is business," informant felt; but he was obviously worried on this point.

In leaner times planter incomes do not seem exorbitant.

One owner who has eight hundred acres under cultivation does not have croppers but rents the land at six or seven dollars per acre. Last year he got about two percent on the $90,000 investment in the farm, that is, $1800. The taxes were $2200, a little over $2.20 per acre. This man makes a particular point of being fair with his tenants, pays all requisitions by check, and makes his tenants countersign the checks as proof they have received the money in question. But there is always the hope of boom times to cheer the operator during a meagre year.

The income derived from cotton, and therefore the planters' share, has greatly diminished since 1929. One effect of this has been to decrease the amount of cash money that the tenants see. A wholesale grocer related that before 1930 most planters furnished their tenants in cash. Since 1930 the planters have begun furnishing through commissaries. Actually they have set up their own grocery stores and are giving the tenants credit at them. The main wholesale purchases of food for Negroes are for salt meat, corn meal or wheat flour or rice, molasses or syrup, coffee, salt, and sugar. A few planters tried to include canned vegetables out of season, such as canned tomatoes. Retail prices are charged for the commissary goods and in addition the regular 20 to 25 percent interest on the furnish. Informant defended this amount of interest; he said it helps defray other necessary costs, such as the cost of sharpening tools, the costly fact that some tenants who are furnished do not actually make a crop, and the medical and other services which are given to tenants (I had supposed that the planters accepted these risks directly as part of the share system). The evidence seems to be that the lot of the planter, the scrupulous planter at least, is not a happy one.

In fact, the rebuttal is quite brisk on the part of the planter who often asserts that the Negroes get the best of it in this situation. A large landowner told me that he has been in contact with the Negro for forty years but does not know him yet. He said that the Negro is the best economist around the place; he always gets a living whether the plantation makes or loses money, but makes money if the place makes it. He added that the Negro provides nothing but his labor. He said the Negroes will not save, that they always spend all of what they get, and that he has known some with a thousand dollars in pocket who would charge a pair of shoes to next year's furnish. In addition he averred that the Negro is not a good manager and that many Negroes on his place now have owned land but have lost it in recent years.

A small landowner told me that one of her Negro servants, male, got angry at her and told her that the white people around Southerntown did not do anything anyway, that they just lived off what the Negroes made for them. She replied with a statement of what she does for the Negro tenants, how she gives them a cash furnish, how they provide nothing but their labor, and how she pays all the various kinds of taxes.[10] Her point was that the Negroes are really better off than she is. Another owner of a medium-sized plantation said that he feels heavily the responsibility of the plantation and the families on it. He does not keep very good books, though he does know what he gives the Negroes. When times are bad he has to take care of the Negroes first, whether they make anything or not; when times are good he has to make all he can in order to catch up on the bad times.

Informant after informant among the middle-class group pointed out the short number of days per year that the Negro tenants work. One said that they work for five months and have to be supported for twelve. One estimated that they work about sixty days a year, another ninety days. A Negro informant said they work about ten months a year, not steadily to be sure, from about March 1 to December when the last of the cotton is sometimes picked. Another well-informed white owner claimed they work about a hundred and fifty days a year and have absolute security of a living. He queried how many white workers in the North can say the same. We must remark, however, that on many of the hundred and fifty days the whole Negro family works, especially during the picking

---

[10] This idea is often used to justify the sales tax which exists in this state: without it a great many people, the lower-class people, would not pay any taxes at all.

season, which adds up to more days of labor than the hundred and fifty per family per year, and this, of course, is all included under the one-share settlement. I noted on July 22, on a trip into the country, that few Negroes were working and many fishing; I wondered if it were true that Negroes fished for food as well as for fun. If so, middle-class and lower-class views would be different on this point.

The northern visitor is bound to comment on the apparent poverty of the Negroes and the poor condition of their shacks, which can be plainly seen from the roads. A white informant answered that the state of the shacks does not reflect on the plantation owner. Sometimes the owner will equip the shack, put in screens, glass in the windows, etc., and in a few days it will be in as bad condition as it was before. The Negroes will tear out a piece of screen in the kitchen window, for instance, in order to throw out the slop. Sometimes, however, the owner will fix up a shack and take pay for it from the Negro's share in the crop. He tells the Negro then that the screen belongs to him and that it goes with him if he moves. Then he may be more careful of it, but on the whole Negroes are just not used to such fixings and therefore cannot take care of them.

A Negro informant agreed to this charge of ignorance and shiftlessness, and asserted that the Negroes make no improvements for themselves, and have to be told every little thing to do; but he added his own rebuttal: The ignorance and shiftlessness is a heritage from slavery days and it is cultivated now by the whites to keep Negroes down.

White middle-class people are quite convinced of the fact, at least, of this shiftlessness. A white informant believed that it was useless to come down and try to organize labor unions among the Negroes. He said that "niggers" have no initiative, that they have to be told what to do, even shown what to do, and you must tell them to do just one thing at a time. If you have two things you want done and give both orders, neither will be done right. If Negroes were on their own, things would be in a mess because they would not know where to start and once started they could not keep going straight.

A scrupulous plantation owner said he had a hundred and fifty sharecroppers on his plantation and that last year they made $150 to $500 in *cash* per family, but that they saved none of this and had to be furnished this year just the same. He asserted that if they could save they would own all the country around and he would be greatly obliged to them because then he would not have to borrow the money to furnish them. A number of owners stated that they have the same number of tenants as in 1930, though they are only planting part of the land in cotton. Some of the tenants have only three days' work a week.

Occasionally one heard of a reliable Negro in contrast to the many stories of shiftlessness. One such Negro is the tenant "Jim." He is very handy, runs a tractor, and is a good cook. He has been married four times, once in another county since he felt that by going into another county he was getting a divorce as well as a new marriage license. Jim will work at any hour and do anything asked of him, such as plowing with the tractor at night. If he is drunk, he will send back word that he is sick or drunk and he never comes then.

A transplanted northern owner questioned the traditional half-and-half sharing of the cropper and the landlord. He thought it unfair to the planter. He is trying to work out a new scheme on various levels, such as forty-sixty sharing, and twenty-five—seventy-five sharing, or rental and share arrangements in which the tenant pays his rent and then shares. It certainly seems possible that this view is reasonable, since the shares for labor and management are traditionally defined rather than worked out in terms of a changing situation. This attempt is a particularization of the view that the tenant gets the best of it, which may indeed be true since 2 percent, for example, is a low share for capital. Furthermore, the number of failures of landowners after the 1929 boom has not been small, proving that the business is highly risky. The low yield on capital, however, is exclusive of the relatively high incomes which middle-class managers, merchants, lawyers, and the like make from the system; it is also a figure given for a depression year when the yield in stable industries like steel was also low. It would not change our conclusion as to a middle-class gain.

We must note that the whites are as automatically caught in this socio-economic situation as are the colored. The middle-class whites are playing their social rôles with no more, but no less, greed and acquisitiveness than any other man in our society exhibits. They are acting as they have to act in the position within the social labor structure which they hold, that is, competing as hard as they can for maximum returns. Planters repeatedly affirm the difference between practical experience with Negro labor and theoretical ideas about social justice, and it is pointed out that the northerner would feel very differently if he actually had to pay for it himself and endure its inefficiency. Theoretical economic justice can only be dealt out, in the sense of our system, to those who have correct working habits involving abstinence and foresight; those who do not have these habits, as the lower-class Negroes do not, would have to be trained by force to have them. Physical nature ordinarily exhibits such force against human indolence; but the Negroes are in this sense a protected group who, at least so far as subsistence is concerned, are released from the actual fear of starvation by the furnish system.

Planters are puzzled and annoyed by the apparently inscrutable way in which Negro tenants leave their land allotments. One said that he studies his tenants rather than farming, that they know how to farm and his problem is to keep them satisfied and working; the big issue is to have a steady labor supply. He said he observes that Negro croppers leave a farm when they are cheated, or when they make too much money. He cited his best Negro tenant of last year who "cleaned up" and then left. Negroes never announce that they will leave a plantation until the settlement has been made because they fear that if they do, there will be no settlement. This migratory trait must be one of the annoyances of Negro emancipation from the planter's standpoint, since the possibility of geographic mobility is one of the certain gains of caste over the slave status of the Negro. This annoyance is abundantly reflected in the literature.[11] At least one thorough experiment has been made to appeal to the self-interest of the Negro tenant and thereby to anchor him more firmly to the land, but it has failed.[12] The reasons for such a failure will be discussed at some length.[13]

A Negro landowner agreed that the tenants try to get all they can out of you; in particular it is difficult to collect bills for medical services. A Yankee planter in the neighborhood became so disgusted that he would not advance money for medical services. The Negro said his policy was to drive a hard bargain with the tenants but to be fair about it. He does not know why the tenants move around so much, even when they are well treated. He said it may be a conviction that the whites are cheating them no mat-

[11] A. H. Stone, *Studies in the American Race Problem* (New York, 1908), p. 109.

[12] "Back of the inception of the scheme was the desire to create a satisfied and satisfactory force of reasonably permanent tenants. Not that we were ever sanguine enough to hope to have them all in this category. We would have been satisfied with a group of 50 per cent. of the total, or even with less. It was hoped to accomplish our object by a direct appeal to self-interest. We demonstrated our ability to make independent property-owning families out of poverty-stricken material. These families in turn demonstrated the fact of their independence by severing relations with us almost as promptly as we put them on their feet. After the termination of three years we had begun to feel reasonably certain that even the most practical appeal we could make to radically improved material welfare would be generally overcome by an apparently instinctive desire to 'move.' After the experience of five years we were quite satisfied of our entire incapacity to make the average plantation Negro realize the remotest causal relation between stability and prosperity." Stone, *op. cit.*, pp. 130-131; quoted by permission of Doubleday, Doran & Co.

[13] "In several instances, hands left because we were unwilling to advance the amount of 'Christmas money' to which they felt themselves entitled. Some departed with the rare frankness of a declaration that they 'just wanted a change.' Family troubles, the separation of husbands and wives, also account for their share. Still others went because of alleged dissatisfaction with the contract under which they had successfully been brought to a state of independence." Stone, *op. cit.*, pp. 143-144; quoted by permission of Doubleday, Doran & Co.

ter what they get, or possibly that they have wanderlust. There has not been so much moving on his place since the depression. He said it is no use to be quixotically generous with the tenants, that one would ruin oneself and not change the system. Major Millsaps[14] has also made an experiment in "trusting the tenant"; both this and Stone's report should be taken as historical record rather than as a statement of current experiment or practice.

A white businessman from outside the community commented on the reasons for mobility in Negroes. He said that they do not, after all, move out of the community, although they may move from plantation to plantation. The labor supply is fixed in the region even though it is wasteful to have the tenants moving from place to place. He believed that the planters are often in league with local merchants, that the planters pay larger bills for supplies than is warranted, sell the goods to the tenants on the basis of these prices, and then get rebates from the merchants. A Negro may make fifteen or twenty bales of cotton and get little or nothing for it. The planters say they have to keep the Negroes poor to keep them here. He alleged also that the planters are wastrels themselves and set a bad example to the Negro; that they too mortgage next year's crop at the bank for advances instead of saving money, doing just the thing they so much deplore in their tenants.

A middle-class Negro hazarded some opinions on why the tenants move. In some instances they will move to get away from plantations where they do not like the overseer. Again the fact that some whites chase their women is a cause for moving. There may also be something in "restlessness" or "habit of moving." This informant stressed the great degree of ignorance and childlike trustfulness of the Negroes in relations with the white landowners; seemingly, as some of our cases have shown, he might have added their ignorance and mistrustfulness as well.

A Negro agricultural teacher commented that there were strains of families who do not move very much and others who are "floaters." The latter acquire the moving habit and

[14] Ray Stannard Baker, *Following the Color Line* (New York, 1908), pp. 102-103.

keep on moving, always expecting to find something better somewhere else. Often it may be a sense of insecurity which drives them from one plantation to another. Many of them actually plan to move every year or so to get a change of scene and possibly a fresh field for sexual operations. He thinks the moving is very bad for whites as well as for Negroes since the Negroes do not take care of their houses, fences, fruit trees, and other valuable property of the owner.

It seems that one of the few aggressive responses that the Negroes may make in the situation is to leave a particular plantation. The planter is vulnerable at just this one point, that is, withdrawal of his labor supply.[15] This freedom to move, as already noted, is one of the gains of the emancipation for them; it is exactly what they could not do in prewar days and it probably represents a confused general distrust, resentment, and hope for betterment which cannot be changed rapidly even by such honest and intelligent experimental action as Stone has taken. If Negroes can move, at least they cannot strike; organization would immediately be interpreted as a threat to white supremacy altogether. We have pointed to the fears on this score, however, and the newcomer in the community, if he has a suspiciously vague purpose, is bound to be warned. This was done immediately in my case. It was said that if I wished to work with tenants, Negro or white, I must be sure to contact the landlord first. There has been labor trouble in nearby states and the landlords fear organization of tenants. It was stressed that there would be no criticism if this stipulation were complied with, but of course it applied only when tenants were seen on plantation land. In this case fear of labor organization melted into the older fear of med-

---

[15] Johnson also has observed this. "Year after year these families continue to live and move about within the county, but rarely leaving it. The tenant turnover is high. Their one outstanding means of asserting freedom is this mobility, although within an extremely narrow range. Planters can never tell which of their tenants will be with them the following year, but of one thing they can be fairly certain—that they will not leave the county, and in time, will rotate, of their own choice, back to the point of beginning." C. S. Johnson, *op. cit.*, p. 25; quoted by permission of the University of Chicago Press.

dling Yankees who have done so much to interfere with labor relations in the South. Emancipation of the Negro slaves was such an interference on a colossal scale. One should not forget, however, that northern employers and factory owners are quite as sensitive to outside organizers. Mining towns are chronically suspicious of strangers.[16]

Landowners take active measures to resist interference with their labor relations and even attempt to protect the Negroes against exploitation, often by members of their own race. A white friend told me there had recently been a "ruckus" on a nearby plantation. A Negro had come down from Chicago in a big car and was getting subscriptions for a trip back to Africa (Garveyism?). The African land was painted in the brightest colors and the Negroes were told that they would all have fine houses and other things to match. To be sure, they were told that this equipment is now in the hands of local Africans who would be driven back into the bush and the American Negroes settled in their comfortable places. The agent said he was sent from Washington to enlist and collect for this movement and that a ship was leaving New York in September with places for 14,000 Negroes. The surrounding planters became annoyed and determined to arrest this man for impersonating a federal officer and running a racket. Two planters and their overseers went to the house where he was staying; they blew the horn (the characteristic way of summoning Negroes), and a large Negro woman came out. When they asked for the agent, she told them that he was sleeping. They wanted her to go in and wake him up; she refused to. One of the men drew a pistol and hit her over the head with it. She was a powerful woman, struggled with him, and tried to take it away from him. In the meantime Negroes came running up, attracted by the scene. The first man retrieved his pistol and was about to shoot the woman when the other white men stopped him. They went back and got some more white help and returned to the scene, but by this time the agent and also the woman were

[16] Hearst's Homestake mine at Lead, South Dakota, is an example. *See* Ferdinand Lundberg, *Imperial Hearst* (New York, 1936), p. 186.

gone. The informant, a planter, agreed that this might have become a very bad situation if it had continued.

This type of informal policing goes on constantly and is part of the vigilance which is necessary to be relatively free from labor organization or seduction of the labor forces into other areas. It is frequently exercised as solicitude for ignorant Negroes and protection of them against exploiters of their own race. This motive cannot be taken at face value because there is no consistent concern over the exploitation of Negroes; it seems to appear only when there is some actual threat of disturbing the status or labor relations.

A very intelligent Negro believed that the furnish system does tend to impoverish the lower-class Negroes, not only in the material sense, but also in a sociological sense, that is, it tends to discourage the type of habit necessary to self-improvement in our society. He felt it was to the advantage of the whites not to encourage thrift or consistency of behavior, because, as long as these qualities are lacking, the Negroes are dependent on the furnish and the landowners are relatively sure of their labor supply. The owner does not care if the Negro spends the cash money he received in a reckless manner since then the Negro becomes economically dependent on the owner, must again apply for furnish and his presence is guaranteed for the next year; if the identical Negro does not come back, some other Negro in the same situation will. In just the same way, if a certain middle-class operator does not own the land and make his class gain, some other white man will; the system goes on, though the individuals may change.

It is perennially asked how fairly the returns on the crop are actually shared with Negro tenants according to the share-crop arrangement. Perhaps a truism is the best summary of the situation—that there are honest and dishonest landlords. If one considers the generality of human meanness, one can hardly see how many landlords could fail to take advantage of the opportunities for cheating Negroes. We have too abundant evidence of the inability to resist a chance to swindle when it comes along.[17] This manner of

[17] Says Johnson on the score of the settlement, "It is, of course, impossible to determine the extent of exploitation of

dealing with the Negroes is of interest since it is so obviously conditioned by the caste barrier which freezes the Negroes' aggression against white men. For example, a white owner told me that the croppers work only about ninety days of the year and that this must be taken into account when considering their small income. The rest of the time they fish, fool around, attend revivals, and follow other trivial pursuits. He said he treats his tenants well, keeps honest accounts, always gives them an accounting. Some owners do not give an accounting and this is one of the ways of cheating. He considers this a low practice because the Negroes are so defenseless (but he laughs in telling about it). An accounting may be refused in the following manner. A Negro may walk ten miles to ask for it but the owner is too busy to talk to him. "Yes, boss." He comes a second time; still too busy. After coming a third time and being put off, the Negro realizes he is not going to get an accounting. A middle-class Negro gives this kind of an example. A tenant may make ten bales of cotton, worth $750, for which his share would be $375, less his advances. The Negro has kept accounts and knows the advances to be, say, $100. The landlord or his overseer calls in the tenant and tells him he did very well this year: he made $10. If the Negro offers a mild challenge, he is told, "Do you mean to call me a liar?" This settles the discussion because to call a white man a liar is extremely dangerous for a Negro. A lawsuit is out of the question in view of the local mores; it would amount to calling a white man a cheat or a thief.[18]

---

these Negro farmers, so long as the books are kept by the landlord, the sale price of cotton known only by him, and the cost and interest on rations advanced in his hands. In the case of many new tenants, however, who could have no standing indebtedness, their 'suspicions' of being paid short were warranted. Said one tenant, 'White folks take it when they git ready and you looking right at them.'" C. S. Johnson, *op. cit.*, p. 120; quoted by permission of the University of Chicago Press.

[18] "Three years ago, when a Negro moved from Uvalda, a small town in the southern part of the county, he tried to get a settlement with his landlord who owed him some money. When the landlord would not settle, the Negro filed a suit

Contrary cases will certainly be exceptional.

Another well-informed Negro thought as a guess that a large percentage of the planters around Southerntown cheated their colored help. It was the same story of the settlement by the forty-five revolver and the "Do you dare dispute me?"[19] and is particularly true of the big planters. He said the country Negroes are coming into the towns and living, when they can, on relief. They say they might as well starve in the city as in the country. The same informant called attention to the bellwether, or pet Negro, on the plantation who is allowed to make some money and whose function it is to induce new croppers to come when the old ones have left. Another Negro informant gave the same information about the pet Negro, usually the one who tattles on the others. The planter will let him make some money, will give it to him in a lump sum, send him into town to show it, tell about it, and negate rumors spread by dissatisfied croppers of the year before. This action is necessary in order that there shall not be a boycott of any particular landlord by dissatisfied tenants. Under depression labor conditions, however, this procedure would seem to be unnecessary.

Some owners, not all, juggle the accounts to keep the

---

against him. The Negro was severely flogged. None of the floggers were ever indicted." Arthur F. Raper, *The Tragedy of Lynching* (Chapel Hill, 1933), p. 201; quoted by permission of the University of North Carolina Press.

[19] "Henry Robinson had been living in the same place for nineteen years, paying $105 a year rent for his land. He raises three bales of cotton a year, turns it all over, and continues to go deeper in debt. He said:

"'I know we been beat out of money direct and indirect. You see, they got a chance to do it all right, 'cause they can overcharge us and I know it being done. I made three bales again last year. He said I owed $400 at the beginning of the year. Now you can't dispute his word. When I said "Suh?" he said "Don't you dispute my word; the books says so." When the books says so and so you better pay it, too, or they will say "So, I'm a liar, eh?" You better take to the bushes too if you dispute him, for he will string you up for that.'" Johnson, *op. cit.*, p. 127; quoted by permission of the University of Chicago Press.

cropper in debt and thus hold him on the land. This is apparently another device for stabilizing the labor force; the man who is in debt has to leave all his goods if he tries to move. Informant said that the cropper is called to the accounting, the boss man sits at the desk, a forty-five revolver beside him, roughly asks what the tenant wants. The tenant says he wants a settlement. "Yes," says the boss man, "you made fifteen dollars last year." The tenant cannot argue or dispute or the boss will grasp the gun and ask him if he is going to argue. If he does, "boom-boom." (Only white juries sit on such cases, or any other cases for the most part; provocative behavior, such as an argument by the Negro, is considered as an adequate extenuating circumstance.) For the most part only the possibility of such an event is needed to discourage the persistent tenant.

Another more indignant Negro reported the same settlement by threat of force. She said some Negroes do not accept being cheated, protest, and are killed. This informant said that it is worse than the old slavery situation, since under the old situation the Negro did not expect anything (had no hope of mobility); now he does and is often cheated and disappointed. She said she could not stand this treatment for herself, seeing money she had earned and needed for her own family going to support someone else who had more.

Another complaint of Negroes is that recently in harder times planters have changed the traditional arrangement by charging for all manner of small privileges formerly given gratis. They charge for hauling this and that, for the right to use a garden plot, and so on. The total economic set of the community has undoubtedly made the situation more harsh for tenants in recent years; also the Negroes have less alternative opportunity to move into other parts of the country.

A Negro manager who saw the problem from the side of the planter thought that many tenants were unreliable about their statements as to what had been advanced them; they forget or do not keep track. They, too, want to cheat the boss man whenever they can. Many planters are honest in their settlements, he thought. A number of them call him or another educated Negro in whenever they have an altercation with a tenant about settlement. Informant said that often the tenant is trying to support a couple of women, and so draws extra from the planter, without telling his family. Later he claims he never received the advances in question.

It is obviously impossible to ascertain the exact truth in this kind of situation; what we have shown is the attitude-set as it seems to be reflected in the opinions and practices of owners and tenants. Not to be left out of account are the simplicity and ignorance of many of the Negroes, and further, their idealization of the planter for whom they work; the patriarchal character of the slavery system has left this attitude as a holdover in present-day field Negroes. The old Negroes' love and loyalty for the master, built up in slavery times, have tended to carry over to the new boss man. This idealization is a matter of major importance wherever the Negro's relation to a planter or other employer is concerned. Apparently he tends to turn submissive affect in the direction of the master symbol of whiteness,[20] be it southern planter or northern factory owner. Undoubtedly the caste barrier, by the status distance it creates and the categorical differences between Negroes and whites it suggests, constantly reënforces these older attitudes.

In earlier days there were, of course, compensatory arrangements, such as the responsibility of the employer for the care of the ill, old, and otherwise disadvantaged Negroes. No doubt the attitude still persists among upper-class white people and is an important force in meliorating the lot of the Negro. It seems to be breaking down, if indeed it ever existed, among the middle-class white people. A Negro woman remarked that the middle-class whites will have a servant for a good many years and, when he gets old or sick, they will just throw him out. She does not believe the story that southern families take care of their servants; maybe they did in the old days but now it is a straight money-wage proposition and the older traditions of responsibility are going. She cited the case of the house serv-

[20] Sterling D. Spero and Abram L. Harris, *The Black Worker* (New York, 1931), p. 467.

ant of a white family in the city. He got sick, they moved him out of the servant's house on Monday, and he died on Wednesday morning. He was very ill, but they sent him to his sister's house on a plain country wagon.

Public relief for Negroes should be mentioned in this connection. There seems to be a good deal of resistance to giving them federal relief in Southerntown. The reason appears to be that such relief would take the pressure off the Negro families to seek employment on the farms or in the white households, and there is fear that the standard of relief offered would compete too favorably with the local living standards of the Negroes.

Negroes seem aware of this fact. One of them commented that Negroes get a very bad deal on relief; it was said that in a neighboring town there is only one Negro man on relief out of three or four hundred families. In looking over W.P.A. projects he remarked that there was not one which was for a Negro institution or which seemed to involve Negro labor. The President had recently signed the Social Security Bill, but my informant did not think this would do the Negroes any good because the old Negro people would be eliminated from the rolls. He recalled having read a protest by a prominent editor in the state against the bill, but the protest was directed toward the fact that a large number of old Negro people would get aid and they in turn would support a lot of worthless young Negroes who should be working on farms. Direct aid by whites to Negroes in trouble, given after the old manner, would not incur this danger because they could give it more discriminately.

It is frequently said by white people that the greatest hostility toward Negroes exists among lower-class whites, and it is similarly implied that the middle- and upper-class whites love the Negroes. The middle-class Negroes, at least, do not confirm this statement. The Negro owner of a small farm said that the hostility lies mainly between the "strainers" (the middle-class whites) and the Negroes, and not between the Negroes and the poorest whites. It is the strainer who resents the Negro having any property or holding a job which he feels ought to belong to a white man. "Strainers" will try to discredit a Negro manager by arousing the jealousy of the Negroes who work for him, or telling them that a white man could do the job much better. These persons are the ones who hate to see a Negro succeed, who curse him when he can buy a better automobile than they. Such whites, my informant said, try to arouse distrust in Negroes of the middle-class representatives of their own race, and to steal the business of middle-class Negroes. Often a Negro will be employed to initiate business with members of his own race; but, as soon as the clientele grows so that there is a respectable income in it, he will be replaced by a white man.

A Negro who had failed in business reported that the whites initiated some kind of quiet but pervasive boycott on him of the whites-trade-with-whites type, that is, business along caste lines. Ultimately, as a result of this, his business failed. If whites brought trade to him, they did it only on the assumption that he would radically undercut the white competitors. When he did not, they would say, "Well, we might as well take it to Smith." This man thinks that there is a type of informal economic council of businessmen in Southerntown which tries to direct purchases in the community, even to the extent of using ridicule on whites who buy from Negroes.

Another Negro said that whites put definite pressure on Negroes to buy from whites and that Negroes' lack of business loyalty is often due to white pressure. One method of doing this is to give Negro tenants orders which are good only at a white store; another is to allow the tenant to go to a Negro professional man, such as a doctor, but at the end of the season claim money was lost on the tenant and therefore not pay the doctor's bill. The caste situation makes it impossible for the Negro to argue, threaten, or sue. Another method is to discredit the reliability of Negro professional people or merchants by claiming that they charge high prices. The latter is often true since Negro merchants lack the capital to have as large a range of goods or as low prices as white competitors. In any case definite pressure is seen here by the whites to monopolize the business and professional opportunities, i.e., the middle-class economic gain.

The question of "white-man's jobs" is a very important one; perhaps this phrase represents as well as any other the competition between the middle-class white and Negro groups and the effort to exclude Negroes from the better paying jobs of higher status. This exclusion of Negroes is a distinct limitation on the bi-racial economic organization which many people see as a possible solution for the Negro in southern society. If the Negro wants any kind of institutional job, he must be careful not to let it seem too inviting, or else it will be reclassified as a "white-man's job."

Negro professional men are very few in Southerntown and they have many difficulties. For one thing their clients are so poor that the conscientious professional does not like to charge the fees he ought to charge. The Negro caste is the only source of their business, and it is a poor group; there is not much money around Southerntown anyway, the Negroes get very little of it, and some of them none at all. A large number are just permitted to exist by the community. This situation has a tendency to force the Negro professionals out of the southern small town into more lucrative opportunities. Professional people are further handicapped by the seasonal nature of the income of the Negroes. They have money only during the three fall months; during the other nine months of the year when the planters send them for any professional service, the white professionals get the business.

A white man told me that Negro doctors in the town have often been in "dope" trouble. One Negro physician has served time in Atlanta for selling dope; it is said to have improved his doctoring. There have been a number of drug addicts in Southerntown and they have put particular pressure on all the doctors for "dope." With the Negroes they have used money, threats, praise, everything, to get drugs out of them. Since the Negro physician's income is likely to be small anyway, there must be a great temptation to sell narcotics.

The Negro professional must be on the alert also to collect his fees. I tried to make a contact with one of them on a Saturday afternoon, but he did not wish to talk. He had to stay on the street below and try to collect his bills. His patients were in town and they had "seed money" and cotton money and he had to be on the alert if he were to be paid at all.

It is quite plain that the most active sources of antagonism between Negroes and whites lie between the middle-class whites and the Negroes. In promoting their own interests the white middle class uses any means at hand to fight competitors; this they do with whites and Negroes alike, of course, but in the case of Negroes the caste barrier and various other un-American methods of competition can also be used.[21]

Apparently the situation among Negro middle-class people was better before the depression. It would seem that the general tightening-up has particularly disadvantaged them, as one would expect from the nature of the social structure. It is said widely that before the depression many more Negroes owned land than now do; many owners of both castes have suffered foreclosure in recent years. There was also a Negro bank in operation in the town for twenty-four years; it failed in 1928.

The most vigorous competition which the white southern merchants experience is from Jews entering the community. It is said, "If there is a Jewish holiday, you cannot buy a pair of socks in this whole country," a remark which illustrates how complete the control of retail dry-goods trade by Jews is supposed to be. This success of Jewish merchants is

---

[21] "These men who crowded the smoking room were Canal employees of the artisan class—engineers, machinists, plumbers, electrical workers, and helpers. They were rough; their language was coarse and profane. But I gave the best attention I could to what they said, because it presented an interesting and important view of life, a view that I was unfamiliar with, a view that disclosed one of the most discouraging aspects of the racial situation. One expression that they constantly used brought to me more vividly than anything else ever had a realization of the Negro's economic and industrial plight, of how lean a chance was his with his white brothers of the proletariat. The expression which I heard at least a hundred times was, 'Never let a nigger pick up a tool,' 'Never let a nigger pick up a tool,' 'Never let a nigger pick up a tool.'" James W. Johnson, *Along This Way* (New York, 1933), p. 355; quoted by permission of the Viking Press.

believed to be due to winning the Negro trade. In the older white stores, when a Negro went in, the owner would say to him, "Well, *boy,* what do you want?" even if the Negro in question were eighty years old. The Jews, on the contrary, let the Negro know that his dollar is as good as anyone else's. One might remark that the Negroes do not receive preferential prices in the stores; the whites do not feel it a blow to social equality that they pay the same prices as the Negroes. Over and over again one hears from Negroes that southern dry-goods merchants have been crowded out of the territory by their rough, hostile, categorical treatment of Negroes. One must remember that it is in the field of dry goods rather than of food or shelter that the Negroes have most freedom to buy and hence their patronage would be most controlling. It was stressed that the Jews have treated Negroes with courtesy, or at least without discourtesy, in strictly business relations. They find some way of avoiding the "Mr." and "Mrs." question, such as by saying "What can I do for you?" and letting it go at that.

Another fact in the success of Jews seems to be that they bargain with the Negroes and the Negroes like this. Other merchants are more likely to follow a strict one-price policy, while the Jews will mark things up and then mark them down as a concession to the Negro buyer. Southern whites tend to be brusque and "take-it-or-leave-it" with the Negroes, while Jews are more considerate, putting business before caste principles. An expression of this bargaining tendency is the saying that "there is not a one-price dry-goods store in Southerntown." Middle-class Negroes comment that the Negro tenants are naïve on this score; they get satisfaction out of the fact that the Jewish merchant appears to allow himself to be beaten. This tendency is by no means, of course, confined to Negroes.[22]

It was said by one of the Jewish merchants that they use more sales pressure on Negroes than they dare do on the whites. If white buyers say "no," they mean "no" and the traders do not insist. But if the Negro says "no," they go on, get the goods out, and try them on him. Thus the merchants

[22] *See* Hanns Sachs, *Zur Menschenkenntnis* (Vienna, 1936), p. 7.

take advantage of their position as members of the white caste in using a certain amount of persuasive coercion.

Very conspicuous in this account of economic gain has been the absence of data on the lower-class white people, namely croppers like the Negroes. It must frequently have occurred to the reader to ask how the lower-class whites fare in the situation. My research has yielded no direct data on this point and it does not pay to guess. There are few lower-class whites in Southerntown; so the chance did not exist to study them in the town itself.[23]

In interviewing planters a small amount of information concerning their attitudes toward lower-class whites was secured. One said he did not like white tenants, that he had a few but that they were suspicious and made trouble; the Negroes are much more tractable. The sense in which they are docile was clearly revealed in talking to the manager of another quite large plantation. He made the familiar remark that he has dealt with Negroes for a long time and the more he deals with them the less he understands them. The Negroes seem to be quite a mystery around Southerntown. His plantation changed from Negro to white tenants in 1924 and changed back en masse in 1928. The reason given was that the white tenants tried to run the place, got radical, tried to vote the taxpayer, that is, the plantation, into expensive school buildings and other improvements. The Negroes are more manageable, so they were reinstated. This planter believed that the Negroes are about as good farmers as white tenants. It is easy to see from this case how the playing off of white against Negro tenants would tend to create animosity between them and also how the presence of the Negroes is a chronic threat to the economic security of the lower-class whites. Low standards of living can be forced on the Negro by utilizing caste prerogatives to suppress any demand for change on his part, and then the lower-class whites can be made to compete on the basis of these low standards. The old competition between Ne-

---

[23] Dr. Leonard W. Doob came to Southerntown with me during part of the summer of 1935. From his standpoint the research motive was not the main one in the trip. He did, however, make some observations on lower-class white people and has consented to give them in the Appendix to this book.

gro slaves and the poorer white workers has not diminished, at least in this area.[24]

There is the question, of course, of the increased use of mechanical power which may replace both Negro and white tenants. On some of the largest plantations tractors are being used increasingly. There is also the threat of a machine for picking cotton. This is the crucial threat since it is the picking of the cotton rather than the planting or cultivating of it which makes the masses of Negroes indispensable. If this invention should prove practicable and be widely adopted, the South would be faced with a radically new problem as regards the Negro.[25] We might expect then an efflorescence of fantasies of colonizing the Negroes in Africa, or of putting them in a separate state. The colonization fantasy occurred occasionally in the minds of thoughtful Southerntowners. Another possibility, of course, is the more even distribution of Negroes throughout the country, should they be needed again in the high-speed industrial machine of the North. While this would solve some of the problems of the South, it would certainly raise new ones in the North and make the American race problem a national instead of a regional issue.

It is interesting to consider whether the allegations that the Negro is slow and shiftless and that his labor turnover is extraordinarily large can be maintained in the northern environment. This does not seem to be the case.[26] Nor does it

[24] Lewinson, *op. cit.*, p. 32.

[25] The successful tryout of a cotton picker invented by John Daniel Rust and Mack Rust has been reported; *see Time*, 1936, Vol. 28, No. 11, pp. 47-50.

[26] "One of the questions contained in the preliminary questionnaire was: 'Has your Negro labor proved satisfactory?' Of 137 questionnaires returned by establishments employing five or more Negro workers, 118 reported that Negro labor had proved satisfactory and nineteen that it had not proved satisfactory." Chicago Commission on Race Relations, *The Negro in Chicago* (Chicago, 1922), p. 373.

"Despite occasional statements that the Negro is slow or shiftless, the volume of evidence before the Commission shows that Negroes are satisfactory employees and compare favorably with other racial groups." *Op. cit.*, p. 378. Both citations quoted by permission of the University of Chicago Press.

seem to be true, all things considered, industrially.[27] And the fact seems to be that most of the Negro migrants to the North have remained in that region.[28] In view of our experience in Southerntown these facts require some explanation. It seems that Negroes actually work better in the North. The following are some guesses concerning an explanation: the hope of status advancement is much greater in the North and this acts as a powerful incentive; the caste barrier, of course, does exist in the North but it is less explicit and probably less rigid. It may be too that the social environment, in particular the mechanical, automatic set of industry, provides a coercive form into which the Negro fits, whereas there is a large individualistic element in agriculture. On the southern plantation Negroes work more on their own responsibility, whereas in the North they work under more mechanized conditions where the coördination of labor sequences supports and coerces them. Another possibility is that the Negroes who migrate are the more capable ones and the more shiftless are left behind in the cotton fields. In any case, it seems to be a tribute to the great power of the social milieu that such different accounts of the traits of the Negro are given in the North and the

[27] "This problem of labor turnover seems to have been particularly acute during those years when Negroes were first moving into northern industries in large numbers. In recent years, since they have had time to become more adjusted to conditions in the North, there has apparently been a lessened tendency to change jobs, although according to most of the recent surveys Negroes still have a higher rate of turnover than do white workers. However, numerous investigations indicate that in establishments showing great mobility of colored laborers, this condition is usually due to poor selection of employees, poor housing, and to unsatisfactory conditions of labor." Louise V. Kennedy, *The Negro Peasant Turns Cityward* (New York, 1930), p. 121; quoted by permission of the author and the Columbia University Press.

[28] "The fact is, however, that few Negroes have returned to the South, even in response to insistent invitations and offers of free transportation and better home conditions made by southern states that were left badly in need of laborers as a result of the migration." Chicago Commission on Race Relations, *op. cit.*, p. 604; quoted by permission of the University of Chicago Press.

South. It may well be, too, that the tendencies of Negroes toward orderly behavior do not receive collective support in the South; rather their inadequacies are tolerated, whereas in the North there are higher expectations and the prospect of social advancement to strengthen their tendencies toward responsible and consistent conduct. In the North Negroes appear to escape to some degree the categorical treatment accorded their caste in Southerntown; probably they do not escape the economic gain which middle-class white people make from them.

CHAPTER VII

The Sexual Gain

∾∾∾∾∾∾∾∾∾∾∾∾∾∾∾∾∾∾∾∾∾∾∾∾∾∾∾∾

A marked reticence surrounds the field of sexual behavior in Southerntown, especially where cross-race ties are concerned. In freeing ourselves to see and speak of these matters we must avoid the opposite fault of exaggeration, a very common one to outsiders. As usual we are not concerned with the personal lapses of individuals but with the manner in which sex behavior is patterned by the caste situation. The problem is to describe how a person may act as a result of his social position, while at the same time realizing that not all individuals who have caste privileges actually make use of them. Objectivity is difficult, the facts are hard to secure, and the discussion is bound to raise some apprehension, even as the realistic treatment of economic matters does.[1] Although it is often difficult to distinguish between sex and mastery impulses in this field, there is nevertheless a state of affairs which may be referred to as a sexual gain for the white middle class.

The researcher cannot avoid discussing sexual matters if he abides by the data as they are visible in Southerntown. Sexual motives play too obvious a rôle in class and caste relationships to be overlooked.[2] Yet the white people of

---

[1] Sumner, with his usual candor, writes, "Nearly all our discussions of our own social order run upon questions of property. It is under the sex relation that all the great problems really present themselves." W. G. Sumner, *Folkways* (Boston, 1906), p. 374; quoted by permission of Ginn & Co.

[2] "The sex passion affects the weal or woe of human beings far more than hunger, vanity or ghost fear. It has far more complications with other interests than the other great motives. There is no escaping the good and ill, the pleasure and pain, which inhere in it." Sumner, *op. cit.*, p. 347; quoted by permission of Ginn & Co.

Southerntown give allegiance to high moral standards and it seems part of this code to suppress all references to the touchy issue. Etiquette and a fair return of hospitality of Southerntown people might seem to demand that I should be as blind as possible on the score of sexual factors, but no such suggestion was actually made. It may be, of course, that the suppression is more intense in Southerntown than in the usual small town because the sexual problem is more acute due to the race factor; indeed, it has been suggested that "sex" is at the root of many problems in the racial field.[3]

Except for the caste situation there is probably nothing exceptional about Southerntown. People are everywhere accustomed to understate, at least formally, their interest in sexual matters. Social scientists are no exception, perhaps because of the suspicion, always ready, that those who study sexual matters are not personally above reproach. It was not easy to test out the sentiment or behavior on this score and the following report is necessarily partial.

In simplest terms, we mean by a "sexual gain" the fact that white men, by virtue of their caste position, have access to two classes of women, those of the white and Negro castes. The same condition is somewhat true of the Negro women, except that they are rather the objects of the gain than the choosers, though it is a fact that they have some degree of access to white men as well as to the men of their own caste. Negro men and white women, on the other hand, are limited to their own castes in sexual choices. This gain probably accrues to lower-class as well as to middle-class white men, although in Southerntown itself the main white group is of middle-class status. We are justified in speaking of a gain here for the reason that our American society does not countenance in theory such nonreciprocal relationships; it will further be indicated that

[3] "Through it all I discerned one clear and certain truth: in the core of the heart of the American race problem the sex factor is rooted; rooted so deeply that it is not always recognized when it shows at the surface." J. W. Johnson, *Along This Way* (New York, 1933), p. 170; quoted by permission of the Viking Press.

this preferential access to Negro women on the part of white men is experienced by Negro men as a disadvantage.

The caste barrier has already been defined as prohibiting legitimate status for mixed-blood persons and sexual contact between women of the patriarchal caste and men of the lower caste. In the latter respect the caste morality resembles the double standard of sexual morality which does, or used to, prevail in Western Europe and the United States. The owner husband conserves his sexual property, accepts gratification elsewhere, and refuses the like privilege to his wife. Other men are, of course, denied the same access to her which he expects to exercise in regard to other women; in this case it is the Negro men who are systematically disadvantaged.

There has long been a tendency toward idealization of white women in the South, originally probably an upperclass pattern but a pattern which has spread widely among the other classes.[4] This ideal image is passionately and even violently defended, and the danger of soiling it is one of the threats which brings out the fullest hostility of southern men, especially when the attacker is a Negro. Actual behavior of whites toward white women does not always correspond with the ideal, but it is most important, nevertheless, to know of its existence. It seems possible that this idealization has an effect on the erotic behavior of white men toward their own white women, and produces perhaps a feeling that they are untouchable, that sexual sentiments are unbecoming in relation to them, and that sexual behav-

---

[4] "One of the rituals of the university dances is that of a fraternity of young blades entitled The Key-Ice. During an intermission the lights are turned out and these men march in carrying flaming brands. At the end of the procession four acolytes attend a long cake of ice. Wheeled in on a cart it glimmers in the torches' flare. Then the leader, mounted on a table in the center of the big gymnasium, lifts a glass cup of water and begins a toast that runs: 'To Woman, lovely woman of the Southland, as pure and as chaste as this sparkling water, as cold as this gleaming ice, we lift this cup, and we pledge our hearts and our lives to the protection of her virtue and chastity.'" Carl Carmer, *Stars Fell on Alabama* (New York, 1934), pp. 14-15; quoted by permission of Farrar and Rinehart, Inc.

ior toward white women must take place, though, of course, it does take place, only against a personal sense of guilt.

On the contrary, the image of the Negro woman in the white man's talk and fantasy seems to be of quite another kind; it is rather that of a seducing, accessible person dominated by sexual feeling and, so far as straight-out sexual gratification goes, desirable. This image of the Negro woman as inveterately sexual may or may not correspond with the facts; we will come to those. What we wish to establish now is that such an image does exist. It is by no means confined to the South, as the currency of sexual jokes about Negroes throughout the North will readily show. Jokes often give the quality of an imagery which would be hard to express in plainer terms. It seemed to me that the sexy stories told about Negroes among Southerntown men are more direct and vulgar than those one customarily hears in the North. These stories bubble up repeatedly and in none of them does one find the Negro women represented as delicately suppressing or veiling her sexual interest; the image of her in the jokes shows a crude, direct person.

A question is then raised about the two sides of this image. Was it really one image originally, case by case, in the lives of men who tell and appreciate these stories, an image that has been split according to well-known psychological mechanisms? It seems possible that the image of the white woman is in part conserved against sexual thought and allusions, whereas the Negro woman tends to draw the full burden of the unsublimated sexual feeling. This is hinted at by Tannenbaum.[5] In this case it would appear that the white men are defending their women not only from the sexual thoughts and attentions of Negroes, but also from their own, and what they deny to themselves in fantasy they will hardly permit Negroes in fact. It is legit-

[5] "You cannot indulge in certain relations toward colored women and expect to escape free from influence in your attitude toward white women. The idealization of the white women in the South is thus partly the unconscious self-protection on the part of the white men from their own bad habits, notions, beliefs, attitudes, and practices." Frank Tannenbaum, *Darker Phases of the South* (New York, 1924), pp. 32-33; quoted by permission of G. P. Putnam's Sons.

imate to speculate about this problem because of the extraordinary influence of this split image on the mental life of southern men; someone must turn up an explanation of a sufficiently crucial character to fit the well-known facts.

From the standpoint of the split-image theory the sexual gain of the men of the white caste would seem to be the luxury of preserving the image of the untouchable white woman and at the same time having available on easy terms the Negro woman as a target for the withdrawn affect. We must remind ourselves that the discussion of the sexual impulse is no simple matter; it is a very complex field of research which, though greatly illuminated by Freud, is still problematic in many particulars. Every society must deal with sexual impulses and somehow manage them, since conflicts centering around sexuality have such great power in disrupting the unity of the in-group. The result is that these impulses everywhere meet with taboo and control. It may be, for example, that the controls on sexuality within the white patriarchal monogamous family are so severe that they tend to taboo, by extension, all white women as sexual objects. Were this true, it would be easier to understand the utility of the lower-caste women as an alternative.

The official opinion of Southerntown on the relations between white men and Negro women was expressed by an informant who stated that only lower-class whites, "rednecks," go to Negro houses for gambling or women. When they do go, interracial trouble often starts. The explanation seems to be this: the white men get "down on the Negro level" by gambling and whoring and then want to be looked up to and treated as white men too; instead the Negroes often make insulting remarks, fights start, and the whole racial issue is raised. The police do their best to discourage whites from going into the Negro quarter for any frivolous reason. The opinion that cohabitation with Negro women is done, if at all, by lower-class white men is apparently quite widespread. There is no doubt that there is social pressure against such cohabitation by middle-class men, but it is doubtful whether the official version represents the facts.

A Negro informant told me that there is still much to

learn on this point and that everyone is protective of information about these relations. He stated that some of the highest-class white men have intercourse with the lowest-class Negro women. He referred to a certain white man who was seen repeatedly in a neighboring town following Negro prostitutes whom respectable Negroes call "alley-bats." In many of these towns, he said, there is a rush from the white to the Negro part of town after dark; white men will set up in a cabin cheap Negro women whom a respectable colored man would not look at. This informant has a bias, of course; part of his own rôle as a middle-class Negro is to stress his disapproval of such behavior and to turn the tables on the whites.

Occasionally an incident occurred in Southerntown which was revealing. A middle-class man who had been a drunkard died; in recent years friends would not offer him drinks because of his well-known alcoholism. It was said that he went to "nigger town" when he was off on one of his "bats." This behavior was viewed by all, however, as exceptional and regrettable since the man was well liked.

A case of a white man protecting his Negro mistress was reported. A Negro informant told me that a certain white man keeps a Negro girl who lives in the slums. Informant recently talked to this girl but was warned by another Negro not to do so. He was told that her white lover keeps a suspicious eye on men who talk to her, for fear they might be making dates with her. He recently beat up a Negro who had had something to do with her.

Testimony seems to be quite widespread to the fact that many, if not most, southern boys begin their sexual experience with Negro girls, usually around the ages of fifteen or sixteen. This may be a hang-over from older days since evidence from the present high-school generation indicates that white girls are not so inaccessible. It was said further that many white men do not have experiences with white women until they finally marry; and the half-joking point is sometimes made that until they were married they did not know that white women were capable of sexual intercourse. The latter remark would seem to be another testimony to the split in the image between white and Negro women. In reference to this matter a number of white informants recorded their belief that there are actually no chaste Negro girls after the ages of fifteen or sixteen. A white woman believed that most white men in the town, and especially the younger ones, have "had to do" with Negro girls; she thinks that practically all do. She remembered one incident from her adolescent training which shocked her. She was in love with a boy who brought her home one night and she kissed him warmly at the door. An older woman saw her and warned her never to kiss a boy that way; she said he might go to "nigger town" afterward. This seems again to emphasize the displacement of direct sexual feeling from white to Negro women.

A lively woman informant told of a middle-class man who was infatuated with Negro girls. Whenever he went downtown he would not notice the white women on the street, but would follow Negro women with his eyes and then pursue them, catch them in an alley where he could talk, and ask to go home and sleep with them. Apparently he was notorious in Southerntown for this, and got a venereal disease from these girls, referred to by my informant as a "terrible disease." She said she did not understand how his wife could tolerate having him in bed with her. Finally his wife did not dare let him go into town alone, but always went with him to see that he did not follow the Negro girls. Here is to be noted the strong disapproval of the people of Southerntown which forced the white man to talk with Negro girls in alleys and which otherwise discredited him in the community.

In popular belief and from such fact as could be gathered, most white men seem to prefer the lighter Negro girls; they do not profess as much attraction for the very dark women. The same seems true of Negro men; they too prefer the lighter women as sexual partners, although in this case there are many qualifications to be made. Here, at any rate, direct sexual competition for the lighter women can occur between men of the two castes and on the Negro's home ground. This fact tends to strengthen our opinion that the sexual affects directed toward Negro women have been attached originally to a white person and that they still seek, in the lighter Negro women, to approximate the original goal. Otherwise why, after all, is not the most characteristic Negroid type preferred? Cohn[6] has noted that white and Negro men share the same Negro women under some circumstances.

It is frequently said in Southerntown that there is much less white blood pouring into Negro veins than was formerly the case. One would like, but hardly dares, to make a census on the matter. It is probably true that acts of intercourse between caste members result in fewer children than in former days and that the bulk of sexual relations does not produce children. This can be understood on several scores: a class of Negro prostitutes who are sophisticated in respect to preventing conception has been segregated; contraceptive knowledge is more general in the whole Negro group; and, finally, the widespread rumor and fact of venereal disease among Negroes has led white men to take their own precautions against mucous contact. These, at least, are the alleged reasons, rather than the fact that it would be thought immoral to have a child whom one could not acknowledge in a legitimate manner. It was said, however, that there is still some white blood filtering into the Negro group, though less than in earlier times. When I expressed surprise at this, white friends pointed out that there are many white men of low moral principles.

It would seem that concubinage has definitely decreased when compared with earlier days.[7] It is possible, of course, to have a mixed-blood child without the permanency of relationship involved in concubinage. Here is the sort of evidence that comes in. A Negro woman said she had heard locally of only one mixed-blood child; at least the child in question was very light and the mother was known to go with white men. In her home town, not Southern-

---

[6] David L. Cohn, *God Shakes Creation* (New York, 1935), p. 84.

[7] "Concubinage itself was fairly frequent, particularly in southern Louisiana; but no frequency of purchases for it as a predominant purpose can be demonstrated from authentic records." U. B. Phillips, *American Negro Slavery* (New York, 1918), p. 194; quoted by permission of D. Appleton-Century Co.

town, my informant knew the situation much better and there she was acquainted with many cases. She referred to a white lawyer in her town who had two legitimate sons and an illegitimate Negro daughter twenty-four years old. The Negro mother of the girl was dark and homely, but the girl was fair and pretty. Informant said the father had always taken care of the concubine and her daughter; he had supported them, sent the daughter to good schools, and seemed to be much interested in her. The legitimate sons were hostile to this relationship. They tried to dissuade the father from having anything further to do with the concubine and daughter, and finally forced the girl to leave town. One of the brothers, however, also had a Negro mistress and a child by her. This child is as fair as any white child, and bears the father's features so strikingly that his legitimate wife got the city to forbid the child's passing her house on its way to school. Informant said that most of the white men who have Negro concubines and children are quite nice to them, give them houses and land, and support them well. They also take good care of the children, better than Negro men could. There is a section of the Negro district in her town where the Negro women who have white lovers live; in some cases the white men actually live with them. Informant thinks this sort of thing is much more prevalent in her town than it is in Southerntown.

A middle-class white woman from Southerntown talked to me about her cook, how devoted they were to one another and how much she had done for this servant. After ten amicable years the cook had a child by a white man. As if this were not bad enough, the cook insisted on calling the child by the name of its father, a member of a prominent family. The family became indignant and the cook was forced to leave town; her employer gave her the money to do so. This cook had defied caste etiquette; what was prohibited was not having the child, but the implication that it was a legitimate child and that it could expect status classification according to its father, which was implied in taking his name.

An embarrassing case was recorded of a white man who had a child by a Negro woman. This child was fair and bore a striking resemblance to a child of the same father by his wife. The coincidence was noted and became the subject of extensive gossip in Southerntown.

The most definite statement was made by a white male informant who claimed to know of six illegitimate children born to white men by Negro women at present living in the town, in contrast to other informants who had said that such cases were very rare. He stressed also that the children are often not completely disavowed; that, although they cannot be acknowledged socially, they can be supported and aided to achieve a preferential position within the Negro group.

One completely declassed white man in Southerntown not only had a Negro mistress but went so far as to live with her in "nigger town" across the tracks. This act could not be tolerated by the white group because open living carries the implication of legitimate association which is tabooed by caste regulations. Concubinage must be more or less furtive where it does exist.

A Negro woman reported with indignation that a number of white men in Southerntown have Negro mistresses. She had been surprised to learn of the fact because some of these very men are the ones who insist on segregation, and preach that the Negroes should have their own life separate from that of the whites. She believed that there is probably genuine affection in some of these relationships because many of them have lasted for years. The net impression from these informants is that neither miscegenation nor concubinage has disappeared in Southerntown but that a rising social pressure has brought people to exaggerate the actual decline in these patterns since slavery days.

One might ask why, in view of the many derogatory attitudes whites have toward Negroes, Negro women are still attractive sexually. It is almost certain that the answer will be too simple if it is stated in terms of crude sexual motive alone. Sexual behavior is almost always more complex than it appears and deep taboos and anxieties are in most cases associated with it; but certainly the factor of straight sexual desire must play a rôle. After all, monogamy involves much renunciation and when society, informally or formally, permits an escape, such as that to lower-caste women, there are many who will take advantage of it. It may be that the character traits of Negroes have a special lure just in the sexual field, especially in the case of lower-class Negroes. The women of this class may take sex more lightly altogether, tend to put less burden on the white man, and may react more responsively and permissively to his overtures. In the case of transitory sexual contacts the element of mastery must also often be involved. The remark is current in Southerntown that a man does not know what a sexual experience is until he has had a Negro woman; this seems to pose the problem as one of proving virility. The virile man would hardly be expected to pass this challenge by. The assertion of mastery or adequacy may creep in by other means too; a man suffering from a fear that he is not genitally adequate or that others may think him passive or that he is too fond of men may demonstrate the falsity of all such opinions by cohabiting with Negro women.

Another dominant element may well be the attempt to make the "other fellow" feel mean by taking his woman or women, to show the racial inferiority of the Negro by the wanton use of Negro women. In a patriarchal society the protection of one's "own" woman tends to be an important point and the conquest of women easily becomes a means of aggression against the men related to them.

It may be again that Negro women are valued because they provide a zone of freedom in an otherwise tight cultural situation as respects sexuality; with them the white man can have a transitory irresponsible relationship, whereas otherwise sexuality is loaded with cares, threats, and duties. In relations with Negro women the psychic strain may be much less.

Possibly the factor of odor plays a rôle, since white people generally profess to be revolted by the body odors of Negroes. The association between odor and sexual attraction is an old and well-known one, and it may be that just those odors which are revolting when one is in a conventional mood may be exciting in the sexual mood. But on this score direct and detailed study of white informants will be indispensable, a study which has been impossible in this research.

In the face of such complexities as these I will pass with bare mention the possibility that there are innate cross-racial forces tending toward sexual attraction. It may be that there are, that the strangeness in color, feature, or form has an allure. This explanation, however, can be given its proper weight only when the considerations already advanced are taken into account.

Certainly one feature of the attractiveness of the Negro woman that must not be neglected is the fact that she cannot be protected by her "legitimate owner." As will be discovered later, the Negro man is debarred from violent expressions or threats in defending his wife, sister, or daughter; whereas within the white caste women are almost uniformly attended by energetic protectors. The threat of the white protector at the invasion of his rights may vary. He may force the aggressor to marry against his will, kill him, or, infrequently but significantly, castrate him. With Negro women these threatening circumstances which attend white women are removed automatically by white-caste pressure against Negro men. In fact, wherever such pressure is removed, and there are parallel cases (such as those of white prostitutes or the "free modern girl"), any man is freer to pursue the woman than when she has a legitimate possessor, especially if he is present. The Negro women fall into the category of unprotected women; their men, the usual protectors in a patriarchal society, are unable to shield them by virtue of the unchallengeable position of the white man, i.e., caste.[8] In the case of Negro women of

[8] "Such laws severely handicap the struggle which Negroes are making—it is they more than anything else that is checking intermixture. In many smaller towns of the South protection of women of their race from the unwelcome advances of white men can and sometimes does mean lynching for the protectors. Governor Hugh M. Dorsey of Georgia in 1921 gave an example of such conditions which is not unusual. He had called together a group of prominent citizens of that state to place before them a hundred and thirty-five cases of mistreatment of Negroes within the state which had come to him unsolicited during the preceding two years." Walter White,

middle-class status the only alternative seems to be a relative seclusion which puts them beyond unwelcome attention.[9] It may indeed be one of the functions of the caste situation to keep the Negro woman without a protector and therefore more accessible; whether or not this is consciously intended, it is in fact a result of the low-caste position of the Negro man. The white man without the courage of his convictions will find it much easier to approach a woman who is not protected in the customary way; and since there are many such men in every community it is unreasonable to suppose that they do not make use of these opportunities with Negro women.[10]

Middle-class Negro women frequently comment on their sense of being under scrutiny by white men when they are on the streets. To be sure, this scrutiny of women, white or Negro, seems to be quite general in every town, but in the case of Negro women it is said to be coarser, more direct, and not limited by convention in the same way. The white man plainly indicates his sense of the greater availability of the Negro woman. Informants say further that

---

Rope and Faggot (New York, 1929), p. 78; quoted by permission of Alfred A. Knopf.

[9] "The beauty of Negro womanhood is not often exposed to the public gaze. School girls may be seen at certain hours of the day; but except as sheer necessity requires an occasional excursion for shopping or business, Negro women of refinement and culture are not often seen in public places, except among their own people. They prefer the protection and shelter of their own homes, for it happens more frequently than even our white friends are aware that such women are constantly exposed to unwelcome and uninvited attentions from a certain type of white men without any sort of redress or protection in the law." R. R. Moton, *What the Negro Thinks* (Garden City, N. Y., 1932), pp. 34-35; quoted by permission of Doubleday, Doran & Co.

[10] "As in slave times, many white men in the plantation area feel that they have certain privileges with Negro girls and women. Near Emelle there is at present a landed white man who lives with a Negro woman, and by her has had several children. It is reported that a prominent citizen of Livingston virtually lived with a well-known Negro woman." Arthur F. Raper, *The Tragedy of Lynching* (Chapel Hill, 1933), p. 83; quoted by permission of the University of North Carolina Press.

white men seem to feel freer to approach a Negro woman on the subject of a sexual affair than they would a white woman in a similar case, perhaps counting on the widespread belief that all Negro women are sexually lax. White people frequently relate that there are "two classes" of Negroes, the one a little more reliable, responsible, and moral than the other. But white people do not discriminate between the middle- and the lower-class Negroes with sufficient accuracy and are constantly offending the former in this way.

When we remember the great number of Negro women who work outside the home in Southerntown we can see how accessible they are to sexual approach. In these cases there is no need to speak to a Negro woman on the street; the matter can transpire informally within the home. There is no doubt that household servants are more exposed to sexual approaches than are women who stay at home. This may have something to do with the middle-class ideal of both Negroes and whites that the wife shall not work. I encountered two cases where Negro women with high personal standards left employment in houses where the husband or son was "always bothering" them. These cases are probably exceptional; in the great majority, if approach is made, there must be acquiescence.

It is conventional in Southerntown to consider sex relations between members of the castes as brief and transitory and to represent them under the guise of a sadistic utilization of the body of the lower-caste woman. Most of the jokes seem to emphasize this casual and exploitive aspect of the relation. This is a true picture, probably, of most of these sexual contacts. The mores among white people against such contacts are slowly gathering force and may be expected in the future to assert an ever more insistent pressure against cross-racial sexual contact. It need not be assumed, however, that love, idealization, and tenderness are always absent from these relationships; in fact, quite the contrary must be assumed in some cases. The dehumanization of sexuality is often only official; warm and lasting personal relationships occur behind this façade. Social pressure tends to force any genuine love affair between white man and Negro woman under ground, since being lovers openly would tend to legitimate their relationship and would thus challenge the caste arrangements. It is difficult to secure testimony on this score from white partners to such relationships; the only hints come from the gossip of other white people and from testimony by Negro women. The middle-class Negro woman, in whom some degree of race consciousness has developed, finds a perplexing situation here. She tends to love, of course, along middle-class principles, which include permanence and a stabilized relationship. Many of the social traits to which she is most attracted are probably possessed in the highest degree by white men; and yet the caste barrier is expressly designed to prevent the realization of the social form which for her is a condition of being in love. One Negro woman told me that she had always been proud of the fact that she never cared about any white man. She had always held herself above any such attraction; because white men do such terrible things to Negro men, burning and mutilating them, and cause Negroes so much misery and act in such a superior way. She said she had never in her life been attracted to any white man in a personal way and had never had any trouble fending off such approaches as were made to her—until a certain man came along. When she saw him, she had the experience for the first time of being strongly drawn to a white man; she did not know why it was but she had many daydreams and thoughts about him. Nothing was said, of course, but when he left Southerntown she became very rebellious against the white people who, she felt, prevented their getting together. This was the first time, she said, she had ever felt any bitterness against the white race and its pretensions; before that she had been able to keep hatred out of her heart and not dislike anyone just because they were white. For a while thereafter she felt very bitter, but finally decided this was not fair and fought it off. This illustrates how the caste barrier may look from the other side, and also serves to show that Negro women can love in the conventional manner.

When concubinage exists, it is quite plain that some more or less permanent emotional tie holds the parties together.

A Negro woman may have a child by a white man as a result of a casual sexual contact; but, when the relationship is sustained over time and the closest permissible approximation of normal family life is built up, we must assume that a genuine love attraction exists between the partners. As already indicated, concubinage is by no means moribund. It is possible that the white man may accept the looser relationship with relief as compared to the limitations of his formal married life; crucial, possibly, is the fact that the concubine cannot legitimately make jealous claims.

It is certainly not unknown for Negro women, and especially middle-class Negro women, to avoid sexual contact with white men. Such avoidance may indeed be very frequent, contrary to folk belief among the whites, if compared with the number of opportunities. A Negro woman said, for example, that there was a white man in Southerntown who wished to have relations with her, but that she had refused and tried to avoid contact with him as much as possible. She did not want the honor of being loved by a white man, as white men so often assumed; she believed that love singles out particular people, regardless of color. The white belief, on the other hand, seems to be that Negro women invariably welcome coitus with a white man and do not feel the lack of the attention surrounding legitimate love affairs. Briefly it may be said that love is not recognized as a sentiment which may be felt across the caste line; here only crude sexual expressions are appropriate.

Middle-class Negro women are firm adherents to the code which demands a more than transitory devotion as a justification for the sex act. One informant with these principles cleverly and bitterly fended off an approach from a white man. Once when she was in his office he proposed sexual relations to her. In response she smiled and said she did not believe in social equality. He was abashed, blushed, and did not know what to say. Finally he told her she was an exceptional Negro. She said she was not; she was just a Negro and proud of it. She was saying, of course, that sexual relations implied for her the love which for the white man would be a sign of social equality. Such solutions as hers may permit the maintenance of the caste situation but they do not solve the problem between the two castes. Undoubtedly there are many cases where sexual relations are attended by idealization, tenderness, wish to be of service, and desire for permanence; these cases must be among the unpublicized tragedies of the caste plan of social action.

An aristocratic white man stated that he felt physical revulsion at the thought of coitus with a Negro woman. He hesitated and recalled that once he was attracted by a very light mulatto woman but never approached her. He gave the usual assurance that nowadays only lower-class white men have sex relations with Negro women. In his grandfather's day, to be sure, it was fashionable to have a Negro mistress, but not now.[11] An upper-class woman reported on old-time concubinage as it existed in her town. The white man, a judge of the supreme court of the state, had a Negro mistress living in a cabin in his back yard. He had three daughters by her whom he treated well; two of them he sent to a music conservatory and the third to a woman's college in the North. Informant said that one of the girls subsequently returned to the town as a grown woman and always said she was the unhappiest person in the world because she could not enjoy both of her parents. The father could not openly acknowledge her, although he supported her and gave her an education. The white wife of the judge lived in seclusion at their home. Informant added that this was antebellum practice and does not happen often in these times. She repeated the assurance that respectable people condemn such things strongly now and that only

[11] "A large planter told me the reason he sent his boys to the North to be educated was, that there was no possibility of their being brought up in decency at home. Another planter told me that he was intending to move to a free country on this account. He said that the practice was not occasional or general, it was universal. 'There is not,' he said, 'a likely-looking black girl in this State, that is not the paramour of a white man. There is not an old plantation in which the grandchildren of the owner are not whipped in the field by his overseer. I cannot bear that the blood of the . . . should run in the veins of slaves.' He was of an old Scotch family." F. L. Olmsted, *A Journey in the Seaboard Slave States* (New York, 1904), II, 252; quoted by permission of G. P. Putnam's Sons.

low-grade white people have sexual traffic with Negroes.[12]

It would seem, nevertheless, that the taboo falls heaviest on social acknowledgment of such relations rather than on the fact of their occurrence. Despite the taboo there seems to be a "boys will be boys" attitude about it. One informant objected to being in Washington for the reason that colored and white mix too freely there. He said that white men were seen with colored women and colored men with white women. In his home town nothing like that occurs; there the "nigruhs" know enough to let the white folks alone. The secrecy characteristic of sex relations everywhere in our culture seems to be steadily increasing where cross-caste relationships are concerned. The jealousy of the white women for the males who have these prerogatives may be a factor in strengthening the pressure against them.

In this connection a rather surprising statement is often made: that white men do not sleep with Negroes very much in Southerntown any more because there are so many white girls available. This statement is unlooked for in view of the idealization of women historically characteristic of the South. Two possibilities occur: one is that this idealization of women was particularly characteristic of the upper-class group, very little represented in Southerntown, and that the middle- and lower-class standards for women were never so severe. A second and more likely possibility is that modern trends which have tended to lessen the severity of sexual taboos on American women in general have also affected the situation in Southerntown. Very often it is claimed that Negro women are accepted only when white women are not available. A casual informant on a train who seemed rabid on the race question cursed the Negroes for "damned black bastards," and the like. Someone asked him if he had ever had a Negro girl. He answered, "Yes, a lot of them," but added that it was always when no white girls were accessible. The other men in the party took a milder position, said that after all they could not get along

[12] "Low-grade" in this case can always be taken to mean people who do actually have sexual relations with Negroes, whatever their formal social position may be; it is not necessarily a synonym for "lower-class" in our sense.

without the "niggers," and pointed out that the speaker was drunk and would not remember the conversation the next day. The important point is that this sense of shame, or loss of caste, at coitus with Negro women seems to be a growing one among white people; it is likely to spread with the further development of education among Negroes and whites.

It is worth asking why Negro women are accessible to such sex relations with white men as do occur. From the standpoint of white-caste beliefs about Negroes this question seems superfluous. They are supposed to be as accessible as animals in heat and always ready for sexual gratification. Defensive middle-class Negroes are likely to underestimate lower-class wishes for pleasure since they prefer to think of all sexual acts as virtual assaults by whites on Negroes. Pleasure wishes must, however, play a great rôle. We know that the sexual impulse is a difficult one to control in any society; everywhere it is proscribed, canalized, and limited. If the social situation permits its more or less free expression, we can hardly expect lower-class Negro people not to be at the mercy of it. Undoubtedly wishes for transitory gratification are a factor in the accessibility of Negro women.

This motive, however, is unquestionably overstressed in the white stereotype of the Negro woman. To make the matter concrete, an informant pointed out what it means to the Negro woman who gets two to four dollars a week as a cook to have the man of the house offer her five dollars for sexual intercourse. She probably has a family to support, certainly has bills to pay, and needs the money. In this sense the white women coöperate in the seduction by paying their servants so poorly. If the Negro women cannot live on their wages as cooks or maids, they will be more accessible to sexual approaches for money.

As another element the prestige of the white man must be considered. This prestige operates in several ways. It is difficult for a Negro woman to turn down a request from such a man; and, in the second place, it is flattering to receive his attention. These values are bound to appeal to lower-caste people and may be especially prized in the sex-

ual situation. Related to this may be positive, often unconscious, wishes for light children on the part of the Negro
women, wishes which pride may reject but which, if grati-
fied, do give the children a preferred value in their own
group.

A further factor to be considered is the possibility that
these sexual affairs with a white man have an element of
revenge in them from the standpoint of the Negro woman,
as if to say, "Well, these white women may high-hat us,
but we sleep with their men just the same. We may have
to cook for them, but we get back at them in this way."
Through the leveling sex act the caste barriers are down
for the moment. A low-class Negro informant said, apropos
of this theme, that a friend of hers "slept in the very bed
of the white man's wife without her knowledge." There
may also be the sense of pulling the white man down,
making him "come off his high perch," and showing him
to be, after all, just another human being.

Little noticed but very important must be the looseness
of marriage ties within the lower-class Negro group. In the
weak, mother-centered family characteristic of this class,
the husband has less control over his wife than in the middle class; and her economic independence carries with it
the usual correlate of sexual independence. She is therefore
less hampered in expressing her wishes toward white
men. Her husband may be jealous, but he cannot revenge
himself by the threat of lack of support, a threat which is
a factor in keeping middle-class women moral. The inevitable result is an increased accessibility to sexual approaches from all and sundry, white men included.

It should not be too easily taken for granted that the
motives of white men are simply desires for excess sexual
gratification. Though these desires play a part, their importance is probably overemphasized in the white reports on
the situation. True erotic motivation here is doubtless analogous with the escapes from marriage which men make
in the direction of prostitutes or other women accessible
without the formal social sanction. Boredom with the legitimate object or unconscious fear of the incestuously toned
white woman may redirect genuine sexual desire to Negro

women. In addition to this wish for release of sexual tension
the status motive also counts; access to Negro women is a
continued testimony to white mastery and caste superiority.
We have said that "sex" is in fact a very complex personality function. It should not surprise us to find hostile and
self-affirming motives mixed in with the direct sexual ones.
Certainly the reactions of many Negro men confirm this
interpretation; they feel wronged, are jealous, and resent
the superior prerogatives of the white man. A Negro informant said that Negro men experience intense jealousy
when they see their women taken by white men and are
unable to defend their homes. Some, among the younger
Negroes, feel desperate about it; they say that they will
die first, that they have to die sometime anyway, and that
it might as well be over this issue. Informant thought that
education for the younger Negroes is making the situation
worse because they are less able to tolerate these indignities
from the whites. Negro intellectuals have made the bitter-
est sort of protest on this score.[13]

It must never be supposed that Negroes are stupid about
matters like this; they may not act or protest for the reason
that they are unable to, but this need not be taken as a
lack of reaction. The taking of other people's women is in
general held an aggressive act in our society and Negro
response along expected lines is not absent but suppressed.

[13] "I shall forgive the white South much in its final judgment day: I shall forgive its slavery, for slavery is a world-old
habit; I shall forgive its fighting for a well-lost cause, and for
remembering that struggle with tender tears; I shall forgive its
so-called 'pride of race,' the passion of its hot blood, and even
its dear, old, laughable strutting and posing; but one thing
I shall never forgive, neither in this world nor the world to
come: its wanton and continued and persistent insulting of the
black womanhood which it sought and seeks to prostitute to
its lust. I cannot forget that it is such Southern gentlemen
into whose hands smug Northern hypocrites of today are seeking to place our women's eternal destiny,—men who insist upon
withholding from my mother and wife and daughter those
signs and appellations of courtesy and respect which elsewhere
he withholds only from bawds and courtesans." W. E. B.
Du Bois, *Darkwater* (New York, 1921), p. 172; quoted by permission of Harcourt, Brace & Co.

One informant said that some years ago the tension between the races increased in Southerntown; white men were coming with a growing frequency into the Negro district to prostitutes and other women. The Negro men became more and more indignant and finally determined on action. They organized a group that went around and beat up the colored women who had been most notorious in receiving white men, and drove some of them out of town. The whites heard of this action, resented it, and were planning to come into the colored district and punish the men. The Negroes sent out the word, got other Negroes in from near-by towns, and prepared for action on their principal street. Informant said that there were more than twenty thousand rounds of ammunition in the houses along this street. For his part he was ready to die rather than have the sexual situation get any worse. But some of the leading white men surmised the state of affairs and forbade any white man to go down into the colored district, otherwise "we will have to kill every nigger down there." Only one white man went down and he was captured and not injured by the Negroes. The leaders of the Negro group were later arrested, taken to jail, and placed on high bail. After about a week the feeling cooled, the bail was gradually reduced, and in about ten days the men were all released. Tension over sexual matters has never been so great since.

Correlative to this antagonism on the part of the Negroes there seems to be a positive satisfaction on the part of the whites in utilizing the women of the Negro group without the reciprocity characteristic of a democratic society. It is not difficult to sense the resentment of Negro men. On one occasion I was invited to a party to meet a distinguished Negro. Middle-class Negroes of both sexes were present, but I was the only white man. The party was stiff and formal. Most of the people played bridge or whist and the conversation was quite reserved. Of course there was no drinking. As the evening went on people began to dance. Although I would certainly have been welcome, I felt some intangible barrier against dancing and did not do it. I was under scrutiny and if I had danced it might have aroused the suspicion "Oh, that is what he is looking for, as usual." The reciprocity point came up here strongly: since I could not, by the caste arrangement, bring a white woman to such a party, it seemed only fair that I should not dance. There was an unexpected sense of pressure which was not obvious or offensive, but rather tense and palpable.

In sum it seems to be true that the white-caste member experiences a sense of gratification in this mark of his caste mastery, his preferential access to two groups of women and immunity to the resentment of the disadvantaged Negro men.

Much has been made of the importance of blood to Negroes, of the chromatic scale within the Negro group, and of the special problems experienced everywhere by the lighter Negroes. The dilemma is that the white caste establishes its characteristics as most desirable for all individuals in our society; and on the other hand, approximation of these characteristics in a physical sense by Negroes carries with it, near or remote, the implication of bastardy. Part of the social insecurity of the Negro unquestionably stems from this conflict often represented in his very person and appearance; the nearer he is to whiteness in his physical features, the more likely it is that his lineage is a result of the tabooed sexual contacts between the castes.[14] The percentage of intermixture to be assumed among Negroes is surprisingly high; Herskovits's[15] study showed that only 22 percent of Negroes were of unmixed lineage, while Johnson's[16] showed only 17 percent pure Negro heritage on both sides. This ambivalent attitude toward physical ances-

---

[14] "The red stain of bastardy, which two centuries of systematic legal defilement of Negro women has stamped upon his race, meant not only the loss of ancient African chastity, but also the hereditary weight of a mass of corruption from white adulterers, threatening almost the obliteration of the Negro home." W. E. B. Du Bois, *The Souls of Black Folk* (Chicago, 1922), p. 9; quoted by permission of the author.

[15] Melville J. Herskovits, *The American Negro* (New York, 1928), p. 9.

[16] Charles S. Johnson, "Racial Attitudes of College Students" (Abridged), *Pub. of the Amer. Sociol. Soc.* (1934), Vol. XXVIII, No. 2, pp. 29–30.

try showed up repeatedly in the reports of Negro informants on their genealogies. They are proud of their white
ancestors, but related to this pride is the sense of being
scorned and rejected. Most of my informants seemed to be
able either to identify a white ancestor or the first Negro
ancestor who bore white blood. Pride in Indian ancestry
was noted in some cases and seemed to detract less from
the satisfaction of the individual. As it happened, all of my
informants were conscious of bearing either white or Indian
blood, in addition to Negro, although in most cases the
point of entry seemed to be remote, none being nearer than
the grandfather's generation.

The presence of a very light child in a Negro family is,
as would be suspected, a constant possible source of discontent since it opens the way to the suspicion that this
child has been fathered by a white man. Lightness in children, though seeming to be desired, can be a disadvantage
from this standpoint. A middle-class Negro informant said
he remembered a great deal more about his father than
about his mother; his mother was rather dark, like himself.
His father, on the other hand, was quite light, and in fact
looked Chinese. He added that light Negroes seem to get
darker as they grow older and that this happened to his
father. His father was the only bright child in his family
and this caused some hard feeling between his parents because of the suspicion that he might really be the child
of some white man or very light Negro. Remoteness in time
seems to take some of the sting out of illegitimacy and
white ancestors are more acceptable the more remote they
are, especially from the standpoint of middle-class Negroes.

In the case of middle-class Negroes who try to approximate white moral standards there is an energetic rejection
of the white view of Negro sexuality. These Negroes tend
to stress the faults of the whites and to represent sexual
looseness within their own group either as exceptional or as
forced on them by white people. It is therefore difficult to
find out from them what the true state of affairs is among
lower-class Negroes. For example, I was promptly informed
by my middle-class friends in Southerntown that there
was a low class of Negroes in town who pandered to cheap

whites, drank with them, went to excesses with them. It was said that I would not see very much of this class, that they were low-down and immoral. Informant added that there were a number of "bad" Negroes in town and that such Negroes are usually "white man's niggers." They toady to the whites, act with the white group against Negroes, often do the entrepreneurial work for a white man who wishes sexual contact with Negro women but is ashamed or afraid to initiate it himself.

It seems that sexual attitudes among lower-class Negro women are different and freer than among the middle-class group. There is constant testimony to this fact from both castes. The whites seem to take particular satisfaction in pointing to "immorality" as an evidence of the inferiority of the Negroes and do not consider the historical situation which has brought it about. Without accepting it as a mark of biological inferiority, we can nevertheless examine the evidence.

My first impression was gained from overhearing a conversation between two Negro servant girls about "men." One of them commented that she had been with an "awful pretty white man" the night before, who had wavy hair and a straight nose and looked like Clark Gable. The other said that she preferred white to colored men because they were so considerate, that Negro men did not have a chance to make enough money to treat a woman right. The first girl responded that Negro men were more boisterous and complaining, that they beat their women, whereas no one ever heard of a white man beating his wife. She added that a Negro would "raise hell" if he came home and found his supper not prepared, whereas white men did not seem to mind.

A Negro told me of a childhood sweetheart whom he had once wanted to marry. He left town for a time and when he returned met this girl again. She had become a prostitute. He asked her if she had known what was in his mind when they were boy and girl together, and told her that he had thought then that she would make a good wife for some man someday. The girl regretted that she had gone too far now ever to be able to marry, and said it was the fault of her godmother who turned her over to men before she was grown-up.

A white man told of a Negro woman who had recently come to him and asked him to retrieve her husband who was over at such-and-such a house in bed with another woman. The man said he could not do anything for her, but advised her to get another man herself.

A lower-class Negro girl, herself illegitimate, said that her mother was not strict or petty with her but more like a sister. When she was eleven, her mother told her the "facts of life" in order that she might avoid what her mother had gotten into. Her mother had not been crabby with her about going out with boys, but warned her for her own good; if she got into trouble after that, it was her own affair.

A Negro woman recounted an incident that happened when she was around eight or ten years old. She lived on a farm and had to work hard, although the family standards were high. There was a young Negro also working on the farm. One day as she was walking over to her grandmother's house, past a patch of cotton that was as high as her head, she heard someone groaning. She listened and heard it again. She went into the cotton field to see who it was and what she could do to help. The young Negro was lying there on the ground. When she got near enough to ask him what was the matter, he seized her and tried to have intercourse with her. She screamed and fought until her grandmother, overhearing the commotion, came and rescued her. The grandmother's interpretation was that it was a meeting between the two and this she reported to the girl's mother, who did not stop to inquire into the truth of the story or would not believe so much of it as she heard, but whipped the girl violently. It has always made the informant angry to think of this incident, even to this day; she felt it was desperately unfair of her mother when she was trying to be good. The point is, of course, the way in which the event was defined by the mother, a definition which evidently accorded with lower-class expectations of a young girl.

A colored teacher illustrated the same moral *niveau* in describing her first school. The head of the trustees met her at the train and declared himself in love with her at first sight. He made vigorous approaches and claimed that his wife was dead. She rebuffed him; but, as she was to stay at his house, she soon discovered that he had a wife very much alive and a nice person at that. It appeared he was telling the truth in a way because his first wife had died and this was his second one. It was said that he was still in love with his first wife. He put pressure on the teacher all the year long and on one occasion tried to grapple with her when she was alone in the house. She could only rebuff him by saying mean things to hurt his pride.

Moral standards of middle-class Negroes, which are of course much more severe than those of the lower-class group, are weakening along with the general loosening of American moral ties. A middle-class woman thought that standards have changed in her group; she believed that most fellows and girls who go together today do have sexual intercourse and think nothing about it. She never thought of such a thing in her day and her husband made no such proposal before their marriage. She added, however, that, if a girl becomes pregnant before marriage, her mother ought not to be cruel to her. Informant said that very often mothers are mean and sometimes beat up their daughters so that they die or the child dies. In the case of middle-class people, high-school and college training serve to perpetuate childhood restraints and to fix standards of discriminate sexual behavior; by contrast we note that many lower-class Negro children have greater privileges in the sexual sphere just because they begin work at adolescence.

If Negro women are represented as sexually desirable in the folk imagination of the whites, Negro men are viewed as especially virile and capable in this sphere. The idea seems to be that they are more like savages, nearer to animals, and that their sexual appetites are more vigorous and ungoverned. There is a widespread belief that the genitalia of Negro males are larger than those of whites; this was repeatedly stated by white informants. One planter, for example, said he had had visual opportunity to confirm the fact; he had gone to one of his cabins, and on entering without warning, found a Negro man preparing for intercourse. Informant expressed surprise at the size of the penis and gave an indication by his arm and clenched fist of its great length and diameter. It was further said that this impression was confirmed at the time of the draft examination of Negroes at the Southerntown Courthouse in 1917. Two physicians from other states have verified this report on the basis of draft-board experience. A Negro professional, on the other hand, did not believe that Negroes have larger genitalia than whites. He had worked in military camps where he had a chance to see recruits of both races naked, and said there is the usual variation within the races, but no uniform difference as between races. An experienced traveler in West Africa who had abundant opportunity to observe did not believe that Negro genitals there are disproportionately larger than the genitals of the white man.[17]

It might not be worth the time of an actual research to determine the facts. One thing seems certain—that the actual differences between Negro and white genitalia cannot be as great as they seem to the whites; it is a question of the psychological size being greater than any actual differences could be. The belief is further suspect because the same point seems to be coming up with respect to the Jews in Germany, i.e., that they are at a competitive advantage in this respect and that sex relations with a non-Jewish woman are likely to be traumatic. This idea about genital size in Negroes is not mentioned because it is a curious belief or for the sake of noting a quaint exaggeration; the notion is heavily functional in reference to the supposed dangers of sexual contact of Negroes with white women.

Before turning to this issue, an incident may be given which will stress the potency attributed to the Negro; the deputy sheriff who related it said it actually occurred. A Negro about to be executed, and who the next day "swung praying," was given the usual option of a last request, and he asked to have a woman with him the night before he

[17] The author and traveler, Geoffrey Gorer, made this statement in conversation.

was hanged. The officials were bound by custom to grant the request, although it was exceptional; but the trouble was to find a woman who would undertake the gruesome task. Finally a Negro woman was found but she demanded a price of $2.50 in consideration of the extraordinary circumstances. It was guaranteed her and she spent the night with the condemned man. The sheriff remembered the incident because the charge was difficult to enter on the books of the county and it was necessary to take up a collection to pay the girl. This virility-in-the-face-of-death is a good symbol of the potency of the Negro as it seems to the white man, and as it may indeed be in fact.[18]

The agitating question of rape on white women came up in connection with the theme of the Negro's potency. The Negro man is held to be perpetually desirous of such contacts and Southerntown seems set to credit the slightest suspicion that they have occurred. Undoubtedly rapes do occur with sufficient frequency, at least, to give color to the unconscious conviction of the whites that this is one of the main desires of every Negro man. The occasional cases cited are jarring since the circumstances of rape are almost always criminally ruthless. As we were riding past the state farm one day, a white friend told me the story of a Negro trusty who killed a guard and kidnaped and raped his daughter; he held her "in that piece of woods over there" for three days and then let her go. The Negro was captured later by a woman planter and burned by a mob. "It was too good for him," my friend said, speaking with deep feeling. The girl was very delicate and I knew, did I not, about the large genitals of Negro men? She was spoiled for social life in her community and, of course, had to leave; no one could ever forget an experience like that.

One dared not inquire if the punishment fitted the crime, if the occurrence were not to be viewed as exceptional since the man was a criminal, if the girl might not have contrib-

---

[18] There are many jokes, usually having reference to plantation days, concerning the breeding of Negroes and of particular stud-Negroes who were loaned or rented out for the work of fertilization. Of course, these are only jokes but they show the reputation for sexual virility which the Negro man has.

uted to the delinquency, and so on, questions which one would have had to ask if the man had not been a Negro. Whence comes this conviction of the lustful and violent desire of Negro men for white women? Why do the infrequent actual confirmations serve to keep it so brightly alive?

A few days later the same point was illustrated in another way. One night after a movie I heard a strange voice calling my name; it turned out to be a local white woman whom I had met casually. She said her family was not at home; would I mind following her in my car and shining my lights on her garage while she put her car away? I agreed, puzzled, but on the way to her house it all became clear. I was expected to understand that this was only a reasonable precaution to take against the danger of assault.

In a little social group a white girl said she was not the least bit afraid of "niggers" and did not even think of being afraid to walk down the street at night; she was sure a "nigger" would not attack her, it would never even occur to him. A white man answered that it would occur to him all right, but he just wouldn't dare do it; Negroes know their place and they know that anything of the sort just is not tolerated.

Rape done on white women is especially abhorred as compared to any other type of rape.[19] It may be that white men have a fear of reprisal for the things they do to Negro women. Fear of retaliation in the same terms as the attack is one of the commonest sorts of fears and it is invariably noticed wherever thorough personality studies are

[19] "The two white men charged with raping the Negro mother were brought into court. The witnesses were called, the case was finished, the jury retired and remained out all night. At ten o'clock next morning it returned a verdict of guilty, and recommended sentences of one year each. Two of the jurors had held out for acquittal, but finally accepted the compromise of a sentence of one year. Thomasville was in a stir; while some people were humiliated at the mildness of the sentences, many more expressed disgust that a white jury should sentence white men at all on such a charge. At this same term of court Homer Taylor, Negro, plead guilty of assault with intent to rape a young Negro girl and received a sentence of twenty years." Raper, *op. cit.*, p. 248; quoted by permission of the University of North Carolina Press.

conducted. People sometimes show extraordinary fear of retaliation simply on the basis of mean or aggressive wishes, let alone acts, toward others. In Southerntown there is the frequent fact and constant possibility of aggressive sexual behavior by white men against Negro women; we may have the counterpart in a conviction that Negro men *must* constantly wish to make a counterattack against white women. Certainly some potent and not obvious explanation for the sensitivity of white men on this score must be found.

A Negro woman threw some light on the subject from her standpoint. She did not believe most of the stories of attacks. She saw no reason why Negro men should go to white women, because there are women just as light in the Negro group and all other shades to boot. She said that the attacks which actually occur can probably be charged to one of two causes; either Negro men are revengeful because they cannot protect their own women, or the white women seduce them and bring an accusation of rape if caught. A Negro might attack a white women for revenge because he knows that this is the place where he can hurt the white man most. Negro men experience constant jealousy and hatred because of the sexual affronts to their women. My informant thought that the element of revenge is very large in such attacks and said further that some of the Negro boys who go North and take up with white women do so simply to revenge themselves on southern men. One such boy actually stated this. It is as if the white men held the women of the white caste collectively in trust and collectively defended them against sexual aggression from Negro men.

There is no point to going into detail on rape or lynching stories; what is really scientifically important is the psychic and social context out of which rapes and lynchings come. Rape is, of course, an atrocious act to everyone in our society; to a southern man, when it is committed by a Negro on a white woman, it is in a class by itself and justifies the severest punishment.

On the other side, white people told stories of a type to illustrate the loyalty of Negroes in defending lonely white women; these stories seem in general to emanate from upper-class white people and to continue slavery-day traditions of the loyalty of house servants. A white planter told of a Negro woman's coming to stay with his wife while he was away; she slept in the same room with his wife and her husband came and slept on the front porch of the house with his gun beside him. The object, of course, was the protection of the woman against the danger of her situation on a lonely plantation surrounded by Negroes.

One cannot take a cavalier attitude toward the problem of attacks on white women by Negroes; they undoubtedly do occur and under circumstances that are especially terrifying. Around this sexual issue centers quite visibly the whole caste problem; it is experienced as the most acute and agonizing of issues and one calling for the utmost in defense and aggression on the part of the white caste.

Despite the infrequent but symbolically important rape incidents, relations between the races seem to flow quite smoothly in Southerntown. The Negro man knows his "place" and stays in it. The occasional lynchings in other areas of the South serve as warnings in the way they are intended to. Negro men are careful not to look or act offensively in the presence of a white woman, and in general attempt to minimize contacts with them in order to avoid the too-ready suspicion of the white men. For example, a Negro informant described a Negro landowner in the county whom he had visited recently, who had five white people working for him picking cotton, because as he said he could not get any other labor. It was bad enough to have whites working for a Negro, but what was worse, three of them were white women. Informant said he trembled at the danger the employer was running. Any little thing might have gotten him into trouble. If one of the women had said that he "shined up" to her, it might have cost him his life; the whites would take the women's word for it without question. But nothing, in fact, did happen.

A Negro told me another instance of the same kind. He was talking to two white girls who came to sell him something. They began joking with him, asking him why he did not study law in the North where Negroes could be lawyers and doctors and some of them even married white women. He warned them against this kind of talk. They continued, saying that he was very good looking, that he was not like these black Negroes, and that several of the girls had been talking about his good looks. He protested again. He told me that the situation had been dangerous for him, since if some white man had heard, he certainly would not have consulted the women but gone right after the Negro.

Another Negro told of representing his college at a conference in Chicago. He made a speech and after he had finished noticed four white girls standing at one side of the rostrum. They came up and introduced themselves to him and he was surprised to learn that they were from his state. He talked and had meals with them several times while at the conference. They showed a great deal of interest in how a Negro student thinks and feels. After he went back home they wrote to him, but he never answered their letters; he thought it would be dangerous if anyone found out he was corresponding with white girls. And in this, of course he was quite right, since belief in the white caste would tend to favor the presumption that he was the aggressive one and that he was getting out of his place.

We have seen white men guarding the border line of their caste, belligerent and suspicious, repelling every overture of a Negro man across the caste line. We might also ask how the white women feel who are defended in this manner. The official attitude is that sexual attraction to Negro men simply does not exist. We can view this as the preferred belief of the society and one which, no doubt, most white women are actually able to accept. A white girl once tried to tell me what her feelings were about Negroes. She did not think she could ever love a Negro man because she feels they are loathsome and inferior; it would be just out of the question. Negroes are for her automatically excluded as love objects. She said several times, "You don't know how we feel about it down here." The fact that the caste taboo is one not only on Negro men but on white women as well is apparently not recognized, because it is assumed that there is nothing to taboo in the case of the women of the white caste. Where there is no attraction but only repulsion and disgust there is no need for a social barrier. The caste line is therefore always phrased in terms of repulsing the advances of Negro men. Very occasionally in the literature one finds complaint which seems to be based on a perception by women of the relative advantages of the men in this situation.[20] Some evidence comes from the Negroes which seems to indicate that attraction for Negroes is not an exclusive prerogative of the white man; it is slim indeed but perhaps significant. In talking about lynching, a Negro woman said that the attacks on white women which are reported are frequently "affairs" which, when discovered, are made out to be attacks. This interpretation saves the white woman from the utter social isolation which might otherwise accrue to her, because, although shamed, she is at least guiltless if "attacked." This woman remembered one case in a near-by town where a white woman had had a Negro lover for a number of years. When they were discovered, however, she refused to let a mob hurt the Negro. She said she had invited and proposed the affair and it was not his fault. The Negro was let go. The same informant knew of another case of a Negro student who worked in a white home. Two of the white girls in the house made advances to him; he refused them, knowing the danger. One girl persisted and said that if he did not oblige her she would scream some day and claim that he had attacked her. He packed his clothes and left the house

---

[20] "Among Southern women, not unnaturally, the feeling aroused by these practices has been especially bitter. Here is a remarkable plea, published in the *Times-Democrat* on June 21, 1907, signed 'A woman.'

" '. . . I am a resident of a large town . . . where miscegenation is common—where, if a man isolates himself from feminine society, the first and only conclusion reached is, "he has a woman of his own" in saddle, of duskier shade. This conclusion is almost without exception true. If some daring woman, not afraid of being dubbed a Carrie Nation, were to canvass the(se) . . . counties . . . taking the census, she would find so many cases of miscegenation, and their resultant mongrel families, that she would bow her head in shame for the "flower of Southern chivalry"—gone to seed.' " Ray S. Baker, *Following the Color Line* (New York, 1908), p. 166; quoted by permission of Doubleday, Page & Co.

that night. A Negro informant said white women apparently like the brighter-colored Negro men and sometimes will make direct advances to them. For example, they will do favors to such a man and let him understand that he can do anything he wants; then if he is caught they will "holler wolf," that is assault.

There is a form of evidence that white women are interested in the matter of Negro sexuality which is quite impressive to me, though I do not know how it will affect others. It is the jokes they sometimes tell. One frequently hears jokes relating to the sexuality of Negro women, jokes which convey an amusement at the freedom with which Negro women do sexual things. They are never a direct play on the situation of the Negro man and the white woman but always refer to Negro women. I take these jokes seriously because they are the fleeting forms in which forbidden interests can be socially expressed although they could not be seriously declared. For this reason I will give four of them which were told at one time or another by white women of the middle or upper classes. The stories seem to express a rather simple sort of envy of the superior freedom of Negro women who, we should remember, have access to men of both castes, as the white women do not.

A Negro woman had six or seven children and one of them was conspicuously light. The other children would not play with him and were always fussing and quarreling with him. At last the mother got irritated, went out to the children and said, "Go on, play with him; he is your brother just like all the others; he would be just as dark as you are if I hadn't gotten behind with my 'surance." This is evidently an economic interpretation of the Negro woman's sexual accessibility.

A story which appeared first in the North and circulated in Southerntown is the following: A Negro woman who appeared in court for some reason told the judge that she was a widow. The judge asked her when her husband died. "Ten years ago, jedge." The judge looked at the row of children behind her and asked, "Whose children are these?" "Mine," said the woman. "What," said the judge, "you say these are your children and yet your husband has been dead for ten years!" "Yes, suh," said the woman. "Ah said he's dead, not Ah's dead." Here death is equated with lack of sexual gratification and "life" with sexual activity.

If the story contains a little dig at the Yankees in addition to its sexual content, it is sometimes more appreciated. Such a story is the following. A rich Boston old maid came to the South to visit friends. The Negro cook in the house was a privileged character and was able to say many things that ordinary Negroes could not. She asked the woman if she were married. The Boston lady was annoyed at this familiarity and said stiffly, "No." Then the Negro woman said, "Is you got any chilluns?" The Boston lady was appalled, drew herself up and said, "Of course not." The Negro mammy said, "Well, you sho is lucky." The southern woman who told the story excused herself by saying that she had read it in a magazine. It seems to show that life without sexual expression is inconceivable to Negroes.

Most characteristic is this story. A doctor going through the colored ward in a hospital sees three Negro women nursing babies. He asks the first one when her baby was born and she says, "June first." He asks the second one when hers was born and she says, "June first." He asks the third and she says, "June first." He goes to the next bed with a knowing smile and says, "Well, I suppose your baby was born on June first too." "No, suh, Boss, it sho wan't," says the woman. "Ah didn' go to de same picnic."

Jokes are, of course, illustrative of a whole cultural set as well as of a particular point. My contention is that the white women who told these stories were imaginatively enjoying the freedom attributed to Negro women; possibly, though this is more doubtful, they envied the contact with Negro men. It is obvious that these stories are less frank and brutal than those frequently told and enjoyed by men. They are the only examples found of interest in Negro sexuality on the part of white women and in order to be fully useful they would have to be correctly set in the psychic lives of the persons who told them. One theory[21] is that

---

[21] At a meeting of the Boston Psychoanalytic Society where I presented some material, Dr. Helena Deutsch made an illuminating comment. In several analyses that she had carried

there actually is a considerable attraction between white women and Negro men, that the white men are unconsciously aware of this attraction but dare not call up the intolerable idea, and that, as a result, they are jealous lest their women should make sexual contacts with the virile (in their stereotype) Negro men; consciously the whole matter is charged off to the sexual aggressiveness of the Negro men and in this way the complicity of the white woman is avoided.

If this theory could be accepted, it would throw much light on the conviction of Negro guilt which inevitably appears among white men whenever a rape charge is raised. It is easier to assume aggression by Negro men than to face the unpleasant possibility that the white man does not occupy the sole focus of sexual attention for white women. If this were the case, the white jealousy of Negro men would seem more reasonable; and the beliefs current about the dangerous size of the Negro genitalia would be intelligible.

It seems clear that any move toward social equality is seen on its deepest level as really a move toward sexual equality, that is, toward full sexual reciprocity between the castes. Social equality would mean that the white men would have to abandon their exclusive claims to women of the white caste and to admit reciprocal rights to Negro men. Apparently the innocent-seeming intimacies of everyday social life have a latent vector; they may lead toward the always-greater intimacies of sexual contact. Repeatedly in dreams of Negro women I noticed the manner in which

---

out on southern women she found marked sexual attraction to Negro men and masochistic phantasies connected with this attraction. I cite, by her permission, a part of a letter she has written me on this score.

"The fact that the white men believe so readily the hysterical and masochistic phantasies and lies of the white women, who claim they have been assaulted and raped by negroes, is related to the fact that they (the men) sense the unconscious wishes of the women, the psychic reality of these declarations, and react emotionally to them as if they were *real*. The social situation permits them then to discharge this emotion upon the negroes."

eating with a white man symbolized other intimacies. Eating together is the sort of act which can be done in a normal courtship situation and is a sign of legitimate social contact which might lead to legitimate sexual contact. Actually, the caste situation guarantees that a Negro woman of high standards can have a white man only with a bad conscience. One cannot help wondering if there may not be an incestuous tone to all such contacts, especially for Negro women. White women, on the other hand, seem jealous of the legitimacy and official character of their status rather than of the superior opportunity of their men in the sexual sphere. The notion that social intimacies presage sexual intimacies, and in particular that food symbolizes other intimacies, has occurred to others.[22]

As repeatedly emphasized, caste is based on marital prohibition and on exclusion from sexual contact of the lower-caste men. There are tendencies in our culture that are deeply set against this type of barrier. Our industrialized society, based on money exchange, tends systematically to obliterate such differences; it can never function on its predicted and logical lines while such marriage barriers exist. In a society like ours people must be functionally interchangeable. Such barriers as caste tend to support the older feudal type of economy and are technologically out of date. Caste tends to block the spread of democratic practices, of division of labor, of mass education, and of reward according to social value. We do not pass a value judgment on the problem but merely point out the fact.

Caste, of course, is not new in the world and the tendencies which create it are by no means dead. Everyone has noted how the Germans are now building caste barriers against the Jews. Recently the papers announced an edict forbidding any Jewish family to employ a German maid under thirty-five years of age. Marriage is, of course, for-

---

[22] "For, in that region, a white gentleman may not eat with a colored person without the danger of serious loss of social prestige; yet he may sleep with a colored person without incurring the risk of any appreciable damage to his reputation." J. W. Johnson, *op. cit.*, p. 312; quoted by permission of the Viking Press.

bidden at the present time between Jews and non-Jews. The above edict seems to indicate that neither will any chance be taken of coitus occurring. This maneuver would seem almost comic if we were not constantly assured how deadly serious it is.

A qualification is necessary concerning the sexual gain of middle-class whites. The fact that the white men have access to Negro as well as white women and fight for the situation which allows them this privilege does not mean that they can enjoy these sexual contacts to the utmost; nor does it mean, we repeat, that all white men who have such privileges make use of them in fact. Many times people are cheated of the enjoyment of hard-won gains by the development of conscience. Impulse, once controlled, may be controlled too well. Marriage, for example, does not always mean release of the sex impulse. The middle-class white men in this town have superior prerogatives. The question remains as to whether the strain of becoming a middle-class individual does not frequently damage ability to enjoy these prerogatives. The lower-class Negroes, though actually more limited in sexual choices, may have much freer psychic capacity to utilize the women available.

CHAPTER VIII

The Prestige Gain

〰〰〰〰〰〰〰〰〰〰〰〰〰〰〰〰〰〰〰〰〰〰〰〰

Every now and then some concrete fact will by its strangeness call attention to a new class of experiences. This can be illustrated in the case of the prestige gain. A Negro plantation manager told how after the death of the northern owner of a local plantation, his son and heir made his initial visit to the plantation. He was amazed at the experience. The Negroes bowed and scraped, "yes-boss"-ed him to the limit, and made him quite drunk with their unexpected adulation. The manager had to warn him not to be deluded by this behavior, to explain that the Negro is a "Dr. Jekyll and Mr. Hyde," and that this deference was not to be taken at face value. The Yankee was dazzled by the customary behavior of the Negroes toward the white boss which seems so much a matter of course once one is familiar with it. The manager added that the whites demand this deference of Negroes, and he thought that the demand is designed to persuade the Negro that the white man is of another kind and comes naturally by his right to superiority.

It is impossible not to respond with self-satisfaction to such an experience as the above. This can be seen most clearly when the traveler compares having his grip carried at the Grand Central Terminal in New York and at a railway station in the deep South. These are quite different experiences. In the Grand Central the Negro is a mechanism for moving weight from one point to another on the earth's surface; in the South he is this, and something more. The southern porter is extremely nice about it to boot and does various things that are flattering and exhilarating. If the traveler approaches the experience as an average individual rather than as a moral philosopher, he is bound to find it a pleasant contrast.

In the North a man may have a prestige position because he has money, or is learned, or is old; the novelty in the South is that one has prestige solely because one is white. The gain here is very simple. It consists in the fact that a member of the white caste has an automatic right to demand forms of behavior from Negroes which serve to increase his own self-esteem. To put it another way, it consists of an illumination of the image of the self, an expansive feeling of being something special and valuable. It might be compared to the illusion of greatness that comes with early stages of alcoholization, except that prestige is not an illusion but a steadily repeated fact. It gives not only the sense of a sweet submissiveness on the part of others, but also a gratifying sense of mastery. For anxious persons it may tend also to create a feeling of security in being, or appearing to be, so well loved. It must always be remembered that in the end this deference is demanded and not merely independently given. From the standpoint of the white man the crucial thing may be that his aggressive demands are passively received; this gives the gratification of mastering the other person. Still more important perhaps is to receive the deference in advance of demanding it, a submissive affection which is freely and automatically yielded.[1]

From the standpoint of the Negro one can see two possible motives in his submissive behavior. The first is based on the familiar formula that repressed antagonism is often replaced and concealed by servile behavior. The repressed antagonism itself is presumably an answer to the initial demand for self-abnegation. A second motive will probably be that of identification with the socially powerful white person accompanied by idealization, pride in the white man, permissiveness, and a wish to serve him. Eventually this second motive gives rise to a wish to be like the white man. These demands for subservience by the whites and deferential responses from Negroes can be understood, of course, only in terms of the class and caste set-up, and the

[1] Lasswell refers to safety, income, and deference as prime values for individual striving. *See* Harold D. Lasswell, *World Politics and Personal Insecurity* (New York, 1935), pp. 3-26.

caste situation in turn must be referred to its historical antecedents. In any case, it is a fact that the northerner has a new experience when he comes into the South and for the first time enjoys, as he does enjoy, the borrowed prestige of the southern white man.

It is doubtful if such prestige is ever accorded voluntarily in adult life, and it is certainly true in this case that subservient behavior is demanded of Negroes and, in the ultimate case, by force. Negroes who do not exhibit it are "getting out of their place," are "uppity," are "getting above themselves," and there is a way of dealing with them.

This demand for submission and adulation from the Negroes is supported by the common human passion for dominating other persons and having them behave in a desired manner. It is well rationalized in the case of Americans by the belief in the superiority of the white race, a superiority innate and not based on culture.[2] A middle-class white informant stated in this connection that the white race will never let any other race dominate its government and that, if present methods of disqualifying Negroes from voting should fail, others will be found. Informant took the foregoing statement as a fundamental of political thinking about race relations. He added that the white race has a will to mastery and quoted something, perhaps from Kipling, that goes like this, "Wherever the white man meets another race, there he is master or finds his grave." Appeal is often made to instincts of racial purity to explain this passion for mastery.[3] This belief in the mission of the white race is one of the most powerful supports of the social regu-

---

[2] "One of these principles is the absolute and unchangeable superiority of the white race—a superiority, it appears to him, not due to any mere adventitious circumstances, such as superior educational and other advantages during some centuries, but an inherent and essential superiority, based on superior intellect, virtue, and constancy. He does not believe that the Negro is the equal of the white, or ever could be the equal." T. N. Page, *The Negro: The Southerner's Problem* (New York, 1904), pp. 292-293; quoted by permission of Charles Scribner's Sons.

[3] William B. Smith, *The Color Line: A Brief in Behalf of the Unborn* (New York, 1905), p. 24.

lations of the South and one to which northerners or westerners respond readily whenever the case turns up. Whether the struggle of racial groups be described ultimately in terms of economic or some other kind of competition, it is certain there is much that is mysterious in the sense of racial integrity. It often seems that race struggles are conducted without regard to economic advantage.[4]

If the race struggle is not acute, deference flows smoothly from the lower to the higher caste and a kindly accommodation develops which was apparently characteristic, by and large, of the slavery regime; loving reactions toward Negroes are still characteristic of the upper-class white group and are often claimed also by middle-class persons. An elderly white man made the following statement which proved to be quite characteristic. Southerners know their Negroes, know how to handle them, have no trouble with them, whereas Northerners do not know how to handle them and have much trouble, as instanced by riots in Chicago, St. Louis, Washington, and elsewhere. Informant said he would not want to live where there are no "niggers" and that they are all right if properly dealt with, that is if the commanding attitude is maintained and the appropriate deference is exacted from them.

We have referred to desires to dominate as human rather than as southern white. Certainly they are exhibited between nations as well as between races, and ethnocentrism centers around many characteristics other than physical form and feature. Extorting deference from other human beings is probably one of the things the human being will do if he gets a chance, unless his culture is so built as to make such extortion impossible. As has been shown, superior prestige often results in sexual and economic gains.

---

[4] "Any race, or group within a race, which is subjected to discrimination or persecution tends to take on the form of a nationality. The natural bonds of union within are strengthened by the opposition from without. A race consciousness and a race pride tend to develop as a defensive reaction. The struggle of races and of race groups is not so much an economic struggle as it is a struggle for self-respect and race preservation." E. B. Reuter, *The Mulatto in the United States* (Boston, 1918), p. 381; quoted by permission of Richard G. Badger.

Caste indeed might be otherwise defined as a systematic program for enhancing the self-abnegating reactions from Negroes. Love from Negroes is certainly not the only gratification involved in the prestige gain. Superiority and mastery and the status associated therewith are important considerations. It may be that submissiveness and deferential behavior are significant only in that the individual so behaving acknowledges his inferiority. It is observable that white people become aggressive as soon as Negro submission is withheld, and many stories are told of the "what I did with that 'uppity' nigger" type. One concerns a Southerntowner and a friend of his who went to Chicago last year. First they tried to find, and located, a hotel where no "niggers" were accepted. Then they went in search of a restaurant of similar tradition and found it; they made this out to be something of a feat. At the restaurant they felt the Negro waiters did not pay them enough attention and my bellicose informant shouted at one of them, "Come here, you son of a bitch." The Negro hurried over and asked, "You gemmun from de Sout'?" "Yes," they answered. "Boss," said the Negro, "dem is de sweetes' words I heard in eight years." The waiter told them he did not like it in the North, but he made so much more money that he stayed there. He was lavish of attention and pleaded with them to be sure and come back. The story as recited illustrates the aggression on one side and the accommodative submission on the other, as well as one way of dealing with a Negro.

There were many opportunities for me to observe the pressure on Negroes for deferential behavior, especially in connection with my own rôle as a researcher. I was suspected, and rightly, of not demanding the usual forms toward myself; and, on the other hand, my Negro informants were suspected of acquiring bad habits by dealing with me. It was never certain that my Negro friends would be courteously handled when they attempted to get in touch with me. On one occasion I was out of town for a few days and an informant tried to reach me. He was told that I was not there and that he need not try again. Apologies do not completely mend such a wound, though it certainly must be said that I put an unusual strain on the situation and those who punished my Negro informants or criticized me were quite within their rights from the standpoint of Southerntown. Still it was plain that powerful pressure is constantly exerted on Negro people to maintain their submissive attitudes. It is certainly no case of mere inertia of culture forms; the situation is rather maintained by active pressures, social and physical.

A method of reinforcing the white sense of superiority, and proving the fact after a fashion, is the satisfaction taken in errors of speech and other *faux pas* of the Negroes. There is much opportunity for such gratification since the Negroes are far from perfectly assimilated into white society. The visiting Yankee indeed may hear so many examples of the naïve mistakes of Negroes as to become bored with them. A common observation is that Negroes misuse the English language, mistake words, and like to use big words. It is said, though, that they often manage to express themselves very well despite their mistakes. A judge told the following illustrative story. Negroes are permitted to attend court under ordinary circumstances; but in rape cases which concern white people the court room is always cleared of Negroes. Such a case occurred and the clearance order was given. One Negro came by the judge's bench and asked what it was all about. The judge put him off with a joking answer. "Oh," said the Negro, "Ah see, jedge, it's one of dem 'fornuopulating' cases." Often really funny and ingenious, these errors are retailed by white people with much apparent pleasure and the inference is drawn from them that Negroes are inferior. Such stories and jokes about Negroes seem to be a source of pleasant self-satisfaction, much the same kind of satisfaction with which amused parents tell stories of the doings of their children. Pride in superior cultural achievement is a widespread fact of which this is a special case. In this superiority there is a distinct element of condescension and it also is used argumentatively, as a mild form of aggression against social pretensions by Negroes.

The tendency among students of culture to consider such acts as tipping the hat, shaking hands, or using "Mr." as empty formalisms is rebuked by experience in the South.

When we see how severely Negroes may be punished for omitting these signs of deference, we realize that they are anything but petrified customs; our illusion to the contrary occurs because we are not accustomed to think in terms of the emotional value of such forms. In Southerntown the use of "Mr." as a white-caste mark and the omission of it in speaking to Negroes have great emotional value. The Negroes know that to omit the "Mr." in referring to a white man would always mean that the addressee could enforce his right in some uncomfortable way. The main fact is that behind deference from the Negroes is the demand for deference by the whites and the ability to secure it by force if it is not willingly given.

Here is the sort of submissive response that white men like: A white man speaks to a Negro, "How are you, Sam?" Sam: "Oh, pretty good for an old nigger." In this case the Negro takes toward himself the derogatory attitude of the white man, calls himself by the name "nigger" which has so much negative affect for Negroes. A Negro responding in this manner establishes himself as definitely knowing his place and puts himself in a good way to get whatever he wants from the white man. Lower-class Negroes are quite expert at managing white people through their vanity. It is apparently a case of making the best of their status and exploiting the whites as best they can, in such ways as by borrowing without repaying, minor thieving, and so on. This is a sort of secondary compensation for the primary loss of self-esteem. A middle-class informant said that Negroes manage whites by self-abnegation. The "Sambo" or "Rastus" type of Negro takes off his hat, grins, strikes the boss for a half dollar, and often gets it in exchange for his submissiveness. This, informant said, is what white men mean by saying that the Negro is a "good psychologist" and that he knows his white folks; he adjusts himself to the inevitable and knows how to take some advantage of the situation.

It is an odd thing, but white people seem pretty completely taken in by this behavior of the Negro. Negroes have developed a definite "white-folks manner" which has become second nature with most of them and which is one of their defining caste characteristics. To adjust, in Southerntown, if colored, one must have it. There is continual flow of agreement by the Negro while a white man is talking, such as "Yes, boss," "Sho nuff," "Well, I declare," and the like.[5] The Negro must maintain a position of continuous affirmation of the white man's wishes and ideas, showing thereby his lack of contrary intent, independence, aggressiveness, and individuality. A "good nigger" from the white man's point of view is one who has mastered this technique.

The white-folks manner referred to is not motivated in the same degree in all Negroes. Some Negroes are so psychically organized that they fall into it easily, and the social rôle seems to fit their mental characteristics. In this case the social behavior is powerfully reinforced from the psychic side and the submissive attitudes seem quite natural. In other cases the Negro is not psychically fitted to develop a white-folks manner out of his own inner life. The rôle is then pressed on him by the community and is adopted, but usually with a certain externality and with internal reservations. In some cases a Negro so mentally constituted will not be able to adjust to Southerntown customs and will either be driven out of the community or otherwise disposed of. These are probably the people who cannot completely repress their hostility, and their rebelliousness shines through the white-folks manner. Life-history materials have given clear examples of such types of character occupying the uniform caste rôle of the Negro.[6]

[5] "So too, when the white man speaks to the negroes, they assume from the beginning the attitude of approval and there is a distinct evidence of sympathy. So it is in most of the meetings if no personal interest is challenged, and many negroes have been seen to nod their assent weakly to everything a white man was saying, though his total utterance was the abuse of the Negro in his political aspirings." Howard W. Odum, "Social and Mental Traits of the Negro," *Studies in History, Economics and Public Law* (1910), Vol. 37, No. 3, p. 551.

[6] *See* Reuter's discriminating discussion of the rôle concept. E. B. Reuter and C. W. Hart, *Introduction to Sociology* (New York, 1933), pp. 53-68.

Brief reference will be made at this place to behavior usually classed as "Jim Crow"-ing because it is related to the prestige gain. An example of such behavior is the use of the word "nigger." The word implies derogation of the Negro and, one often has reason to suppose, gives a correlative sadistic satisfaction to the user. In establishing the other person as inferior the user comments at the same time on his own superior position. All such designations of minority groups have a strong aggressive and hostile coloring; the words "hunky," "wop," "mick," and so on, illustrate the point. A middle-class Negro woman who was soliciting funds from plantation owners and managers commented that in her presence they omitted references to "niggers" or "darkies," both of which terms are offensive. She thought this unusual because many solicitors have to bear heavy insults. The white men around Southerntown do not appear to press the point, with her at least. The term "nigger" has the effect of isolating the Negro from human society and establishing him as an inferior, animal-like being. On the other hand, we notice how rigidly Negroes say "sir" or "boss" or "cap'n" to white men. Apparently these terms have replaced the "massa" of earlier days. Any failure on this score is immediately noticed and a demand for the deferential titles is made.

Failure to use the title "Mrs." for middle-class Negro women is a particularly sore point. There seems to be a vague feeling that middle-class Negro women deserve this title and they certainly feel so themselves. On the other hand, custom is strict in refusing it; it demands that Negro women, regardless of education or status in their own group, shall be addressed by their first names by any and all whites. There are many jokes about the problem of how to treat a prominent Negro man without calling him "Mr." One of the ways out is the title of professor, of which the Negroes are very fond. All their high-school teachers seem to be professors; this title is not begrudged by the whites. There are many minor occasions when the white man demands unusual and submissive behavior from Negroes. A case occurred one night when we were driving to another town; we lost our way and decided to ask someone for directions. The driver stopped beside a dimly lit cabin and blew his horn loudly a number of times until a Negro came out. He then asked the way, and we went on. The status assumption underlying this behavior is obvious.

We have learned from Freud[7] that the first love object of the human individual is his own physical self; a phase of "primary narcissism" is postulated at the base of the genetic sequence. If we grant this assumption, we assume that the individual's body, features, and color are accepted as natural and authentic and that other persons are judged in a derogatory sense in proportion as they deviate from one's own characteristics. If this be true, a considerable achievement is demanded of Negro persons in adjusting themselves to white society. They must accept the narcissistic wound of learning to prefer white color and features to their own; all that is designative of the primitive Negro self is judged "bad" by society. Most Negroes accept the superiority of white characteristics and the inferiority of their own, and attempt to edge over toward the white model. Two examples of the last point come to mind: one is the preferred value of white characteristics, such as color or feature; the second is a tendency to "marry white" within the Negro group. Both of these types of action indicate acceptance of white standards and admission of inferiority. White superiority is conceded not only by the deference but also by the imitation of Negroes. This point has been frequently observed by psychiatrists in cases of Negro mental patients.[8] When we remember that in the psychoses, for one

---

[7] Sigmund Freud, "On Narcissism: An Introduction," *Collected Papers* (London, 1925), IV, 30-33.

[8] "It is the conscious or unconscious wish of every negro to be white. This is brought out in his dreams, the hope of being white and snowy being in the eternal life and in psychoses in which he *is* or *was* white." W. M. Bevis, "Psychological Traits of the Southern Negro," *Amer. J. Psychiat.* (1921), I, 71.

"The whole psychosis seemed to consist of a confused mass of delusionary ideas, the most constant of which were those about his color. He stated that he had assumed his present disguise a number of times in the past, in order that he might mingle freely with the negroes to carry out certain business

reason or another, the disavowed trends of the personality are most likely to appear, we will be the more impressed by this testimony. It is said by some that the Negro idea of heaven is that there the Negro will become white,[9] a notion doubtless associated with cleansing from sin as well as achieving a white skin and features. The association of superior attributes with increasing degrees of approximation of whiteness within the Negro group has often been commented upon;[10] the scale seems to go from white through various shades of brown to black, and in Southern-town at least, the color black is euphemistically called "stove-pan brown." Prestige and deference seem to be dosed quite carefully in accordance with these distinctions.

So far as mixed marriages are concerned, and these can occur only in the North of course, we learn they are largely cases of marriage of Negro or mulatto men and white women.[11] The probability is that, if the cases were care-

---

and political projects. He had also adopted, so to speak, a negro family of the same name as his own and when he was wearing this disguise he lived with them the more completely to fool people. . . . Practically every morning he accosts the physician on his rounds and makes some request relative to his main delusionary idea. Now he wants a half pound of Epsom salts with which to bleach himself, again some fish-oil which may remove the paint, etc." J. E. Lind, "The Color Complex in the Negro," *Psychoanal. Rev.* (1913-1914), I, 410.

[9] "But these are exceptions and the rule which will be verified by any one who has had considerable dealing with the negroes is that the future blessed state according to their ideas is one in which they will display a spotless integument and the first ceremony in the ritual of their entrance to Heaven is the casting aside of the ebony husk." Lind, *op. cit.*, p. 404.

[10] "Beginning in early life, the pale child notices differences between himself and his darker playmates. He compares his color with theirs as well as with that of the white children and soon arrives at the conclusion that he is more like white than colored. This realization generates early the attitude of superiority which is usually associated with white, and this attitude is carried on, ever increasing, to that stage in life at which an adjustment must be attempted." C. F. Gibson, "Concerning Color," *Psychoanal. Rev.* (1931), XVIII, 420.

[11] "The large majority of the mixed marriages are of Negro or mulatto men and white women. In one hundred and fifty-

fully examined, the class position of the Negro man would be found above that of the white woman, either because she was depraved or disadvantaged in some manner or because she was a foreigner who did not realize the kind of trade she was making. Since the proposal of marriage in a patriarchal society is reserved to men, it is clear that such marriages involve a gain in status for the Negro and a loss for the white woman. Considering that these marriages are legal in the northern states, they have been very few, probably a testimony to the power of the informal caste line in the North. The upshot of the matter seems to be that recognizing one's own Negro traits is bound to be a process wounding to the basic sense of integrity of the individual who comes into life with no such negative views of his own characteristics. This is indeed one of the basic frustrations for Negroes which generates hostility toward the white caste.

In a situation like this where Negroes are compelled to exhibit submissive behavior toward whites, it is not surprising that few have the courage to express open resentment. It need not be thought, however, that they do not feel it, and this is especially true of middle-class Negroes. One spirited informant said that the southern white man expects the Negro to eat dung and like it; they eat it all right, but they do not like it, even if they pretend to. He imitated ironically a Negro coming into a white man's office, saying "boss," taking off his hat, smiling so as to show every tooth in his mouth. If a Negro will do this, he can get privileges from the whites. The aggression problem will be discussed in detail later, so we will merely note it at this point and indicate the possibility that the self-abnegating behavior of Negroes is a substitute for an aggressive response. The aggression in the Negro is called out in the first place by injury to his basic pride in himself.

Any minor Negro official, such as a social worker or teacher, must express an often-reluctant deference in all re-

---

eight of the one hundred and seventy-one cases reported by Baker, the groom was a Negro and the woman white." E. B. Reuter, *The Mulatto in the United States* (Boston, 1918), p. 135; quoted by permission of Richard G. Badger.

lations with his employer. He will not be able to talk with
the boss or interrupt him when there are white people with
him; he is not asked to sit down in the office. If white
people come in when the boss and the Negro are having
a conference, the white man stops and talks to them. Sometimes the Negro will have to stand and wait for several
hours to get a two-minute decision while streams of white
people come and go. If the employer's office is elective, the
problem is difficult for both, since the boss cannot be seen
talking to a Negro while a white person is waiting. It would
be bad in the next election. Negroes often say that if they
could vote they would not have to tolerate these humiliations; they could talk when their right turn came. A vote
is here seen as an aggressive instrument which would alter
the necessity of automatic submissiveness for Negroes.

It is often assumed that it is Yankees who put aggressive
ideas into Negroes' heads, and southerners who wish to
excuse the behavior of Negroes during the reconstruction
period will say that it was not their fault, rather it was the
Freedman's Bureau and the carpet-baggers who put them
up to it. This is the old argument that "outside agitators"
stir up a peaceful situation. What is more likely is that Negro hostility is constantly present, but it is compensated for
by passive behavior; this submission is enforced rather than
freely given and, if the situation permitted, the primary
aggression would reappear.

It struck me repeatedly that the deference of Negroes, in
addition to being pleasant, has the function of allaying anxiety among white people. By being deferential the Negro
proves, in addition, that he is not hostile. Whites are not
satisfied if Negroes are cool, reserved, and self-possessed
though polite; they must be more than polite; they must
be actively obliging and submissive. It would seem that
there is much fear behind the demands of white people
for submissiveness on the part of Negroes. My first intima-
tion of this came when a white informant told me about
two classes of local Negroes who had been away to school.
The first type hangs on white folks, fawns, wants to show
how much he knows; the second is offish, cool, and keeps
to himself. The latter group will hardly speak on the street,

according to my informant, and sometimes will not speak first; not, of course (with a blush), that one wanted to be spoken to by "niggers"—"but you know how it is." It seemed to me that he did very much want to be spoken to by Negroes and deferentially treated by them, and that he had unpleasant threatened feelings when the required favor was not forthcoming.

It struck me repeatedly that many landowners use the term "my niggers" as though they still actually owned the Negroes. The expression did not sound like "my factory hands" or "my staff," but appeared to be much more possessive. Actually to own the body of another person and to control it completely is probably the most exalting possibility from the standpoint of the owner's self-esteem. It is suggested that in addition to the property loss to the upper- and middle-class whites occasioned by emancipation, there was a sharp narcissistic wound; their gratification in owning and controlling Negroes so completely was taken away by force. The northern armies took more than property away; they changed in a fundamental manner the mastery-and-deference relations between the races. The man who is owned must behave to his master's taste; when the looser caste control was substituted for slavery, all such prerogatives of ownership were weakened.

The subservience of the Negro is obviously a heritage from slavery days, and many Negroes maintained attitudes of love and loyalty long after emancipation. This was particularly true of house servants, that is, those Negroes whose chances for personal contact with the white group were greatest. Such Negroes also felt, apparently, a marked sense of superiority by virtue of their superior tasks and contacts with the white masters, and expected deference in their turn from the Negro field hands. As a system, the slavery arrangement would be forced to crush individual boldness and resistance and would tend to breed subservience. Submission is necessary to the type of labor organization demanded by plantation slavery. At the same time as resistance is suppressed, dependent and submissive attitudes must inevitably be created. These attitudes in turn are socially transmitted and are visible in large numbers of

Negroes today, especially those living still under plantation conditions. Very little external force is needed to maintain them. One may say that subservience is an attitude corresponding to the limited conditions of safety for slaves, that it has been built into the personalities of individual Negroes, and that thereafter it is culturally transmitted from one generation to the next. These attitudes correspond too well to the known slavery conditions for it to be suggested that they are biological traits or transported African habits.[12]

These deference relationships in the South are not viewed as especially characteristic of this region. It is believed, on the contrary, that most people tend to want to use others in this way and would make the gain if they could; as a feature of our social order, such automatic prestige is passing, and democratic practices based on reciprocal rights and duties are growing. Nor is this behavior seen as a series of cases of individual meanness on the part of southern white people. It is rather that the system operates this way and, by and large, people conform to it, both white and Negro, because they must. The white person in Southerntown has no more option about calling a Negro "Mr." than the Negro has to demand the title. Very likely race equalitarians have exactly the same tendencies to extort deferential reactions from others, but probably they are more afraid of making such demands and have more resentment about being humiliated themselves. Perhaps an increasingly democratic organization of American society would begin to function psychologically by forcing increasing numbers of people to suppress their hostile and exploitive tendencies toward others, in all spheres, the economic, the sexual, and that of prestige.

[12] In discussing this material with Dr. Eugen Kahn of Yale University he described the deference patterns in Germany before the World War. He remarked that in Germany soldiers and officials had extraordinary prestige and received signs of submissiveness and self-abnegation from the public. Evidently it was assumed that the public existed for the officials and not the other way around. A curious example was the case of a man who worked under a German official and who, when he came to call on his chief, would always knock at the *bottom* of the door as a symbol of his awe and respect.

CHAPTER IX

Caste Patterning of Education

∞∞∞∞∞∞∞∞∞∞∞∞∞∞∞∞∞∞∞∞∞∞∞∞∞∞∞

The shadow of caste falls over the school in Southerntown no less than over the courthouse and the church. Control of the schools and school opportunities is a crucial matter to American citizens and has long been viewed as such. Mass education is in the American mores and it is the door which has traditionally been open to those seeking to better their social status. It is this fact that has made the education of the young one of our major occupations and has led to the high value we place on schools and schooling. The symbol of the schoolhouse is the public guarantee that American society is actually offering the equality of opportunity which is the pivotal conception in our social order. Since the Civil War Negroes have increasingly participated in school opportunities.[1] This is true no less of Southerntown than of other sections of the United States. In Southerntown, however, there is more conflict over the offering of educational opportunities to Negroes. It is inevitable that this should be so since the southern regional mores place the Negro in a lower caste, where social opportunity is much more limited and where the hope of indefinite advancement for all persons must be denied in fact, whatever be the national theory. If equal opportunity were offered, Negroes and whites would tend to divide up according to ability and social value and not according to caste prescriptions. Since the latter outcome cannot now be accepted, the only alternative is to attempt to act on both of the

[1] In 1866 one Negro out of ten was literate; in 1930 nine Negroes out of ten could read and write. U. S. Dept. of the Interior, Office of Education, "Secondary Education for Negroes" (1932), Bulletin No. 17, Monograph No. 7, p. 12.

conflicting definitions of the Negro's rôle; the result is a compromise.

Education means much more than formal schooling. It may be defined as the assimilation of an individual into a culture not originally his own. Thus one may speak of educating a child, since this is a process of indoctrinating him with our own mores and folkways. The education of an immigrant means familiarizing him with the features of our variant of Western European society so that he can adjust himself to our social life; the immigrant already has learned many of the basic habits which are common to the Western European culture area and the process is a much briefer one than in the case of the child. More difficult is the education of an American Indian or other member of a preliterate society, since such an individual is keyed to a social structure quite different from our own and has to change his major life orientation quite radically. It is well understood today that much of the most crucial educational work is done before the individual comes to a school at all.

It is not true to say that the people of the South have resisted the "education" of the Negro altogether. They have had to educate the Negro in order to fit him for a place first as slave and then as caste man in southern society. His education began as soon as he learned to talk English, when he heard the passionate preaching of Baptist evangelists,[2] and when he saw the manner of life in the white households where he served. Acquisition of language alone carries with it access to the major features of American culture; and the daily participation in work, even with slaveowners and overseers, has been a constant force in the education of the Negro. If it be a favor to him to transfer his allegiance from local African cultures to our own, this process has been going on for several centuries, unsystematically, for the most part, but quite inevitably. Through it he has come to share American speech, clothes, religion, family form to a degree, and in particular of late, aspirations for social advancement. In this sense the major educational problem with the Negro had been solved largely, though imper-

[2] C. G. Woodson, *The History of the Negro Church* (Washington, 1921), pp. 19-20.

fectly, before emancipation and the initation of formal schooling. Formal schooling replaces for Negroes as well as for whites the older informal methods of indoctrination and is a phase of our stage of social and technological development. Apologists for the older status order in the South put the very highest value on educating the Negro, sometimes phrased as saving his soul; and they thought it well worth his while to submit to slavery in exchange for it. Time and historical perspective may very well prove them right, though the question is unarguably complex at the present time. Increasingly in recent years the formal order is taking over the task of indoctrinating the young into our folkways. This practice has the effect of overshadowing the contributions always made and still made through informal participation in social life, especially in the family.[3]

So far as the Negro was concerned, his assimilation into American life was spurred, as indicated, by the physical, external necessity of adjusting to the slave system; but soon also by another factor, his own wish not to be different, not to be looked down upon as a stranger and a savage. As soon as the process was set going there was a powerful premium on assimilating American folkways and this, all things considered, has been done to a truly amazing extent by the American Negro. Although it was not the object of southern society to educate him for *full* participation, but rather for slave or caste participation, it is difficult to check the educational process once it is set in motion. When one has the language, for example, the major idea patterns characteristic of American civilization are accessible; and if, in addition, one can read, there is opportunity for full assimilation and identification with the highest values of our culture. Literacy especially is an enormous step since it breaks the bonds of social isolation and enables the individual to state his claims in terms of the full American social ideal: access to indefinite economic and status advancement for any individual. This has been done by the middle-class Negroes in recent years.

It is just this claim, however, which the southern system

[3] John Dollard, *The Changing Functions of the American Family* (Thesis Abstract; Chicago, 1931), p. 30.

cannot admit on the part of the Negro. He has his place and he is to know it; the intent of the supportive social institutions like education is to keep him in it. This purpose was clearly, if intuitively, realized by the upper-class white group in slavery days. They objected in most cases to literacy for the Negro and in some cases even to verbal religious instruction[4] on the ground that it would disturb the status relationships then existing. The situation has changed in the last seventy-five years and the Negroes have rapidly come within the circle of the literate. The change is due in part to the War and the educational endeavors by northern groups in behalf of the Negro; it is also due in considerable part to the perception by the South of the advantage to be gained by the social system through a restricted education of the Negro. The caste principle functions in education in this way: it stresses especially craft and vocational training for the Negro, a type of training which would prepare him for, but not beyond, the opportunities of lower-caste status. White people are said to be won over more easily to this type of education for Negroes and it is the symbol constantly used by the many influential white men in the South who are advancing Negro education. Even so, a white informant said, people fear that education for Negroes will make it possible for them to pass state educational tests for voting and thus make them a factor in politics. Informant saw this danger but did not take it seriously.

It will be remembered that Booker T. Washington greatly advanced the cause of Negro education by meeting the white-caste stipulations on this point. He took what may have been the only constructive attitude in his day by asking for industrial and agricultural training for Negroes. Informants in Southerntown pointed out how much

---

[4] "These workers, however, soon found that there was a strenuous objection even to the verbal instruction of Negroes for fear that the oral exercise would inspire a desire for literary training, which was out of harmony with the status of the Negro in a slaveholding commonwealth. Thinking that it might lead to such a state of affairs, most masters in some parts of the South opposed all instruction of Negroes during the thirties and forties." Woodson, *op. cit.*, p. 155; quoted by permission of the Associated Publishers.

impressed planters were when humble Negroes were taught how to do useful things about the farm, such as mending harnesses, sharpening plows, and the like. The inculcation of orderly habits of work and development of relevant farming skills have brought increasing support for Negro education from the middle-class white group.

A Negro teacher living in Southerntown, but teaching in another city, illustrated the other side of the question. Her school needed, or felt it needed, a general science laboratory. The city refused to provide any money for this laboratory and limited its appropriations to the work of the domestic science department. From the caste standpoint it was self-evident that "domestic science" was the type of training needed by Negro women. There is much ridicule of any other kind of knowledge for Negroes and many illustrations are given by white informants of their inability to make use of it. Negroes are frequently said to be spoiled by advanced training and there is probably truth to this, at least from the viewpoint of their continued unprotesting adjustment to the caste situation. The figures for the county showing percentage of children in school at various age levels reveal the influence of caste very clearly; in considering them it should be recalled that the Negroes outnumber the whites by about two and a half to one in this county. Between the ages of seven and thirteen 89 percent of the Negro and 94 percent of the white children are in school. Of children fourteen and fifteen years of age, 81 percent of the Negro and 85 percent of the white are in school. Similarly, for the ages of sixteen and seventeen, 48 percent of the Negro children and 60 percent of the white children are in school, and for the ages eighteen to twenty years, 10 percent of the Negro children and 27 percent of the white children.[5] In the earlier ages percentages are almost equal; in the ages representing later high-school and college years the white percentages are almost three times that of the Negro.[6] Participation in advanced schools,

[5] These data have been worked up from census reports.

[6] Southerntown and county are very progressive if compared with the state as a whole. In the state the percentage of white children enrolled in high school to children of high-school age

largely as a preparation for upper-class and middle-class status, still tends to be markedly less for Negroes than for whites; it is only in this sense that southern society seems to show reluctance to the education of Negroes.

Educationally Southerntown is very enterprising and offers unusual opportunities to Negroes as well as whites. This advanced position is due to unusually effective leadership on the part of the school administrators. There is a colored high school in the town, not at all a common thing, which offers a three, instead of a four, year course; this means that the graduates from it cannot go directly to college but must spend a pre-college year away from home.[7] For the Negroes who are demonstrably least well-endowed economically, this is a heavy handicap to the educational and status advancement of their children. While I was in Southerntown, a county high school for industrial and agricultural training was in the process of organization; there had been no county high school which admitted Negroes. The remedy of Negro parents has been, incidentally, to send their children away to colleges, which perforce offered high-school as well as college training.

One of my Negro informants told of going away to college and doing high-school work there. This was puzzling at the time. He explained that in those days there were no high schools for Negroes in his community or county and that Negroes had to go to college to do high-school work. Informant said this made professional or advanced training much more expensive for Negroes since they have to pay for from one to four additional years away from home. In

---

is ten times as great as the similar percentage for Negroes. U. S. Dept. of the Interior Office of Education, "Secondary Education for Negroes" (1932), Bulletin No. 17, Monograph No. 7, p. 15.

[7] The figures from the state showing participation in various high-school years make the same point, that the percentage of Negroes enrolled in the *first* year of high school is ten times as great as the figure for the *fourth* year; in the case of whites the percentage for the first year is about double that for the fourth year. This probably reflects a lack of fourth-year facilities as well as normal dropping out. (*Op. cit.*, p. 17.)

Southerntown, as matters stand, it would be only one additional year.

The high-school building in Southerntown is a handsome one, which is often pointed out by white informants as an evidence of their fairness to Negroes. Apart from the lack of a fourth year and some defects in curriculum, it seems to be doing good work and offering opportunities that are exceptional. It must be understood that high-school and college education are the portals to middle-class status for those who do not have other types of claims on it and that facilitation or retardation at this point plays a great rôle in tightening or loosening the caste and class boundaries. Leadership by those who believe that an educated Negro caste will be more efficient and easier to live with has brought about the present opportunities for Negroes. It is not to be thought, however, that the education of the Negro child has been placed on a par with that of the white child in Southerntown or county. For one thing, there is a great reluctance to spend money for Negro education. It is really the fervor of Negro belief in education as a means of advancement that has been responsible for much of the development. After all, from the standpoint of the white caste, why spend money for Negro education if it tends, as most suspect, to unfit them for their caste and class rôles?

The situation differs, of course, town by town. In a neighboring town the Negroes were given a shell of a building for a school and in one way or another the salaries of the teachers were eked out. The rest of the work was done by Negroes, and an unexpected lot it was. Negro carpenters and masons contributed the work on remodeling the building. Negroes collected the funds to furnish the school with desks, blackboards, and other accessories. No money is provided annually for supplies or fuel by the town; so Negroes contribute for the school supplies and cut and haul their own fuel. This is done in a community where Negro working habits are generally reported to be bad; it is done, of course, by zealous individuals with the bright American goal of social advancement before their eyes.

A rural Negro teacher paused a moment while talking to me, then explained that he was thinking about the difficulty of getting in the supply of wood for the winter; it would be hard if an early fall came and it rained a good deal, for the swampy forests would become impassable. But he was glad, on the other hand, of the prospect that the bulk of the cotton would be picked by October first. This would permit the rural Negro children to go to school.

A school organizer in a rural community expressed annoyance at having to raise five hundred dollars from the local Negroes. It seemed that the Negroes had recently built a school and money had been loaned them on notes by well-to-do white friends; these friends were asking for their money. He thought it was a pity it had to be squeezed out of the Negroes, the poorest people, when tremendous amounts of W.P.A. money were being spent for improvements of various kinds, including school grounds and buildings. This informant was being educated politically without realizing it since the caste situation, and the political order which represents it, determine both the desirability of spending W.P.A. money for white schools and projects and also the relative undesirability of the same expenditures for Negroes. It was not merely that officials did not wish to make such expenditures; it was literally true that they could not since their official tenure was dependent on the white voters who vote on caste lines. Negro enthusiasm for education and social advancement must indeed be intense to press along as it does against such obstacles.

The percentages on enrolment already given are a little misleading because the Negro schools do not have terms as long as the white schools nor are the school units themselves as efficient. A Negro rural teacher commented unconsciously on the short term in the following way. He said that he had a lot of problems at his school because so many of the Negroes are renters and tenants and have their work actively supervised by white bosses. His race is in a bad situation, he said, because they have to do what the white men say. For example, during cotton-picking season every member of the family who is mature enough has to pick cotton and rural Negro children may not go to school until the picking is done. This means that the majority of students enter in November and December. The school opens October 1, but only a few students are enrolled at that time; the real enrolment begins when the cotton is finally picked. An interesting additional fact is that the percentage of females under ten years of age gainfully employed in agriculture is unusually high.[8] School terms vary over the county both for white and colored children; in the case of the whites, between 160 and 180 days, in the case of Negro children, between 100 and 160 days.

It was something of a surprise to learn that in the county there are about ten times as many Negro as white schools. I tended to think of a school as a school and it seemed from the figures that the Negroes were better taken care of than the whites. The paradox is resolved by noting that the white schools have been consolidated into large efficient units, and transportation to them is furnished; the colored schools, on the other hand, are small, scattered, and numerous. Often abandoned churches are fitted out as schoolrooms. The number of schools is partly a testimony to the eagerness of Negroes and to their tacit demands on plantation owners that schools for children be provided; schools are a necessary factor in holding the Negro labor supply. In this connection the development of county high schools (evidently for whites) in the state is shown by the relatively high number of school busses operating in 1933.[9] The above considerations apply primarily to the rural schools; the Negro grade and high school in Southerntown is much nearer to the level of the white school.

Another feature of the school situation is "caste pay" for Negro teachers. Salaries for white teachers in the county vary from $75 to $200, while for Negro teachers the range is from $25 to $75. Some writers, such as Moton,[10] report

[8] Howard W. Odum, *Southern Regions of the United States* (Chapel Hill, 1936).

[9] *Ibid.*

[10] "The poorest paid teachers where separate schools are maintained are found in the states of the lower South where salaries range from $900 to $2,500 for whites and from $290 to $500 for Negroes. The best paid are in the border states, where white teachers receive from $900 to $4,500, while coloured teachers receive from $700 to $3,000. In considering these figures allowance must be made for the shorter terms

low average salaries for Negro teachers over the whole South. The depression has, of course, affected the level of local salaries for teachers and reduced somewhat the already small incomes of the teaching Negroes. This is best seen from an illustration. An informant who is doing clerical work is considering changing her job to teaching, which she likes very much; she is a competent primary-grade teacher. Her salary in her present job is $40 a month and she is offered $50 to change to the teaching position. Still, the $40 a month salary is for twelve months in the year, but the $50 salary for teaching is for seven months only, the rural Negro school term. Even though the Negro standard of living may be lower, it is certainly not low enough to correspond with this salary difference. It will be noted, though, that even this wage is markedly above that of the lower-class Negro woman who is doing housework; it establishes the possessor of a teaching salary definitely in the middle-class group.

It has been suggested that education is not exclusively an affair of formal schooling. In this connection we may note that educative personal contact between white and colored has decreased since slavery days, at the same time that the formal contacts with white culture, through the schools, have increased. The effect has been to expose Negroes more fully to the total American mores and to withdraw them somewhat from the regional mores of the South; their aspirations are formed by the national ideal of social advancement rather than by the well-accommodated acceptance of their inferior position characteristic of slavery days. The fact is of momentous significance from the standpoint of culture conflict in this area. Despite the tendency to limit the Negro's education to skills appropriate to his caste position—agricultural and mechanical skills—it is impossible to carry out this program. Other types of information are in-

---

for coloured schools and the general absence of the higher grades where the higher salaries are paid, and the practice also of grading pay according to the professional equipment of the teacher." R. R. Moton, *What the Negro Thinks* (Garden City, N. Y., 1932), pp. 103-104; quoted by permission of Doubleday, Doran & Co.

cluded, as well as social goals for the Negro differing from those of the southern white caste. Furthermore, the teaching is done by Negroes who are middle-class people and much less well accommodated to the caste situation than are the lower-class Negroes. Even when the teachers are not aggressively race-conscious, which is seldom the case, they are bound to be more objective than is the local current of tradition in Southerntown.

In recent years there has been a remarkable improvement in educational facilities for Negroes in the county, notwithstanding the fact that they have not reached the white level. Ten years ago educational tests were given to the Negro teachers and it was found that more than half of them tested around the fourth-grade level. An energetic campaign to raise the level of the teaching force was instituted and today more than half of the teachers are college graduates, a quarter have had two years in college, and most of the rest are high-school graduates. It must be remembered that this achievement represents the good will and fairness of a southern white community. Seven years ago there were 20,000 Negro children of school age in the county of whom 5,000 were in school. The average daily attendance was 2,000. At the present time there are 16,000 Negro children, 12,000 of them are enrolled in school, and the average daily attendance is 9,000. This is a truly remarkable achievement attesting the tolerance and foresightedness of the white people as well as the zeal of the Negroes for educational opportunities.

We have noted the importance of literacy since it opens the door for the Negro individual to the wider American culture. It is further important in that it serves as a substitute, like the school, for the informal educational contacts between Negroes and whites which are steadily being reduced by caste limitations. The caste, as compared with slavery, forces on the Negro a greater isolation from southern white people. This is an area and state which rank high for both Negro and white illiteracy.[11] In the county, census figures show that about a quarter of the Negroes over

[11] Odum, *op. cit.*

ten years of age cannot read or write; testimony to the relative efficiency of white schools is the fact that less than 3 percent of white people, including poorer whites, in the county are illiterate. We should remember that in the case of the Negroes these figures mean that a quarter of the Negroes are cut off from the fullest type of participation in American society. In the town only one twentieth of the Negroes over ten years of age cannot read and write, a testimony to the better schools and probably to the selectivity of the town for the literate Negroes.

Literacy is important not only as the door to the wider American culture but also as a factor in the many tangible affairs of daily life; for example, literacy is the almost exclusive portal to middle-class status. One Negro businessman told me he did not know how to read and write when he began his business career. He found it a great disadvantage, for instance, in keeping books. Slowly over many years he learned to write, first by copying people's names out of telephone books. Now he writes pretty well but does not spell well. His illiteracy has been a marked handicap in his business and social relations.

Literacy and education are a certain protection for the Negro in the caste situation. It is more difficult for ill-disposed whites to take advantage of caste privileges with the educated Negro. A middle-class Negro informant gave a detailed story of his difficulties in renting land from a neighboring white man. The man was unscrupulous and tried to trick him on at least three separate occasions; each time he stood his ground and firmly but politely refused to yield. He was better educated than the white man and felt that only this superior advantage enabled him to stand off against the other's superiority on the prestige side. He believed that if he had been ignorant, as many Negroes are, the white man could have done anything he wanted.

Negro parents say repeatedly that they "cannot afford" to send their children to advanced schools. Since our society encourages each individual to get as much schooling as possible, failure to continue in school is often a result of lack of capital on the part of the parents and of a need for the earnings of the child. This may well remind us that skills of management and operation, habits of thrift and caution, are themselves accumulations of capital laid down in the character of the individual. In this sense the acquisition of middle-class status requires a little platform of capital to stand on. Social advancement for children is only possible when they do not need to work in childhood and can be allowed to acquire skills while others support them, thus keeping out of productive activity for the time. Since we deal mostly with lower-class Negroes in Southerntown and county, we observe that they lack these accumulated skills of management and foresight, and hence cannot compete with middle-class white people. Lack of schooling and inferior opportunities operate as pressures to maintain the present-day lower-class group as it is.

The value of education in the Negro group is well appreciated and is often vigorously advocated by the clergy. It is frequently, too, a passionate hope of Negro parents in lower as well as middle classes. The "I will arise" clubs which were a feature of post-War Negro life, have already been mentioned; they showed in their very name the wish for social advancement. A Negro informant pointed out this desire for education in the Negro families who leave plantations for the towns; one of the biggest attractions is the better schools for Negroes there. Negroes will live huddled and half-starving in the cities so that their children can be within sight of the school. Good rural schools are one of the major factors in holding the farm labor supply to the land. Recently a state-wide movement was conducted to cut down Negro illiteracy. The teachers, mainly white, who conducted night classes for Negroes, were greatly impressed by their eagerness to learn. This "eagerness to learn," of course, is a feature of the social mobility of the Negro; he realizes to what degree education is a condition precedent to status rise; most Negro families share the common American aspiration to have their children "better off" than they were.

We have little data on this point, but it seems that most of the traits characteristic of the rural Negroes will disappear as educational advantages are made available to them. One such characteristic often remarked is that of superstition. The schools, of course, actively explode superstitions and constitute a force working against this cultural hangover in the Negro. A Negro teacher said that he used to be very much afraid of ghosts and "hants" but that he no longer is nowadays; his superstitions have evaporated. He gives a course in general science which, he says, explains many of the superstitions, and the students seem to like it. Often they will bring up cases and he will be able to give them a scientific explanation. This means, of course, that the Negroes are steadily being inducted into the rational, materialistic world view characteristic of our formal society, despite the many eddies in the Negro folk culture in which the older beliefs continue. With the aid of the schools the Negro is increasingly becoming an American in the full sense of our society.

This offers one very striking problem. If Negroes are to continue to live, for the most part, in southern states, it could be argued that the white group is unwise to educate them at all. What is desired locally is that they accept the regional mores of the South and maintain the caste rules without friction. On the other hand, the dominant pattern of American life, which is presented through the schools, does not recognize caste and tends to apportion social awards and status on the basis of efficiency. These are, then, two divergent trends in the mores. It must be remembered, however, that the white southern people are also members of the major American culture and share the dominant views about the desirability of mass education. Therein lies the conflict and it explains many of the inadequacies of the Negro educational system and the half-heartedness with which Negro training is often conducted. Education for the Negro tends to break down an unprotesting adjustment to caste status; acceptance of inferior position seems more natural and tolerable as long as cultural differences (like lack of education) can be cited to make caste seem reasonable. Educated Negroes become more fully aware of their formal rights and of the gains of the white middle class; as they increase their social efficiency by education they compare themselves with white people and perceive that their lower status is categorical and not based on a factual inferiority. This perception tends to raise the resentment which unjustified discrimination always does raise. It must be a potent factor in the development of conflict between Negroes and whites in the southern states.

A second paradox connected with educating Negroes is that they tend to become better competitors with middle- and upper-class white people and this potentiality of competition sharpens caste antagonism. As matters stand, the bi-racial adjustment, limited largely to education and religion, does not provide an adequate outlet for the number of middle-class Negroes who are being trained. Education dresses them up and they have no, or little, professional place to go. The caste system seems, by its logic, to prefer a large and passive population of lower-class Negroes who are accustomed to do the most strenuous and ill-paid work. Educational needs for this class are very simple, provided it accepts its caste status and does not make the general American demand for social advancement. If, on the other hand, formal education for these Negroes is developed and steadily improved, we will find them straining increasingly against the limiting caste barriers.

One Negro boy perceived the situation quite clearly in his own way. His parents had sent him to a liberal arts college at eighteen. He wished he had gone to Tuskegee instead. If he had gone to Tuskegee, he could have learned a trade and would have had "something to stand by" him. He was thinking about a college in the North and asked the pertinent question, "Do they get jobs for their graduates when they finish?" He seemed very much at sea about what to do with his life and felt blocked in the present situation. His dilemma is the one of whether to accept the caste situation and make the best of it or to cherish the hope of mobility characteristic of the wider American society.

We may expect an increasing pressure within the southern region as a result of this conflict, a pressure from the growing Negro middle-class group clamorous for social opportunity and anxious to escape caste limitations. For the moment there seems no solution in view of the solidity of southern society on the caste issue and we have to note, rather than solve, the contradiction. It may seem in the future to be a fortunate thing that this middle-class group is developing within the Negro caste; for the moment social tension will be increased by the fact.

Taken all in all, it must be said that the education of the Negroes to the degree at present possible is a remarkable achievement in view of southern sentiment. Slavery did not countenance the formal education of Negroes. The advance all over America has been very rapid since emancipation. In 1870, 9.2 percent of the Negroes between five and twenty attended school; in 1930, 60 percent of the Negroes between these ages did.[12] This is a truly astonishing change in social practice and it has resulted in a rapid assimilation of Negroes into American folkways and the development of a considerable middle-class Negro group. This change has been wrought in the South as well as in the North by the activity of thoughtful and foresighted persons who felt that education was an advantage as well for the white as for the Negro caste and who were, in any case, in the grip of the powerful American pattern of mass education which carried them forward despite the regional suspicion of the South. Comparative limitations in educational facilities in our state and county are general for both whites and Negroes, if one compares it to a larger northern state. We learn[13] that the whole state budget would be consumed if the schools were brought to the national average. Expenditures for education are therefore high considering the wealth of the state; the education of the Negro in these straitened circumstances is the more of a feat.

The seeming purpose of the educational system as modified by caste and class in the South is to train whites for their class and caste positions of mastery and responsibility; hence, on the whole, they are better trained. Since Negroes in turn are trained for their expected lower-caste positions in the system, they receive the simpler, more manual and practical forms of training. As we have noted, this difference in training is not always realized in fact and doubtless

---

[12] *Negroes in the United States* (1920-32), U. S. Dept. of Commerce, Bureau of the Census.

[13] Odum, *op. cit.*

a little algebra and history filter in along with the manual training and applied agriculture. Caste training is, nevertheless, the theory if not the fact of educational practice in Southerntown.

CHAPTER X

Caste Patterning of Politics

It is a liberal political education for the average northerner to live for a while in a southern town. He comes to see for the first time what it means to be able to vote, and, quite as important, not to be able to vote. What may have been previously a mere ceremony to him suddenly snaps into significance as an effective method of determining how local government will influence his personal life and interests. In the North only persons who pay considerable amounts in direct taxes and members of political machines seem to grasp this point clearly.

A tolerant Southerntowner told me that the white caste has two types of ways of excluding the Negroes from voting. The first is that a two dollar poll tax must be paid two years before the vote is cast and that all taxes levied against the person must be paid before February of the year of voting. The second is "the interpretation of the Constitution" clause; judgment as to satisfactory interpretation is left to the local (white) registrar. Informant remembered the days before such orderly methods were in vogue when white voters simply policed the polling places and refused to let Negroes enter to vote.

The history of these restrictions is well known and frequently elaborated in political science texts. The major problem from the standpoint of Southerntown has been, of course, to find a legal way to evade the implications of the Fifteenth Amendment[1] and the phrase in it which forbids

[1] It reads: "The right of citizens of the United States to vote shall not be denied or abridged by the United States or by any state, on account of race, color, or previous condition of servitude. The Congress shall have power to enforce this article by appropriate legislation."

the United States' and any state's debarring anyone from the right to vote on account of race, color, or previous condition of servitude. There are two ways out; someone other than a state may debar the Negro voter, or it may be done on some other ground than race. Both ways are used. The understanding and "reasonable" interpretation of the Constitution clause has been one of the most effective ways of excluding Negro voters, and it has been decided by the Supreme Court that such a stipulation does not violate the Fifteenth Amendment; the contention was that an educational qualification is not a barrier on the grounds stated by the amendment. Certainly the intent of the Abolitionists' Congress which passed the amendment is not effectuated at the present time, but, as is so often the case, the formalities are upheld while the regional culture has its way.[2] When all is said and done about the legal formalities, the local white registrar is obedient to the mandates of his local culture and his task is to exclude Negroes from voting; this he does by imposing the most extreme educational demands on the would-be Negro voter.

A second and very effective device has been the organization of the Democratic party as a private concern which has the right to set its own stipulations for membership;

---

[2] "The legal position established by the Supreme Court is, briefly, as follows: No positive grant of the suffrage is implied either in the Fifteenth Amendment or in the Enforcing Acts passed under it. A denial of the right to vote by the States must, to make a case for the Federal Courts, be on grounds of race, color, or previous condition of servitude, and such discrimination must be alleged in any indictment under the Amendment or what remains of the Enforcing Act.

"It has been further established that the constitutional prohibition runs only against States, and individual offenders against franchise rights, on whatever grounds, must be sued in State courts. A commentator adds that when the rights of Negroes are curtailed by discriminatory State action, probably 'the Federal Court can only declare that the State statute is unconstitutional,' but can afford no remedy. Finally, disfranchisement has been held not to be a tort, and the Federal courts have refused to entertain actions for damages arising out of a denial of the franchise." Paul Lewinson, *Race, Class and Party* (New York, 1932), p. 59; quoted by permission of the Oxford University Press.

the real battle is then fought out over the Democratic nomination in an exclusive white primary. Every candidate is pledged to abide by the result of this election. After the decision is reached in the primary, it does not matter whether Negroes vote in the open election or not. The Democratic party, of course, is not a state in the sense of the Fifteenth Amendment and therefore is not under federal control;[3] it can and does exclude Negroes from membership. There are now eight states which debar the Negro from participating in the nominating processes.[4]

This bit of history illustrates very clearly the conflict between the regional mores of the South and the passionate but irresolute attempt of the post-Civil War Congress to set the pattern of political life in the southern states. So long as the fascistic rule of the northern armies prevailed in the South, about ten years, it was possible to keep the bottom rail on top; thereafter, with the rise of the Klan, the former status relationships were restored and local self-government was returned to the southern states. Local self-government is, of course, based on the postulate of white domination. Apparently after a few years the northern states were glad to find a *modus operandi* which would permit them to coöperate again with the southern states. They had no taste for another war or for a further military occupation of the

---

[3] "Three cases were taken to the United States District Court under the new law and party rule. In all, the decisions went against the Negro plaintiffs, on the ground that the Democratic party was a private organization, and therefore not subject to the limitations of the Fourteenth and Fifteenth Amendments. The same decision was reached by the State courts in Arkansas." Lewinson, *op. cit.*, p. 155; quoted by permission of the Oxford University Press.

[4] "In 1930, it was possible to point to eight States in which the Democratic party by a definite State-wide rule barred Negroes from a share in the nominating process. These were Alabama, Arkansas, Georgia, Louisiana, Mississippi, South Carolina, Texas, and Virginia. In three more—Florida, North Carolina, and Tennessee—there was no State-wide rule; but the rules of county and city Democratic committees took its place, with a few important exceptions in the two States last named." Lewinson, *op. cit.*, p. 112; quoted by permission of the Oxford University Press.

South in the interests of the Negro voter. This would have required a type of centralization in American government of which our democracy is quite incapable. The consistent pressure necessary to change the Negro's status in the South was not possible after the war passion died down. It is, of course, quite another question whether it would have been desirable even if the required consistency of policy had been operative. Southerntown and county have participated in all of these processes. The War is remembered here and with considerable keenness; it is felt that "reconstruction," a hated term, and Negro domination were worse than the War itself. This domination was, of course, based directly on Yankee force. Southerntowners take pride in the fact that the Negroes have again been submerged, the Yankees outwitted, and their political arrangements for the South abolished.

There is a nominal Republican party in the state, in fact two Republican parties. One of them, the black-and-tan party, represents more or less the northern attitude toward Negroes; the other, the lily-white Republicans, has the standard southern attitudes toward Negroes and would like to be simply a rival white party competing with the Democratic party. Neither has made much headway in the state, and Republicans, either black-and-tan or lily-white, are as rare as large incomes. The black-and-tan party, of course, inherits the antagonism of southern white people for the North, abolitionism, reconstruction, and Negro rule; in short, it stands against the southern white caste. Naturally its shrift is short. The black-and-tan Republicans are an artificial party which is merely a device for distributing patronage in the southern states when the Republicans control the national administration. A white Republican complained about the difficulty of building up a lily-white organization in the state. He said that the white Democrats were quite content with the black-and-tan Republicans because they could control the "niggers," whereas they could not control white Republicans. He thought the state was missing something in not having a Republican party to watch the Democrats. Instead there is factionalism within the Democratic party. It has been legally proved, according to this informant, that black-and-tan Republicans have sold federal offices; but a white jury sat on the case and acquitted the defendants nevertheless. Explanation: the black-and-tan defendants were in league with the white Democrats, the latter, of course, controlling the organization of juries.

There are occasional echoes of the days before this *rapprochement* had been worked out, when Negroes were likely to be appointed to federal offices. A Negro related that during a Republican administration his father was appointed to the postmastership of a small town in the state. The white people there threatened to lynch him if he stayed, and he fled the town for a year. During the interval a barn full of cotton on his farm was burned, presumably in revenge by the whites. At the end of the year he returned to the town and took up his work again. Apparently the black-and-tan Republicans are resigned to the fact that Negroes cannot be appointed to important federal posts; instead their politicians get what personal concessions they can for delivering the offices to white people picked by the Democrats. This is the state and federal political context in which Southerntown is set.

We can see the situation very concretely from the census figures on the number of voters in the county. The census goes to the trouble, for example, of enumerating the number of Negro males and females who theoretically could vote. They number about 24,000; of whites who could vote there are about 9,000. Voting is handled strictly according to caste principles. It is possible for any one of the 9,000 in the white caste to vote if he complies with the stipulations; it is virtually impossible for any of the 24,000 in the Negro caste to vote no matter what their qualifications. Only about 27 percent of the people in the county, therefore, have access to the means of controlling the governmental machine. We may note also from the census that almost all of the white voters are native white of native parentage, the foreign-born or native white of foreign or mixed parentage being negligible in number. The importance of this fact is that the caste principles are not attenuated by outside influences; Southerntown white people have experienced directly, or through their ancestors, the historical process which has consolidated caste and have lineally inherited the social attitudes relevant to caste. It is not to be assumed, however, that all of the 9,000 potential white voters do actually vote; the number who take advantage of the opportunity is probably much less. In Southerntown itself there are about 900 whites eligible to vote and 1,000 Negroes theoretically eligible to vote. The difference between the "American plan" and the southern regional pattern is nowhere seen more clearly than in the fact that only the members of the white caste can actually vote.

Who wants to vote anyway? Is it not just a boring obligation, a chance to oblige some really interested friend or to get a share in the offices or other privileges flowing from the successful party? Most people do not seem to realize that voting is a way of affecting their own real interests. Perhaps this is just as well since it seems to be dangerous to try to change the *status quo* very much by voting; the armed conflict which voting has replaced seems to reappear when voting gets serious as an instrument of social change.

The position of the Negroes in Southerntown throws an altogether new light on voting. Like many other things that we take for granted, we realize what voting means only when we miss it or see others missing it. Voting is concerned with whether the streets in a given part of town are paved and whether the town spends money for lighting these streets. Voting determines the treatment that the citizen may get from the courts. It may save him from being beaten if the police or county officers arrest him for any offense, since the voter always has in reserve the threat of helping to oust from office those who misuse him. A voter has easier access to the legal machinery, and the officers representing "the law" are more likely to listen to him; if a voter says that he did not get a correct settlement from a planter, it is a matter of public concern. It is less so in the case of a nonvoter. The voter is more likely to receive the full protection of the law in regard to the sanctity of his home and person; that is the function of peace officers, to heed the needs and wishes of those who elect them. The voters, and the successful voters of course, share in the spoils of offices; the nonvoters naturally do not. The last consideration is an important one for the middle-class Negroes who would naturally receive many elective offices if Negroes could vote. Then there is the matter of taxes which are always most discriminately levied when the voters have control of the tax levying and collecting officers. Although probably few Negroes in this county could pay formal taxes in any case, some can and do; in the case of the informal taxes which are passed on to the lower-class Negroes through the "settlement," they are, of course, as a group, the largest taxpayers; these taxes are paid in a lump sum in the form of a smaller annual income. Then there are the sales taxes which affect the lower-class group particularly and fall with disproportionate incidence on it. Those who cannot vote must accept the will of others in these matters. It does not follow from this that the Negroes receive no protection from the law, no personal respect, no paving, lighting, sewerage, and so on. But it does follow that what they get is given through the benevolence of the white group rather than through the usual coercion implied by voting. It would take an inhuman fairness on the part of administrative officers to distribute the burdens and perquisites fairly when the element of coercion by voting is lacking. Of course, no such extramundane fairness exists. The Negroes in Southerntown perceive quite clearly that voting is not merely an honorific matter; by their exclusion from it they are unable to exercise "democratic force" on the state as it affects them.

It is not true that not one single Negro is allowed to vote in Southerntown; a couple were pointed out. But it was added that these Negroes are old and well known as "good Negroes"; it does not set any bad precedent to allow them this symbolic privilege. Further, they vote only in the meaningless national elections and not in the primaries. Informants said that young Negroes are not allowed to vote since it would induce others to demand the same privilege. If a Negro is aggressive about his theoretical rights and, for example, tries to register, he may be peaceably rejected; or, on the other hand, he may be asked to leave town, "asked for his room"; or, in still other cases, an assault on him may be arranged by some (supposedly drunk) Negro or white men. It is part of the Negro's caste "place" that he does not vote and does not complain about being unable to do so.

There is, however, a substitute for voting among Negroes that is an alternative method of influencing the formal political order. A Negro may get a white "angel" or patron who will speak for him and in case of trouble protect him, even against other whites. To be truly appreciated this must be seen as a political method. An informant detailed the matter as follows: Say that a Negro gets put in jail for a minor, or even a major, crime; he calls on his white boss or protector to get him out. The white man calls up the jail and says, "What is the idea of putting one of my niggers in jail; let him out, I need him out here to pick cotton." And the jailer usually does. Needless to say, middle-class or upper-class men are the only ones who can do service to Negroes from this standpoint, since only they have the necessary access to the political machine. Negroes are said to have been known to kill other Negroes and get off without punishment when they have a white protector. This fact tends to make life more dangerous within the Negro group, since ordinary protection of the person by the state is not fully operative there. My informant gave an example of how Negroes suffer in dealing with the law as compared with white men. He said that, if a Negro is arrested, the policeman or sheriff is not beholden to him in any respect, does not fear that the prisoner's friends or relations will gang up and vote against him next election if he behaves badly toward the prisoner.

One might think to ask why the Negro vote is so much feared today. The historical answer is clear enough since the South had a really bad experience with voting by illiterate Negroes, influenced by exploitive northerners in addition. Both of these facts, however, have changed; the carpet-baggers are gone, and many Negroes are literate and responsible persons. From our standpoint there is an easy answer as to why Negroes are not allowed to vote: it would upset the present-day caste relationships and the gains dependent on them, it would damage white prestige, and it would open the door to social (sexual) equality. An intelligent white man pointed out the danger in letting Negroes vote since they are so irresponsible and could easily be bought. In this case I argued, saying there are many Negroes capable of voting by educational standards, that it is not a matter really of educational qualifications or personal fitness, but of the caste barrier. The informant responded that the number of Negroes is great, in Southerntown and county almost three out of four, and that, if they could vote, they would naturally vote for members of their own race. This would turn public administration over to the Negroes and the old and feared situation of Negro domination would be returned.[5] Where Negroes would not actually dominate, they would have a "balance of power" position that would give them undue influence. The contention that Negroes are ignorant and easily influenced is used over and over again, and the truth in it is exaggerated; not all Negroes are as ignorant as represented, nor are they all morally depraved and purchasable. There is much ridicule of these arguments among Negroes. One middle-class woman informant told of being in a class of Negro women which was addressed by a white woman. The class was gathered to consider what it could do for the cause of world peace. The teacher advised them to pray. One of the members of the class queried: Why could they not vote and directly affect the political mechanism? The white leader replied that they could not vote because the Negroes are so ignorant that white politicians would take advantage of them and buy their votes for a nickel or a dime. My informant refused to be intimidated by this argument and

[5] "The reasons for this general state of affairs were obvious. The Black Belts and the southernmost States of the South were most easily impressed with the 'Negro domination' and 'balance of power' arguments. The country districts, isolated and unprogressive, were least touched by recent developments like the interracial movement; had lost the more active and open-minded element of their white population to the cities; and had the least evidence of Negro advance in the shape of professional men, teachers, and successful business men. Negro leaders capable of openly or subtly aggressive protests also left the country." Lewinson, *op. cit.*, p. 121; quoted by permission of the Oxford University Press.

responded that there were many ignorant whites in the state who were not above the level of many Negroes either in character or education. The argument resulted in the usual stalemate, the truth being, of course, that the caste barrier is unarguable.

It has long been known that it is the race issue which keeps the South solid and it is equally appreciated that the issue is frequently dragged in by the heels in political situations where there is no actual threat from the side of the Negro.[6] At the time I was in Southerntown there was a good example of this type of behavior. Huey Long was recommending one of the candidates in a state election; the opposition forces printed pictures of Negroes balloting in Louisiana with headlines asking if the reader wanted this to happen in his state. The local white people took the matter very seriously and were much impressed by the pictures of Negroes registering to vote. One of them said that thousands of Negroes in the state belonged to Huey Long's "Share-the-Wealth" clubs and that conscientious Southerntowners could hardly vote for a man allied to Long. This informant plainly felt that Long was disloyal to southern custom. Was there a distinct absence of regret among middle-class people when the news came that Long had been killed? Evidently the pictures showing the Negroes registering were good campaign material, but it seemed very questionable that Long really stood for political equality for Negroes. A Negro informant reacting to the same situation thought it ridiculous the way the race issue had been brought into the campaign and a pity that the Negroes who cannot vote at all were being used in this way. An-

[6] "The events occurring under 'Negro domination' in the South once more obliterated class and party divisions among the whites, as the Secession crisis had done before. Furthermore, the course of 'Negro domination' left behind it a persistent spectre to be conjured up—sometimes on meagre provocation—by political and economic interests bent on preserving some advantageous *status quo*. To understand both the party solidarity of the South and its susceptibility to the Negro bogey, it is essential to realize what happened in the South from 1867 to 1876." Lewinson, *op. cit.*, p. 46; quoted by permission of the Oxford University Press.

other Negro was much worried over the use of the race issue; he felt it was stirring up race hatred and might result in further violence and even lynching of Negroes. In relation to the local political situation he also commented on the news that Ethiopia was being invaded by Italy, and agreed with Haile Selassie that, if the powers let the invasion go on, there might be another World War. He thought the darker races would sympathize with Ethiopia and the lighter races would collect around Italy. He felt also that this attack would result in increased racial tension all over the world; it was clear that he was comparing the Italian conquest of Ethiopia with the disenfranchisement of Negroes by the white caste.

As an example of how such an issue as the election appeared in the context of a Negro's life, there follows a dream of a Negro and the comments associated with it:

A Negro man from a neighboring town was being chased by a white mob and came to dreamer's house. Dreamer took him in and told him that he might remain. The man needed to be outfitted with shoes and dreamer noticed that his feet were much bigger than dreamer's; so he took a pair of his shoes and cut them out in places so that the other's big feet could get into them. Dreamer hid the man in his house.

I shall give only the recent experiences which contributed to this dream. It was quite plainly a response to the Negro's fear as a result of the local election campaign which had raised the race issue that is always so threatening to Negroes. Informant said that he had the dream just after election day and that the newspapers were bringing in the race issue more strongly in this contest than they had since reconstruction days. A newspaper had printed the picture of the very Negro friend who appeared in the dream; the accompanying text explained that he was a leader of one of Huey Long's "Share-the-Wealth" clubs for Negroes. He was therefore, for the moment, a marked man, one who had threatened to participate politically by joining a Long club. Informant said that in actual life, as in the dream, he would have taken the man in if he had been pursued by whites. Of course, he was not certain that his Negro friend had not consented to have his name and picture used on the understanding that local whites would not revenge themselves by taking his job away. The picture would be useful to at least one faction of local white Democrats who could be expected to protect the Negro. If this were not the case, they would certainly punish him.

Inquiry was made as to the feeling tone in the dream about the fugitive. The dreamer responded that he was hiding the man at some risk to himself; he was willing to do so because it was not a crime to belong to a "Share-the-Wealth" club. If the fugitive had been a real criminal, the informant himself would have arrested him. For example, there was a Negro criminal who was recently shot in a near-by town. The dreamer would not have taken that man into his house but might have helped him by giving him directions, food, or water, if he had asked for them. He would do this because there was no chance of an orderly trial for Negroes. If Negroes fell into the hands of a white mob, the mob would at least shoot them, possibly mutilate or maim them. Since this was the case, the only thing that Negroes could do was to stand together. Just picture, he said, a mob of five hundred Negroes chasing a white man and determined to deal with him on the spot. He believed that whites under such circumstances would stand together, if there was no hope of a fair trial. It is evident that an anxiety process of considerable strength had been set off in this Negro by raising the threatening race issue in politics; he responded to the threat by affirming his solidarity with Negroes. Much more might be said about this dream, but it is utilized here to show how attitudes are mobilized in the face of changing real situations. The social and political events in Southerntown were constantly echoing in this way through the dreams, fantasies, and daily behavior of Negroes. In this instance, the race issue in politics suddenly made the world seem more threatening to the dreamer.

Another Negro, in a bitter mood, commented on the use of the race issue in politics. He said that formerly one of the best ways for a politician to get notoriety was to kill a Negro; such an act would speed him on the way to getting office and reveal that his sentiments on the race question were sound. Certainly if a politician can be shown to be anything but orthodox on this question, his political chances are small. One local politician sued a newspaper for a large sum because it had printed his name between the names of two Negro lawyers and had not explicitly stated that he was not a Negro. When we remember the nature of caste sentiments and the lower-caste role of the Negro, we shall find his indignation readily intelligible.

With reference to voting it is well to remember that in our democracy all officeholders are transient embodiments of the state. Their business, first and foremost is to serve those who elected them and in most cases to get reëlected. During the period of my research in Southerntown a political campaign occurred which offered me an opportunity to hear political speeches and to participate in the energetic discussions and emotions that attended it. When one sees with what anxiety nominees campaign for office and how they test out every possible source of votes, it is not surprising that once in office they very carefully represent prevailing white viewpoints on all caste issues. Naturally they dare not take any independent or suspicious stand on any racial question, no matter how much the merits of the case may diverge from the stereotyped view. Elected officers are keenly responsive to the sentiments of the white caste; indeed the lives and economic welfare of their own families are involved in rigidly accepting them. The smallest actions which might indicate pro-Negro sentiment are noted and may become powerful arguments in an election year. Many other considerations figure in the election, of course, such as religion, class position, the personal life of the candidate, his fitness for office, sentimental factors, and so on. On election night the streets were full of white people and they seemed to be people from the county as well as from Southerntown. A good many of them were celebrationally drunk. They gathered in the offices of friends who were up for election and stood around while the returns came in. There were very few Negroes on the streets; there was no reason for them to be downtown since they had only indirect stakes in the election.

In recent years, especially during the time of Negro migration to northern cities, the group of lower-class white people in the county has grown. They were imported from elsewhere in the state to replace migrant Negro laborers and possibly also to serve in competition with those who remained. A number of middle-class people deplored the influence of these voters on political affairs, called attention to their ignorance and to the fact that unscrupulous office-holders rushed them into the status of voters. Frequently the poll taxes would be paid for them by one or the other of the factions in the local Democratic party. It is well worth noticing these voters because they are the local contingent of that great group of propertyless southern white people who support leaders like Huey Long. Their socio-economic position is weak, they are at the bottom of the status scale in the white caste, but they have the consolation of "at least being white," and they get an experience of social equality through the electoral process; if at no other time of the year, they can slap middle-class politicians on the back and call them by their first names at political rallies and barbecues. When we remember that the census shows over 80 percent of the people of this state to be rural, we can guess that the typical politician is a friend of the farmer and, of course, of the poor white farmer.

One wonders what would happen in the United States if the "taxpayers" in the northern states were as oppressively taxed as are the people in this state and county. The ratio[7] of direct taxes to value of land and buildings is relatively high for farms operated by full owners. To be sure, much of this taxation is passed on to the tenant farmer. This is shown by the fact that the hard conditions of life for tenants are frequently justified by owners on the ground that they have to pay the taxes. There is a high state gasoline tax and, in addition to that, more recently, a sales tax. A further item which tends to bear out the severity of taxation in the state is that it is among the group of states which relies most heavily on federal contributions to relief. Heavy taxation, of course, tends to throw voting and political par-

---

[7] Howard W. Odum, *Southern Regions of the United States* (Chapel Hill, 1936).

ticipation into increased prominence and we may be sure that directly or indirectly the Negroes are heavy contributors to the tax funds; their complaint in this respect is the historic one of "taxation without representation."

In conclusion we might take a look at the legislature[8] of the state as it appeared in a recent year. It included, of course, no Negroes, but several women; the average age was rather younger than that in neighboring states. Most of the members were born in the state and five sevenths came from rural districts. Most of the rest came from urban districts under 40,000 population. About 10 percent had seen war service, 92 percent were members of secret orders, and 90 percent were church members. None were college trained. A little under one third were lawyers, about 15 percent were farmers or planters, a similar percentage were businessmen; only a few came from laboring groups. It is this legislature which is the general trustee for the political interests of the people of Southerntown; it arises out of their pattern of life and in turn influences it again. The legislature is obviously dominated by rural, white, religious, middle-class people. Evidently our finding as to the significant rôle played by the middle class in Southerntown has value for the state as well.

[8] *Ibid.*

CHAPTER XI

Caste Patterning of Religion

⋙⋙⋙⋙⋙⋙⋙⋙⋙⋙⋙⋙⋙⋙⋙⋙⋙⋙⋙⋙⋙⋙

On Sunday morning Southerntown is in a dream waiting for church. Presently on the white side of town cars begin to cluster around the two large churches, Baptist and Methodist. Through the open windows the voices of the congregation float out. The churches will be filled, with white people of course, for the caste line applies to religion too. The main features of the service are, as usual, the singing, the collection, and the sermon. The latter is customarily addressed to the personal sinfulness of the members and does not deal with current social issues. The northerner notices with a little surprise the vehemence of the preaching and the gestures. The white minister does not mind stirring his audience if he can; but by comparison with the lower-class churches it is a tame business. Nevertheless more freedom of expression is permitted in preaching than is usual in Northern Protestant churches. Those who attend in Southerntown are almost exclusively the middle-class white people. Politicians, of course, find it convenient to appear at churches regularly and conspicuously, as do businessmen and others dependent on community sentiment; perhaps most of them really want to.

About the lower-class white churches I have only the vaguest impressions. The attendants in this county are mainly rural people and they make more of a day of it than do the middle-class urban group to whom church-going is only one of the events of Sunday. Lower-class ministers preach with apostolic passion, attempting to stir their audiences to genuine personal remorse and to give them a thrilling emotional experience. As in the middle-class groups the type of appeal seems to be quite remote from any here-and-now interests, except those involved in the guilt of the parishioners over breaking various commandments and rules of the church, relevant, to be sure, when one accepts these strictures as guides to behavior.

Christian belief is a very lively pattern in this area; nationally symbolic personages must always remember that they are speaking to these people as well as the religiously less committed urban populations and should be careful to cast their public utterance in a form that is intelligible in Southerntown. The power of the religious institution in public life was brought sharply home to me one day when I called upon an official in the State Department of Education. It was about eleven-thirty of a Monday morning and it became apparent that I had reached my friend's office just at the hour when a prayer meeting was to be held. I was, of course, invited to stay. The meeting was attended by all available persons in the offices. My host was a bit shamefaced about it, but nevertheless conducted the service himself. We sang a hymn, all four verses, heard a reading from the scriptures and a five-minute talk on the lesson. The little sermon was thoroughly religious in spirit, postulated absolutely the personal existence of God, and was on the theme of freely loving your neighbor. It was said that this prayer service pattern has been going on in the department for eleven years and all the leaders are expected, though not required, to attend; legally, of course, church and state are separate institutions. Politicians in Southerntown do well to know their Bible and to salt their speeches with references to it.

A lower-class white farmer told me about the revivals in his community, one of which had just occurred. He preferred to have the local preacher conduct the revival because those who came out of curiosity might be attracted by the permanent minister and stay on after the revival; whereas if an outside preacher, such as Brother Smith, held the service, people would attend while he was there and drop out after he left. He said he "glorified" in the work of the revivalists. They meet twice a day and have two sermons, one in the morning and another in the evening, or one in the afternoon and one in the evening. Revivals are said to do much for the moral tone of the community. A number of white informants affirmed likewise that the church performs a very valuable service by keeping up the morals of the people, which are always to be suspected without this aid.

It must be remembered that the church has been a mighty influence in inducting the Negroes into American society. The basic conceptions of a culture seem to be carried by any of its major institutions and the church is no exception. For example, the democratic idea is implied, probably foreshadowed, in the religious doctrine that all Christians are equal in the sight of God; social mobility, so important in our society, may be prefigured in the religious doctrine of winning salvation and merit in the heavenly world by doing good works in this one.[1] Apart from these leading conceptions, the Negro's knowledge of our language was undoubtedly greatly improved by his religious participation since the ministers who came to preach to him were among the most literate men of the time. That this ever-fuller participation of the Negroes in our society might some day be regretted did not everywhere escape actual record; there was some vigorous initial opposition in the English colonies to the conversion of the Negroes at all, and just on the ground that religious education would make slaves intractable.[2] There was apparently a similar trend of

[1] Max Weber, *The Protestant Ethic* (translated by Talcott Parsons; London, 1930), p. 108.

[2] "An item significant of their attitude upon race relationships is the following from the journal of the Crown's committee of trade and plantations, Oct. 8, 1680: 'The gentlemen of Barbados attend, . . . who declare that the conversion of their slaves to Christianity would not only destroy their property but endanger the island, inasmuch as converted negroes grow more perverse and intractable than others, and hence of less value for labour or sale. The disproportion of blacks to white being great, the whites have no greater security than the diversity of the negroes' languages, which would be destroyed by conversion in that it would be necessary to teach them all English. The Negroes are a sort of people so averse to learning that they will rather hang themselves or run away than submit to it.' The Lords of Trade were enough impressed by this argument to resolve that the question be left to the Barbadian government." U. B. Phillips, *American Negro Slavery* (New

feeling in the American colonies since slaveowners perceived, perhaps not very clearly but nevertheless vigorously, that according Negroes equal access to our religious ideas and ideals would pave the way for subsequent demands in other spheres.[3] At first Negroes attended white religious meetings and churches where the caste line was preserved by segregating them in a part of the church or at the outskirts of the revival crowd. Later, in the first quarter of the nineteenth century, the necessity for a stricter exclusion of Negroes from participation with whites in religious exercises led to the organization of separate Negro churches and religious institutions.[4]

The Negro churches have grown greatly in the last century and have operated separately from those of the white group. They provide the best example of bi-racialism, that is, of a social order divided in all its functions along caste

York, 1918), p. 48; quoted by permission of D. Appleton-Century Co.

[3] "At first the whites had seriously objected to the evangelization of the Negroes, feeling that they could not be saved and, when the latter had been convinced of this error, many of them were far from the position of conceding to the blacks equality in their church organizations. Negroes in certain parts, however, were at first accepted in the congregations with the whites and accorded equal privileges. During the American Revolution when there was a tendency to give more consideration to all persons suffering from restriction, this freedom was enlarged. After the reaction following the American Revolution when men ceased to think so much of individual or natural rights and thought more frequently of means and measures for centralized government, the Negroes, like most elements far down, were forgotten or ignored even by the church. In this atmosphere of superimposed religious instruction the Negro was called upon merely to heed the Word and live." C. G. Woodson, *The History of the Negro Church* (Washington, 1921), pp. 71-72; quoted by permission of the Associated Publishers.

[4] "Complete separation of the Negro Baptists in this church was, therefore, deemed a necessity during the first quarter of the nineteenth century when there was an increasing prejudice against free persons of color because of the rapid migration of freedmen from the South to Pennsylvania." Woodson, *op. cit.*, p. 87; quoted by permission of the Associated Publishers.

lines. They provide also a splendid opportunity for the social and political training of Negroes; and in fact, a corps of Negro speakers, executives, planners, and leaders has been developed around the church. It does not matter that up to the present time they have done little leading outside the religious field; what is important is the sociological asset of the trained personnel. We have already noted that religious leadership is one of the primary activities of the Negro middle-class group, although it should be emphasized here that not all Negro ministers are middle-class persons, as one could expect in northern white churches. In the church a Negro has the opportunity for complete individuation without the wounding comparison with white achievement to stir feelings of inadequacy. Humble people receive opportunities for valuable self-expression and are allowed, along truly democratic lines, to develop their talents competitively.[5] This state of affairs is no less true of Southerntown than of the history of southern Negro churches as a whole.

It is impossible to say from census materials what percentage of Negroes and whites are members of religious bodies in our county. We do know for the state[6] that about half the adult Negroes are church members and of these, four fifths are Baptists. We do not know how far these pro-

[5] "The opportunity found in the Negro church to be recognized, and to be 'somebody,' has stimulated the pride and preserved the self-respect of many Negroes who would have been entirely beaten by life, and possibly completely submerged. Everyone wants to receive recognition and feel that he is appreciated. The Negro church has supplied this need. A truck driver of average or more than ordinary qualities becomes the chairman of the Deacon Board. A hotel man of some ability is the superintendent of the Sunday church school of a rather important church. A woman who would hardly be noticed, socially or otherwise, becomes a leading woman in the missionary society. A girl of little training and less opportunity for training gets the chance to become the leading soprano in the choir of a great church. These people receive little or no recognition on their daily jobs." Benjamin E. Mays and Joseph W. Nicholson, *The Negro's Church* (New York, 1933), p. 281; quoted by permission of Harper & Bros.

[6] Howard W. Odum, *Southern Regions of the United States* (Chapel Hill, 1936).

portions hold for Southerntown and county but Southerntowners say that if a Negro is not a Baptist someone has
been tampering with him. Apparently the Baptists and
Methodists were most energetic in their early measures to
capture Negro allegiance by means of their itinerant preachers.[7] Furthermore, the religious behavior of these denom-
inations was less formalized and stereotyped than that of
the Presbyterian or Episcopal churches, and the evangelical
mode of preaching seemed to have a spontaneous appeal
to the Negroes;[8] perhaps they were disposed toward emotionally toned group meetings by their African background.
They seemed to have a marked selectivity for the tensity
and emotionalism of the Baptist and Methodist preaching,
and it is competently held that they introduced African
patterns in modifying the Baptist form of Christianity in
their own churches.[9] These religious exercises of the Ne-

[7] "Wherever the Presbyterians had the opportunity for prose-
lyting the Negroes they usually embraced it. Yet there were
hardly 20,000 Negroes in the Presbyterian church prior to the
Civil War. One of the important reasons is that the Methodists and Baptists were the first to reach the Negro. The
Methodists, moreover, had an itinerant system serving like
scouts to go out into the wilderness to find the people and
bring them in. Then this disinclination was due also to the
fact that the Presbyterian church, somewhat like the more
aristocratic churches, disregarded the 'emotional character of
experimental religion.' Its appeal was too intellectual." Woodson, *op. cit.*, p. 97; quoted by permission of the Associated
Publishers.

[8] "The Negroes in these meetings appealed especially to the
white ministers because of their quick response to the appeal
to come out of darkness into light. While an Episcopal clergy-
man with his ritual and prayer book had difficulty in interesting the Negroes, they flocked in large numbers to the spontaneous exercises of the Methodists and Baptists, who, being
decidedly evangelical in their preaching, had a sort of hypno-
tizing effect upon the Negroes, causing them to be seized with
certain emotional jerks and outward expressions of an inward
movement of the spirit which made them lose control of themselves." Woodson, *op. cit.*, p. 143; quoted by permission of the
Associated Publishers.

[9] "Negroes in the United States are Christians, yet it is possible to see among certain groups of them expressions of
Christian worship that are unknown in Europe. The songs of

groes, especially at the revival meetings where they are most arresting, have been described frequently. Readers will notice in the following descriptions some of the elements which Herskovits has indicated are likely to be African importations and modifications of the Baptist ritual. The Negro revival service is emotionalized to an extent hardly credible to the average churchgoer of the North or to anyone familiar with the heavily ritualized churches of Rome or England. Both preacher and audience play extraordinarily expressive rôles and the opportunities for emotional release are unusual. The description of the revival ceremonial is of great importance since it is one of the most expressive of lower-class Negro patterns and one which doubtless helps to make life tolerable for them.

Here follows an account of a revival meeting which happened to be particularly stirring. The group was singing vigorously but not especially harmoniously when we entered the church and sat down on the back benches. The men were seated on the left and the women on the right. In the front and center was an open square facing the pulpit, and along the side nearest the congregation was the "mourner's bench." There were three or four little boys on it on the men's side and five or six little girls on the women's side. The preacher, a very confident-looking young man, was sit-

---

the American Negroes—the spirituals—have long been thought of as African, though there are many today who hold that these are merely borrowings of well-known European hymns. Whether or not these represent in their imagery simply borrowings, or have taken on 'accretions,' the place of the song in the religious service, and its accompaniment by hand-clapping, tapping the feet, the instruments of percussion such as the tambourine, do not partake of European religious cultural behavior. Spirit possession (by the Holy Ghost) manifested through dances—'shouts'—in which the motor behavior is clearly African, is found in some Negro churches, while among these 'shouting' sects the communion service partakes largely, in both psychological implications and outward ritual, of very different elements than are found to mark the corresponding rite in white churches." M. J. Herskovits, "Social History of the Negro," *Handbook of Social Psychology* (edited by C. Murchison, 1935), pp. 254-255; quoted by permission of the Clark University Press.

ting on a chair on the platform. Shortly after we came in, the singing died down and he advanced to the table, calling out in a leading voice the song, "Have you got good religion?" and the audience answered, "Certainly, certainly, certainly, Lord." They sang this spiritual together.

The preacher then started by reading a part of the scripture, with the text "The joy of our heart is ceased; our dance is turned into mourning." From this he went on to the story of "Norah" and the "Nark." He spoke vividly, starting peacefully in a calm and quiet voice and working up gradually until he was practically chanting his words, clapping his hands, and stamping his feet. He described the flood, told how God selected Norah as a just man and a good carpenter and gave him specifications for the Nark and meanwhile the people were dancing and giving in marriage. Norah kept on building the Nark and God decided, once it was finished, to lock the door and pin down the windows himself, because he was afraid that Norah would not be able to withstand the pleas of his fellowmen once they began to drown. God then loosened the springs of the earth and the water rose waist-deep. God opened the heavens and the waters rose to the first story. The people kept on marrying and dancing and giving in marriage. Then Norah called all the "beasties" of the earth, pair by pair, and the elephants came and the fierce lions of the jungle and all the animals. Then the water rose to the second story and still the people kept on dancing and giving in marriage. Then the water rose to the third story. At this point God himself locked the door to the Nark and pinned down the windows. People began falling off the housetops, mothers with their children in their arms crying out for Norah to save them. The water got so deep that people were hanging on the tree tops and one by one being hurled into the water, all hollering for help from Norah, as long as they could holler at all. But Norah could not help them because God had locked the door and taken the key and pinned down the windows. The preacher was getting more and more excited, and at this point he came down from the preaching stand into the square between the men and women and the mourners. He addressed himself to the boys and girls. It became more and more difficult to understand him as he intoned phrases, clapped his hands, and stamped his feet. During all this time, from the first of the sermon, the congregation was responding. One massive Negro kept saying "Well?" at various points; others punctuated the sermon with "Amen," "Yes, Lord," "Isn't that true?" "Sho 'nuff," and other expressions. At the point when the Nark was floating free and the people were drowning, a sister jumped up, flung her arms out in a stiff wild gesture, let her head fall back, and swayed but made no sound. Immediately a group of women tended her. She began moaning in a low voice and throwing herself about. She was really dangerous to herself and others as once she struck a kerosene lamp swinging from the ceiling. Finally they got her back to her seat and as she quieted down she sat with her head bent low, still mumbling and moaning. Suddenly the preacher stopped preaching and the church officers knelt at the center of the square and began to pray. The first was the massive Negro who had kept saying "Well?" He testified his faith in religion, probably as an example to the young mourners.[10] Then a sister began to pray, becoming more and more hysterical as she did, and finally bending back and flinging up her arms and beginning to shout and sob. Again the women gathered around and carried her tense, straight body to the back of the women's side of the church.[11] Then another of the men prayed,

[10] Mourners are those who are mourning for their sins, who expect to have or have had a verifying experience and who will shortly be baptized and inducted into the church.

[11] Miss Helen Watson, my research assistant, who was present at this meeting, happened to be outside when this sister began to shout. Miss Watson reports: "At the time when the sister who shouted became hysterical I left the church and stood under the window near which they were bringing her to. They were fanning her, patting her, and repeating, 'Wake up, Mandy, wake up now.' In five minutes or so she had recovered and gone back to her seat in the front of the church." Miss Watson says further: "This was a stirring emotional experience and I can easily see how the Negroes become hysterical. At times when the singing became very loud and the rhythm sharply marked with clapping and stamping, I was carried away by it myself. After all this strong emotional

evidently a church leader. In the meantime songs were sung and led by various men. Often the words of these songs were not understandable, but a tremendous volume of somewhat discordant sound was let loose. Evidently when the singing is impromptu, it is more likely to be noisy and discordant; when it is a well-practiced spiritual it is likely to be better. After the testifying phase was over, the preacher came and addressed the boys and girls; finally one of each came up and sat down on a chair before him. The preacher asked the boy if he had religion. He answered that he did. The preacher said, "M-m" in a friendly manner, which seemed surprisingly off-hand. Then he asked the boy's name and what he had to say to the congregation. The boy stood up, said he had had a change in his heart, then began to babble that he was so glad, so glad, so glad, so glad; his face seemed transfigured and joyful. The preacher turned to the girl and asked her name and again said, "M-m." She also answered that she had religion. He asked her if it had happened this evening or during the day. She said during the day she learned she had it. The little girl was very shy and had no more to say than this. The preacher commented, to comfort her, that that was all any of them could say really, that they "had it." The deacon took a vote on each case separately, asked the congregation if after baptism this person would be accepted as a full-breasted member of the Calvary Baptist Church.[12] The congregation voted "yes" in each case. The boy was then led to the deacon's row on the men's side by one of the deacons and the girl was led to the grown women's side. Thereafter the deacon turned and addressed the remaining boys and girls who had not been able to testify and began singing a spiritual to them very softly, in which the rest of the congregation joined, also softly. It was in effect that "You got to get religion while the blood runs warm in your veins." He told the youngsters in a kindly way that he was going to let them go tonight, but he hoped they would

---

preaching, singing, and praying, the singing of the last spiritual so softly was doubly impressive."

[12] Not the name of the church, nor a reference to any church of that name.

come back tomorrow, that they could all get religion and that, if necessary, they should just stand up and say so, as the little girl had done (by which he meant that they did not have to have any elaborate experience). His voice was very tender and friendly as he talked to the children. Then the deacon said he saw some "white friends" in the back of the church and asked if we wanted to say something. We thanked them for being able to join in the exercises and said that we considered it a real religious and spiritual experience. The deacon exhorted the audience particularly to come to the Friday meeting and to come with some contribution for the preacher, saying "We don't want to let him pay for his own gasoline, do we?"

It seems indubitable that there are aspects of this experience which did not originate in the religious history or psychology of Western Europe. It seemed clear also that the separation of men and women is functional in the church; the orgastic excitement developed during the shouting might lead to personal entanglements if the men were to take care of the shouting women. If one were to judge by the mourners who were present that night, it would seem that this is a rite having primarily to do with adolescent children. All the mourners were of this age. The whole point of the service seemed to be to induce the younger people to seek membership in the church. Once membership is accepted the child is led to the adult section as if he were now regarded as a grown person; though, as we learned later, if a sinner falls from grace, he may have to be reconverted.

The reader can form his own judgments of the effectiveness of the sermon. It is, of course paraphrased, but certainly not in such a way as to make it more effective than it was when delivered. After the meeting we talked with the preacher and found him to be a tenant on a plantation some miles away, a typical lower-class Negro worker. His control of English, of course, was nothing like perfect, although it was germane and powerful. I marveled that he could have invented such a sermon and suspected that possibly he had learned the main organization of it from someone else. Johnson has indicated that stereotyped sermons are relatively common among Negro preachers, which tends to bear out my suspicion.[13]

The next morning I attended the day revival service at the church reported on above. The scene was quite different. There was one man and about a dozen women there, one little male mourner and four females. The deacon, who was the man present, read a text from the Bible; then the adults began a chanting type of antiphonal song where one member announced a phrase and the others repeated it in a rising and falling unmelodious bellowing. The person who had initiated the phrase went to pray before the others in the center of the church. While the supplicant was chanting his imperfect (but conventionalized) prayer, the other sisters were moaning and singing as almost to drown out his voice. This was still going on when I had to leave. No one had hysterics this morning (i.e., there was no "shouting"), perhaps for the lack of the precipitating sermon and the authoritative preacher. Incidentally, the church service, set for eleven o'clock, opened at eleven forty-five. The chapel bell was tolled at eleven fifteen to announce it.

Here is another brief account of the last session of a revival meeting in another church. It was an evening meeting

[13] "I remember hearing in my boyhood sermons that were current, sermons that passed with only slight modifications from preacher to preacher and from locality to locality. Such sermons were, 'The Valley of Dry Bones,' which was based on the vision of the prophet in the 37th chapter of Ezekiel; the 'Train Sermon,' in which both God and the devil were pictured as running trains, one loaded with saints, that pulled up in heaven, and the other with sinners, that dumped its load in hell; the 'Heavenly March,' which gave in detail the journey to the faithful from earth, on up through the pearly gates to the great white throne. Then there was a stereotyped sermon which had no definite subject, and which was quite generally preached; it began with the Creation, went on to the fall of man, rambled through the trials and tribulations of the Hebrew Children, came down to the redemption by Christ, and ended with the Judgment Day and a warning and an exhortation to sinners. This was the framework of a sermon that allowed the individual preacher the widest latitude that could be desired for all his arts and powers." J. W. Johnson, *God's Trombones* (New York, 1927), pp. 1-2; quoted by permission of the Viking Press.

in a small wooden church in the country with about one hundred and fifty people of all ages present, a good many men, mothers with small children, small girls and boys, post-adolescents. Overhead were swinging oil lamps. They were singing when we went in and took our seats in the rear. The preacher was leading, catching up the words when the various phrases ended, beginning the new lines. This repetitive singing continued for fifteen or twenty minutes, apparently warming the audience up. It was fairly harmonious but more in the nature of a chorus all singing the melody, than of part singing. The audience was composed largely of rather dark persons, evidently "croppers" from the neighboring plantations. The preacher began his sermon, then interrupted himself for the collection. It was taken at the front of the church, people coming forward with their gifts. One heard a steady murmur of "thank yous" from the collector to the contributors. The preacher then continued his sermon. It was the story of a murderer whose punishment was to have the body of the murdered strapped to him, foot to foot, knee to knee, nose to nose, and eye to eye, and to be put on a vacant island. Between this island and the mainland was a perilous stretch of water full of dangerous animals. No one took pity on the murderer, except, finally, his mother. Her journey across the channel was described and all the risks she took to rescue him. Her first act was to unstrap the dead man he had been carrying. "We all have that corpse tied to us," said the preacher, "the corpse is our sins which come to follow us in just the form we have committed them. We have an account with God. Is it settled?" And analogies were made to the accounts members have with the stores in Southerntown. The preacher moved through the range of speaking in an ordinary voice, through heightened emotion and passion, to a veritable chanting at the end, preaching as if singing. There were frequent "Amens," "That's right," "Preach good tonight," and so on. Very stirring were the currents of song that surged up while the preacher was speaking, rising at one side of the hall and threatening to drown his voice, dying away and surging up again; this song was a constant low undertone during the service. There were four or five young girls with headbands marked U S H E R; they aided in seating people and also held and fanned the shouters. There were two of the latter who, toward the end of the service when excitement was highest, gave piercing screams, stood up, and threw their arms up and outward. The persons nearest seized them, and the ushers ran to them. The second shouter, her face contorted, cried, "Hold me, hold me!" The preacher's talk was not connected logically, but it was continuous and fluent. There were frequent introductions of biblical phrases out of context, such as "Come unto Me all ye who are heavy laden,"—such phrases elicit the "Yes, Lords" especially. There was effective use of simple metaphors, such as that of the master and slave,— Christ is the master and you the slave, he frees you from sin as the master freed his slaves, he settles an account not his.

The interaction between the preacher and the audience is very simple and dramatic, and some of the orator's tricks are extremely impressive. One such is the following: At a meeting the preacher stood up and very calmly put his coat on backwards; then he asked the audience if it was on straight. They were amused and answered "No." Then he asked them what he should do to get it on right and they told him, movement by movement: pull out the left arm, pull out the right arm, and so on. He followed instructions and under their persistent direction took it off and put it on right. During all these actions he moved slowly and with dignity and asked questions as he went along, requesting guidance at every turn. When they answered that his coat was on straight he went on and made his point: some people think that they have salvation but do not realize that they have made a mistake; they are really not saved, but just deluded. Quite regularly there is the element of rejoicing that the group is "saved" and that they have been preserved from sin. One preacher, after such rejoicing, said at the outset of the sermon that he was the brother of Jesus, and the son of God, but no relation to the devil; if any of the congregation were related to the devil, they were not related to him. He had a boy read from the Bible and several times turned to this boy and asked him to look up texts, saying, for example, "Find me the fifth chapter of Lamentations." Sins that he enumerated as particularly to be avoided were lying and "coming out of a neighbor's house." His great point was the difference between being converted, which might be to any belief, even a wrong one, and being saved, which meant to his belief. On one occasion I heard humor used in a sermon—a rare thing. It happened this way: The revivalist had done his best to arouse the congregation, but no one shouted and no one came forward to confess religion. In this emergency the preacher had to beat a retreat and he did it by lightening the tone of the meeting. He told several humorous anecdotes, joked with the congregation, and actually made them laugh. It was, of course, an atypical performance.

One series of revival meetings differed somewhat from the regular practice in the Negro churches and I shall describe in part the meetings of this sect. The first item at one meeting was the singing of a hymn, something on the lines of "I've got Jesus." Next all the members turned and dropped on their knees with faces toward the backs of the chairs. Then there was a kind of intoning or singing in which one after another of the sectarians took the lead. It was something between an intoning, a prayer, and a song. A leading voice would take up the theme, saying "Jesus, my savior," or "Hallelujah," or "We thank him for the rising and the setting of the sun," or "He is in my arms." The rest of the group would repeat the phrase, drawing it out and singing it, this time in very good part singing. A number of younger members were posted near various sisters who were apparently expected to become emotionally excited, and would fan and talk to them, sometimes anticipating the actual shouting. Apparently each of the kneeling members took the lead once in the intoning and the others joined in a kind of choral response, repeating in part harmony, "He is in my arms," or "Hallelujah." One young man in the singing group, apparently an acolyte of the minister, beat a tambourine which gave a jingly rhythm to the singing. The singers in this case were obviously a practiced group; I noticed that they came most regularly to the meetings. After this ceremony the preacher began. On one occasion in the same sect the meeting began with testimony. Various of the members stood up and told how they had been saved, on what day, and how grateful they were. Each went through a little pattern, for the testimony is highly conventional, with many "Amens" and "Thank Gods" from other members. The opportunity to testify in public and hold the lime-light is evidently an expected and much-appreciated privilege for the audience. When the preacher wanted to omit it the next night, he made a lengthy point of asking permission since the time was needed for other parts of the service. Most of the sectarians in this church are women; certain men do come but usually sit back in the shadows. The singing is markedly better than that in the generality of rural churches.

During the collection frequent calls may be made by the chief collector, as for two more cents, three more cents, and so on. On one occasion a collection was being taken up for Elder So-and-so, a church officer who had become ill and had to go to a sanitarium to recover his health. The preacher asked who "loved the elder a dime's worth." After much exhortation fifty-five cents was accumulated, whereas the congregation was responsible for raising a dollar. White visitors are allowed but by no means coerced to contribute; they usually do because there is such a good chance of being significantly benevolent at a small expense from the white man's standpoint. Once I gave a half dollar. It was immediately announced by the collector that the "white gentleman" had contributed fifty of the ninety-five cents so far raised. Then a request was made for the members to give whatever small change they happened to have. Fishing in my pocket I found thirteen cents and complied with elder's request. He thereupon announced with great appreciation that the "white gentleman" had increased his contribution to the total of sixty-three cents. One cannot run a church without money and, if there are any who get their money's worth from the churches, it must be the lower-class southern Negro group.

In view of the daily behavior patterns of lower-class Negro people, the sins which are denounced in church are very interesting. They are, of course, the traditional sins of Baptists and Methodists—breaking Sabbath by games or sports, playing cards, dancing, gambling, and the like. The most significant breaches of the mores, at least from the white standpoint, are not conspicuously denounced in the churches, although one hears an occasional allusion to them, such as the "coming out of the neighbor's house" already referred to. Middle-class whites and Negroes frequently ridicule the lower-class people on this score and point out by how far theological denunciation misses the mark of sinful daily behavior. A middle-class Negro denied that the condemned dancing and card playing were actually so bad, but pointed out at the same time that the preacher would not excoriate the adulterer and the murderer. Another said that he did some of the things which the church calls sinful, but that to him the greatest sin was lying which he thinks worse even than immorality, though that is bad enough. If anyone lies to him, he can never trust that person again. This does not mean, of course, that there is not some condemnation in the lower-class Negro group of drunkenness, adultery, and violent acts toward others; there is, but they are not preferred subjects for denunciation by the minister. We will find that in many other respects the Negro church in Southerntown tends to avoid the reality of current social life.

Following the revival meeting, testimony, and induction into the church, comes, for the new member, the baptizing, a feature of the widespread Baptist ritual. I saw such an event one bright Sunday morning, which had called religious Negroes, and families and friends of the baptized, from a wide area. A crowd of Negroes, eight or ten deep, stood along the bank at a bend in the Pine River. Over their heads one could see the water and in it were four or five men standing waist-deep. They had on a kind of white, shirt-like garment over their regular clothes and white headpieces with four knotted corners. Each of these men was apparently a church official. Those to be baptized were standing on the shore, also specially dressed, and were convoyed to the baptizers by men on the shore, three at a time. First one of the preachers in the water made a loose but impassioned speech, in which the Pine River was often compared to the River Jordan. He indicated the unusual character of the ceremony and worked the audience up to enthusiastic participation. Then two men seized each person to be baptized, held his arms, and clapped a hand over his mouth and nose. One of the baptizers intoned, "In the name of the Father—of the Son—and of the Holy Ghost." The baptizee was firmly ducked backward into the water and completely immersed, then promptly brought up again. Most of those baptized took it calmly, but some were frightened and screamed, especially the little girls. A woman on the bank, evidently someone's relative, screamed and began flinging out her arms and reaching into the air. She was hastily attended by a group of those near her who held her and began to fan her. After her peak of emotion was reached, she continued to bubble in the crowd, occasionally raising her arms. In the early part of the ceremony the introductory speeches were long; later, and after a number of the baptized came up on the bank shrieking, the rest were done swiftly and without speeches. If a person came out of the water raving, a song would often be started to cover the disturbance. People in the crowd kept recognizing those being baptized and would say, "That is Bill So-and-so." Most of the participants were adolescents; only a few were older people. The crowd came to the baptizing either in wagons or in old junks of automobiles, cars with one headlight and no spare tire.

The baptizing next recorded[14] took place on another Sunday beside another stream. There were "thirty head" to be baptized. The watchers were standing on the shore and the preacher came down, followed by the thirty all dressed in long white cotton robes with their heads tied in white kerchiefs. It was difficult to tell men from women. The deacon, dressed in a black robe and black "tam-o-shanter," saw the visitors, and came over, saying he wanted the white folks to get down to the water's edge where they could see the whole baptizing. Then the preacher, dressed in a long blue robe, and the deacon led the procession into the water; they walked in about waist-deep, formed a semicircle, and

[14] Observed and recorded by Miss Helen Watson.

all joined hands. As they walked in, they were singing a spiritual but the words were not clear. A man on the shore started praying. One large man in the water—not a mourner —kept jovially shouting, "Come on, help him to pray good!" Then they started the baptizing. The mourner stood between the preacher and the deacon. The preacher told his name and how he had gotten religion, and then orated for a while, ending up with, "I baptize you in the name of the Lord." After that he took charge of the mourner and carried or helped him back to the shore, where he was covered with a blanket or towel and rejoined his family. Several as they came out of the water screamed, "Thank you, Jesus," "Hallelujah," or "Oh, Lord, I'm saved," and several on the shore would shout and carry on. Apparently the parents or family of the one being baptized did most of the shouting; perhaps they were overjoyed by the certainty of being united with their loved one beyond the grave. The preacher, in his talk as he baptized, repeated, "The water is a witness," "The heavens are a witness." Once he remarked that every time he baptized someone, he knew everyone on the shore wanted to jump right in and be baptized too. This drew a long and loud response from the audience. The whole atmosphere of the rite seemed to be jovial and happy; the onlookers were all amused and laughed a good deal, but it was probably because of the "great occasion" and the thrill of having the family and friends "get religion," rather than because they regarded it as a show. After the baptizing they returned to the church and presumably spent most of the day there. More than half the mourners were adults; only some six or eight of them were adolescents. Perhaps the adults had had religion, lost it, and found it again.

It would be a gross misunderstanding to assume that the behavior of the participants is "put on" or artificially staged. It is evidently seriously and significantly experienced. As a way of religious life it seems emotionally charged to the limit. Frequently the white observer feels that the Negroes even drag out the ceremony and make the most of it; there is a certain tedium in the uncertainty of the arrangements and the repetitious character of much of the ritual. One must remember, however, that the rural churches meet only once a month, but then sometimes from twelve to four in the afternoon. Before and after the service, of course, a social atmosphere prevails; there is visiting, lunching together, and exchange of news in the manner typical of rural people everywhere. The preacher is not always on time since he may have other engagements on the same Sunday, and it is said that if he is not there when the congregation gathers, a "jack-leg preacher" may rise and hold the fort until he comes. In this way aspirants to the rôle of preacher may serve their apprenticeship.

After the first baptizing ceremony reported above, the group went back to the church to give the "right hand of fellowship" to the new members. I did not see this rite, but was told that the candidates go to the church and stand before the pulpit. Then the congregation marches past them, the preacher and elders first, and shakes hands with them.

No opportunity occurred for me to witness a funeral in a lower-class Negro church, though reports indicate that the ritual is different from the white custom. I shall not try to report it from hearsay.

At several revival meetings at rural churches there was a church official who acted as policeman. Once we asked the sexton why he had not gone inside to the service. He said it was his task to stay outside because there were a lot of youngsters who would otherwise hang around and "court" instead of going to church. They would smoke cigarettes during the service and sometimes go off to make love in the church yard. It was his duty to see that this did not happen during the service.

The custom of "testifying" before the church as a proof of a valid conversion has already been indicated. One Negro said that in former days people had a private "praying ground" to which they went at night to pray, apparently in search of a mystical experience; very often they would have the experience there. For example, they would ask the Lord to have a song put in their mouth, and it would be done. (When they reported this fact in church they would lead off with the song and the congregation would join in—of course it would be a well-known one.) Or they would ask that, if they were really saved, they be allowed to see a star fall, and this would happen; some again would have a vision of a white man, or would hear a voice which said something special, such as "Go in peace and sin no more." The mourners would report these experiences dramatically while testifying in church. My informant also had an experience, but it was quite pale beside any of these; she just had a strong conviction that she had accepted Jesus Christ as her personal savior and, when she went to church in the evening she simply stood up and stated this with great sincerity. She asked forgiveness for her sins. The preacher was evidently impressed with her testimony because he gave a reassuring answer, "Your name is written down!" If the minister was in doubt about the sincerity of a convert, he might phrase it, "*Be sure* your name is written down!"

A man reported that he was converted at seventeen and thereafter became a more sober individual. He did not have the great experience that some Negroes report; his father was a Sunday-school teacher and said that the way to join the church was just to make up your mind to live a certain kind of life. Informant remembered that he was impressed particularly by the weird singing of people at the church.

Another informant said she did not have any spectacular experience when she joined the church; it was just a continuation of Sunday school. She never had any feeling of being changed or of being any happier after her conversion, although these two elements are frequently reported by converts as a warrant of their sincerity.

The Negro ministers, usually preachers rather than pastors, are remarkably well fitted to their jobs; on the platform they are graceful, secure, and have the highest histrionic talents. They hit their stride easily in talking, and preach smiling, occasionally sizing up the audience and varying the attack at will. The object, of course, is to master the crowd and bring it to a high pitch of emotional participation in the service. The crowd expects it and the competent preacher is able to do it. The fact that there is a fine tradition of public speaking in the African areas from which these Negroes come may not be irrelevant.[15] For the most

[15] "As a result of their interest in court procedure, most African men have great proficiency in argumentation and in

part, in Southerntown and county, the preachers do not seem to be educated men. The following is an account of an exception. The preacher was a partially bald Negro, light brown in color, and seemed to be well educated. In his talking he stressed the importance of learning something from the sermons (very unusual) rather than merely having an emotional experience. He undertook to reconcile the scientific account of the origin of man with the biblical account. In this he followed[16] the Jesuitical version of the separate creation of each species and development within the species, but not development from species to species. It was wonderful to see this brown man in a simple church become the living image of God, take his rôle in various steps in the creative process, call into being with appropriate voice the various phases, and describe the junctures and dilemmas which God faced in creating the world. He was so dramatic and verbally astute in building up the marvelous story as to rouse envy of the Negroes for his splendid artistry.

Yet another preacher proved himself very clever and gifted on the platform; he excelled by the simplicity of his devices and figures of speech. On one occasion he acted out a number of episodes showing how a sinner is like a man who toes out and cannot walk the straight and narrow path. In another sermon he used ironical negative statements very effectively, such as "Maybe God was just fooling when he promised us salvation," "Maybe he didn't mean it." The congregation denied his assertions the while, saying "Yes, yes he did mean it," "No, he wasn't fooling." Again he held an imaginary altercation with one of the sisters in the

---

skillful presentation of a case before a judicial body. This argumentation is carried on with a wealth of allusion, characterized by the use of a vivid and often poetic imagery and the employment of many proverbs. The effect of this style of presentation is that it enables the African, in displaying his histrionic ability, to make his points much more strikingly and persuasively than a bare presentation of facts could possibly do." Herskovits, *op. cit.*, p. 230; quoted by permission of the Clark University Press.

[16] As L. W. Doob, who also heard the sermon, was able to tell me.

audience, "You's lied," "You's a back-biter," "Can you be sanctified this way?"

The preacher, of course, does not make such a connected discourse as would be expected by a better educated audience. He is allowed to repeat himself without fear of reproach and he utters frequent stereotyped phrases while he is collecting his thoughts. Furthermore he has probably learned many of the sermons and has carefully worked them up very much like an actor learning a part, although no doubt he is constantly amending and enhancing them with new images and devices. His talk is often punctuated with the audience's responses. As in the white churches, the preachers in the county were exclusively men; I heard of no women preachers.

The intensive participation of the audience is seemingly required by the minister and is obviously of greatest aid. I had never truly understood the meaning of the term "collective experience" until participating in a well-planned Negro revival service. One's image from white Protestant churches is that every member sits in quiet isolation from every other member and that it is a case of every man against the preacher. In the Negro churches it is a case of every man with the preacher and the boundaries of the self are weakened. There is an obvious eagerness for sympathetic contact, a willingness to be stirred and caught up in a powerful story and to abandon in song, speech and spastic gesture the strictures of the controlling self of everyday life. With special preachers and special audiences it is possible to achieve an unusually intense communal experience. It has already been reported how the sermon is peppered with the responses of the audience. These seem to be an indicator to the minister of the way he is achieving his collective delirium; if the confirmatory responses are lacking, the preacher may say to the crowd, "How am I preaching?" or "Can't you give an amen for Jesus?" He must persuade and coerce every single member to abandon his individuality and to give himself to the circuit of emotion generated by the sermon.

From afar, that is, from the back benches, I had witnessed this phenomenon and with a certain amount of envy.

Certainly, I thought, no more exhilarating form of leadership of other human beings exists than that possible between the Negro preacher and his congregation. Several times I was asked to "say a few words," as white guests usually are, and always I stood up in the back pew and briefly expressed my thanks. I determined, however, that if it happened again I would take the pulpit and expose myself to the congregation. It did, of course, happen again and when the next chance came I took it. It was all that I had expected and more too. Not familiar enough with the Bible to choose an opportune text, I talked about my own state, described the country through which I had passed in coming south, spoke of the beauty of their land, and expressed my pleasure at being allowed to participate in their exercises. Helped by appreciative murmurs which began slowly and softly and became louder and fuller as I went on, I felt a great sense of elation, an increased fluency, and a vastly expanded confidence in speaking. There was no doubt that the audience was with me, was determined to aid me in every way. I went on to say that in my country the rain soaked people as it does in Southerntown, that the cold bit through broken shoes in the same way, that poor people have the same desperate struggle for a living, that the scorn of the mighty is as bitter, that the loss of those we love lays a whip across the heart in the same way. This brought a murmuring flood of approbation, of "Well," "Hallelujah," "Isn't that the truth?" and so on. I said then that against these dangers men have always come together to share their experiences and to draw comfort from common warmth and strength. The little talk ended with a round of applause which, of course, was permitted in this case; but more than that, the crowd had enabled me to talk to them much more sincerely than I thought I knew how to do; the continuous surge of affirmation was a highly elating experience. For once I did not feel that I was merely beating a sodden audience with words or striving for cold intellectual communication. Here the audience was actually ahead of me, it had a preformed affirmation ready for the person with the courage to say the significant word. Of course, there was no shouting, and mine was a miserable performance compared to the many Negro preachers I have seen striding the platform like confident panthers; but it was exactly the intensive collective participation that I had imagined it might be. No less with the speaker than with the audience there is a sense of losing the limitations of self and of unconscious powers rising to meet the unbound, unconscious forces of the group.

The disparity between the somewhat theoretical sins preached against and actual breaches of the mores is an old issue between ritualists and freethinkers; the latter are always willing to point out that the faithful observe the punctilio of church rules by neglecting obligations nearer to the sincere conscience. Middle-class Negroes are frequently shocked at the behavior of the lower-class faithful and in particular at the preachers who come out of this group, and they are careful to distinguish their personal habits from those of such Negroes. There is a general charge of rascality and venality against Negro ministers and it is made with particular vehemence by middle-class Negroes. The whites, of course, are in general amused at this behavior and admit that it is about what might be expected from a Negro. So far as I could tell, lower-class Negroes do not uniformly deplore such immoral behavior in their ministers; rather they tend to take them on the basis of their pulpit performance and to expect that they will not in general be any better than their parishioners. The Negro minister, to lower-class Negroes, is much less a model to his flock than a powerful exhorter and impresario in the pulpit. Here, for example, are some sentiments of middle-class Negroes on the score of the morals of the preacher. An informant said that a number of approaches of a sexual nature have been made to her by preachers. In fact, practically every one she has known has sooner or later gotten around to it. She does not think that preachers are any better than other folks. Furthermore, they have very special advantages. For one thing, everybody admires preachers; for another, every door is open to them in their own congregations and nobody knows when they go to a house that they are not going on church or community business or for special religious work. In short, they have preferred access to women and they make use of it.

Another woman informant said that the preachers do not practice what they preach, that most of the Negro preachers drink and have extramarital relations at the very time they are advising others against them. One preacher tried to explain to her how to lead a Sunday-school class. He stated that he always preached about his own sins because he was able to denounce them with particular vigor and expressiveness; he selected his own weak spots in order to save others from the sins he was himself prone to.

As a concrete example this woman informant told of an experience with a strange minister, a man about sixty years old. She joined the church and this preacher admitted her. The next day he called up and asked her to do some typing for him. She objected because she could hardly type, but he insisted and said that he did not mind if she were slow, he wanted her to do it and no one else. She went to his home after work and discovered that he did not have any typing to be done at all, but wanted to make love to her. She refused, apparently very indignantly. She did not like this hypocritical type of preacher. I reminded her of the spiritual "Do you call that religion?" and of the line which reads "I know I've got religion, know I was called to teach; you don't pay no 'tention to what I do, you just practice what I preach." She agreed that this is the attitude of many ministers.

Another very conservative informant said that she received a stunning shock several years ago when she learned that several of the men and women who were leaders in her church were doing low and dirty things and were also playing politics. She felt that very religious people are hypocritical and that many people who live outside the church are better than those who live in. Her father would never join the church because of the bad lives which some members led.

We are cautioned by these cases not to lump all Negro ministers together. Those who are of middle-class status, who have had special college and theological training, are likely to have the standards of the middle-class group. Those who are self-selected, who have simply had a private "call," and who have retained the social habits of lower-class people, have also the lower-class moral code. This latter fact shocks middle-class Negroes and amuses the white people who observe such paradoxical behavior in a religious leader.

Of course, the individualistic strain characteristic of Protestantism is visible here also; the individual ultimately sets himself up as the judge of social institutions. This movement is widespread among middle-class Negroes who will often say that they are not blind followers of the church, that they do not take everything the minister says for truth, and that they make their own interpretations of the Bible. Although they follow Christianity in general, they have many private reservations and often disapprove of the human agents of the faith.

Among middle-class Negroes there is marked objection to many of the religious forms of the lower-class churches. One informant said that he did not like the way people act in the churches these days, the mystical experiences, the excited singing, the stamping and "shouting," the tearing off of clothes and experiences of possession. This informant never approved of this sort of thing from childhood on and never accepted it as his own. He felt that a religious experience could come quietly within the self and that the best expression of it might be the peace and joy which arise from knowledge of fulfilment of duty. The middle-class Negroes know that these ecstatic performances in the church are the subject of ridicule on the part of white people and they are attempting to approximate the quieter and more restrained patterns characteristic of the white churches.[17] It can be

[17] "Mr. X told me that he had endeavored, with but little success to prevent this shouting and jumping of the negroes at their meetings on his plantation, from a conviction that there was not the slightest element of religious sentiment in it. He considered it to be engaged in more as an exciting amusement than from any really religious impulse. In the town churches, except, perhaps, those managed and conducted almost exclusively by negroes, the slaves are said to commonly engage in religious exercises in a sober and decorous manner; yet, a member of a Presbyterian church in a Southern city told me, that he had seen the negroes, in his own house of

observed that the middle-class churches in town are much more reserved and have much more the frozen, restrained characteristics of the white churches. There seems to be also the perception among middle-class Negroes that the emotionalized patterns of lower-class religion have a sexual element in them and that there is something orgastic about the high-tension performances of the preachers and congregation. Often I had occasion to point out to such informants that they were really more moral than their religion, since on the basis of their own characters (middle-class formations) they rejected the emotionalized, even sexualized, elements of the lower-class ritual.

There appears, among middle-class Negroes, as already noted, the usual revolt against a literal interpretation of the Bible. One informant said that she had her own views on many points, and found it very uncomfortable to be in a Negro church where people say they believe the Bible from cover to cover. She could not believe such a story as Joshua's making the sun stop; science taught her that the sun does not move anyway, but the early Christians did not know this. She thought there could be errors in the way the scriptures were written down, just as there would be if she and I reported on the same incident. She was no coward about her divergent religious views, and whenever she got a chance to teach or speak before a religious class she defended her convictions. This informant said that her family was very religious and from the time when she was five she went to religious revivals. The first prayer she learned was "Now I lay me down to sleep." At the age of eleven she accepted Christ as her personal Savior. She believed in the Virgin birth, though she did not understand it; neither, she said, did she understand how plants grew but she believed in "that." One miracle was just the same as another to her. One of her brothers became a minister and from childhood

---

worship, during 'a season of revival,' leap from their seats, throw their arms wildly in the air, shout vehemently and unintelligibly, cry, groan, rend their clothes, and fall into cataleptic trances." F. L. Olmsted, *A Journey in the Seaboard Slave States* (New York, 1904), II, 80-81; quoted by permission of G. P. Putnam's Sons.

always took a special interest in religious things. She remembered how they would go to church together and come home and "play church." Her brother would mimic the minister and press her into service as deacon. It would seem that there is a steady attrition on the "old-time religion" as a result of the spreading of the scientific world view through the schools.

Certainly religion among the Negroes has been important in making life tolerable around Southerntown. The slaves evidently adopted Christianity with great enthusiasm and their descendants still carry it on as one of their prized institutions. They have made of it a highly expressive affair, not only because the Negro is individuated in the church and can play a significant rôle, but also because he has there an opportunity for intensive, and often ecstatic, impulse expression. From another point of view it may also be true that the Negro church has been serviceable to the whites. A clue to this is given by a local informant. He said that the planters have always welcomed the building of a church for Negroes on the plantation; but their enthusiasm has not been so great for a school. The church, he felt, helped to keep the *status quo* by offering an illusory consolation to the Negroes; the school threatened, on the other hand, to make accessible to every human being ideas of personal dignity which were dangerous to the caste system. Another informant commented that religion centers the attention of the Negro on a future life while negating the value of this one or the importance of effort here and now designed to better conditions. From this standpoint religion can be seen as a mechanism for the social control of Negroes.[18] If taken as

[18] "To be sure, it was not always financial aid in the building of churches or the renovation of old ones that the 'safe, sane' minister received, but personal gifts such as clothes, money and public acclamation on the part of leading whites. In this study, cases were found where the site for the Negro church was given by the white landowners. Economically, it was profitable to the landowners to keep Negroes satisfied and have them honest. The Negro preacher and the Negro church were instruments to this end. And the methods most often employed were to boost and encourage the Negro preacher who taught the Negro the 'right' doctrine, and to allow the Negro religious freedom in his church. In any tense situation,

the only explanation, this is certainly too narrow a view of its function. It is a form of collective activity which gives pleasure and is a center of social solidarity for Negroes. The control view stresses its function in keeping the peace, not only in smothering revolts economically motivated, but in suppressing discontent with the mores in general. Granted this function, the religious institution obviously offers consolation to individuals and much gratification through its expressive patterns. One might note also that in the case of the Negroes[19] the religious institutions have been the door to education. With one exception, all the Negro higher educational institutions in the state are denominational. Perhaps by this means—by stressing the religious motif—they escape the opposition which might otherwise be directed at higher education for Negroes; but, in fact, while directing due attention to the Negro's soul, these institutions have not neglected his mind.

Negroes often show the type of conscience which is easily externalized and projected onto an institution like the church. The lower-class Negroes do not seem to suffer the severe internal pressures of the middle-class group, so widespread in white Protestantism. They seem able to an extraordinary degree to free themselves from guilt with the aid of a highly emotionalized religious service which, of course, is able to thunder against sin with all the lurid imagery of old-time revivalism. It may be that this detachable conscience of the Negro is a feature of the often-observed poise and freedom which lower-class Negro individuals seem to enjoy in the ordinary doings of life. Religious institutions, in this view, play exactly the opposite rôle from that usually ascribed to them in a Puritanical society; instead of stressing self-control and bringing pressure toward impulse renunciation, they aid the individual in increasing his daily satisfaction in life by the ceremonials which relieve his guilt.

---

these Negro preachers could be relied upon to convey to their Negro congregations the advice of the leading whites of the community. Examples of this kind could be multiplied indefinitely." Mays and Nicholson, *op. cit.*, p. 7; quoted by permission of Harper & Bros.

[19] Odum, *op. cit.*

CHAPTER XII

Accommodation Attitudes of Negroes

❊❊❊❊❊❊❊❊❊❊❊❊❊❊❊❊❊❊❊❊❊❊❊❊❊❊❊

Accommodation attitudes[1] are those which enable the Negro to adjust and survive in the caste situation as it is presented to him. Originally the alternatives to accommodation were successful conflict with the whites or extinction. There was little prospect of success in conflict, as the occasional slave revolts demonstrated. The desire to live was strong, so that the only possible alternative was adjustment to the situation. It is of the greatest importance to know what kind of psychological process the social fact of mass accommodation is.

To what must the Negroes accommodate themselves? The answer is simple; they must accustom themselves to the caste situation which guarantees to the middle- and upper-class white groups the three types of gain we have already discussed. Negroes have succeeded in making this accommodation in the past with a high degree of completeness, and it is still a major factor in the stability of social life in the southern states. The full power of this adaptation of the Negroes was shown at the time of the Civil War when the Negro slaves and servants continued loyally to work on the plantations while the white masters were away with the southern armies. A slave accommodation once achieved is a highly durable fact. In Southerntown and county, which approximate today the older plantation regime more nearly than most sections of the South, these attitudes are clearly visible, especially in the lower-class Negroes. Of course the physical force which compelled the Negroes to make this adjustment in the first instance has never been completely

[1] For discussion of this concept see Robert E. Park and Ernest W. Burgess, *Introduction to the Science of Sociology* (Chicago, 1924). Chap. x, pp. 663–666.

withdrawn and is always potential; whenever nowadays there is a threat of too rapid dissolution of these attitudes on the part of Negroes, the force reappears and plays its historical rôle. For example, there are always at hand methods of "treating" Negroes who belligerently insist on their constitutional rights in regard to voting; they are seldom used because Negroes do not care to put themselves in the dangerous situation of evoking force.

In this connection a word more must be said about the gains concept. The concept works best when the two groups concerned are the middle-class white people and the lower-class Negroes. The middle-class whites are in a position by virtue of their caste and class status to make the maximum of all three gains from the lower-class Negroes. Individuals in the white middle class may often mitigate their demands at one point or another. They may refuse, as many do, to utilize their position for sexual ends; they may deal fairly on economic matters with the Negro; and they may show him a proper reciprocal deference. It should be clear, however, that such individuals are not utilizing the opportunities offered by their social position. It would be reasonable to expect that most people would make use, especially, of the prestige and economic advantages; due to a countervailing social pressure fewer than formerly make the sexual gain.

As has been pointed out, a certain class loyalty exists between middle-class whites and middle-class Negroes, and the gains are all less marked between these two groups. Middle-class Negroes get a better economic deal, are less accessible sexually, and are more respected by the whites than lower-class Negroes. We must, of course, ask what situation exists between middle- and lower-class white people. It would seem that middle-class whites have an economic advantage as in the case of the lower-class Negroes; nevertheless they are not able to utilize their superior position to make the sexual or prestige gains in anything like the same degree. The lower-class white man can defend his home and his women and he can vote; he thus guarantees himself a much higher status in the eyes of middle-class white people. It seems to be true that the lower-class whites make a certain caste gain from the lower-class Negroes.

Certainly they are able to enforce the deference forms, and this differential is quite clear; it is frequently alleged also that they are the ones who make the most use of sexual opportunities with the Negroes. So far as the economic position is concerned, they are about on a par with the Negro. Middle-class Negroes do better economically than do lower-class whites, but they must obey the deference forms characteristic of their caste position when dealing with lower-class whites. They are certainly much better able than lower-class Negroes to defend themselves against sexual infringements.

In this discussion of gains we must always remember that the gains are not exclusively on the side of the white caste. It will be urged, as southern white people do urge, that the Negroes also gain from the situation, and in ways which are inaccessible to white caste members. This is a matter of fact and will be extensively discussed. The gains concept is a mere instrument of analysis and not a battle slogan; it is used because it serves to clarify the social mechanics of class and caste relationships which otherwise seem mere outline forms of action.

Even though their personalities seem well accommodated to the caste system, it should not be thought that the Negroes are too stupid to realize the nature of the situation. They understand it quite well, in fact much better than do members of the white caste who naturally wish to disguise and extenuate it out of loyalty to our democratic theory which does not countenance caste and class gains. During the reconstruction period the news was circulated adequately to the masses of Negroes that there were some people who did not accept the caste situation as inevitable; the result has been that the perfection of the slavery accommodation has broken down and many Negroes are able to see the class and caste gains quite clearly, even though they do not formulate them in technical language. We may believe, then, that Negroes will perceive the caste and class distinctions as a chronic frustration situation. In such a situation we should expect aggression from them. What, in fact, do they do?

There seem to be five possibilities of action on the part of the Negroes in the face of these gains. They can:

(1) Become overtly aggressive against the white caste; this they have done, though infrequently and unsuccessfully in the past.

(2) Suppress their aggression in the face of the gains and supplant it with passive accommodative attitudes. This was the slavery solution and it still exists under the caste system.

(3) Turn aggression from the white caste to individuals within their own group. This has been done to some extent and is a feature of present-day Negro life.

(4) Give up the competition for white-caste values and accept other forms of gratification than those secured by the whites. This the lower-class Negroes have done.

(5) Compete for the values of white society, raise their class position within the Negro caste and manage aggression partly by expressing dominance within their own group and partly by sheer suppression of the impulse as individuals. This is the solution characteristic of the Negro middle class.

The element of force in evoking accommodative behavior from Negroes must never be lost sight of. Negroes did not come willingly to America, nor did they part with their ancient cultures out of a desire to share in the superior social values of the whites. They came as a result of conquest and initially, at least, they began to adjust to American culture because there was no alternative except death. It is due to our superior force and ruthlessness that the Negroes are slaves here and not we in Africa. Force was only slowly replaced by a routine of life to which the Negroes became accustomed; and gradually the routine made alterations in the personalities of Negroes. Only when these inner adjustments to white force were accomplished could we speak of accommodation and it is to be noted always that force was never totally withdrawn, though it could be withdrawn to the extent that Negroes became accustomed to their rôle and way of life. Once the accommodation was fairly complete the necessity of coercion was markedly reduced; this is a factor which is never sufficiently taken into account by commentators from the North who identify themselves with the slave or caste man. Once accommodation was a fact, other incentives could make themselves felt, such as loyalty and pride.[2] The result of force and routine was in the end a change in Negro character; these factors formed character and resulted in the accommodated Negro, i.e., the one who had made his choice to live rather than die in a fruitless resistance. "Resistance" on the part of the Negro in slavery times could only terminate in expressions of physical violence, and these, of course, were not tolerated,[3] though there was probably a kind of passive sabotage expressed in waste of time and materials.

The alternative to any effective resistance is acceptance of the new conditions of life. In its simplest form accommodation is the principle of "safety first"; Negroes who valued their pride or culture too much to adjust themselves to the slavery regime had, as the alternative, extirpation. Accommodation is not an exclusive mechanism of Negro people, although they have perhaps been forced to use it to an unusual degree; we must all accommodate ourselves to various unpleasant situations, for example, to the fact of being small when we want to be big, to the fact that others may be stronger, more favored, or talented than we, to the facts

---

[2] "The theory of rigid coercion and complete exploitation was as strange to the bulk of the planters as the doctrine and practice of moderation was to those who viewed the regime from afar and with the mind's eye. A planter in explaining his mildness might well have said it was due to his being neither a knave nor a fool. He refrained from the use of fetters not so much because they would have hampered the slaves in their work as because the general use of them never crossed his mind. And since chains and bolts were out of the question, the whole system of control must be moderate; slaves must be impelled as little as possible by fear, and as much as might be by loyalty, pride and the prospect of reward." U. B. Phillips, *American Negro Slavery* (New York, 1918), pp. 293-294; quoted by permission of D. Appleton-Century Co.

[3] "To strike a white man was death by lynch law, in Gardiner's shipyard; nor was there much of any other law toward the colored people at that time in any other part of Maryland." Frederick Douglass, *Life and Times* (Hartford, Conn., 1882), p. 207.

of disease and death, and to all the aspects of our culture which are perceived as limiting. For instance, if a man does not accommodate himself to the *mos* against murder and renounce his private revenge tendencies, he is likely to suffer the fate of the proud African who could not adjust, and be eliminated (by the electric chair).

Accommodation involves the renunciation of protest or aggression against undesirable conditions of life and the organization of the character so that protest does not appear, but acceptance does. It may come to pass in the end that the unwelcome force is idealized, that one identifies with it and takes it into the personality; it sometimes even happens that what is at first resented and feared is finally loved. In this case a unique alteration of the character occurs in the direction of masochism. Each Negro as he is added to the group must learn to accommodate himself to the caste situation, regardless of whether he lives in the South or in the North. He must renounce the theoretical equality of opportunity and accept the actual social situation as it is defined by the regional culture. He must learn to devalue his personal physical characteristics; he must "remember his place." If resentment is produced by these renunciations, it must be squelched and the façade, at least, of a smooth acceptance must appear in its place. Since the Civil War the element of plantation routine which was an important factor in guaranteeing Negro accommodation has weakened; the result is that in order to maintain the Negro in his caste place the social milieu has had to become more threatening against him. Immediately after the War the Klan and similar terroristic organizations replaced the routine of life under slavery.

The process of socializing Negro people cannot be a smooth one; actually they are caught in a conflict between total American and southern regional definitions of their rôle. It is because of this fact that Negroes have had to be more forcefully dealt with in the years since the War than in the years before it. Observation in Southerntown and county makes it clear that the Negro does accommodate himself by and large to the situation and accepts his rôle as defined by the white caste.[4] This accommodation is evidenced wherever the Negro is seen if he has been under the influence of southern regional culture. It is observed, for example, no less in mental hospitals than in the cotton fields.[5] Accommodation attitudes are, of course, best established in lower-class Negroes and in those with minimal formal schooling, that is, those who have the least access to a divergent conception of the Negro's place in American society.

We may inquire concerning some of the characteristics of the accommodated Negro.[6] One is, of course, his speech. I

[4] "Without any permanent place in the economic life of the community, the Negroes are thoroughly cowed, meek, humble and generally silent. Of course, Negroes can and do adjust themselves to the situation." Arthur F. Raper, *The Tragedy of Lynching* (Chapel Hill, 1933), p. 171; quoted by permission of the University of North Carolina Press.

[5] "A word here in regard to the management and control of these colored individuals: in the hospital the colored patient is much more submissive and amenable to discipline than the white. As slaves they were docile, tractable and subordinate, and these instincts of obedience which have been transmitted from their immediate forefathers remain with them. The traditions and influence of slavery have made the disposition of the colored more pliant than it would otherwise have been. Their native cheerfulness and good humor are unchanged, and as a rule are always with them; when angered they are not cruel, but impulsive. In their daily associations they are rarely violent with each other. They occasionally use impulsive physical force, but the violence of their language is at variance with their actions, and the most extravagant verbal engagements always terminate peacefully when the power of their tongues and their lungs is exhausted. The tumult begins at a high pitch and after lasting one or several hours gradually dwindles to silence. As these periods become quiescent, familiar and amicable relations are at once resumed until an occasion arises for another outbreak." Mary O'Malley, "Psychoses in the Colored Race," *Amer. J. Insan.* (1914), Vol. 71, pp. 334-335.

[6] "The negro of pure blood, especially in the far South, is naturally unambitious, tractable, and easily satisfied. He does not lie awake at night brooding over the loss of inalienable human rights. Politics have no great charm for him and 'grandfather clauses' or questions of civil rights seldom disturb his primrose path. He does not look upon the 'Jim Crow' car as a humiliation and the writer's observation is that the free-

ave heard dozens of middle-class white people imitate the
speech of Negroes in telling an anecdote. They always give
a image of a high-toned, pleading voice, full of uncer-
inty, begging for favor. Evidently this whining, cajoling
ane is one of the badges of inferiority which Negroes accept
ad cultivate. The whites imitate it with an evident hostile
slish. It establishes at once by its difference from ordinary
hite speech the inferior position of the Negro as a sup-
liant. If the reader has ever seen Stepin Fetchit in the
aovies, he can picture this type of character. Fetchit always
lays the part of a well-accommodated lower-class Negro,
hining, vacillating, shambling, stupid, and moved by very
mple cravings. There is probably an element of resistance
e white society in the shambling, sullenly slow pace of the
egro; it is the gesture of a man who is forced to work for
nds not his own and who expresses his reluctance to per-
rm under these circumstances.

An informant already cited has referred to the Negro as
"Dr. Jekyll and Mr. Hyde." He was making an observa-
on that is well understood among Negroes—that he has a
ind of dual personality, two rôles, one that he is forced to
lay with white people and one the "real Negro" as he ap-
ears in his dealings with his own people. What the white
outhern people see who "know their Negroes" is the rôle
hat they have forced the Negro to accept, his caste rôle. I
ave sometimes referred to this as a "white-folks manner"
nd have had much opportunity to observe it operating in
eference to myself. The same point has been made by
ther observers.[7] It is perhaps this fact which often makes

---

tom of a car of his own colour is infinitely preferable to one
vhere the presence of members of the white race would be
elt as a restraint. When protests do come, they are in the
reat majority of cases from mulattoes." J. M. Mecklin, *Democ-
acy and Race Friction* (New York, 1914), p. 154; quoted by
ermission of The Macmillan Co.

[7] "His attention to circumstances is passive and sensuous;
is social self has not developed the love of home and family
ior the desire to accumulate property. Withal, the Negro has
wo distinct social selves, the one he reveals to his own people,
he other he assumes among the whites, the assumption itself
aving become natural." Howard W. Odum, "Social and

Negroes seem so deceptive to white people; apparently ov white caste wishes the Negro to have only one social pe sonality, his caste rôle, and to *be* this with utter complet ness.

Negroes become quite adept both at concealing the feelings and dealing with white people. A Negro informar said that Negroes learn to get along with white people b outwitting them, by studying them closely, and by markir the points at which they are susceptible to influence. H affirmed that there are many good Negro thinkers, thoug they are not school-learned, and many who are clever managing the whites, at least within limits; but, he add most of the time the security of the Negro lies in his—fee pointing to his shoes. When the Negro cannot fight, his onl recourse is to run.

The white caste is quite aware of what it wants in N groes. It idealizes the "old-timy" Negroes and, in its turr was well accommodated to them, accepting responsibilit for their welfare, loving and directing them. The image raised by the idea of the "old-timy Negro" are those of th bandana around the head, the Sambo and Rastus types, be lief in spells and conjures, love of their white folks, and highly cultivated white-folks manner. In short the phrase a direct reference to the slavery Negro of the well-accom modated, house-servant type. It should be noted that thes Negroes had their primary allegiance to the single, maste ful white man and still tend to trust him; the emotional tie run vertically to the patriarchal head and not horizontall to the sibling caste members. This is a fact of the greate importance as the Negro comes more into the sphere of ur ban and factory work.[8]

The value of accommodation is actively propagandize

Mental Traits of the Negro," *Studies in History, Economic and Public Law* (1910), Vol. 37, No. 3, p. 565.

[8] "The International Ladies' Garment Workers have had t face all of the usual difficulties in their efforts to organize th Negro. They have had to overcome distrust of the white work ers and to change the Negro's traditional loyalty to the em ployer into a loyalty to his fellow workers." Sterling D. Sper and Abram L. Harris, *The Black Worker* (New York, 1931) p. 344; quoted by permission of the Columbia University Press

within the Negro group. An excellent example is a sermon on tact which was reported by one of my informants. He said that the preacher gave a very good sermon about a king who had the Jewish people in his power, and selected Ruth, a Jewish woman, as a mistress. She was so beautiful that he resolved to grant any request she made. She did not make her request the evening of the first banquet but waited until the second night, tactfully fixed him another fine banquet, and then asked him to spare the lives of the Jewish people. He granted her wish. The point made by the preacher was that those who behave tactfully often have wishes fulfilled which otherwise would not be. The preacher mentioned, for example that the Ethiopian people might have their wish for victory granted. Informant said there was much talk about the Ethiopian War among Southern-town Negroes, that it was often mentioned in the churches, and that some of them read about it in the newspapers. He thought the Lord might still work a miracle and save the Ethiopians from the Italians. There are many Negroes whose basic characteristic is tact, and who study the world constantly from the standpoint of securing privileges by guilefulness.

Deference forms will not be considered at great length here, except to indicate them as part of Negro accommodative behavior. Negroes are practiced in saying, "Yes, sir," "No, sir," to white people. Although I personally disregarded the deference code in many respects, they would constantly drop into these patterns with me. For example, one night on the street in Southerntown I met two members of a Negro quartette whose singing I had long admired. I recognized them from a picture I had seen in a song book, and greeted them. The big Negro who sang bass tipped his straw hat when I stopped to speak to him and again when I went on, and used all the deference forms; he was perfectly practiced in accommodation attitudes, although this group had been abroad for two and a half years, had broadcasted over the National Broadcasting chain, and is widely known.

It may be that one of the persistent accommodative attitudes of lower-class Negroes is lying; at least this charge was constantly made by whites, often as a challenge to the validity of any results I might get from interviewing Negroes. One informant said that Negroes cannot be trusted, that they will invariably tell a white person what they think he expects them to say. If we postulate that people lie when they are afraid, this is equivalent to saying that dealing with a white man is always viewed by the Negro as a potentially dangerous situation in which he does not feel he can afford to be honest. Perhaps with the northern white person this situation may look different to the Negro; it certainly does to the Negro who is highly placed and secure.

A good example of the value of lying is given in the following incident. A middle-class white informant related that his cook did not come to work on Sunday, and further, that there was not a cook in town who did; they were all "sick." He added that there was a baptizing down at the river, hence the "illnesses." "The bastard, if she had chills and fever, I had lockjaw." From the Negro's point of view the matter might look like this: if white people do not respect Negro religion and do not recognize the wish to attend a baptizing as a valid motive for not coming to work, the only alternative is to lie. The cooks perhaps felt they had as good a right to attend religious exercises on Sunday as did anyone else.

One aspect of the accommodation behavior of lower-class Negroes affects the researcher particularly. He must be very careful concerning what he says to them and how he acts with them since they may well report any unconventional behavior (i.e., unconventional from the caste standpoint). Middle-class Negroes explain this by saying that many of the Negro servants are treacherous and would tattle on anybody including their own people; an informant stated further that they are probably afraid and trying to curry favor with the white folks. Very likely in view of the total situation this is expedient behavior since the researcher or middle-class Negroes are able to do very little for them, whereas their white employers are able to do much and are always there to do it. It should further be noted that lower-class Negroes are probably afraid to be interviewed and easily feel that they may be suspected of incorrect behavior from the caste standpoint.

The caste attitudes of Negroes are, of course, particularly keyed to southern white people. A startling example of this occurred one night after a revival meeting. Four of us waited to interview the preacher, two northern white men, a northern white woman, and a southern white woman. We wanted to ask whether the baptizing which was to follow the revival could be held in time so that one of the members of our party would be able to witness it before going back north. I made the request and the preacher told me that it probably was not possible, that people could not get their clothes together, and that it would be rushing matters. The formal time was quite a long distance ahead and could not easily be advanced. Finally the southern girl spoke up and made the same request. The preacher executed an immediate rightabout-face, answered, "Yassum, yassum, I think it can be done," and promised to advance the date. In this, of course, he was deceitful because he knew he could not move his people much ahead of the time already set; but he also knew that it was dangerous to refuse to do anything a white person wanted him to do, even if it was impossible. The response to the southern voice was immediate and striking.

At the revival meeting the next evening the preacher arose and exhorted the congregation to put forward the time of the baptizing to the next Sunday. No one seemed enthusiastic; parents apparently had to prepare clothes and otherwise get ready for the event. Then the preacher played his trump card, namely that the "white gentlemen" wanted it to be held when they could see it. This left me acutely embarrassed since I had already tried to discourage him and urged him not to put the interests of one or two persons over those of the whole church group. The preacher showed here very clearly where his own loyalty was; he felt it was up to him to try to oblige us at all costs and that he should act as an agent to move his congregation in the direction that we wished. Possibly he knew that he could not do it anyway, but he wanted the merit of making a vigorous attempt. The northerner often finds it embarrassing to be the object of such special solicitude, since he is not accustomed to the notion that no amount of trouble for Negroes is too much to gratify one of his wishes.

In another connection we have mentioned the practice of white patronage of Negroes; as is so often the case in this analysis, the same material can be seen, and needs to be re-cited, from several points of view. To have an "angel" is one of the Negro's means of accommodating himself to the caste system; he gets extra privileges and the whites are secure in his allegiance. For example, a white lawyer told me that Negro attorneys have practiced in the local courts but they do not seem to succeed. Negro clients do not flock to them, and he wondered why. He himself said that Negro lawyers do not get "good breaks" before white juries. He also stated that Negroes seem to trust white men more, that they probably get their work done better, that ethical standards are better consolidated in the white group, and so on. It seems entirely likely that Negroes take cases, legal and medical, to whites because of their greater skill; but there is another point. They never know when they will be in need of a white friend, and these business relationships consolidate the friendship and protection which the Negro always needs. This is another type of pressure which undoubtedly operates against a bi-racial economic organization of south-ern society. The condition of protection is, of course, sub-mission and servility to middle-class members, planters, or businessmen. The "angel" will protect only a properly def-erential Negro.[9]

---

[9] "Within the past quarter century several of the large plant-ers have sold land to Negroes. Some were personally interested in certain Negroes having homes of their own, others found the successful Negro tenants the best available market for their less valuable tracts. The Negro purchasers are very conscious of their dependence upon the white men who made ownership possible for them; and, though not as servile as the landless Negroes, they are far from being independent farmers. Their avenue into ownership, as well as their security in ownership, was and is contingent upon their being acceptable; and being acceptable in this Black Belt county means that they will be punctiliously servile to the whites and find no fault with exist-ing educational, social, political, and economic conditions." Raper, *op. cit.*, pp. 83-84; quoted by permission of the Univer-sity of North Carolina Press.

A Negro teacher, presenting the matter from his point of view, said that he has finally learned that the only way to get along is to have a white patron. Improvements for Negroes, such as a school building, do not just happen. The white people have to be shown how it is to their advantage. Informant wanted a new school and advocated it with the businessmen of his town on the grounds that children are less disorderly on the streets when they are well schooled; more intelligent servants do not have to be dragged out of bed every morning; the better class of Negro workers will not come to a community unless there is a good Negro school for their children; more of the better class of goods can be sold to a better class of Negroes. With these arguments he enlisted adequate support among the influential people of his town. He happened to be particularly close to several of these on the basis of other contacts extending over a considerable time; they were his "angels."

There is another means of accommodating to life when it is not arranged according to one's wishes. This is the use of magic. Of course, one can think of magical practices among the Nergoes as lagging culture patterns, which they are, but one can also think of them as forms of action in reference to current social life. Magic accepts the *status quo;* it takes the place of political activity, agitation, organization, solidarity, or any real moves to change status. It is interesting and harmless from the standpoint of the caste system and it probably has great private value for those who practice it. These psychological satisfactions are important, even if they do not alter the social structure and are mere substitutes for more effective efforts to alter it. Education tends to discredit magic by showing up more clearly the nature of the actual life situation and indicating the effective, practical, though perhaps impossible, means by which it might be changed. Magic, in brief, is a control gesture, a comfort to the individual, an accommodation attitude to helplessness. There is no doubt that magic is actively believed in and practiced in Southerntown and county. For example, there is the belief in being jinxed. An informant said that a jinx is when you have a run of bad luck, when everything goes against you, in cards, in love, in business; when things turn out this way you try to lift the jinx. Middle-class informants laughed at magical practices and thought it funny that I took them seriously. But another Negro stated that some prominent people around Southerntown believe in charms and that I would be surprised to know who they were.

A Negro informant, who had worked in a drugstore, said that Negroes used to come to him for love magic. He remembered one time when he told someone that he did not have any love magic, and the man pressed him for it, promising never to tell and offering to pay any price. Informant continued to protest that he did not believe in such things and to refuse to sell any harmless powder as love magic. Later one of the other clerks laughed at him for passing up the chance; if he did not sell the love magic, some other druggist would. Evidently in this case the man expected a kind of powder which he could sprinkle on the pillow or clothes of the person who was to be made to fall in love.

Another Negro said that a man had recently tried to sell him for twenty-five dollars a charm that would double his business. Informant laughed and commented that some of the whites get their cotton crops blessed or prayed over with the idea of insuring a good crop.

Magical practice is a very complex theme which has been admirably treated by Puckett[10] from the standpoint of culture patterning. There is no need to present more evidence on it, except to remark that it is concerned with charms, fetishes, amulets, lucky and unlucky days, and the like. The plain purpose of the magical act as seen in the life-history context is to gratify some wish, for love, revenge, or power, which is not attainable in the person's actual life. The existence of such practices among Negroes is by no means displeasing, apparently, to white people; magical acts probably tend to absorb some of the discontent which would otherwise be directed at the system itself, although, to be sure, in many cases the Negroes strive by magical means to avoid evils which are common to persons everywhere. We do not need to blame unrequited love or bad weather on the caste system.

[10] Newbell N. Puckett, *Folk Beliefs of the Southern Negro* (Chapel Hill, 1926).

There is another type of accommodation which does not yet exist in Southerntown, although it is known on a considerable scale in other sections of the South: the discussion of issues and an attempt to arrive at mutuality of view. Very probably discussion does not exist because the white caste regards as its own the privilege of decision; discussion would admit a claim on the part of Negroes which cannot as yet be tolerated. The white caste may make concessions to the Negroes and may often do generous and intelligent acts for Negro advancement, but they are done at the wish of the white people and without any sense that they are a concession to aggression on the part of Negroes. This state of affairs is often deplored by middle-class Negro informants. One of them remarked that there are some evidences of "better times" for Negroes in Southerntown; for example, Negroes used to have to stand in line in front of the post office and wait before getting their mail until all the whites had been served; this practice is ended. Other types of discrimination, such as the gains already discussed, are as galling. Informant resented such things and has often tried to discuss them with his white friends; usually the white people pull away or fend off the conversation. Informant wished the time would come when whites and Negroes could at least talk over their differences: "Let a group of each come together, make speeches, and outline their points of view." But this time has not come.

There is some coöperation between the groups for various collective ends. For example, during the War Negroes were solicited to do war work, buy bonds, and the like. Occasionally now the Negroes will participate in civic events. Very often they are asked to sing. A Negro leader spoke in this connection of a program that she had organized for "Better Homes Week" at the request of a white woman. She had planned an act in a pageant, showing a middle-class Negro home and its interest in good furnishings, art, music, and literature; a Negro family was gathered around with friends invited in; there was singing, piano playing, and reading of selections from poets. This program was designed to be representative of the best of Negro life in Southerntown. Its organizer remarked that she always does anything she can for the white people, and she is careful to remind them that she is going to call on them when she needs something done. This type of accommodation—collective effort for common ends—is most valuable in mitigating racial strife and friction. It is the object of effort by thoughtful white people and Negroes over wide areas, although, to be sure, it is unlikely that any essential caste issue can be arbitrated in this type of discussion group. Discussion is profitable only when the fundamental assumptions of the participants are more or less the same; and in this case they are obviously widely different, as one can see if he reminds himself of the nature of the caste line.

One of my most striking experiences with local caste attitudes came when a Negro told me about his first visit north. His southern accommodative attitudes became clear as he listed what had surprised him about the North. In the first place, he was frightened at the things he was allowed to do with white people; he was surprised at seeing only one entrance to the railroad station instead of two, and almost appalled that a white family sat at table with him, gave him and his wife their guest room, and took them both around to see their friends. He said that it felt like "being treated as a man." Informant added that those who live around Southerntown and never know anything different do not realize their situation, but those who have been away do. This is a type of experience which liberates aggression and tends to translate a passive accommodation to the *status quo* into an active demand for new opportunity. Accommodation to the caste system tends to be broken up as new ideals of personal dignity and freedom are concretely understood by Negro individuals. Many, of course, have such ideals but believe it hopeless to strive for their realization under present conditions; they accept the caste rôle with the best grace possible and accommodate themselves to the situation in order to survive. Acceptance of inferior status is always more difficult when the culture presents a conflicting ideal of personal dignity, as our dominant American pattern does to Negroes.

CHAPTER XIII

Aggression Within the Negro Group

∞∞∞∞∞∞∞∞∞∞∞∞∞∞∞∞∞∞∞∞∞∞∞∞

Let us examine more in detail the nature of the aggression problem. The Negro individual occupies a socially stereotyped caste position in which he suffers certain systematic disadvantages. He is aware of these disadvantages because he knows the difference between his actual status in Southerntown and his theoretical status as defined by the dominant American folkways and mores. His situation, therefore, is one of frustration because he perceives the contradictions in his situation and prefers his theoretical rôle as an undifferentiated member of American society to his actual rôle as caste man. The usual human response to frustration is aggression against the frustrating object. In this case the frustrating object is the American white caste which maintains its dominance over the Negro caste in various ways. Our problem then becomes: what happens to the aggression which is inevitably germinated in this situation? Our first answer has been that it is translated into accommodative behavior toward the ruling caste. The method is very simple: aggressive tentatives by the Negro bring out marked counter-hostility in the dominant group; this puts the Negro in a dangerous situation to which he adjusts by submission and sometimes love of the white caste. The white caste, it should be remembered, means all white people in America, since the caste line is drawn in the North effectively, if not as formally, as in the South.

There is another method of dealing with this aggression which is too dangerous to express; that is, to divert it from the provoking object to some other object. It will be argued in this chapter that some of the hostility properly directed toward the white caste is deflected from it and focused within the Negro group itself. There are two advantages to this procedure. First, it is expressive from the Negro standpoint; Negroes are able to react in a biologically satisfying manner. Second, it is safer than taking up the hopeless direct struggle against the white caste which is so severely sensitive to all hostile expressions from Negroes.

This is the negative of Sumner's famous proposition.[1] The Negroes are not able to isolate the white caste as an othersgroup; survival for them depends on maintaining peaceful relationships with the dominant caste. The evidence seems to be that they have chosen the opposite alternative, namely that of conflict within the group and peace without. One of the splendidly realistic aspects of Sumner's analysis of group life is his recognition that in-group peace and out-group hostility are correlative facts. We can fortify his conclusion in the case of the Negro caste by showing that accommodation with the out-group and conflict within the group are also positively associated. It is not forgotten that in the case of the Negro we are dealing with a caste within our society and not with a separate culture; it is just this fact which makes it impossible for the Negroes to establish the white caste as an out-group. They are too utterly involved in the white social and economic structure to be other than dependent on it and passively accommodated toward it. Strong in-group loyalties are impossible where aggression toward the out-group may not be expressed and where, on the contrary, there is a genuine dependence on out-group (that is, white caste) relationships.

Southern white informants believe that there is much more aggression and violence within the Negro caste than there is in the white caste, and the evidence for this assertion will presently be set out. Informants are less interested in the fact of this disproportionate aggression within the Negro group than in the reason for it. Some are inclined to charge it to emotional instability among Negroes. Here, incidentally, white informants invariably mean lower-class Negroes, since they say that they know that there are some

---

[1] "The relationship of comradeship and peace in the wegroup and that of hostility and war towards others-groups are correlative to each other." W. G. Sumner, *Folkways* (Boston, 1906), p. 12; quoted by permission of Ginn & Co.

orderly and disciplined individuals and families within the Negro caste, by which, of course, they refer to the middle-class Negroes. Properly reinterpreted, something can be made of this explanation of "emotional instability"; it may well be that the caste culture of lower-class Negroes does not offer a mold for the type of character in which aggressive expression is controlled to the degree required by the dominant patterns of American civilization. Other white informants are inclined to view excessive violence in the Negro group as a racial trait. It is said that Negroes are nearer to "savagery," and it is assumed that "savages" are more aggressive than we ourselves. There may also be some truth in this but probably not very much in view of the fact that under certain circumstances, i.e., middle-class position, Negroes are able to mute their direct aggressive expression in the manner required by our society. A preferable view would seem to be that, since the hostility of Negroes against whites is violently and effectively suppressed, we have a boiling of aggressive affect within the Negro group. The essential point is, again, "safety first."

We shall inquire more directly into the nature and sources of Negro hostility for Negroes. One of these, and a very important one, is that of sexual jealousy. Old lawyers in Southerntown seem invariably to assume in a cutting or shooting case between two Negroes that there is a woman in it—that some man has been sleeping with some other man's woman. It is added that violence between Negro women is also quite common and for the same reason—some woman's snatching some other woman's man. Whenever such a case comes up in court, even though the jealousy motif may not be obvious, it is invariably searched for by judges and lawyers.[2] Local Negro informants commented on the frequency

[2] "Jealousy and the violent expressions of this passion are manifested by both men and women during the courtship period, by legally married couples and by companions in a common-law relationship. Because Ben Mason began courting Alice Harris' daughter another woman shot him five times. But Ben Mason had not himself the best reputation. A few years earlier he had accidentally killed one girl while shooting at another who had spurned his attentions. The gossip of the community for the greater part of a month centered around

of violent expression, and there are many references to it by observers of Negro life.[3]

There is obviously a connection between the frequency of sexual jealousy in the Negro caste and the fact that the hold of the Negro man on his woman is institutionally very weak; this has already been pointed out in the chapter on the sexual gain. Since the Negro cannot hold his woman by force, say, of a strong family institution, he must do it by personal force instead; and jealous aggression is one of the ways in which he expresses his claims. The weaker the institution in guaranteeing the woman to the man or the man to the woman, the stronger efforts the person must make individually to hold what the institution does not secure to him. This certainly accounts for a part of the trouble over unfaithful love partners in the Negro caste.

More in line with our theory of aggression deflected from the white group is the following hypothesis: part of the jealousy which motivates the fights between Negro men is actually directed against the whites who take Negro women or have them accessible; this jealousy cannot be expressed and must be suppressed so far as the whites are concerned, but it is vented with additional fury against any Negro aggressor of the same kind. Another alternative to punishing the white rival is punishing the Negro woman; much of the sus-

---

the murder of a young woman at one of the frolics, by a man who came in a blind rage of jealousy to kill his wife because she was 'runnin' 'round with other men.'" Charles S. Johnson, *Shadow of the Plantation* (Chicago, 1934), p. 51; quoted by permission of the University of Chicago Press.

[3] "A further analysis of the negro's anger indicates that a very great part has its origin in jealousy over persons. This is not only true of the women, who fight and quarrel because of jealousy and envy, but it is also true of the men, and it would appear that at least eighty per cent of the fights and personal encounters among the negroes are ordinarily caused by the woman in the case. And just as jealousy leads to intensity of the animal passion peculiarly in the case of the negroes, so with this emotion go laughter, shrieking, singing and various expressions of wanton recklessness and morbid pleasure in the pouring-out of the animal passion." Howard W. Odum, "Social and Mental Traits of the Negro," *Studies in History, Economics and Public Law* (1910), Vol. 37, No. 3, p. 550.

picion and aggression against Negro women by their husbands or lovers may be accounted for in this way; it is too dangerous to take it out on the white man, but the woman betrayer is at hand and may be punished.

In the case of aggression between Negro women there does not exist the complication of rivalry with white women, since it is one of the features of the caste status of Negro men and white women that they may not have social or sexual contact. The hottest rivalries, however, are engendered over the question of Negro men. Here again the weak hold of the Negro woman on her man from an institutional standpoint brings forward jealous aggression as a means of claiming possession of the loved object and keeping rivals away. One Negro woman related how she had unwittingly gone out with a married man who had represented himself as single. She liked him very much and would have wished to continue the contact. Finally, however, he broke down and confessed his marriage. The important thing was the informant's attitude toward this event. She said that he had put her in a very dangerous position and that he was actually risking her life by his lie. The man's wife might easily have killed her and, since she would not have recognized the woman, she could not have protected herself in any way. She wrote the husband a long letter telling him that she would not see him again. This letter apparently fell into the hands of the wife and her threat toward the informant was withdrawn. This active danger connected with rivalry situations is characteristic of life in the Negro caste in Southerntown and county. The danger will become more intelligible when we remember that the personal security of the Negro is by no means so well guaranteed by the law as is that of the white person.

A surprising feature of the situation is the assertion by local informants that lower-class Negro women are frequently armed, at least in the sense that they carry ice picks or razor blades as weapons. Apparently we have here a kind of frontier where the law is weak and each person is expected to attend to his own interests by means of direct personal aggression and defense.

A white informant stated that there are many brutalized

Negroes in Southerntown and supposed it must be because they are so near to tribal life. He said that they often beat their children fiercely and that physical combat between husband and wife is frequent. He guessed that three quarters of the Negro women carry some weapon, usually a razor, for defense. The men are likely to carry knives. Informant stated that the whites try to keep guns out of their hands but are of course unable to do this.

Gambling between Negro men is a frequent occasion for violent expressions, especially where strangers meet over the gambling table.[4] A white planter said in this connection that there was not much disorder on his place among the hands; they shoot craps on the plantation and he allows this because he would rather that they do it at home. If they went to neighboring plantations, shooting and cutting scrapes would be much more likely. Southern white people are familiar with these tendencies toward violence in the Negro group and contrast them with the idealized picture of the lower-class Negro often held by northern white people.

In connection with the theme of in-group violence among Negroes, it is useful to refer to the matter of magical practices. There is good evidence[5] that such practices are still

[4] "In the lower class of Negroes a predilection for petty gambling amounts almost to a passion. Their opportunity of indulging it depends upon their command of ready money. A majority of the murders committed in this section arise out of gambling. Therefore, I would attribute the difference in the relative number of homicidal crimes committed by the Negro . . . to the Negro's greater command of money. . . . Around these tables, especially on Saturday nights and Sundays, gather crowds of men and boys of all ages, scarcely one in five without a knife or pistol. It takes but a word to bring one or both into the game." A. H. Stone, *Studies in the American Race Problem* (New York, 1908), p. 107; quoted by permission of Doubleday, Doran & Co.

[5] "Most generally a human image is used. A good piece of sympathetic magic is the following . . . method of disposing of a person even when he is absent: On the change of the moon take a newspaper and cut it out in the shape of a person, naming the image after the man you wish to kill. Stick a brass pin in this image working it down from head to foot (so as to 'bear him down'). Then get a small box 'sech ez thread comes

fairly widespread among lower-class Negroes. What is to be noted here is the exceptional frankness with which death wishes toward other people may be expressed and carried out in magical acts. Apparently these wishes are tolerated in that diminishing section of the lower-class Negro group which clings to magic. As a contrast one should remember how reluctant most American white people are to acknowledge frankly their hostile wishes toward others, let alone attempting to effectuate them, even by magical means. This denial of aggression in individuals may account for the fact that our wars all have to be described as "defensive." The point is, of course, that the possibility of such openly acknowledged wishes indicates a much freer level of aggressive expression within the Negro group. The same wishes are presumably activated but repressed in personalities formed by the larger American social pattern.

There are other behavior patterns in the lower-class Negro group that apparently often lead to quarreling and outright aggression. One of these is the type of aggressive banter and boasting that goes on where groups of men are gathered together. I know little about this pattern directly and cannot enlarge upon the idea from firsthand experience, but references to it have come from informants as well as from other observers of the Negro.[6] Very often this banter

---

in' and lay the man out in it like a man in a coffin. Just as the sun is going down, dig a hole in the cemetery and bury the box. Your enemy will surely die—'goes down wid de sun.' Or else you may dispose of him by getting some of his old dirty clothes and corking them up tightly in a brown jug. Bury this jug in the graveyard on the breast of the grave. In nine days your enemy will be dead, but the process may be hastened somewhat by burying in the back yard a new half-gallon bucket filled with ashes from his grate." N. N. Puckett, *Folk Beliefs of the Southern Negro* (Chapel Hill, 1926), pp. 242-243; quoted by permission of the University of North Carolina Press.

[6] "The outward markings and physical manifestations of the positive self-feeling have been indicated: Holding the head high, stepping high, throwing back the head and shoulders, strutting, or on the other hand, walking in a wanton, reckless swagger, and general bumptiousness; gesticulating, being puffed up with conceit, attempt to attract attention—bluff in all of its forms." Odum, *op. cit.*, pp. 560-561.

takes the form of a competition in making insulting remarks about the other person's status, performance, and even about the virtue of his wife, sweetheart, or mother; although it begins in jest, this activity sometimes goes over into murderous behavior.[7] The analogy that comes to mind from the wider American pattern is the boasting among boys of the late adolescent period, although among the Negroes it seems to be a much freer form of behavior in which direct pleasure is taken in open aggression. Self-aggrandizing action of this type is perhaps one of the thrills which more disciplined individuals must abandon in the course of development.

Recognition of these banter patterns leads to another consideration. There seems to be within the Negro group an actual idealization of personal violence. This idealization is apparently differentiated from the furtive compensatory admiration for an outlaw like Dillinger or Jesse James which appears in some sections of our wider society. Among the Negroes it seems to be more open and explicit.[8] It is much more like the admiration felt on the frontier for the individual who is physically and morally competent to take care of himself. The analogy here is stronger than might at first appear. The formal machinery of the law takes care of the Negroes' grievances much less adequately than of the whites', and to a much higher degree the Negro is compelled to make and enforce his own law with other Negroes. The inevitable result is an atmosphere in which ability to

---

[7] David L. Cohn, *God Shakes Creation* (New York, 1935), p. 161.

[8] "There is a tradition of violence which seems to mark personal relations to a high degree. Although strictly speaking not a matter of health, reference to the setting in which these violent deaths take place is important as a phase of the social life as well as the mortality. They include accidents of various sorts as well as homicides. The violence of life was an inescapable fact in a large number of families of the county. In another connection reference has been made to the violence attending jealousy in sex relations, but violence is not confined to love affairs. The large amount resulting in death in this group of 612 families may be considered simply another index to its cultural status." C. S. Johnson, *op. cit.*, pp. 189-190; quoted by permission of the University of Chicago Press.

defend one's rights or to be the successful aggressor is highly prized.[9] As Negroes approach or achieve middle-class status, they apparently value the contrary point—that they "have never been in any trouble" with the law. Lower-class Negroes, on the other hand, do not appear to be at a social disadvantage in their own class as a result of prison experience for a cutting or shooting affair; rather they seem to have a touch of Homeric attractiveness about them. They are envied their freedom of aggressive expression as well as their superior ability to take care of themselves.

This relative freedom of aggression is undoubtedly linked to the weakness of the monogamous family among lower-class Negroes. Where this family form is strongly in-trenched, it develops the character patterns for checking violent expression and, by cutting down reasons for sexual jealousy, diminishes as well the reasons for aggression. Seen from the standpoint of the white-caste mores, the lower-class Negro family is much less tightly organized to control impulse expression. Testimony on this score comes from both white and Negro informants. A white law officer de-scribed the frequency of violence of lower-class Negro men with their own women and gave as an example the fact that recently a white man in Southerntown had to intervene to save a woman when her husband was about to kill her. He commented on the inconsistency of Negro behavior; a Negro man and woman will have a fight or cutting party, the woman will get her husband thrown into jail, but the very next day she will be down begging to have him out. Inform-ant believed this argues for the capricious and temperamen-

---

[9] Read, for example, the words of a Negro father with re-gard to his two daughters and their children: "Ain't none of my daughters got married but dey is my chillun, and I take care of all of dem. The fathers of dey chillun don't come here less dey come right. I tell 'em all to stay way from my house. I don't git into no trouble with nobody. I am dis old and never been to jail, never been handcuffed or had a fight. My brothers git into trouble, but I ain't never had a fight. I keep my gun near 'cause if anyone tries to bother me, gonna shoot 'em shore. Gonna shoot 'em shore." C. S. Johnson, *op. cit.*, pp. 80-81; quoted by permission of the University of Chicago Press.

tal character of the Negro who is ever puzzling to the white man.[10]

The following story about her family difficulties came from a lower-class Negro woman. Her father and mother were divorced and her father married again; she continued to live with her mother. She said she used to visit her father during the summers at his tenant farm near Southerntown. At first his second wife was very nice to her. This was when she was about eleven. Two summers later, however, when she went to visit her father, his wife was mean; so she never went again. It came out subsequently that the reason for her meanness was fear that the girl would poison her on instructions from her mother. Actually, informant said, her mother never thought of such a thing. Significant, of course, are the suspicion of the second wife that such direct and violent means might be taken, the jealousy present, and the type of stress in the family situation.

The stepmother problem seems to be a troublesome one among lower-class Negroes, especially since there is so much shifting about of marriage partners. In the more nearly monogamous family this occasion for jealousy and hatred is much less likely to be present. The appearance of jealousy, hostility, or violence in the family is of the greatest importance from the standpoint of the character patterns of the children; if these factors are openly present in the lives of the adults, it is not very likely that the children will develop along lines different from their parents.

A powerful light is cast on the amount of in-family aggression in the Negro group by the comments of middle-class women on their family experience. It was repeatedly stressed by such informants that their husbands were "kind" to them. For example, one woman said that she had a terrible time with her husband in some ways, he drank terrifically, but still and all he was very kind to her. If he had not been so kind, even when drunk, she would never have been

---

[10] I have heard, however, the same affirmation from an officer in a domestic relations court in the North, this time with regard to white people. Mrs. Frances L. Roth, Assistant City Attorney of New Haven, has recited a number of instances of this type.

able to stand him as long as she did. I had heard this remark about "kindness" a number of times and finally asked the informant what she meant. She said that her husband always talked nicely to her and never beat her, that even when he was most drunk he would never abuse her, curse her, or threaten her. She would sometimes rail at him in his drunken moods, but he never answered angrily. Occasionally he would even be able to straighten himself out and make a friendly response.

Another middle-class informant said that shortly after her marriage she was carrying a child and during this very time she had direct proof of her husband's infidelity. She reacted by seeming to be physically sick, but knows now that she was mentally sick and heartsick. She said, however, that she was able to put up with all this and similar incidents over many years because her husband was very kind to her and the children. His kindness finally came to an end, however, and, in some trivial quarrel, he struck her. Later he said he was sorry and asked her to forgive him because he was not himself. She told him that she could well believe it if he could beat her that way. These middle-class women make such a point of the fact that their husbands do not beat them that one can see they are stressing their difference from lower-class people. The contrast between this and the wider American pattern must be plain with its consequent implication of freer aggressive activity in the Negro group.

Revenge by a Negro woman on a deserting husband or lover is by no means infrequent. The following story shows this behavior and some interesting aspects of the social situation as well. A Negro man took a fancy to a colored girl who, informant said, was half crazy anyway. He had intercourse with her, impregnated her, and then broke off the relationship. She wrote him letters, visited him at his work, did everything she could to get him back, and finally, when she was persuaded that he was not going to come back, sat down and wrote a love letter, full of impertinent expressions and solicitations, to one of the most prominent white women in town. She signed the name of her former lover to it. The white woman got the letter and turned it over to her husband; they were both quite incredulous about it. Informant said it happened that the white people were nice people, which was lucky for the Negro. The husband handed it to the police and here the Negro man had a second bit of good luck; one of the policemen was a friend of his. Instead of taking immediate action, the officers stopped to check up on the matter. They rounded up the Negro man and compared the letter with known samples of his handwriting, and, of course, discovered that it was not written by him. Then, according to pattern, they questioned him about "woman trouble" and finally discovered the former mistress. She got a prison sentence of a number of years, baby and all. Informant added that when she came back she had another child, this time by a white man. But what he stressed was the luck of the Negro man; very often a Negro is not questioned, he is just assumed to be guilty. Revengeful actions of this type having direct aggressive form or intent seem to be much more common in the Negro group than in the comparable white group.

Gossip, of course, is a universal form of aggression against others as well as a means of social control. It consists in telling the mean, embarrassing, insulting, and injurious things about other people, the things they would prefer to conceal.[11] Such gossip is extremely common in the Negro group which seems to be split and sectioned in every direction with distrustful people. Instances of this behavior came up repeatedly in the life-history materials, especially in relation to Negro leaders. It is very disheartening for the leader of a Negro group to experience the amount of annoying and destructive tattle that constantly goes on about him. My unchecked impression is that hostile and malicious gossip is more common than in the white caste. If so, it is an evidence of freer aggressive expression, since holding one's tongue is a major feat of renunciation of hostility toward others.

Should a researcher go to Southerntown and come in contact only with the middle-class Negroes, he would quickly be informed by white friends that these Negroes do not give a proper impression of the Negro group as a whole; they try

[11] This idea was first suggested to me in a course with Prof. Ernest W. Burgess of the University of Chicago.

to put the best face on it and to show only the "civilized" side of Negro life. It is frequently added that such middle-class Negroes are the only ones northerners get to know and are the basis of mistaken northern stereotypes of the Negro; that really to understand what the Negroes are like, one should see the slum section after twelve o'clock on Saturday night. A constant series of cases of shooting, cutting, beating, and occasionally murder, comes out of this area. All white people seem to agree that there is an unusual amount of violence nascent in the Negro group. Personal contact confirms the statements of white informants. Middle-class Negroes do want to put the best face on the situation and wish to make it appear that their class is really representative of their caste. In one sense they are right; their class shows what Negroes can do, but it does not show what lower-class Negroes are like right now.

White informants frequently point out another type of aggressive behavior among Negroes: middle-class Negroes frequently exploit their own people. They take advantage of the ignorance or superstition of their lower-class people and run skin games of one kind or another on them. Surprise is sometimes expressed at this behavior and it is felt that Negroes should be more loyal to one another. In skin games, however, the Negroes have too good a permissive example from the whites—and not southern whites alone—to make the behavior seem unusual.

It is impossible to see the more violent patterns of Negro behavior in the right perspective unless one understands that there are different standards of justice for the two castes. White persons are held much more strictly to the formal legal code; Negroes are dealt with much more indulgently. It is not a question of different formal codes for Negroes and whites, but rather of differences in severity and rigor of application of the code that does exist. This is true only under one condition, however—when Negro crimes are committed on Negroes; when they are done on whites, the penalties assessed may rather be excessively strict. The result is that the individual Negro is, to a considerable degree, outside the protection of white law, and must shift for himself. This leads to the frontier psychology already alluded to and to its consequent idealization of violence. Indeed, this differential application of the white law is often referred to as a merit of southern white persons; one will be asked to notice that they are lenient and indulgent with Negroes, and that Negroes are not nearly so severely punished as whites would be for the same crimes. It is clear that this differential application of the law amounts to a condoning of Negro violence and gives immunity to Negroes to commit small or large crimes so long as they are on Negroes. It may be indulgent in the case of any given Negro, but its effect on the Negro group as a whole is dangerous and destructive. One cannot help wondering if it does not serve the ends of the white caste to have a high level of violence in the Negro group, since disunity in the Negro caste tends to make it less resistant to the white domination. If this should be a correct observation, it need not follow that the tolerance of violence is a matter of conscious policy on the part of the white group; instead it would seem to be pragmatic, unformalized, and intuitive, but nonetheless effective.

A lawyer, for example, illustrated the point by telling me of a Negro woman he had defended. She was a cook about twenty-five years of age who had had a young lover. When he left her, she decoyed him back to her house and stabbed him to death. Her attorney got her off with a sentence of three years; he pleaded that such behavior was customary among Negroes, that their actions were unaccountable anyway, and that his client should therefore not be held to a severe standard. The same informant stated his belief that white juries do not tend to take Negro cases very seriously; they only hang Negroes for murder of Negroes when it is exceptionally brutal, or cold-blooded, or has some peculiar barbarous twist to it. The idea seems to be, "What can you expect of Negroes anyway; they are a mysterious lot, impulsive and primitive; and they should not be held accountable by white standards." It is commonly said, also as an evidence of white indulgence, that when Negroes have any chance to adjudge the offenses of other Negroes they are much more severe than are whites. One can well imagine this would be so, since they understand clearly the danger of unchecked aggression in their group. I have heard it openly urged among a group of lawyers discussing Negro crime that there should be a special criminal code for Negroes which would follow Negro folkways; it was said to be foolish to try to treat them like white people. It may be true that it would be vexatious for the time being to have to deal seriously with all of the Negro crimes that occur, but it is also true that so long as the law does not take over the protection of the Negro person he will have to do it himself by violent means.

A trial scene in the mayor's court will illustrate the point. It was a case of a shooting and cutting between two Negro women; the sheriff said privately that they loved the same man who vacillated between them. The testimony of the Negroes was relevant and sensible so far as it went; one of them, called "Chicken," just professionally did not know anything that he should have known, could not offer a report on matters that had happened right under his nose. There were currents of amusement through the dense Negro audience as the testimony progressed. Evidently there were many private understandings among the Negroes. It appeared that woman B made an obscene remark to woman A. A challenged her to come downstairs and repeat it. B came down a flight of ten steps; A fired a gun five times at B; B closed in on A who was still firing, pursued her, caught up with her, and stabbed her with an ice pick. A was fined ten dollars and costs for firing at B. The white officials talked to the Negroes in a normal manner, not using a special dialect, as sometimes alleged. The judge seemed fair and reasonable with the Negro witnesses. The defense attorney alleged that the obscene remark was not felt by the Negro as it would have been by a white woman since Negroes were always saying such things to one another. "If these had been two white women, A would have been justified in the shooting." The defense attorney occasionally referred to the audience as "these niggers." This trial is an example in miniature of the attitudes of white officials and attorneys toward Negro crime. They are fair, but they simply do not take it as seriously as they would the same offense by whites. It is this attitude on their part that makes life dangerous in the Negro group. It seems quite possible that lack of adequate legal protection of the Negro's life and person is itself an incitement to violence.

Control of violence in the Negro group is further complicated by the patron-protégé relationship. We have already referred to this "angel" pattern. It amounts to this: if a Negro belongs to the feudal group of some influential white man, he may have extraordinary liberty to do violent things to other Negroes. This fact is bitterly complained of by middle-class Negro people. In reference to this sheltering of the Negro henchman behind his white boss, an informant said that a Negro, so intrenched, has been known to threaten to kill another and say that he knows he will not be punished for it; he will "farm another acre," that is, do extra work for his boss in exchange for the protection. Incidentally, the boss who can offer this kind of protection to a Negro can exchange it for economic advantage to himself.

A confirmatory statement comes from the white police. They complain that many bad and dangerous Negroes are pets of some influential white person in the community and that, when they go out and round them up for a crime, the white "angel" comes in and "does not understand" how the Negro could have done what he was accused of, swears that he is a "good nigger," and gets him off. The police say this is a considerable barrier to literal justice in the community and prevents them from cleaning up on bad "niggers." Southerntown is small enough so that this personal influence is very important and has great effect on theoretical justice. It seems that every white family has some Negro or Negroes whom it protects. The dangerous element in the situation for Negroes is that white people interfere in justice between them. Evidently the whites do not consider security of life and person for the Negroes a very important issue.

An influential white attorney, puzzled, told me that reputable white men will appear as character witnesses for Negroes whom he personally knows to be disreputable, killers, and very dangerous men. He wondered why this was so. He said the whites will swear on the witness stand that the Negroes in question are obedient, pay their bills, do not bother anybody, and the like. He was bearing unconscious testimony to the point already made. Very probably from the white standpoint these actions seem benevolent, since the whites know the accused Negroes as good servants or field hands. From the white standpoint it is a feudal protectoral relationship, an extension of family ties to "their" Negroes. No doubt it often costs white people a good deal of trouble to take the witness stand and make these asseverations, and very probably they frequently believe them. The result of this type of influence, however, is greatly to increase the danger and thrills of life in the Negro caste and especially in the lower-class group.[12]

Oftentimes, however, the reason for such benevolent behavior on the part of the white "angel" is more tangible. Negro informants say that if a white man gets a Negro off a murder charge "because he needs him on the plantation," that Negro is indebted to him in a peculiar way; very often he is more or less bound to this benefactor in a kind of servitude. Perhaps "servitude" is not the right word, but as long as he is in the community he is under a peculiar obligation to his protector. It is almost as if he were bound out to his boss rather than sent for a term to the state farm. Both of these factors—the relative indifference to crimes of Negroes against Negroes and the feudalistic protection of favorite Negroes—lessen the pressure of our formal legal standards of justice against Negro crime. It would be convenient if there were local statistics which would formally define the differences between white and Negro crime rates. There are

[12] "Ask any Chambers County nigger about Wade Finley and he will keep his mouth shut unless he knows and trusts you. If you can get him to talk, he will tell you that Wade Finley is a bad nigger. Ask any white man and he will tell you Wade is the best nigger in the county—a real white man's nigger—the highest compliment he can bestow on him . . .

"It is a long time since Wade Finley killed his first nigger, and no one seems to know just what it was about. He said it was in self-defense, and old man Huckaby and a lot of his friends testified that Wade was a good hard-working boy, so the judge let him go. Chambers County niggers were afraid of him after that and he had and still has a great power over them." Carl Carmer, *Stars Fell on Alabama* (New York, 1934), p. 212; quoted by permission of Farrar and Rinehart, Inc.

only a few general facts which may be alleged in support of our contention. One thing is that Negroes pay life-insurance rates 10 to 20 percent higher than those for whites of equivalent age and hazard of occupation. The reasons alleged are greater liability to disease due to complex socio-economic factors and greater prevalence of violence in the Negro group which makes life more dangerous. We learn also[13] that the state is high in the list of states for the offense of "aggravated assault." Negroes are not segregated in these statistics, but Negro violence against Negroes must be a large proportion. The state is in the highest of four groups in the number of homicides and lynchings. The Negroes, of course, do not do the lynchings, but they probably provide a disproportionate number of the homicides. An additional fact, difficult to interpret, is that the state was ranked low in number of suicides per 100,000 population in 1929. If suicide and homicide were regarded as antitheses from the standpoint of aggression, the figures would make perfect sense, since social patterns permitting or encouraging homicide would direct outward the aggression which might be internalized as suicide. Considering the state of the evidence, however, this hypothesis is exceedingly tentative. It should follow from our conception of the two classes in the Negro group that homicide would be much more frequent in the lower class and suicide in the middle class. The informal local evidence from all sides and for both castes suggests, however, that violent and aggressive behavior is disproportionately present in the Negro caste. A shred of confirmation exists in the relatively high homicide rates for Negroes in certain southern cities.[14] Further, the general evidence seems to be that Negro crime rates the country over are comparatively greater than those in the white group.[15]

[13] Howard W. Odum, _Southern Regions of the United States_ (Chapel Hill, 1936).

[14] Arthur F. Raper, _The Tragedy of Lynching_ (Chapel Hill, 1933), p. 33.

[15] "Examination of available records of Negro crime prompts these observations as a preface to further analysis:

1. It is difficult to secure dependable data on Negro crime,

It seems very likely that aggression within the Negro group has increased since slavery days because white slave-owners could hardly afford to permit the type of behavior now exhibited by Negroes. It also seems probable that even in slavery days discord within the Negro group was facilitated by the system. While the overseer was usually a white man, the actual "slave driver" was a Negro in most cases. Further, the hierarchy within slavery which distinguished house servants from field hands was an important matter. House servants apparently customarily despised the less acculturated hands who did the manual labor in the fields.[16]

The concluding impression is of a much greater freedom of aggressive expression among Negroes, a freedom which seems to be related to the value of Negro disunity from the

---

because (a) general crime records are poor and comparative figures less dependable, and (b) racial factors enter, influencing the agencies of law enforcement most frequently to the disadvantage of the Negro and the Negro records of crime.

2. The Negro crime rate as measured by all comparative records is greater than that of the white.

3. The difference varies widely and according to geographical location and population ratios; it also varies by types of offenses.

4. There is a much higher Negro rate for homicides than white, even when the emotional factors referred to are taken into account.

5. Negro arrest rates are higher than white for petty offenses and lower than white in commitment to prison for serious offenses.

6. There is obvious discrimination in the administration of laws on the part of the police, magistrates, judges, and pardon boards, which explains an undetermined degree of the disparity between white and Negro rates.

7. It is possibly true that Negro rates of crime are more nearly actual crime rates of Negroes than white recorded rates are of crimes committed by whites.

8. Illiteracy, unfavorable environment, age distributions, and unfamiliarity with city and urban life, are factors to be seriously studied in relation to present Negro crime." C. S. Johnson, *The Negro in American Civilization* (New York, 1930), p. 316; quoted by permission of Henry Holt & Co.

[16] *See*, for example, these relations as represented in the excellent novel by Margaret Mitchell, *Gone with the Wind* (New York, 1936).

standpoint of the master caste. The differential is likely to exist as long as the caste pattern of relationships itself, since it seems to be functionally related to white superiority and Negro subordination.

CHAPTER XIV

Negro Aggression Against Whites

Most of the time it is the part of wisdom for the Negro to suppress his resentment at the superior advantages enjoyed by white people. We have seen how this aggression is converted into a passive accommodation and how it is displaced onto persons within the Negro group. It must not be supposed, however, that Negroes show no direct resentment toward white people; they do, even though this form of reaction is not of major importance.

For the sake of contrast we should remind ourselves of the normal outlets for aggression available to a minority group which wishes to change its economic or social status. They are political behavior, in-group organization, and active protest against undesired conditions. Some members of the minority group achieve political status and are able to represent the interests of their social segment. In the case of the Negroes in Southerntown, as we know, this conventional form of striving is not available. A common result is to drive hostile protest under ground, to keep it a lurking and latent force in the social order. It is doubtless the failure to describe this fact and to see in proper perspective the aggressive tensions within societies that makes so many social developments and movements surprising to social scientists.

Southern white people, however, do not make this mistake in respect to Negroes. On the contrary, they show the greatest sensitivity to aggression from the side of the Negro, and in fact, to the outside observer, often seem to be reacting to it when it is not there. Still, it is very convincing to experience in one's own person the unshakeable conviction of the white caste that danger lurks in the Negro quarter. Only constant watchfulness, it is believed, and a solid white front against potential Negro attack maintain the *status quo*. This behavior on the part of the whites suggests the following proposition: they realize the gains they are making from the Negroes and expect the Negro to react as they themselves would if they were arbitrarily assigned an inferior caste position. As we know, they are mistaken in this assumption since there are other ways out of the dilemma than direct aggression.

It is astonishing, when any little incident occurs, how unerringly aggressive intent on the part of the Negro is assumed. The following event described by a middle-class Negro informant will illustrate. A Negro boy's automobile was sideswiped by another car, and the impact threw it against a white worker on the road. The worker was slightly injured. The boy was brought to jail, tried, and given thirty days at the county farm. Informant intervened in behalf of his protégé and talked to an officer of the law who thought that the boy had come off lucky not to be killed for hitting a white man; the fact that the accident was caused by the other driver did not appear to matter. It seemed to be taken for granted that a Negro would hit a white man if he could get away with it under cover of an "accident." A further detail about the case may be added. The boy was sent to the state farm, worked, beaten, and came home in bad condition with his buttocks scarred from whip marks. Informant went to the doctor who had taken care of the injured white worker and arranged to pay the bill, which was only five dollars. Later the injured man tried to collect fifteen dollars from him for the doctor's bill, and was surprised to learn that he had already been to the doctor and paid it. Informant said that this is the sort of thing a Negro is not supposed to do, viz., to think and to act for himself; he says this white man still holds the incident against him.

One might notice that the above case could easily fall under the classification of reckless driving and also that the Negro informant may not be unbiased. The incident, nevertheless, is typical in at least one respect, that of positing a destructive impulse in the Negro's act. Where there is so much smoke, there is bound to be some fire. Certainly the whites are attuned to notice the slightest forward pressure on the part of the Negro, and the white caste is little disposed to accept even the feeblest direct action from the Negro's side. A white middle-class informant in a softened mood once told me that Negro men have to take a lot and are helpless to complain or fight back. Even when a husband finds a white man in bed with his wife he may not retaliate. The principle seems to be that nothing justifies aggression by a Negro against a white man or woman. My informant was reluctant to talk about this issue and persistently passed on to other matters. But he later made the point in another way. He said that some white men will bait a Negro and then smash him down if he answers back. Informant does not do this; when he jokes with a Negro, he also lets it be understood that he can take as good as he gives. In the case of baiting, it seems as if there were an attempt to provoke the Negro by sadistic joking and then, when his counter-aggression is mobilized, to come down hard on him. The sensitivity to any assertive move on the part of the Negro is immediately recorded in threatening judgments of his behavior of the type we already know; he is said to be "uppity" or "getting out of his place."

Since the Negro may not retaliate openly, he must have recourse to furtive means if he is to retaliate at all. This we shall find to be the case where direct aggression is expressed. It is done, if possible, so that the aggressor is unknown; the direct challenge would provoke certain vengeance. We shall find also that, since explicit hostility is so dangerous, Negroes have recourse to indirect, circuitous, and symbolic methods of conflict with whites. In the following discussion we shall indicate some of these, enumerating them in a series from the most direct to the most roundabout means of expression.

It is worth noting as a general point that within the caste situation Negro women can be somewhat more expressive of their resentment than can Negro men. In comparing life-history data of Negro men and women it was quite clear that much more antagonism is tolerated from the women; they can do and say things which would bring a severe penalty had they been men. It may be that white caste members do not fear the aggression of women so much, especially since it cannot take the form of sexual attack; or the chivalry expected of men in our society toward women in general may come into play. There are, of course, distinct limits to what a Negro woman may do, but they are not so narrow as for men.

The Negro's threat to the whites is that of furtive individual acts of violence. In this day and age an uprising does not seem a real danger; it is the sporadic individual attack or reprisal which has threatening significance for the white caste. It would seem indeed that only the rather direct forms of aggression from Negroes are feared or even appreciated; ridicule is a difficult weapon for the lower-caste member against an upper-caste man, and mere wishes do not hurt anybody. The individual reaction has not always been the only type; there have been, of course, slave uprisings[1] and these have been of some importance in the history of American slavery. There have been no successful revolts in North America, but the occasional uprisings that did occur were the source of violent reprisals, fear, and intensive precautionary measures.[2]

There are two possible explanations for the lack of organ-

---

[1] "Its cost was too great, and one of the causes of this cost was the slave insurrections from the very beginning, when the slaves rose on the plantation of Diego Columbus down to the Civil War in America. Actual and potential slave insurrection in the West Indies, in North and South America, kept the slave owners in apprehension and turmoil, or called for a police system difficult to maintain. In North America revolt finally took the form of organized running away to the North, and this, with the growing scarcity of suitable land and the moral revolt, led to the Civil War and the disappearance of the American slave trade." W. E. B. Du Bois, *The Negro* (New York, 1915), p. 158; quoted by permission of Henry Holt & Co.

[2] "The several arguments had varying degrees of influence in the several areas. In the older settlements where the planters had relaxed into easygoing comfort, the fear of revolt was keenest; in the newer districts the settlers were more confident in their own alertness." U. B. Phillips, *American Negro Slavery* (New York, 1918), pp. 133-134; quoted by permission of D. Appleton-Century Co.

ized hostility on the side of the Negroes at the present time. One is that the war-like front presented by the united white caste leaves no hope of success. A second is that there is an alternative available now which was available only with great difficulty in slavery days,—physical mobility or escape toward the North. It is understandable that escape would be preferable to the prospect of a suicidal attack. We have already noted the conflict within the Negro caste which makes any type of collective effort difficult, and most of all, of course, any effort against the armed and determined upper-caste group. At any prospect of a united political front on the part of the Negroes, such as membership in Huey Long's "Share the Wealth" clubs, the white alarm is immediate and the event becomes a political issue; the vigilance which is the price of dominance is keen.

Among secretive hostile acts is included "shooting from the bush," that is, murdering a white man either under the cover of night or from ambush. This is a recognized peril and is, to some degree, a limitation on white aggression toward Negroes. It does occur occasionally and the assailant never goes unsought for, though he is often not found. Sometimes a substitute sacrifice is required. A white middle-class informant who represented vigorously the growing attitude against white sexual contacts with Negroes said that whenever a white man is shot from the bush, it is because he has been fooling around with Negro women. He added the opinion characteristic of his class that only lower-class white men do this and quoted a Negro approvingly on this score: "You caint be a white man during the day and a nigger at night." Occasionally the white man will feel the disapproval of the community on his behavior with Negro women sufficiently so that he dare not appeal directly, and on this issue, for caste revenge on the Negro;[3]

[3] "Grant had lived in McIntosh County all his life and was without court record. It is established, however, that some months before the lynching, Grant had ambushed and shot a white man for 'running with his woman.' The man though seriously wounded and disfigured, did not have him arrested. It was not learned how much schooling Grant had had or what his general intelligence level was." Arthur F. Raper, *The*

in such situations there are other methods and other issues which can be raised to reaffirm the point that Negro aggression is not tolerated.

A middle-class Negro speaking on this topic was quite pessimistic about the situation of the Negro in America. He thought that Negroes are becoming ever more restless under the constant pressure from the whites. In his town recently there was a man hunt and a Negro was shot; the Negroes did not show by their faces or behavior how much this angered them, but if they got a chance, they were ready to fight back. He also cited the case of a Negro man who was "friendly" with a certain Negro woman; then a white man began coming to see her. The Negro caught the white man there and "beat the hell" out of him. Of course, the Negro had to leave town after this because a white posse went out looking for him. Informant said he did not think riots would do any good, but they do leave a certain sting. He thought that resistance for the Negro is hopeless.

Occasional surprising instances occur in Southerntown where the "circumstances of the case" are taken into account and caste solidarity is not invoked. A Negro relative of one of my informants ran a small store. A white man came in, ordered some goods, got them, and then refused to pay for them. The storekeeper brought the white man into court and forced him to pay. The white man took this as an intolerable affront and came to beat up the Negro. The Negro fought with him and beat him up instead. In this case the other whites did nothing, but said the white man should have paid his bill in the first place. A sense of fair play based on the business morality of the community here came into effect; and there may have been other factors, such as that the store owner had a white friend at court, or that the white assailant was disliked. All such factors alter cases when caste punishment of Negroes is concerned. In general, however, the feeling of the necessity of solidarity among the whites is so strong that the nature of the case is not examined; all that is seen is militancy in a Negro, and this, it is agreed, cannot be tolerated.

Tragedy of Lynching (Chapel Hill, 1933), p. 210; quoted by permission of the University of North Carolina Press.

Occasionally, of course, the spirited Negro and the intolerable situation come together and the result is a stand against the white man. One Negro informant told a story about his father. A fence was down between his father's farm and that of a neighbor, and the white neighbor persistently let his horses run into the Negro's field. It is against the law to let horses run loose in this way. The animals got into the Negro's corn a number of times and were destroying a large part of it. Several times the "old man" drove them back and finally sent one of his sons to complain. After the boy returned, the horses were promptly back in the corn again. The Negro asked his son what had happened. The boy said the white man paid no attention to the warning and told his hired man to let the horses loose again. Informant's father became intensely angry, took a gun, and walked with it in his hand to the white man's house. He had an angry talk with the owner of the horses; finally the white man's wife intervened and told him they would keep the horses away. A lynching party formed at the white house later in the day; the owner eventually stopped it on the ground that the Negro did not really know what he was doing. Informant said his father became so angry under such conditions that he did not care what happened to him; he said he would sooner die than have the food which he was raising for his children and for which he had worked so hard destroyed in this way. The would-be lynchers here were reacting on principle and not according to the circumstances of the case.

Apparently aggression of Negro children against white children is not taken quite so seriously as that of adult Negroes. A Negro man recalled how he and his idolized brother went around and did mischievous things together when they were boys. They used to fight with the white boys in the neighborhood and especially with four German boys who lived on the adjoining farm. Since there were only two Negroes and four whites, the Negroes were often beaten. They would have fist fights by rounds and "rock" each other, and once there was a near-tragedy. The Negro boys' father had a .22 rifle with which he used to shoot the heads off chickens. The boys would sneak it out when he was not at home and practice with it until both became good shots. Once they decided to even things up for good and all with the German boys, and took the gun in a bag down to the line fence where they usually fought. It was planned that the older brother would engage one of the neighbors in a fight, then step aside and let the other shoot. This very day the white boys did an unusual thing. They came up and asked the Negro boys how their grandfather was; the brothers answered that he had died the night before, which was true. "Well, then," said one of the white boys, "I think we're foolish for fighting all the time this way." Peace was made and no shooting took place. It may be noted that this story was a treasured fantasy of this informant, and its function undoubtedly was to affirm his own integrity as over against white men. He did not conceive of himself as forever passively accepting affronts from the whites.

A highly placed white man expressed a widely held view when he said that Negroes have neither malice nor gratitude; they will do anything in the heat of passion, but once rage is burnt out they do not carry grudges. It is this sudden blind "passion" which the whites fear in Negroes, and against which they feel they must defend themselves. It is as though they were saying that Negroes have the ruthless, nonacculturated character of children, but with grown-up bodies. Perhaps white people do not realize how desperately they often drive the Negroes and that the "passion" alluded to is a last embittered stand after sore and repeated trials.

Now and then the worst fears of the whites are confirmed. For example, a case of cannibalism occurred in a near-by town. A Negro killed a white man and his wife and ate part of their bodies. After much searching he was finally caught by federal officers for making obscene use of the mails; he had been writing suggestive letters to women in a northern town. As evidence of the discipline of the area we note that the man was legally tried and hanged, and that fifteen hundred national guardsmen were on hand to see that the law took its course. The incident was later written up in one of the pulp magazines quite as my informant had told it. It seemed clear that the murderer was a psychopath. The difference between the sentiment in Southerntown and the view of a similar atrocity in the North is that in the South it supports the stereotyped view of the Negro as a savage and meets a preëxisting conviction that this is the sort of thing one expects from Negroes. In the North it would be compared with other cases of such atrocities and the men would be put down as morally defective (i.e., nonacculturated). His behavior would no more be viewed as typical of Negroes than similar behavior by a white man would be considered characteristic of whites. The expectation of hostility from the Negro caste and the use of every incident to confirm this stereotype are tremendously important in Southerntown.

A personal observation on a mental hospital was enlightening in this connection. Of course, the caste line is strong in the hospital; there are separate buildings for Negro men and women and it was my impression that the equipment was somewhat inferior in the Negro wards. It was said that no Negro patients, either men or women, are allowed ground privileges at any time, but that some white patients are. Since a certain amount of freedom on the grounds is considered by progressive psychiatrists[4] important in rehabilitating the mentally ill, this lack of privilege is no trivial matter. No reason was alleged for the practice. It may well be that attendants adequate to supervise the Negro patients are not available, that is, that it is a financial matter; the white patients, of course, are supervised. But it seemed likely to me that fear of "crazy Negroes" had something to do with it. The attitude seemed to be that they are enough to be feared when they are officially sane; when they are proved insane, special caution must be used. I could not help noting that the women's wards in the Negro hospital seemed quieter than women's wards in mental hospitals usually do. There was not the stormy clamor that often greets one in a disturbed ward of women patients. Of course, there was no telling what happened when white officials or visitors were not present; still the presence of such visitors was no deterrent to excited behavior on the white wards of the same hospital. Another trivial point noticed

[4] Such as Dr. William A. Bryan of the Worcester State Hospital, Worcester, Massachusetts.

in the mental hospital was the fact that Negro patients never regain their former titles. In considering this matter we must keep in mind a practice which may perhaps be followed unconsciously in white mental hospitals. When white patients are very sick they are likely to be treated as children by the psychiatrists and called by their first names, even if they are old people. As they improve, the psychiatrist seems to adjust himself to the increasing social normality of the patient by restoring his title to him, calling him *Mr.* Jones instead of "Tom." The Negro patient can never expect to win back normality along these lines; he is "Mose" so long as he is in the hospital. The caste pattern proves a differentiating guide to behavior throughout the smallest details of the culture.

The most notorious type of individual Negro aggression is rape of white women. Indeed this is used as a generalized justification of white aggression against Negroes. Just why this is so has been altogether insufficiently wondered about, and it is doubtful whether as sociologists we can provide an answer. It is sufficient for our purposes to know that rape is the most intensely hostile act a Negro can perform within the purview of southern regional culture. In another connection it will be shown that statistical evidence of the frequency of rape cases does not support the assertion that sexual assaults are the uniform inciting cause of illegal violence against the Negroes. Rape cases were by no means unknown, as is frequently alleged, before the emancipation of the Negro,[5] although they have probably been more

---

[5] "The statistics of rape in Virginia, and the Georgia cases already given, refute the oft-asserted Southern tradition that negroes never violated white women before slavery was abolished. Other scattering examples may be drawn from contemporary newspapers. One of these occurred at Worcester, Massachusetts, in 1768. Upon conviction the negro was condemned to death, although a white man at the same time found guilty of an attempt at rape was sentenced merely to sit upon the gallows." Phillips, *op. cit.*, p. 459; quoted by permission of D. Appleton-Century Co.

"Such evidence shows that the crime of rape directed against white women was not unknown prior to 1860. As regards other crimes frequently committed by negroes during the period of slavery, apparently it formed a rather small proportion. It

frequent since. Rape and the wish to commit it seem to be constantly posited by the white caste as features of the Negro psychology.[6] Certainly this is not true if the conscious intentions of the mass of Negroes be taken into consideration; there is no evidence for the widespread *overt* prevalence of such wishes. If the unconscious, repressed and seldom-realized wishes of Negroes are taken into account, it may be that the white caste is correct in this assumption. For example, the superior prestige position of the white woman and her categorical inaccessibility may be a challenge to the Negro along quite American lines; from this view the proof of social advancement and mobility would be sexual contact with a white woman. And there is undoubtedly the element of revenge in such crimes, when they do occur; the Negro is wreaking on a symbolic member of the white caste the impotent rage which he so frequently feels at the seduction of his own women by white men. This point has not escaped the attention of white observers[7] who have often good reason to know the basis for

---

was far from being a crime that was more frequently committed than any other, and yet it was one for the perpetration of which the negroes showed a marked propensity whenever an opportunity presented itself. Under the institution of slavery, however, such opportunities were few. From the nature of slavery, the negro seldom had an opportunity to ravish a white woman." James E. Cutler, *Lynch-Law* (New York, 1905), p. 216; quoted by permission of Longmans, Green & Co.

[6] "As the crime of rape of late years had its baleful renascence in the teaching of equality and the placing of power in the ignorant Negroes' hands, so its perpetuation and increase have undoubtedly been due in large part to the same teaching. The intelligent Negro may understand what social equality truly means, but to the ignorant and brutal young Negro, it signifies but one thing: the opportunity to enjoy, equally with white men, the privilege of cohabiting with white women. This the whites of the South understand; and if it were understood abroad, it would serve to explain some things which have not been understood hitherto." T. N. Page, *The Negro: The Southerner's Problem* (New York, 1904), pp. 112-113; quoted by permission of Charles Scribner's Sons.

[7] "The Hon. Alex. C. King, of Atlanta, Georgia, was introduced as the first speaker. Mr. King spoke as follows upon the subject, 'The Punishment of Crimes against Women, Exist-

such revenge tendencies. The expectation of retaliation from Negroes must do much to strengthen the fixed belief in Negro wishes for sexual aggression against white women. This is a special case of the talion principle which is so deeply rooted in our cultural and educational procedures. We can make sense of the conviction of the white caste, then, only in terms of the unconscious rather than the conscious wishes of Negroes; it must be true here, as in other unconscious wish formations, that they are of quite unequal strength in different individuals and that consequently some strongly assaultive Negroes would be found and many others who would be in no position to attempt to carry out such a wish. An elaboration and confirmation of these hypotheses could come only from a more minute study of the life histories of southern white informants, by means of which one might determine, for example, what share seductive behavior on the part of white women plays in releasing sexual aggression in the Negro man. This behavior again need not be conscious on the part of the woman, but can be quite as effective when the socialized self does not formally ratify it. There is, at any rate, enough sexual aggression on the part of Negro males to constantly evoke defensive measures and reinforce the belief of the whites.

A second form of aggressive behavior which has been tolerated in Negroes since emancipation is the effort to improve their socio-economic position. Strange as it may seem, this effort on the part of Negroes is perceived by the white caste as an affront. Holding a prestigeful job, owning a large

---

ing Legal Remedies and Their Sufficiency': . . . An emotional race, belonging to that which the German Bluntschi styles the childish races of the world, he resents what he deems a denial of his rights. In the lawless this incites a tendency to strike to damage, in order to show their power for revenge. To criminal tendency is added race animosity, and this in the brute with passions of the lowest order, incites to the assault on women of the other race. He will triumph over the other race in the person of a woman of that race." *Race Problems of the South,* Report of the Proceedings of the First Annual Conference Held under the Auspices of the Southern Society for the Promotion of the Study of Race Conditions and Problems in the South (Montgomery, Alabama, 1900), pp. 162-163.

tract of land, having a special talent by which the Negro competes with white people are forms of activity which are defined as aggressive. It is plain to see how the caste situation tends to discourage or prevent vertical social mobility in Negroes. In Southerntown, at least, resentment at Negro "rising" is felt not only by lower-class white people, but by the middle-class people as well. Statements indicating these resentments are often and naïvely made by conservative white people. They will object to any educational or other "frills" for Negroes by saying that they do not want to do anything for "niggers," that the only place in which they like to see them is in the fields working. In some neighboring towns, though not in Southerntown, it is said that Negroes are challenged if seen dressed up on the street during week days; again their place is in the fields. Every Negro who has achieved advancement beyond lower-class status in Southerntown has been made aware of this envy and resentment at his aggressive mobility. Such Negroes are said to get ideas beyond their station, that is, to threaten the fixed inferior and superior positions of Negro and white castes.[8] The individuality and independence which go with landownership, for example, seem to be defined as aggressive behavior on the part of a Negro; however absurd it may seem, the

---

[8] Such a statement as that of Moton is, from the standpoint of white Southerntowners, a very aggressive manifestation. It follows: "At the bottom of his heart the Negro believes that he has capabilities of culture and character equal to those of any other race; he believes that his gifts and endowments are of equal worth to those of any other people; and even in the matter of the mingling of racial strains, however undesirable it might seem to be from a social point of view, he would never admit that his blood carries any taint of physiological, mental, or spiritual inferiority. However long it may take, therefore, through however many generations of social progress it may extend, the Negro expects ultimately to live in America with such freedom of movement, such equality of opportunity, and such measure of common respect for his person and personality as will leave him, even though distinguished in physical characteristics, without any lower status than that of the average American citizen." R. R. Moton, *What the Negro Thinks* (Garden City, N. Y., 1932), p. 239; quoted by permission of Doubleday, Doran & Co.

fact is that Negroes believe this to be the case and whites act as if it were so. A middle-class Negro informant well acquainted with this situation was much concerned about the tendency for Negroes not to struggle to own land of their own. He said that around Southerntown in earlier days they had a great ambition to own land; now they seem just to drift with the tide. He thinks one cause is their general insecurity. If they work hard for material possessions, they never know when they will have to leave them suddenly. Although it does not happen often, the threat of being driven off one's own land is always there; "the less you have, the more easily you can leave if threatened." He said that whites often attack responsible Negroes as well as irresponsible ones when a race incident occurs; the homes or barns of the innocent and upright may be destroyed. The knowledge that this can happen has a tendency to discourage the capable Negroes from saving and building up farms of their own.

Take the cases of two Southerntown Negroes who own land to illustrate. One of them is an extremely capable man who ran a large plantation very competently; he received a good salary, saved his money, and bought a few hundred acres of land as well as some other property. He continued to prosper, would have liked to buy more land, had the money and the administrative ability to run it well, but he was cautious and thought it dangerous to "pop his head up too high." The whites did not like the idea of a Negro with a large amount of land. He decided he had just about the safe amount; he would rather operate on a smaller scale and be personally secure than own a larger tract and be in danger. The other Negro owned a large plantation; he was careful not to have the land all in one place but rather in parcels in different parts and counties so that his prosperity would not be too obvious in any one region.

Another aspect of the same problem is the conception of the "white man's job" already referred to. For a Negro to hold such a job is viewed by white people as a threatening gesture on his part. Needless to say these jobs are the less laborious, more remunerative ones with higher prestige attaching to them. Despite these hindrances, however, Ne-

groes are inevitably pressing toward advancement in status
and therefore exhibit a kind of aggression against the caste
system in Southerntown. In this they are responding to pressures in our dominant American pattern which admit of
social advancement as a goal even for the humblest individuals. All too frequently success and actual mobility of Negroes are punished as aggressive acts. Without much doubt
the same envy is aroused among white people when a white
man advances in status or betters himself in an economic
sense; but within the white caste the face of the society is
set formally against the expression of it, and a white person
may not be punished for his temerity, industry, ingenuity,
or luck.

Continuing our descending scale of overtness of aggression, we shall refer briefly again to withdrawal of trade from
white businessmen as a form of hostility open to Negroes. A
boycott is a distinctly aggressive act, as he knows who has
ever experienced or witnessed one. In Southerntown, at
least, it would be too dangerous for Negroes to declare a
formal boycott since it could easily be broken up, but individual Negroes do withdraw their patronage if they are
not treated to their satisfaction in white stores. One informant reported that she had refused to buy in stores where
they call her "sister," after the church custom, or "aunty,"
according to the older plantation custom. She could at least
show her resentment by this means. It is generally held by
middle-class Negroes that one reason, though not the only
one, for the success of the Jewish merchants in the dry-
goods trade is that they do not draw the resentment of
Negro patrons in this way; Jews do not treat business as a
caste matter and do not stress the inferiority of the Negro.
The boycott could be an exceedingly powerful weapon, as
is obvious, but the difficulty about using it, as has frequently
been noted, is the lack of in-group organization among Negroes which would enable them to stand solidly behind it.
Very probably, too, if attempted, it would bring in its train
forms of counteraggression from the whites against leading
Negroes which would be exceedingly unpleasant. For the
moment withdrawal of trade has more significance in man-
ifesting the aggressive self-esteem of individual Negroes

than in affecting the caste situation in any general way.

We must also consider the high labor turnover among plantation Negroes in this new perspective. Moving away is a form of retaliation that exasperates planters who want an efficient but stationary labor force. It is troublesome and expensive to have a constant shifting of tenant families. But one of the few things made absolutely secure to Negroes by emancipation was freedom of geographic mobility, and this they use in part to express their discontent with the conditions under which they work. It may not be a very effective means of retaliation and it may even be against the interests of the Negro himself, but it evidently gives some satisfaction. Oftentimes just to go away is one of the most aggressive things that another person can do, and if means of expressing discontent are limited, as in this case, it is one of the few ways in which pressure can be put on. The alarm of the whites and the exultation of the Negroes at the mass migrations to the North are evidence of how effective this pressure can be; it will continue to be so as long as the Negroes are needed for plantation labor, but of course no longer.

White women frequently complain that their Negro cooks and servants never have the courage to let them know before they leave. They just disappear some day after a pay day. One housewife, a good natural psychologist, said that she always suspects they are about to leave whenever they come around to praise her or "make over her" especially. It is a sort of apology in advance for what they intend to do. The only explanation of such behavior is that the Negro woman views leaving as an aggressive act and fears to confess her intention lest she be stopped somehow or argued out of going. Many of the unaccountable moves that Negroes make from homes and plantations could probably be understood if they were viewed in this light. It is as if the Negro were saying, "I may be inferior and you may have many advantages over me, but at least you do not own my body."

Another type of aggression open to Negroes is the withdrawal of deference forms and prestige acknowledgments to white people. Nothing is more immediately sensed as hostile and the whites never neglect to stress the correct behavior. A Negro who had worked in northern territory for some years gave his personal experience of this. In the Yankee town Negroes voted as well as whites, and altercations were handled on a person-to-person, not a race-to-race basis. He said he could not get used to things when he came back to Southerntown after many years away. He would say "yes" and "no" instead of "yes, sir" and "no, sir." His wife and other Negroes remonstrated with him and warned him of the danger he ran, but he found it hard to change the habit he had built up over eight years. Whites had several times corrected him when he failed to observe the caste code.

Humility and lack of direct demands are elements of caste etiquette for Negroes. We have already noted that women are given more license than men. For example, a middle-class Negro informant was asked to talk before a women's discussion group in one of the white churches on the topic "Our Manchurian Friends." The chairman of the club introduced her as a *friend*. When she rose to speak, she said that she was glad to be introduced as a friend and hoped she was one. She went on to take as the major issue of her discussion the fact that it was nice to be interested in Manchuria, but that the club might also be interested in its Negro friends in Southerntown. Right over on the other side of the tracks were plenty of problems nearer home than Manchuria. Probably no local Negro man would be asked to speak before a group of white men, unless perhaps a Negro minister, who can always be trusted to be tactful and deferential; but if a man were invited he would hardly dare to be as lacking in humility as this woman was.

Another woman informant, strongly conscious of her middle-class status, commented openly on the cowardice of white people who do not have the courage to call her "Mrs." She said she knew herself to be worthy of the title. She felt especially that white Christian ministers were hypocritical on this point, since they ought to set a good example. Of course this informant will not be allowed her title, but she apparently gets some satisfaction from expressing herself pointedly in defiance of the caste pattern. In various ways

Negroes may slight, elide, and make a mockery of the deference forms, but they must observe them nevertheless; not to do so is actually an aggressive and even dangerous act.

A middle-class Negro informant said he was no "Sambo" nigger. He respected whites for what they could do, but he thought every white man respected a brave man; he said that he would not show any undue deference, smile in a servile manner or scratch his head or the like. He followed the main forms because he had to, but he would not add to them by a jot and he carried them out in a cool and reserved manner. The aggressive element is quite obvious in this, the more so when one thinks that whites expect Negroes not only not to be aggressive, but to be positively ingratiating at every turn.

Lower-class Negroes seem to make few reservations with regard to carrying out deference forms toward white people. They do it automatically and punctiliously and often with right good heart as well. We have already noted that their sabotage is more passive and takes the form of slowness, awkwardness, and indecision about their work. After all, this is a slavery accommodation; the slave may not show his resistance by stopping work altogether, but he can at least slow up. It may also be that the carelessness of white time and goods often attributed to lower-class Negroes is another evidence of resistance. The fact that there is something aggressive in such behavior will readily be seen when the annoyance of the boss in the face of it is observed. This partial refusal to accept the worker's rôle is viewed as the equivalent for the lower-class Negro of the refusal of deference signs by the middle- or upper-class Negro.

Telling tales about southern white people to northerners and other democratic sympathizers is another form of resistance by the Negroes. We have noted that northerners are peculiarly susceptible to such tales and that the careful researcher must guard against distorted information due to this tendency. Of course, I am included among those to whom such stories have been told. After all, the Negroes have good historical evidence for the efficacy of this action. It amounts about to this: if you cannot take direct militant action against the white-caste patterns, perhaps you can get someone else to do it for you, i.e., the North. Southern people are conscious of this form of hostility and meet it by trying to discredit the Negroes as reporters, and by various subtle forms of intimidation. In the North itself Negroes can and do carry on an active propaganda against the caste situation. Since the northern ox is not gored, due to the relative scarcity of Negroes in the North in the past, there is no very active resistance. It will be noted that the official attitude of southern Negro leaders, like Booker T. Washington, has been conciliatory and accommodative, whereas the most active hostility to caste has come from northern Negroes and their various associations, of which perhaps Dr. W. E. B. Du Bois and the National Association for the Advancement of Colored People are representative. One might say that the difference between Washington and Du Bois is due to a difference in regional culture; Washington wanted to do something in the South, while Du Bois wished to mobilize hostile sentiment against the caste institution and make clear the contradiction between the formal American definition of the status of the Negro and actualities of his situation. All writers, researchers, and officials who consult with Negroes in the South should be aware of this pattern and realize that there is an element of revenge and protest in the information received from Negroes. This is, of course, inevitable, since more direct forms of protest are not allowed.

The displacement of aggression is a well-known mechanism which has already been discussed in connection with the conflicts within the Negro caste. The Italo-Ethiopian War provided another type of opportunity for such a displacement. This conflict aroused great interest among local Negroes, and was discussed both by individuals and church groups. One middle-class informant who was much exercised by the Italian attack on Ethiopia thought it would produce bad feeling between white and Negro races everywhere. He said that the Negroes were very conscious of it as another assault by the whites on Negro freedom. Another well-informed Negro said that the current excitement in Southerntown about the war was probably a result of the continuous local tension in relationships between Negro and white men. American Negroes identified themselves with Ethiopia and saw in Italy's actions the arrogance to which they were so accustomed from local white-caste members. Poor little Ethiopia symbolized the disadvantaged Negro and superior, explosive, masterful Italy the white man. The realities of Ethiopian life as a feudal and slaveholding land did not enter into the evaluation. Very likely the interest of the Negro intellectual in the cause of the darker races is of the same nature; his partisanship is really an expression of his discontent at his own status in America; and lurking threats of revenge by the "darker nations" on the "white man" are actually concealed expressions of his own hostilities toward his immediate life situation.

A form of local revenge which has to be used carefully and sparingly, but still is used, is the telling of gossipy tales about the Southerntown white people. Negroes have excellent opportunity to become familiar with the shadier aspects of local white behavior. For one thing, many of the intolerant, sadistic, and other disapproved types of act are done directly to them so that they appreciate white failings from their own experience. For example, Negroes may know before whites do that such-and-such a leading citizen has a Negro mistress, or that so-and-so is a drunkard. Living as intimately as Negro women do in the white homes, they see and hear much that the whites do not wish known, and this, of course, forms the best material for gossip. White-caste members themselves are very protective about such information and Negroes have to be extremely careful in retailing it; still they do and it gives an opportunity for expression of animosity. With the outsider Negro gossip is usually masked and there is great reluctance to indicate specific persons and places. This is intelligible since such gossip is naturally felt as extremely hostile by the whites.

It would be remarkable if, under the circumstances, Negroes did not occasionally blame the caste line for personal failures which are actually not concerned with their disadvantaged position. For example, a Negro businessman described his failure in business as due to discrimination against him by the whites and a virtual boycott on his

business. Fellow Negro informants attributed the failure
rather to his defective character; they said he did not attend
to his affairs wisely, did not watch his business, and did
not modernize his service. He let his clerks steal from him,
did not give people the type of service they wanted, and
was away a good part of the time on other matters. In
examining information from Negroes one must be intensely
aware of the tendency to blame on race prejudice and discrimination what is actually a character defect. This is a
general pattern, but, where race discrimination is absent,
there is no systematic façade on which to project the blame
which one actually deserves oneself. If the tendency to
avert blame is present, it must then be attributed to mean
behavior on the part of single individuals.

We all know that the withdrawal of the interest, attention, and love of others can be experienced as a form of
aggression. If a former friend does not speak to us on the
street, we are aware of hostile intent on his part, some of us
perhaps more so than others. Suspicion and distrust of white
people are quite marked in Negroes, although they usually
lurk behind the deceitful rôle of caste accommodation.
Open distrust is much more in evidence among middle-
class than among lower-class Negroes. All white people,
North and South, who deal with Negroes must count
with this fact; however good individual relations may be,
the experience of the Negro in dealing with whites in the
past justifies him in taking a distrustful attitude. He coolly
surveys the other person and his actions, implying that he
has to be watched, and at the same time not accepting
his apparent fairness at its face value. Thoughtless white
people are constantly baffled at this attitude on the part of
Negroes.

A middle-class Negro said that there are always reservations in his relations with white people. Sometimes whites
appear to be very nice and give every sign of liking him,
and yet they will turn around and do something "dirty."
If he were to tell them everything about himself or his
feelings, there would be the danger that they would use
it against him in some way. A white man recognized this
when he said that "niggers" do not trust the whites any

more than the whites trust them. This informant was a bill collector and he gave the following example. He said a "nigger" will come to him and get him to figure out his bill, ask if he can have the paper on which the figuring was done, and take it home with him. Next week he comes back and asks to have the bill figured out again. If the figures are even a few cents more, he pulls the old slip from his pocket and points out the mistake. People are often deceived by the accommodation attitudes which Negroes show and so underestimate their distrust. It is there, however, as an historical reminder of long-standing relationships between the castes.

Closely related to distrust are the attitudes of withdrawal and secretiveness about their affairs which Negroes show. Secretive withdrawal is the nearest thing to an in-group attitude that one can find among Negroes; one might call it a passive in-group attitude. It comes out very clearly in the contrast between the behavior of Negroes in the presence of whites and when they feel themselves to be alone in their own group. When they are dealing with whites, they exhibit the well-known, cheerful accommodation attitudes and, if one is intuitive, one feels behind these a considerable measure of distrust and withdrawal of genuine feelings; but if the visitor is well recommended as a friend and guest at a Negro picnic, he will have a quite different experience. There is little strain in the relations of the Negroes to one another. They talk freely and easily and seem to be able to have a good time with little help from others. The conversational ball is chucked rapidly about and there is a sense of high good feeling and freedom. This spontaneous naturalness of Negro in-group relationships is in notable contrast to their withdrawal and reserved behavior with white people. Perhaps this is why the whites profess to find Negroes so mysterious and why they so often say, "The longer I live with them, the less I know about them." Negro deference is often the mask which conceals hostile aloofness. The "good nigger" from the white man's standpoint is the one who "comes across" rather completely emotionally and in whom this protective reserve is less detectable.

Everyone has noticed at one time or another an aggressive element in jokes; for example, jokes about dictators inevitably arise once other forms of aggression are suppressed. The joke, of course, conceals its aggressive intent behind the façade of the little story, and oftentimes it takes a bit of analysis to make it clear. In sarcasm, on the contrary, the aggressive element is plain. Negroes do not omit jokes from their arsenal of reprisal against white people. White informants frequently comment on the unaccountable manner in which Negroes laugh. Very often when whites suddenly come upon Negroes laughing and the Negro refuses to explain, it is not because he cannot give a reason or that he is a mere idiot laughing at nothing, but rather that the joke is on the white man and an explanation would be tactless.

There is a story of a white man who overheard a Negro in the field singing something that sounded at first like just a mumble. He would sing for a bit and then laugh to himself. Finally the white man made out the words of the song: "Lazy white man sits on the fence, don't do nothing all day long." The Negro had his little joke, and also his little revenge.

Negro humor often has a delicate suppressed quality, perhaps because of the danger of allowing the aggressive component to come through clearly. A Negro informant told the following story. A Negro named George went into a white store to buy a hat. The clerk said, "Well, *Bill*, what will you have?" The Negro guessed he would have nothing. At the next store, "Well, *son*, what will you have?" He said nothing. And so on, through a list of names such as "uncle," "Mose," etc. Finally he came to a store where the clerk said, "Well, *George*, what will you have?" "A hat," he answered and bought it. This is also an example of the stubborn self-respect of this Negro who could "fix it with himself" to accept being called by his first name only if the white man got it right. This story deserves a bit of thinking over; the least that can be said about it is that the fragile joke is on the white man. Negro humor is often so delicate that it is hard to locate, and one comes off with the baffled general feeling that the whites have been lampooned without knowing quite how.

The following story deals with the terrible theme of lynching and manages to make a joke out of it. It was told at a public meeting by a Negro speaker and it brought a hearty laugh from the house. The speaker said that a man was lynched in Texas and a sign was attached to his neck while he was still hanging by the wayside. It read, "In statu co." The Negroes in the town were frightened and wanted to know what the sign meant. Some thought it meant they should gather up their belongings and leave town right away; others had different opinions. So they called the preacher and asked him. He looked at the sign and said the words were not in the Bible and since he knew only what was in the Bible, he could not be expected to know. They called on various others who were also helpless, and finally they called on the "'fessor". The professor looked at the sign and he didn't know either; but he had to know because he was the professor, so he said, "Well, I can't tell you *exactly* what the words mean, but in general they mean that this man is in a hell of a fix."

To take cheerfully a matter of such terrible moment is really to turn the joke back on the white man; some fun is squeezed even out of his warning. The phrase "In statu co" is probably garbled Latin. It should be noted, of course, that, though the joke may relieve personal feelings, it does not alter the real world as more direct forms of aggression would; it should also be noted that joking may serve other purposes besides the expression of hostility.

In the face of a frustrating world the mechanisms of dreams and fantasies are open to all mankind; they, too, may express divergent motives and among them, hostility. Without attempting a minute analysis I will cite a few dreams of Negroes which show aggression. The following dream of a woman deals with the derogatory attitudes of whites toward Negro women. Informant said that she dreamed of being at a meeting of white people and of being introduced as "Mrs." A white man arose in the audience and objected. She was terribly angry about it and argued, saying that she *was* married, that she was a mother, and that her standards of personal behavior were as high in every respect as those of white women who are called "Mrs." without question. In real life this informant would not have dared to protest in this way in a public meeting about not being given her full title.

The following is a dream of a Negro man relating to the situation of defending his wife from the attentions of white men. Informant is in a car with his wife beside him and they are driving along a country road. They turn sharply to the left and see three white hunters crossing the road at a little sand flat. Informant stops the car and the motor goes dead. The white men pass before the car. Informant gets out to crank the car and notices that his wife is standing outside the car and that one of the hunters has come back and is standing near her. The white man has a shot gun in his hand. Informant is afraid that he is going to make a sexual approach to her, and he advances to get his own rifle which is in the car. Then he stands between the white man and his wife. The hunter spits in his face. Informant is going to kill the man but his wife warns him not to, saying "You wouldn't be a murderer, would you?" She pleads so pathetically that he does not kill the man but he tries to curse him. Instead of curse words, all he can say is, "I will kill you, I will kill you." In the light of the foregoing data on the sexual situation, the overt content of this dream is clear. It refers to the danger situation always threatening a self-respecting Negro—that he may be called upon to defend his woman at the price of his life. Of course, this situation confronts white men too, but not so frequently or with such real danger as in the case of a Negro.

The guilt of the same informant is expressed by the following dream which was coupled with the preceding one. Informant is going down to the post office for his mail. He finds the post-office building larger than he had expected and it turns out to be a courthouse. In the courtroom a trial is going on. There are some accused Negro prisoners who seem to be trying to testify to their innocence. A white judge is taking it all very lightly and laughing. This dream seems to show a Negro culprit going to court, being tried by whites, offering futile explanations, and meeting the cynical assurance of the judge. Supplementary material showed that it was informant himself who was on trial. This is exactly the situation of the Negro attempting to explain any type of aggressive behavior to whites. In the first dream above he had permitted himself the luxury of showing his full hatred.

It is much harder to get fantasy material than dream material because we view a person as responsible for his fantasies, whereas his dreams just "come over him" and are largely disavowed by the socialized self. One clear aggressive fantasy is the following. The same Negro and his wife went into a grocery store and were looking over various kinds of meat. She refused one kind after another which the white clerk offered her. Informant began to wonder if the clerk would become angry and insult her, since Negro people are not supposed to be too "choosey." In that case he would have to defend her and he resolved that he would, because she was his wife and a woman. He looked around the store and observed that it was full of white people and reflected that a lynching party might easily follow. It was the kind of incident which could set off a white crowd. The clerk, however, was pleasant to his wife and did not take offense at her failure to buy. Very likely this informant is a little oversensitive on the possibility of affront to his wife and overanxious to show himself a man; still, in view of the actual social situation confronting Negroes his apprehensions were not unreasonable.

These several incidents cannot do more than suggest what an enormous rôle aggressive dreams and fantasies must play in the Negro group. To an unusual extent Negroes are debarred from direct action; and, since we cannot suppose with them, any more than with other human beings, that they naturally endure frustration and humiliations submissively, we must look for the actual outlets for their aggression. Sociologists who do not take this possibility into account are bound to misunderstand the personalities of Negroes; dreams and fantasies are as much social acts as blows and manifestoes.

In the same connection we might refer again to magic

as a valve for social hostility. For my part I did not come across any attempts to do injury to white people by magical means, but they are referred to at least once, to my knowledge, in the literature.[9] The growing assimilation of Negroes into the white cultural universe and the immunity of whites to magical acts will probably tend further to decrease their employment. Such acts are related rather to the dreams and fantasies above than to genuine methods of altering life conditions and are at once an inheritance from a more helpless past and an innocent means of ventilating hostility. Needless to say the use of fantasy, dream, and magic helps to confuse and conceal the actual issues and social problems; it may be the only way out when real aggression is too dangerous.

Possibilities of socially effective aggression for Negroes in Southerntown do not seem to be increasing. This is all the more true since depressive economic conditions have taken a heavy toll of Negro business. A middle-class informant said that Negroes used to play a much larger rôle in the town than they do now; this was in the days when the Negroes had a bank and business was more prosperous generally. Still Southerntown is known as a good town for Negroes and the general advance in Negro status in America is reflected here also, for example, in improved schools. One informant said that the colored people have been inching forward, asserting themselves a little more, winning this and that small concession, but he feels that the progress is very slow and that only a little gain has been made since slavery days. This is inevitable since Negroes are debarred from the more direct forms of organization and action which

[9] "Even the wind may be the innocent bearer of 'devilment.' Find out the direction of the wind and stand so that it will blow from you towards your enemy. Having dusted your hands with powdered devil's shoe string and devil's snuff, hold them up so that the wind will blow from them towards the man coming towards you. The dust will be carried into his eyes and your opponent will be at least temporarily blinded. My hoodoo friend uses this on white men with whom he is afraid to deal more roughly." N. N. Puckett, *Folk Beliefs of the Southern Negro* (Chapel Hill, 1926), p. 224; quoted by permission of the University of North Carolina Press.

have the power to change status relations in a democratic society, i.e., political activity. In this sense aggression is not only a biological excitation expressed through a social form, but also, sociologically seen, a force tending to alter real-world social relations. It is the paralysis in the second sphere which accounts for the almost imperceptible changes in Negro status in Southerntown.

CHAPTER XV

White Caste Aggression Against Negroes

〰〰〰〰〰〰〰〰〰〰〰〰〰〰〰〰〰〰〰〰〰〰〰〰

It will not be news to any northerner that southern white people show aggression against Negroes; it is almost as well advertised as the plantation stereotype of the goateed planter with his mint julep, the pillared big house, and the happy Negroes singing in their quarters. The latter image, to be sure, has been built up in the North since the Civil War and serves as a means of reconciliation with southerners.[1] By adopting the current legend of "The Old South" we northerners agree not to notice the hostility toward Negroes which southern people tend to understress and which the older abolitionist's ideology in the North overestimated. Protesting Negroes and northern liberals have continued to emphasize southern hostility, and it stands out in jarring contrast to the sentimentalized version of southern life and history prevalent in, say, film representations.

White aggression against Negroes and the social patterns which permit it are forms of social control; they are instrumentalities for keeping the Negro in his place and maintaining the supraordinate position of the white caste. We know now from our study that the whites do not fight for social superiority just for fun; on the contrary, they are attempting to minimize or eliate Negro competition in the spheres of economics, sex, and prestige. Competition appears, when it does appear, in the form of aggressive demands or acts on the part of the Negro which are directed toward the modification of the superior advantages enjoyed by the white caste. We have discussed some of the forms of this aggression on the part of the Negro. Now the defenses

[1] B. Schrieke, *Alien Americans* (New York, 1936), pp. 112-113.

erected against it by the members of the white caste are to be considered. As is so often the case, attack is the better part of defense, and the aggressive manifestations permitted to white-group members are much more overt and decisive than those enjoyed by the Negroes. So far as conscious intent goes, white-caste members justify the measures they take against Negroes on the familiar principle of "safety first." It is said, for example, that it is safer to lynch Negroes than to endure a spreading epidemic of attacks on white women and murders of white men. The white group, intrenched in its caste position, attempts to appal and discourage the Negro and thereby to mute pressure for status advancement from his side. From the unconscious side, it is probably true that social patterns of the white caste permit sadistic pleasures to those in the population who are especially disposed to enjoy them.[2] The fear of being in the hands of such a sadistic person has a particularly terrorizing value for any victim, Negro or white.

It must not be supposed that the major or perhaps even the significant part of white aggression against Negroes consists of the few dramatic acts of lynching featured in the newspapers. Massive and continuous pressures of other types are far more important in achieving social stability. Lynchings are not dismissed as trivial, of course. The terrible thing about them is that they allow impromptu and self-appointed executioners to work out their unrestrained hostilities on the lynched person and that few precautions are taken for ensuring the connection between the victim and the crime. These are the revengeful features of lynch law which it is the aim of the legal process, the stipulated manner of execution, and the official executioner to avoid. Much more important than the actual lynchings is the effect on Negro personality of the threat of lynching; this is as it is intended to be. One can never expect *all* of the members of a society or caste to refrain from savage and sadistic acts if social patterns condone them, although, surprisingly

---

[2] The reader must turn to Freud to learn how hostile acts against others may be experienced as pleasurable. *See* Sigmund Freud, *Three Contributions to the Theory of Sex* (New York, 1930), pp. 21-23.

enough, many persons are so socialized that they do refrain.

I remember a conversation with a naïve Negro who had been thinking about this point. He stated that in his belief the white people actually hated the Negroes. I expressed surprise at this, but he insisted that they look and act as if they did anyway and that is all that matters to him. He was aware, of course, that southern white people say they do not hate Negroes and sometimes even assert that they love them. His view seemed to be that maybe once they did love the Negroes when the latter were all comfortably in their places and seemed likely to stay there permanently. But nowadays, when Negroes are stirring for personal advancement, hatreds are constantly raised in the white people whom they have to oppose.

In the end it seems a better statement to say that white people fear Negroes. They fear them, of course, in a special context, that is, when the Negro attempts to claim any of the white prerogatives or gains. Since the wider American social pattern, however, offers to the Negro the hope of personal advancement and so directs his striving that he is in continuous actual or potential opposition to the caste system, the whites must constantly fear him. Negro opposition to white gains can only be manifested in aggressive action; and this is the source of white fear. This fear, of course, has a long history, fear of revolt,[3] fear of Negroes' running away, and fear of isolated assault or terrorism. Before the Civil War efficient policing institutions and the isolation of plantation life reduced these fears, although even then the white owner and overseer apparently watched Negro be-

---

[3] "The general trend of public expressions laid emphasis upon the need of safeguards but showed confidence that no great disasters were to be feared. The revolts which occurred and the plots which were discovered were sufficiently serious to produce a very palpable disquiet from time to time, and the rumors were frequent enough to maintain a fairly constant undertone of uneasiness. The net effect of this was to restrain that progress of liberalism which the consideration of economic interest, the doctrines of human rights and the spirit of kindliness all tended to promote." U. B. Phillips, *American Negro Slavery* (New York, 1918), p. 488; quoted by permission of D. Appleton-Century Co.

havior very carefully for signs of recalcitrance.[4] It is urged that, when the North interfered with existing social and property relationships in the South, this fear became much more intense and continuous. It is so to the present day, especially in rural black-belt areas of the type in which Southerntown is located. White people fear that Negroes actually will demand equal status, equal economic opportunity, and equal sexual chances, including under the latter the right to protect their homes and women from sexual aggression. By a series of hostile acts and social limitations the white caste maintains a continuous threatening atmosphere against the possibility of such demands by Negroes; when successful, as these threats are now, the effect is to keep the social order intact. Minor caste taboos are here viewed as indirect forms of aggression exercised against the actual or potential claims for advancement on the part of the Negro, claims which would disrupt the existing caste and class relationships. Many minor taboos will seem senseless unless this principle is constantly kept in mind. The Negro is allowed only the feeblest of efforts to realize the American ideal of vertical social mobility; efforts that would be considered normal in others are experienced by white men as fabulously aggressive when they are made by Negroes.[5]

There are two important considerations to raise in the

[4] "It was the interest and business of slaveholders to study human nature, and the slave nature in particular, with a view to practical results; and many of them attained astonishing proficiency in this direction. They had to deal not with earth, wood, and stone, but with *men;* and by every regard they had for their safety and prosperity they had need to know the material on which they were to work. So much intellect as the slaveholder had round him required watching. Their safety depended on their vigilance. Conscious of the injustice and wrong they were every hour perpetrating, and knowing what they themselves would do if they were victims of such wrongs, they were constantly looking out for the first signs of the dread retribution. They watched, therefore, with skilled and practiced eyes, and learned to read, with great accuracy, the state of mind and heart of the slave through his sable face." Frederick Douglass, *Life and Times* (Hartford, Conn., 1882), p. 178.

[5] Is the "aggressiveness" often believed to be a personality characteristic of Jews an illusion of the same kind?

matter of white fear of Negroes. There is a reality element in this fear, viz., that our major American institutions encourage the Negro to leave his "place" as defined by southern regional culture. If debarred, as he is, he is likely to express his legitimate resentment in some drastic way. The cases of shooting from the bush and rape that we have already discussed are sources of real fear on the part of real people. Such acts are constantly alleged to be the sole inciting source of white aggression and intimidation of Negroes.

There is, however, another form of fear which must be discussed. This is not based on real acts of aggression by Negroes or the expectation of them; it is rather the unconscious expectation of retaliation for the hostile acts of whites on Negroes. The justification for this assumption is the fact that white people seem to be much more afraid of Negroes than there is any real reason to be. The Negroes seem, in fact, to be rather well adjusted to the situation and to have, by and large, renounced aggression and organization as means of changing their status. The fright shown by white-caste members seems disproportionate to the threat from the Negro's side; in such a case we may invariably postulate that unconscious mechanisms are functioning, in this case a fear of retaliation for the gains aggressively acquired by the white caste at the expense of the Negroes. Only on such a basis may the unreasonable, often panicky, fears which the whites have toward the rather helpless Negroes be accounted for. The lesson that hatred may be expected from those attacked is learned early in life and is one of the most enduring attitudes planted in the individual by our society.[6] Wherever it is possible, and not too dangerous, the best defense against a feared aggression from others is an aggression on one's own part which keeps the others from going

---

[6] "Fear is the mother of hatred. I have shown in a previous chapter that the white man in the South is saturated with race hostility to the Negro, and that though the Negro responds in kind, his animosity is not nearly so virulent, nor does it take on such violent forms of expression." Maurice S. Evans, *Black and White in the Southern States* (New York, 1915), p. 192; quoted by permission of Longmans, Green & Co.

into action.[7] Real fear and neurotic fear are compounded to build up a permanent necessity for severe measures against Negroes on the part of the white caste.[8]

An example of the fear of retaliation is the constant assumption by white people, already cited, of aggressive intent on the part of Negroes. Any accident or minor mishap may appear to whites as a cover for latent aggression, so that whites often respond to such incidents with what seems a disproportionate severity. This harshness is intelligible only on the theory that they are expecting hostility from the Negro. The accident story is a frequent one. A middle-class Negro told me he had almost had an automobile accident. As it happened a policeman was sitting in such a position that he could directly view the near-collision. The white man began to abuse the Negro, but the policeman was fair, criticized the white driver, and said he ought to be arrested. Informant said that, if the policeman had not been there, the white man's word would certainly have carried against his own. There is in this incident obviously also an element of transfer of blame to the Negro and it is, of course, not out of the question that Negroes may take advantage of seeming "accidents" to injure white people or property on occasion. Out of such fear of Negro animosity grows the surge of hostility which makes white-caste members so belligerent in their dealings with Negroes.[9]

Actual events occasionally give a certain reality to these

---

[7] This reminds me of an election advertisement for Hindenburg which I once read in a German paper; it praised the nominee by referring to him as the man who *"defended* the Fatherland on *foreign soil."* (Italics mine.)

[8] Frank Tannenbaum, *Darker Phases of the South* (New York, 1924), p. 167.

[9] "These discriminations, of course, are simply the crystallization of public attitudes. The bases of lynch law reside in these same attitudes which find expression in the cultural, political, and economic exploitation of the Negro. Another irresistible conclusion is that lynching is an evidence of the white man's fear of the Negro and lack of faith in his 'own' government." Arthur F. Raper, *The Tragedy of Lynching* (Chapel Hill, 1933), p. 51; quoted by permission of the University of North Carolina Press.

chronic fears of white people. A white woman said that she had heard talk of a feared uprising when the Negro soldiers who had learned to fight came home from the World War. It was thought that they would come back armed and furthermore disciplined to some type of collective activity. The situation, however, passed without trouble. Informant said that if there had been any local trouble, trainloads of whites would have come in from neighboring cities to put down any Negro revolt; there is a strong sense of alliance between white people over the whole area. Still such fears lead to reprisals and reprisals there were in the increased severity in treatment of Negroes just following the War; this was often surprising to the Negro soldiers who came back expecting appreciation for their service. The arming and disciplining of Negroes in case of war will be a troublesome issue in the South so long as the caste pattern is maintained. It may always lead to the in-group organization of Negroes and mass attack which are so much feared.[10]

Reality fears of Negroes are based on the furtive, isolated attacks that were referred to in the preceding chapter. These may be feared from specific Negroes who have been injured by an individual white man; and there is always the danger that an individual white man or woman will be the target for a symbolic attack on the white caste by an enraged Negro. In the latter case, of course, it seems justifiable for the whites to act as a unified group in outlawing attacks by Negroes. We have noted, however, that among Negro forms of aggression direct attack plays a relatively small rôle, and it seems by no means to explain the apprehension of the white group.

The notion that white people fear Negroes is often ridiculed in times of race peace when there have been no re-

---

[10] "A people, like a class, to advance must either be strong enough to make its way against all hostility, or must secure the friendship of others, particularly of those nearest it. If the Negro race in the South proposes, and is powerful enough to overcome the white race, let it try this method—it will soon find out its error; if not, it must secure the friendship of that race." T. N. Page, *The Negro: The Southerner's Problem* (New York, 1904), pp. 306-307; quoted by permission of Charles Scribner's Sons.

cent "incidents." One white informant represented the situation as quite peaceful: Negroes are not afraid, whites are not afraid, whites do not feel the necessity to have guns, and there is no reason at all for apprehension, especially if the Yankees would let things alone. Such a statement is open to the objection that people generally attempt to deny their own aggressive tendencies and to minimize their fears of retaliatory action. Still there is much truth in what this informant said, so long as the caste taboos are strictly observed, so long as whites have little economic competition with Negroes, and so long as the whites have no irrational personal need to do violence to Negroes. But these are a lot of "ifs" and unfortunately such conditions seldom prevail. The alternative is the constant smolder of race hostility and the occasional hot flame of violence.

If southern white people were all thoroughly socialized, we might expect that their aggression against the Negroes would be proportionate to the cause inciting it. This, however, cannot be assumed in the South, or anywhere else. There are bound to be many in any group who have private reasons for needing a target for sadistic expression, someone to threaten and curse, and occasionally someone to torment and punish. These persons will take full advantage of the permissive character of the white-caste customs which do not resolutely prohibit scorn, ridicule, and torture as weapons in the extralegal subordination of the Negro caste. White persons who are sadistically motivated due to childhood experience will find this social pattern a comfortable one. On the other hand, there are large numbers of southern white people who do not torture or ridicule and who could not be incited to do these things simply because the social structure is not strongly mobilized against them. These people will often deplore such actions on the part of their fellow caste members. Their position as caste members, however, is such that they cannot escape a kind of complicity in sadistic actions since such acts serve to consolidate the caste position of the liberals quite as well as that of the sadistic offenders themselves.

Let us consider now the use of direct force by white people on Negroes for the purpose of maintaining their superior caste position. The formula is that this force represents a counter attack delivered in advance of the attack by Negroes. It is punitive, to be sure, but it is also, and in a much more important sense, a threat and a warning.

As everyone knows, the occurrence of rape is the excitation usually alleged by the whites as the cause of lynching. Nonsouthern white men and women must remember that these rapes actually do occur. They are not mere fictions or excuses. They are said to happen frequently enough so that they give a grounding of fact to the stereotyped belief. Let us realize also that rape is an exceedingly unpleasant affair, that it tends to arouse irrational passion to an extraordinary degree, and that murderous lusts will be found in any man whose woman or women are attacked in this manner. It is firmly established in our mores that sexual contacts may take place only by consent of both parties. What seems to be true is that in the North murderous rage on the part of an aggrieved man may not flow over into vengeful action, whereas in the South it may and does. Further, white-caste solidarity seems to function in the following way: every southern white man has a claim on every white woman, at least to the extent of defending her against a Negro, and he may experience and express his full hostility against the raper of another man's woman just as if she were his own. The point is that the emotions excited by rape are not peculiar to the South; but the caste situation, the special horror of rape,[11] and the permissive social patterns which allow vengeance are features of the southern regional culture.

There are some other considerations attending this crime. It has been suggested that it is not permissible for a white woman to have a conscious perception of sexual excitation in reference to a Negro man. This does not mean, however, that such excitations are not experienced. It is equally impossible for a southern white man to assume any such mo-

[11] *Race Problems of the South*, Report of the Proceedings of the First Annual Conference Held under the Auspices of the Southern Society for the Promotion of the Study of Race Conditions and Problems in the South (Montgomery, Alabama, 1900), pp. 170-174.

tive on the part of his idealized white woman; still he may unconsciously respond to the fact if it does exist. Some evidence has already been given that there is such excitation, even though it is not rationally experienced and ratified by social values. In this case the following state of affairs may exist: instead of punishing the white woman for any seductive tendencies that she may have, the white man refuses to face these tendencies and attributes the whole blame for the contact to the Negro man. The Negro is then punished both for his own aggressive share in the act of rape and for the fact that white women are not completely able to reject a Negro man unconsciously as well as consciously.[12] This view of the matter spares the white man some anguish since he is not brought into the position of hating his white woman for her share in the transaction, but instead vents the full measure of his rage against the Negro male.

There has been a little, though not much, thinking about the sexual aspects of the race problem among psychoanalysts, and the idea has, of course, been brought forward that the white man may experience jealousy in reference to the supposed or actual superiority of the Negro as a sexual being.[13] It can certainly be established that beliefs about

[12] "Though Professor Siegfried refers particularly to lack of physical repulsion of white men towards coloured women, much more disturbing is the suspicion that the absence of repulsion applies to both sexes of both races. There is no doubt that most of the inter-mixture has come from relations between white men and coloured women. But the suspicion that it is not confined to that class motivates to a large extent the sadistic features of many lynchings and burnings. It has caused the enactment in twenty-nine states of anti-intermarriage laws —legislation which would be most unnecessary if the boasted repulsion were really true." Walter White, *Rope and Faggot* (New York, 1929), pp. 67-68; quoted by permission of Alfred A. Knopf.

[13] "In my opinion the phenomenon of 'lynch law' against negroes can only be explained by supposing the idea of sexual intercourse between his women kind and a negro stirs in the depths of the white man's mind a fury that is the entire product of sexual jealousy. It is a general belief that the negro not only possesses a larger penis than men of other races, but is capable of maintaining it in a state of erection for a longer period than is possible for a male of any other race. This

the superior genital adequacy of Negroes are widespread among southern white men and it can also be shown that the attitude toward the rape problem is irrational and unrealistic. The notion that sexual jealousy is in part the reason for the extraordinary sadism accompanying lynchings is not absurd. The only satisfying evidence on this score would come from intimate life histories of white men; but we can learn on any street corner that sexual jealousy plays a part in white aggression against Negroes.

The difference between the statistics and the popular views of the causes of lynching is very illuminating. When explaining a lynching southerners almost invariably bring up a case where rape has occurred and they give the impression that this is the standard excitation. Of the 3,724 people lynched from 1889 through 1930, more than four fifths were Negroes, and of these less than one sixth were even accused of rape.[14] There is no explanation for this confusion on the level of overt social patterning since whites know perfectly well through immediate experience that most lynchings begin with other events than rape. Yet the belief is held and the disparity between belief and fact gives new point to the explanations offered above of jealousy and suspicion of unfaithful inclinations on the part of the white woman.

The irrational elements of jealousy and suspicion just indicated can receive their emotional support only from events far back in the life histories of the white individuals concerned. They gather so naturally around the Freudian conception of the Oedipus complex as to make it seem an inevitable mode of perception at this point. Individuals who emerge from the Oedipus ordeal as jealous adults will grasp more eagerly at the southern social patterns which permit revenge for a sexual affront; individuals with most doubt about the chastity of in-family women will be most

---

sexual jealousy of the negro's potency drives the white man temporarily mad, to the end that he inflicts the most horrible retributions on his unfortunate rival." Owen A. R. Berkeley-Hill, "The 'Color Question' from a Psychoanalytic Standpoint," *Psychoanal. Rev.* (1924), XI, 251-252.

[14] Raper, *op. cit.*, p. 1.

certain of Negro guilt whenever a rape charge comes up. Confirmation of this hypothesis again will require minute study of suitable white informants; it is a study, however, which would be most illuminating from the standpoint of race prejudice and hostility. Just this prejudice which is the key fact in the caste situation is until now unexplained and unintelligible. For this reason we are justified in advancing any explanation that will aid in reducing the mystery that surrounds it.

Proof of the fact that there is a powerful group of well-socialized white people in the South are the very figures from lynching practice itself. Of about 1,400 threatened lynchings between 1914 and 1932, one half were prevented by conscientious white citizens and law officers.[15] This is a convincing expression of southern sentiment against the unleashing of illegal violence and sadism through the lynching pattern. It is true, to be sure, that the legal process following a prevented lynching is by no means as free from social pressure as our Anglo-Saxon ideal demands. Local sentiment, though avoiding a lynching, may, and frequently does, distort the process of a fair trial so that the difference between the trial and the lynching is more formal than factual.[16] This vengeful justice only makes more clear the unanimity of the white community against rape, threat of rape, or suspicion of rape on the part of the Negroes.

There is another very clear indication that the group of sentiments centering around sexual attack on white women is not rational; this is the fact that negative cases fail to convince holders of the rape stereotype. The following is a case in point: I was talking one day with two state officials about a white social worker who had been in Southerntown for a number of months before my stay. They told me that she

[15] Raper, *op. cit.*, p. 46.

[16] "And usually, after being kept from the overt act of killing, the mob members have successfully demanded of public officials that the accused person be tried in the local county, that the death sentence be imposed, and that no delay of execution be sought by the defendant's counsel—in most cases a local lawyer appointed by the court." *Ibid.;* quoted by permission of the University of North Carolina Press.

had gotten along very well and they marveled that she had been in town for two months, gone around by herself, even alone at night, visiting Negro homes and churches, and had never once been molested. The important fact was their astonishment that this should be the case; they added that if a Negro woman had been doing the same work with a white group she probably would have been bothered; they stated with fairness that they felt ashamed of this. I am sure, however, that this experience did not affect their belief that no white woman is safe after dark.

It is truly amazing that it does not occur to white people that Negro men would have a similar sensitivity about rape of their women. As we know, there is no such supposition, although very probably there are many more such acts by white men on Negro women than by Negroes on white women. It is, to be sure, a well-established belief that Negro women cannot be raped because they are always willing; but this is undoubtedly not a matter of fact. Perhaps, indeed, one must again have reference to unconscious factors and assume that white men do unconsciously posit on the part of Negroes a tendency to avenge the sexual assaults on their own women and that this very fact is a powerful component in the "conviction of guilt" which whites have about any Negro accused of rape. They are just as certain that the Negro is guilty as they are certain that he has a moral right to be vengeful.

A middle-class Negro made the point very well. He was talking about the limitations on his sexual life due to the caste situation and the difficulties of enforcing respect for Negro women. I reminded him that, although the limitations on his sexual wishes are dramatic and arbitrary, there is no man who escapes such limitation; there are always women who "belong" to somebody else and there are always sexual situations in which one can get into a fight and even be killed. To be a white man is no rosy paradise of license. Informant said he knew the only difference between a white man and a Negro was that a white man can back up his remarks by fighting while a Negro cannot. If a white man did something to *me* going down the stairs, I could fight; if the white man did something to *him*, he could not.

He was expressing the already familiar idea that the Negro man is prevented from protecting his women while the white man may be overzealous about defending his.

During the time that I was in Southerntown only one incident occurred in the whole area of report in which a Negro's sexual approach to a white woman was the cause of white retaliation, and on this occasion the punishment was a whipping. This case did not occur in Southerntown itself. The other offenses which precipitated mob action in the area were all related to defiance, assault, or killing of white people. Naturally in the few months of the research it would be impossible to experience directly many such cases and, since this is a relatively quiet region, I was perhaps lucky to have a chance to observe any at all. One day vague rumors came from various informants that a Negro had been killed in a neighboring small town. There was some uneasy excitement and a good deal of tense conversation in Southerntown. It is hard to say if this event could properly be called a lynching since it involved the killing of a Negro who was resisting arrest. The psychological results, however, seemed similar to those of an unconditional lynching. It appears that a Negro in the neighboring town informed a white policeman that there was a stranger around who had a gun and was intimidating the local Negroes. He pointed the man out and asked the officer to take his gun away. Upon being challenged, the stranger stopped and, without warning, shot at the policeman; then he ran around some buildings and escaped into a clump of woods. A posse or mob of men, said to be some three hundred in number, gathered quickly. They got bloodhounds from the county farm and trailed him. It was so hot that one of the bloodhounds died of the heat during the chase. The Negro, running through woods and swamps, kept taking off his clothes as he went. When they finally caught up with him, he had only a pair of shorts on. He shot it out with the white deputies, narrowly missing several of them. Finally one of them put a charge of buckshot through his chest and killed him. The incident apparently caused little excitement among the Negroes because the victim was actually dangerous to them and was not a local Negro. There were slight differences in the reports from Negro and white informants. For example, a Negro informant told me incorrectly that the Negro had actually killed the white policeman, whereas the bullet had only grazed his wrist; and secondly, he said that the Negro had shot the bloodhound when in fact the dog had died as above reported. In this case, of course, the Negro was killed because he had resisted arrest and had shot at a white officer. All that was characteristic of a lynching was the formation of a large crowd, the use of bloodhounds, and the joining of so many people in the man hunt. Probably the Negro was shot rather than lynched because he was fighting to the end and therefore too dangerous to catch.

News of the event kept ebbing and swelling in both Negro and white groups in Southerntown for several days. So far as I was concerned, white informants did not seem to care to talk about it; Negro informants were a little scared but gave more information. There was one detail about this case quite horrifying to Negroes. The cadaver of the slain Negro was given to a near-by college, the flesh was stripped from the bones, and the skeleton arranged and used as an anatomical exhibit. Apparently skeletons should be nameless; at least the Negroes felt it was insulting and degrading to their group to have a Negro so used.

A case of an unsuccessful man hunt was reported by a white woman informant. She said that on the previous day she had gone on a "nigger hunt" near Southerntown. A "nigger" who had killed his manager about three years before, and since then another white man, was hiding on a near-by plantation. The plantation owner, deputy sheriff, policemen, and three or four interested men went out on the hunt, in addition to informant who was left at a store several miles from where the Negro was supposed to be hiding. Mose, a white man's "nigger," had reported that the killer had been hiding in a tree in the woods all day and at nightfall had come to the house of Mose's mother. It seems that a few years before this the killer had fallen in love with Mose's sister and taken her away with him. When she found out what a "bad nigger" he was, she ran back home. He followed her and took her away again. She came home three or four times and every time he came after her. So ever since the girl had appeared at home a few months ago, they had been lying in wait for the killer. This looked like the time to get him. Mose was sent into the house to see if he was there. Then one white man followed Mose in and the rest covered the house outside. But the killer had gotten away again; evidently he had somehow learned about the posse. A white woman who lived in the neighborhood of the plantation wondered if the killer really ever had killed anybody or whether Mose had reported him so that the whites would catch him, slay him, and thus get him out of the running as a rival for the sister, of whom Mose was said to be extremely fond. In any case, there would apparently have been little inquiring done if the whites had caught the man. In reporting the above story informant stressed the intense excitement, speed, and conviction with which the hunt was carried out.

Reports from white people about lynchings are likely to resemble the foregoing one. The guilt of the Negro is taken for granted and the man hunt itself seems a reasonable and even indispensable type of action. From the angle of the Negro it is very different. A Negro woman told of an incident she witnessed about ten years before on a train coming to Southerntown from the North. When she got on, she noticed a certain light Negro man who was in the same car. After the long ride, the train was stopped about thirty miles from Southerntown by a group of ten or fifteen evil and fierce-looking white men, all armed. They entered the coach and covered the Negro with their guns. They made him hold up his hands, treated him roughly, and refused to give any information as to why they were taking him. When the train pulled into the next station an old Negro woman on board ran frantically out into the street and met a white man she knew who, by good luck, knew the Negro. This man got on the train and asked the would-be lynchers what the Negro had done. They said a white man had been beaten up the night before and that the prisoner appeared to answer the description of the attacker—a light Negro with small ears. The white man insisted that it must be some other Negro; he could swear that to his certain knowledge this Negro had been in the North for two years and could not have been the assailant. Eventually the white men got off the train and let the Negro go. Informant said she was terrified by this scene and still remembers it vividly, especially the angry and hostile determination of the mob. They were poorly dressed and seemed to be low-class farmers. It is all too clear, in a case like this, how easily the wrong person could be punished; the possibility makes the life of a Negro man particularly hazardous. The terrifying fact is that lynchings not only do occasionally occur but *may* occur at any time, sometimes without provocation, and that one may suddenly be put outside the protection of legal process and exposed to the unpatterned hatreds and revenge tendencies of a mob.

The threat of lynching is likely to be in the mind of the Negro child from earliest days. Memories of such events came out frequently in the life histories of Negroes. One informant said that his earliest recollection of such an event was when he was eight years old. A Negro came panting up to the house one day, his shirt open and his body dripping with sweat. He asked the boy for a drink of water, which the youngster got for him from the well. Instead of leaving by the front gate the man leaped over the back fence and ran away across the fields. In about fifteen minutes a group of white men came up to the house and asked the children if they had seen a Negro run by. It happened that informant's father had come in in the meantime. He told the posse he had not seen anyone and the boy did not tell about the drink of water. The white party went on and in a few minutes informant heard quite plainly the dull thud of guns. He learned later that the Negro had been caught and killed. Apparently he had committed a crime in a town about twelve miles away the night before. How many of these semiofficial shootings are actually disguised lynchings one cannot tell. It is interesting that the small boy appreciated the situation sufficiently to abet the escaping Negro; he was already a part of the weak and passive Negro in-group.

Some white families and individuals are known to Negroes as being particularly touchy and addicted to violence. An informant spoke of one such family whose members are known to have killed, at one time or another, six or seven Negroes. They had the reputation of being mean in other respects, frequently whipping and beating Negroes. Informant could not help adding that people like that get punished themselves; the father of this family was killed in a shooting affray with another white man, a newspaper editor, who had printed something against him. Such families and their members are, of course, avoided by Negroes when possible; but they should be noted because they are the ones who take personal advantage of the permissive white patterns which permit uncensored violence against Negroes. No member of the above family, for example, had ever spent any time in prison for killing a Negro, and apparently the question was never seriously raised, partly because it would be assumed that the white man is always right in such a case, and partly because the killing of Negroes has a certain exemplary value. One cannot help recalling here the saying that in earlier days a politician could show his standard white-caste loyalty by killing a Negro.

The attitudes already indicated for whites are certainly characteristic of lower- and middle-class white groups. Upper-class white people really do not approve of lynching, often actually deplore it, and in some cases take vigorous personal action to protect Negroes against it. I encountered casually an upper-class white man who had been going around armed for three or four days, not to "get" a Negro but to protect one of his Negroes against fellow white men who were after him. Upper-class people are apt to say that lynching is done only by lower-class whites. One upper-class man who had witnessed a lynching in his home town said he did not recognize a single face in the mob; it seemed to be composed of persons from surrounding counties who had come in for the occasion. In the lynching in question the Negro was tied alive behind an automobile and dragged around the town until dead; the horror of my upper-class informant was quite genuine and probably indicative of the attitude of upper-class people and the sensitive and conscientious people in all classes throughout the South. Still, the upper-class man is helpless even though he does deplore individual cases of lynching. He cannot change the system or the organization of sentiments which support lynching, nor can he disavow his caste solidarity with other whites.

We must remember that the crux of the matter is the white control of formal force, the police, sheriffs, justices of the peace, judges, and juries. Much of the direct action against Negroes is indeed taken through these very agencies; extralegal force supplements and supports the legal action if it is considered uncertain or inadequate. All forms of Negro adaptation are ultimately based on the prospect that this force will be utilized. Extralegal forms of forceful control are the most feared by the individual Negro. In areas like the one in which Southerntown is situated there are no socially effective patterns which confine violence to the rational and measured tread of the law. The only protection the Negro has is the conscience of the individual white man and, as we know, this barrier cannot be relied upon throughout the whole population. Some white people possess the necessary restraints, others do not. The asocial, sadistic, or psychopathic white person is a real danger, for few of the culture-old restraints on individual aggression apply to his acts against the Negro. It is probable that in the southern region, due to the presence of the Negro minority, force has always been more overt than in the North,[17] and concomitantly, control patterns against it have failed to develop.

In well-socialized white people whose personal conscience does not countenance direct violence, there is an echo of the lynching situation in the more sadistic fantasies that may be tolerated in reference to the Negro. Heartless proposals to export them en masse to Africa or other isolated regions seem reasonable. A full humanity with all the emotional responses posited for whites is not attributed to Negroes, and cruel acts may be justified because Negroes are believed not to feel as acutely as whites. A white informant once spoke with great affect about the problem of sterilizing the unfit and gave as an example a psychopathic Negro man whom he had recently seen. He felt that sterilization ought to be put in use at once, starting with those on whom

[17] Paul Lewinson, *Race, Class and Party* (New York, 1932), p. 8.

everyone could agree, like mentally defective Negroes. This probably meant, in his mind, castration of the defective Negroes.

A Negro woman informant came forward with the unexpected idea that white women play a very aggressive rôle in the violent acts toward Negroes. She felt that white women have worse race prejudices than men and that they give "a worse deal" to the Negroes. Informant did not know why this was true but reaffirmed that women are more hostile to Negroes, and especially to female Negroes, than men. She thought that white women were behind or connected with most of the lynchings and could stop them if they wished; often the complaints of women incite what the men do at the lynching party. In relation to this idea I cannot refrain from guessing that the accusations of the Negro man by the white woman may oftentimes be a denial of her own excitation directed toward the Negro. Surely no one who protests so much could be suspected of such loathsome feelings. It seems reasonable too that white women would particularly detest Negro women since the latter are so often actual rivals for the sexual attention and time of the white men.

One of the most effective checks on acts of violence by Negroes against whites is the reprisals which may follow against the family of the Negro man. If the man himself gets away, it has been known to happen that the white crowd will go to his home, perhaps rape the woman and shoot the woman and children, perhaps burn down the house or loot it and destroy the furniture. In such a case the Negro family often does not suspect why the white mob came. This would be another example of the now-familiar displaced aggression and of the dreadful need on the part of the mob to make an example of every case.

Another facet of the situation is that social controls differ even within small units of the same area. In Southerntown and county, for example, no Negro has been lynched for a long period of years. A small neighboring town, on the contrary, is known as one where the whites are particularly mean to Negroes. In such towns violence is more frequent and the provocation needed to set it off much less.

No one should judge even the most incredible of these acts of violence. We should attempt to identify and understand rather than to deplore them. No one is justified in pointing with scorn at mob behavior in the South unless he is disposed to have a personal share in any trouble and sacrifices necessary to revising the basic social situation which generates it. It might be, for example, that a government which could effectually stamp out lynching would have to be far more ruthless against the southern white caste than the white caste is today against the Negroes. One should consider well and be certain of thorough understanding before taking sides; can we be so sure that we would do differently if the problem of dealing with masses of Negroes were to come home to us locally?

It is not always necessary for a white man himself to act if he wishes to punish a Negro. Negro informants are quite aware that some of the many killings reported in the Negro group are caused by white men. One Negro asserted that when white men do not want to make a fuss and kill a Negro themselves, they may give some Negro a couple of dollars to do it; and Negroes can be found who are foolish enough to do such things.[18] A woman informant thought this might occur if a Negro tried to fight when a white man wanted his sister or wife; in this case it would be difficult for the white man to avow the true cause for his hostility toward the Negro. Some charge can always be trumped up or some other Negro can be secured to kill the rival. This is a peculiarly threatening sort of situation since the Negro cannot be secure in his own group relations, but has as a constant danger the "bad nigger" in his own group. The "bad nigger" to the Negro almost invariably turns out to be the "good nigger" from the standpoint of the white man.

We have been discussing forms of violence where killing is the outcome. Much more conspicuous are those aggressive acts which fall short of killing but which include whipping, tarring and feathering, and minor injuries. The latter punishments are used in the case of lesser offenses. We shall present now two reports of a whipping incident by the same

[18] A case of this kind is recounted in a recent novel: Robert Riley, *Deep Dark River* (New York, 1935).

informant. The reports came on successive days and the second modifies the first in a very interesting way.

First report: a middle-class Negro woman said that the local Negro group was stirring with frightened gossip over something which happened in a neighboring town. She explained that all such incidents are feared beyond their immediate locus because of the danger that the bad example will release white aggression in other places. It seemed that in the neighboring town a white woman with a Negro woman in the car beside her drove up and stopped by the side of a road. The white woman called to a Negro bystander and asked him to get change for a dollar. He came over, took the dollar, got the change at a near-by store, and brought it out to the car. He handed it to the white woman who looked at him and said sharply, "What do you mean, winking at me?" He answered, "Ma'am, Ah wuzn't winkin' at you, no ma'am, Ah sho did not wink at you." The woman insisted that he had. Informant said that she knew the Negro and he did have a funny little twitching movement in his face, which might be mistaken for a wink. She has seen him often and knows this facial movement very well. Informant knew for a fact that this Negro man never did anything out of the way, never ran around with other women, was always jolly, friendly, and a "good scout." The white woman, however, went home and told her husband. He immediately collected a "mob crowd" of white men and set out to look for the Negro. In the meantime the police heard about the incident, went out after the Negro, and picked him up before the mob got him. They put him in jail in protective custody. The husband and his crowd came to the jail and told the officers that they wanted to lynch the man; however, they stated two other alternatives. They would not lynch him if they could be allowed to whip him or could be sure he got a long prison sentence. Here there was a gap in informant's story. She did not know whether the man was released and then picked up by the mob or whether the authorities turned him over to the husband to be whipped. At any rate the husband and his crowd got hold of the Negro, took him out to the edge of town and gave him a hundred and fifty lashes. Apparently when the husband saw the blood beginning to run, he went mad and wanted to kill the Negro. Why he did not, with the Negro in his power, was also omitted from the story. The man's hands and feet were securely bound while he was being whipped. He was released in a very serious condition and taken home—by whom was not reported.

A bit of history about the supposed winker and the husband-defender is the following: both were cabinetmakers and rivals for the local cabinet business. The Negro had had constant work during the last two years while the white man had been out of work. Apparently the Negro was a very good worker and very satisfactory to his customers, largely white. The white woman who accused him was, therefore, the wife of his business rival. I asked informant if the white woman knew the Negro by sight. She did not know but said it was possible that the Negro woman with her was there to point him out. At first the Negro woman is said to have denied that the man winked, but later she changed her story and agreed that he had. Informant did not understand why the Negro woman did not defend the Negro man by claiming that he was winking at her. One possible reason is that she intended to accuse the Negro and was in on the game. Another possible economic reason for the trouble is the fact that the winker's wife also had a very good income; she collected rent for a white man who owned a large number of Negro cabins in the town and got a percentage of all she collected. Grudges against her may have been behind the accusation against her husband. The Negro man felt it unsafe to remain in the town since another mob crowd might form and actually lynch him, even in his brutally beaten condition; so he was removed to Southerntown. He planned to leave home permanently and go to a big city. Informant thought this was a pity because he owned a beautiful home and was getting along very well. I could imagine, informant said, how the other responsible Negroes in the town felt; if the man had been a rascal and had committed any crime, she would have had no sympathy with him, but it seemed intolerable that such a thing could happen to an upright and innocent man.

Here we have a recital of events and an interpretation of

them which are based on economic competition but made possible by the tic-like facial gesture of the Negro man. One indubitable fact was that the Negro was whipped.

My informant was an extremely conscientious person and did not withhold the new and more authentic information which she shortly received. She had been talking to the wife of the whipped man, who told her that in the last two years her husband had taken to drinking and was drunk a good deal of the time. He was no longer anything resembling the responsible man he used to be. The wife said that the white woman in question drove up to the curb and spoke to a number of Negro men who were there. The whipped man volunteered to get the change and was not directly asked by her to do it; this disposed of the notion of a plot. His wife thought he had been drinking and probably did wink at the white woman; at least she would not put it past him. In the car with the white woman was her cook. This cook was having sexual intercourse with the white woman's husband, and it was further said that the white woman was having intercourse with Negro men at the cook's house. Only recently the cook had told the whipped man of this. So it seems probable that the half-drunk Negro winked at the white woman because he thought she was accessible to Negroes, and that the white woman in turn told her husband because she took the wink for an assertion that her accessibility was generally known among Negroes, and she wanted to prove her innocence to her husband by this gesture. Another addition to the story is that a kind of crude court was held before the Negro was whipped. Both the Negro and the husband of the white woman were present. The Negro also had a "friend at court," namely the white man who employed him and his wife (his angel). This court gave the Negro the alternatives of death by lynching, a long prison sentence, or a whipping, and stipulated the number of lashes. The Negro chose the whipping. The "friend at court" was present at the whipping and restricted the husband from giving the Negro more than the stipulated number of blows. Informant seemed much less apprehensive about this incident now that she had learned that it was vice which was rewarded by the whipping and not virtue. She felt that middle-class Negro people in the town might feel safe since the retaliation of the white husband was not unprovoked, although it seemed disproportionate to the offense. In this account the tic finds no place in the interpretation, nor does the element of economic rivalry stand out. Much more intelligible is the hypothesis offered by the whipped man's wife, viz., that the Negro frightened the white woman into virtuous protestations by making an actual advance to her.

All the little details of this incident, the panic among the Negroes, the sexual affront, the indignation of the white woman, the rage of the husband, the informal trial, the whipping, and the flight of the Negro, give a better picture of the situation than any amount of formal description. This sort of incident, with the double report, also helped to strengthen my faith in the veracity of a Negro informant who was willing to correct a false picture even when it was damaging to her caste interests and loyalties.

Assaults upon Negroes occur for varied reasons; the following is a case where organization in connection with protesting northern Negro groups was suspected. A local informant told the story about his home town, not Southerntown. Some of the Negroes were taking the *Chicago Defender* and the *Crisis*, militant journals advocating the racial interests and advancement of the Negro. Apparently the white people did not like this. One day some men called on three of these Negroes, a minister, a schoolteacher, and a businessman. They asked each one if he took any Negro literature; each said he did. Then the white men said they were forming a club and invited the Negroes to come down at a certain hour. All complied, though with considerable fear. When they got to the appointed place they were seized, bound, and blindfolded. Then they were put in the back of a car to be taken out to the country and whipped. One of them, the minister, managed to get his knife out of his pocket, cut his bonds, and escape from the car. He came back to town and told his wife that he was going away and would send for her very soon. The others were mercilessly flogged. Informant saw the schoolteacher the next morning when he came to school with pieces of sticking plaster all over his face where the whip had hit him. The minister left the state; he knew that life would be too dangerous for him in his home town.

Violations of caste custom may also lead to the beating of a Negro. A local informant told me of a Negro physician who came down from the North to practice in a southern town. He had resolved to accept the situation and do the right thing. But one day in talking to a drugstore clerk he occasionally forgot and said "yes" and "no." The clerk flew into a rage and bellowed at him, "Say, nigger, can't you say 'Yes, sir'?" The doctor corrected his mistake. That evening a group of young white men called at his house, took him out into the country, and beat him severely. Subsequently he had to leave town. Very possibly the clerk knew of his northern origin and was all the more keenly on the lookout for signs of defiance and independence. Of course, it takes time to become accustomed to the deference forms required of Negroes.

Southern white informants are not reticent about the use of assault on Negroes; rather they talk about it with a self-confident satisfaction. One declared, for example, that the "nigger" is all right in his place. There are, of course, some mean and ugly ones, especially those who return from the North. He mentioned the case of a "nigger" who once worked for him and refused to do something he was told to do. Informant got his blackjack and beat him about the head until he was unconscious. When the "nigger" woke up informant asked him if he wanted any more. The Negro replied, "No, boss, Ah's got enough." Informant did not discharge the Negro but sent him back to the job and "he was one of the best niggers I have ever had." Informant said he has, on occasion, broken all the knuckles of his right hand, exhibiting same, hitting "niggers." Another white man said that the only thing to do with "uppity niggers" is to smash them down. If they get "sassy," hit them; that is all they understand.

A Negro man related the story of a friend who was appointed postmaster of a little town in the South. The white people resented the appointment and threatening rumors began to circulate concerning what the whites would do if the postmaster did not get out. Informant worked occasionally with his friend but finally, in the face of the hostility of the white people, decided to quit. The postmaster stayed on. A few weeks later he was caught by a gang of whites and beaten so badly that he died shortly afterwards. This informant was an elderly man and the act reported happened a number of years ago when it was still possible for a Republican administration to appoint local Negro postal officials. This is, of course, not the case today; but it illustrates the kind of issue which calls forth extralegal force against Negroes.

A pattern very near to physical aggression but by no means identical with it is that of violent and abusive talk toward Negroes; instead of blows, curses. Certainly every white man feels more free to curse or threaten a Negro than he would a white person in similar case. This behavior is undoubtedly experienced as satisfying from the standpoint of the whites and as threatening by the Negroes. Coupled with it in the following instance we see the motive of economic competition operating. A middle-class Negro informant told me that he owned some land; if his stock should wander onto the land of a white neighbor and do some damage, he would have to talk very softly, probably take a cursing, and certainly pay the landowner's estimate on the damages. If, on the contrary, some white man's stock roamed onto his property, he would have no sure recourse. Very likely he would get the cursing, at least if he tried to make claims. Informant said that the Negro here has to learn to "take it" all along the line; his opinion was that things can improve only when the colored people become more economically independent. Frequently economic success on the part of a Negro will draw aggressive responses from the whites[19]

[19] "The third flogging was that of a Negro boy who operated a pressing club at Mount Vernon. White people across the street from his stand reported that he was very polite, and would not permit any boisterousness about his place. He did good work, and was liked about town. At length a white man from Tarrytown, northern part of the county, came to Mount Vernon and opened a pressing shop; he got but little business. After a few months he died; his widow opened his place for business; she got but little patronage. One night a masked

without his having attacked white-caste principles at any other point. It would seem, as already noted, that the Negro's success itself is perceived as a defiance of white people.

In general one may say that Negroes experience much less security in their own homes and pursuits than do white people. Physical invasion of Negro privacy is not taken too seriously. One gets the contrast most clearly by personal experience. On one occasion I went with an officer to have a look at the Negro slum district, which I had frequently been advised to do. We walked along an unlighted, unpaved street between two rows of poor, unpainted houses. Some of them had rooms fitted up for shooting crap, others were brothels. It was early and there were not many people around. The marshal strode into various houses without knocking, and looked around, telling the Negroes to be at ease. I was embarrassed at this unbidden entry onto other people's property and at the contempt for their privacy involved. This sort of "entering without warning" seems singularly aggressive to a northerner.

Whipping is, of course, permitted in the State Prison, as is emphasized by verbal and visual testimony. In the case of the unknown Negro who shot at the police officer, already reported on, this fact came out clearly. We were talking to a seven-year-old boy in the town where the killing occurred and the little fellow said that he had been taken out to the county farm to see the dead Negro. He had a big hole in his chest and there were stripes on his back as though he had been whipped. At this point the boy's father intervened and told us it was the theory that the Negro was an ex-convict because of these stripes on his back. Indeed, the stripes may explain why he shot so readily at the white officer who tried to arrest him; he would rather be killed than go back to prison.

There are, of course, other forms of aggression besides the direct physical violence which we have been discussing.

---

mob broke into the Negro's pressing room and took him 'for a ride.' They beat him badly and dumped him in Toombs County near the spot where Mincey was later left." Raper, *op. cit.*, p. 201; quoted by permission of the University of North Carolina Press.

One of them is undoubtedly moral intimidation, that is, an attack on the self-esteem of another individual. This type of aggression is a chronic policy of the white caste in the South; its aim seems to be to humiliate the Negro, to put him on another and lower scale of humanity, and thereby to paralyze his aggressive tendencies by making them seem hopeless. The personal derogation of the Negro is acutely aggressive on the part of the whites and is so experienced by Negroes; it is used in the maintenance of "social distance" in Southerntown and county. Here we must call to mind the common saying of white people that Negroes are like children and have to be treated accordingly. Such treatment, which is a social fact, probably tends to call up for Negroes the parental images against whom resistance is futile and indeed impious, and furthermore to reinstate childlike attitudes of docility. This form of aggression is one of the most powerful defenses of the white caste against active opposition by Negroes. It tends to stamp the hostile gesture as futile from the outset and to put the white caste hopelessly out of range of counteraggression. We shall examine some of the forms of this personal derogation of Negroes.

One of these, of course, is the caste etiquette which is compulsory for Negroes. A white friend gave me some instruction on this score immediately after I arrived in Southerntown. Never, he said, address a Negro man or woman as "Mr." or "Mrs." and do not refer to them thus in talking to a white person; don't shake hands with a Negro (except in the case of an old Negro friend who has been gone for a long time, and this would be rare); don't tip your hat to a Negro, man or woman, but call him or her by the first name whenever you know it. If you walk on the street with a Negro keep a serious demeanor as though talking business. You may go to a Negro's house on business and even sit down, but Negroes are careful in this case to offer you the best chair, not to sit near you, and, if they are your tenants, not to sit while you are sitting. After this familiarity or the handshake cited above, the Negro must be careful not to presume on the exception the next time you meet, but must show that he recognizes caste etiquette. In speaking

to or of a Negro, use the first name only, or the first and sur-
name, as John, or John Jones. In the case of Negroes of superior status you may refer to them as Smith or Brown as
a mark of special recognition. All of these customs, bearing
on what is referred to as "social equality," are apparently
designed to put the Negro in the familiar child rôle and to
emphasize his dependence and helplessness before white
people. Of course, at first I made mistakes and on one occasion a white friend gently reminded me, "You know, down
here we never refer to a Negro as 'Mr.' or 'Mrs.'; they don't
expect it and we never do it. We always call them by their
first names no matter if they are doctor or preacher or
teacher or anything else. If we should call them 'Dr.' or
'Mr.' or 'Mrs.', they would get the idea that they were somebody and get real cocky." It is quite clear from this statement that not using deference forms to Negroes is thought
of as aggressive on the part of the whites and as controlling and avoiding Negro aggression. "Cockiness" from a Negro would be felt as intensely hostile by white people.[20]

Another form of personal derogation of Negroes is to apply the special and unfavorable designation, "nigger," to
them. It stamps the Negro as an inferior man and seems to
isolate him from the community of human sympathy and
coöperation. At first it was jarring to hear the word used,
but I heard it repeated so often that eventually it lost its

[20] In discussing northern culture patterns, people frequently
cite hat-tipping, handshaking, and the like as meaningless items
of behavior, mere routine forms which we go through. On
theoretical grounds one would tend to deny this since all acts
that men do are probably invested with affect, great or small
in quantity. It is only in the South where the use of these
forms has become a point of caste differentiation that one sees
how tremendously important they are as lubricating gestures
in social interaction. A Negro may be killed or a white ostra-
cized for failing to follow the *minutiae* of the code in respect
to such forms. Even in the North, when we stop to think
about it, we realize that the omission of these deference signs
can become dramatically important; as in the case where someone calls us by the first name too quickly or refuses to coöperate in shaking hands. The safest assumption is that all such
behavior forms have emotional value, even when they seem
most routinized.

shock for me. Several northerners of one or two years' residence have picked it up and use it unthinkingly. The Negroes in Southerntown seem to prefer to be referred to as "colored people" rather than as "Negroes," perhaps because that is too near to "nigger." Many middle-class colored people have accepted "Negro" as an inoffensive designation and some even use it with pride. Such an informant commented that lower-class Negroes do not mind being called "niggers," but that middle-class people do; he said that white people seem to enjoy using the word, particularly in reference to the latter. It is doubtful whether even lower-class Negroes enjoy hearing the term from whites. They may, in joking or hostile moods, use it toward one another; but it probably carries the sting of inferiority for every Negro who hears it, although he does not have the freedom to protest.

There are many forms of personal derogation of Negroes which are hard to classify. One of these, for example, is that Negroes are expected to "wait" or to stand at the end of the line until white persons are through. In the case of Negroes and whites waiting in a professional or business office, it is taken for granted that whites are served first. A Negro employee of a white boss was much irked by having eternally to wait for conferences until no white people were about. The white employer understood quite well, as indeed did his employee, that he could not afford to let it be said that he let a white person wait while he talked to a Negro. This sort of thing is extremely discouraging and disheartening, as probably it is meant to be. It is difficult to keep up a tone of active self-feeling and self-respect when one constantly receives these signs of negative evaluation from others.

Again, a white person may not be too friendly with Negroes. A white government worker was criticized on the ground of her too great friendliness with Negro women, as evidenced by her driving them in her car. She once scandalized a white man by referring to a Negro girl as a "sweet young thing." He commented to me that it was too much like the phrase one would use of a white person. He would praise such a girl by saying, "That's a right smart nigger gal." In all manner of trivial ways like this the caste point is obsessively stressed.

A similar unclassifiable but important case was an experience in a courthouse. It was during a term of circuit court when three juries were impaneled, all white, of course. There were about fifty Negroes in the audience, sitting isolated on the left-hand side of the courtroom; the whites sat on the right-hand side. Of course the Negroes were not represented in any way in the proceedings. After the juries were selected two rival political speakers addressed the audience. One of them attributed the fortitude of the local populace in bearing the depression to the "good old Anglo-Saxon stock of which our state is composed." The Negro stock was completely neglected in his reference. The other, to illustrate a point, told a joke which ridiculed the Negro for his superstitiousness: a "nigger" was afraid of a corpse which somehow popped up in its burial box and threw him into a fright. Here the derogation was publicly and repeatedly stressed, and the speakers had no reluctance to use ridicule directly in the teeth of the Negro audience.

The use of the first name for Negroes is quite systematic. Here again the parent rôle of the white caste and child rôle of the Negro caste come strongly to mind. Whites treat Negroes just as strange grownups treat the children of their friends, automatically assuming the dignity of the adult age grade. It is always a shock to experience this custom for the first time, even with lower-class Negroes, and to have a Negro tell you his name is "Jim" or "Wash" and not give his last name. It is particularly trying in the case of middle-class Negroes. If one has such a Negro as an informant and then hears him called "Jim" in one's presence by the next white man met, one cannot help sharing the humiliation of the Negro. I once had the experience of being asked to talk to a group in which one of my special Negro friends was a leader. The white man who introduced me was forced to refer to this Negro by his first name, a name which I myself would never have thought of using, although we were good friends. This family-feudal pattern of putting the Negro in the child rôle becomes more difficult when it is obvious that the Negro is a mature human being from the standpoint of social achievement. There was a prominent white man in the state who had to meet a talented Negro woman from

Southerntown on various occasions both in town and out of it. He solved the dilemma by calling her "Mrs." when they were away, but by her first name in Southerntown. She said he lacked the courage to be consistent about it. He was actually caught between two divergent patterns and challenged by the fact of her enviable personality and achievement. Informant marveled, nevertheless, that he was always able to get it straight and call her the right thing in the right place. It seems likely that this man had been under alien influence which accounts for the lack of courage and consistency in following the southern pattern.

There are still other ways out of the dilemma of calling a Negro by his first name; sometimes one is forced to them. For example, one of my white informants in riding around the country addressed any Negro he saw as "preacher." "Uncle" is frequently used, as are "elder," "aunty," and "sister." All these appellations have the effect of dismissing the Negro as a concrete, fully equipped human being and of relegating him to a foolish rôle as a plantation stereotype or a comical religious figure. The titles used by Negroes for whites when they are not acquainted with the name of the white person indicate the converse point; such titles as "boss" or "cap'n" express the correct caste deference.

The custom of calling Negroes by their first names doubtless began in slavery days when first names were all they had. After emancipation they generally took the surnames of their former white owners. Perhaps the white people felt that they had no right to such names since they did not acquire them by legitimate descent and socially regulated sexual contact. Furthermore, slaves were property and did not have the personal identity characteristic of the fully individuated white person; without this individuality they had little claim on the august family name. You may call your horse "Bill," but you would hardly refer to him as "Bill Smith." Arising in this context, the custom is now supported by a rigorous caste etiquette and deviations from it are not tolerated.

Another point should be remembered in respect to first names. Elsewhere in America the reciprocal use of first names is a mark of intimacy between two people; if one person uses a first name and the other a title, there is always a claim of superiority on one side and an admission of inferiority on the other. One of the best examples we have of this unbalanced relationship is in our pattern of age grading; younger people cheerfully admit their youth by the use of titles indicating deference to older people. The inferior relationship here, however, is only a temporary one; the younger person will grow out of his age grade and may then expect full status with accompanying prestige tokens. In the case of the Negro this is not true. It is the essence of caste that he may not slough off the inferior rôle.

I have become an expert on the contradictory emotions centering around the use of titles of respect for Negroes. My dilemma has already been explained: without using such titles, I could not have an adequate rapport with my Negro informants; if I did use them, as I discovered, I got in trouble with the white people. I chose the first alternative and experienced considerable social pressure. Realizing that I was seriously combatting white-caste etiquette, I did not resent this pressure; it may fairly be said that my white hosts were indulgent rather than the contrary.

The use of the telephone was a constant source of difficulty. I tried to mollify my white friends by not using "Mr." or "Mrs." in reference to a Negro in their presence; in part this was managed by not talking about Negroes at all, but there were occasional telephone conversations when I had to ask for a Negro by name, and in this case I used titles of respect. A white friend was very indignant when she heard me call a Negro man "Mr." over the telephone. She did not complain to me directly but to other friends who told me. She could not help withdrawing her confidence and approval of my work at this point. Doubtless I was exposing her also to criticism since she had befriended me. The news spread rapidly around Southerntown and the definition of me as a "Yankee" emerged with growing sharpness. Occasionally I would say in reference to the charge of breaking the caste code that I had not intended to affront any white person; that I had used the name over the phone when no one else seemed to be at hand; that, if people took offense, they had to go out of their way to do it. Although this behavior on my part seemed necessary, it is questionable whether I did any favor to my Negro informants. They undoubtedly experienced increased criticism and stood out more sharply before southern observers because of their alliance with a Yankee. Some defenders of my position did agree that a given Negro informant was a superior person, but they did not admit that this was an adequate reason for altering custom with regard to titles. Sympathetic white friends would listen to my side of the story; it seemed to help when I said that I was an outsider, that I was not used to calling Negroes by their first names, and that in the case of certain Negroes I could not use anything but the respectful titles. My idiosyncrasy was more or less accepted, although it was never approved. Such a point as this, however, may be the downfall of a researcher working in the South; when the resentment attached to breaking the caste code is directed at one's own person, the true dynamics of the caste relationships become clear and one realizes the aggressive power with which the white caste clings to all the signs of its superiority. Personal derogation of the Negro is then not a mere phrase but a palpable pressure which is deflected toward any white who does not comply. One of my white friends made a charming exception and put me at ease by herself breaking the code. Meeting me one day, she said she had just seen "Mrs." So-and-so, whom I knew to be a Negro woman. I was astonished and showed it. She went on to say that this woman was sitting in a car with another Negro woman to whom she also referred as "Mrs." I offered to buy her a coca cola in honor of her wickedness. Later I learned that she had told a friend about this event and had said she would not say it to anyone but me, that she wanted to relieve some of the tension which arose from my use of respectful terms for Negroes.

Negro informants in the main seemed to agree that I had better observe southern white-caste manners in public situations. This agreement was never expressed, except by indirect reference. There were opportunities, however, for certain of my Negro friends to put me in an extremely embarrassing position. One of them came up jovially and put out his hand to me in front of the post office, a much frequented place. I had to shake hands but was extremely conscious of the many white witnesses to the act. I am still wondering whether this man forced me to shake hands in an excess of enthusiasm, defying custom, or whether he did it "accidentally on purpose" in order to embarrass me. I experienced the cultural dilemma very clearly in such incidents as these; when meeting Negroes I would feel the twitch of the shoulder muscles tending to put my hand forward and instantaneously the countervailing caste pressure against giving the Negro such a sign of social equality. Such a situation necessarily breeds many insincerities in the outsider. The white people enforce caste rules with ominous unanimity and one is compelled, by one's white-caste membership, to assist to some degree in the personal derogation of the Negro and the expression of hostile pressure against him.

Closely allied to personal derogation, but not identical with it, is the social isolation of the Negro. Difference and inferiority are implied in fact, if not in theory, in the segregation of Negroes, and it is also inevitably experienced by them as a hostile gesture from the white caste. It establishes a "social distance"[21] between members of the caste. The reason given, and the best reason that can be given, for segregation measures is that they make for harmony in race relationships and cut down the friction that would otherwise exist.[22] This "friction" is, of course, aggression between the races. The establishment of social distance is a taboo on Negro aggression as well as an act of hostility on the part of the whites; it is the latter because it imposes

[21] Robert E. Park and Ernest W. Burgess, *Introduction to the Science of Sociology* (Chicago, 1921), p. 440.

[22] "As a matter of fact, such legislation is the embodiment of enlightened public policy, and is the surest guarantee of a minimum amount of friction between the races. In almost every instance of separate car legislation, public sentiment was crystallized into law as the immediate result of intolerable local conditions, not infrequently accompanied by concrete acts of racial violence." Alfred H. Stone, *Studies in the American Race Problem* (New York, 1908), p. 64; quoted by permission of Doubleday, Doran & Co.

a limitation on Negroes not conventional in the rest of our society, a limitation which carries with it the implication of inferiority. In its most real form aggression always involves physical contact as an ultimate measure. The various Jim Crow customs which isolate the colored people socially make Negro aggression more difficult and reduce the occasions for white retaliation. Let us note in passing that we are not, again, deploring or criticizing these customs, but rather attempting to see how they function in patterning individual emotion. The southern conception of the matter plainly is that without such segregation patterns for Negroes the amount of open violence between the races would be greatly increased. Their existence is therefore a manner of holding aggression in check. These customs do actually carry to the Negro, whether intentionally or not, the sense of being inferior, of not being worthy to participate fully in American social life, and also of being a feared and dangerous object in a fearsome and threatening situation.

The commonest of these taboos are those against eating at a table with Negroes, having them in the parlor of one's house as guests, sitting with them on the front porch of one's home, and the like. Any of these acts would imply social equality instead of social inferiority for the Negro. The white-caste view on this matter is simple and logically consistent. It is felt that social equality would lead directly to sexual equality.[23] We already have a suggestion of the painful cluster of ideas centering around sexual acts between Negro men and white women, and so we can understand that the white caste will react to the notion of "social equality" as they would to the conception of "sexual equality."[24] This is probably no delusion. After all, our traditional techniques of courtship center around the dining table, the parlor, and the front porch, as well as freedom of access by the front sidewalk and the front door. One who cannot share these privileges can hardly expect to court the daughter of the family. This is as true for servants in an English country house as it is for Negroes in Southerntown.

[23] William B. Smith, *The Color Line* (New York, 1905), pp. 7-8.

[24] White, *op. cit.*, p. 54.

From the life-history material comes an interesting line of confirmation on this point. The dreams of middle-class Negroes, at least, suggest that eating together with white people in the dream is symbolic of other intimacies, in the same way that courtship is symbolic of marriage and sex relations. One does not attempt to discourage an unwanted suitor from sex relations when he is already married to one's daughter; one begins long before by denying him the house. The white people seem to feel the matter in the same way and are quite as direct in their statements about it. We must always bear in mind that historically and constitutionally such systematic exclusion from contact as exists in Jim Crowing is outlawed and that the southern regional practices do not have the total sanction of the American mores. The result is that the Negro's acceptance of his inferior place can never be automatic and unquestioning, even in the remotest rural areas. The white-caste exclusion of the Negroes, therefore, runs counter to the dominant mores and must be aggressively and locally enforced. It is for this reason that Jim Crowing is classified as an aggressive manifestation.

These patterns imposing a relative social isolation on Negroes are the most immediately striking features of the southern social landscape. I noticed at once that Negro men walking along the street seem careful not to look at the white women sitting on the porches they pass. Negroes are not in general allowed in restaurants where whites go; in the case of some of the poorer restaurants, there is a separate entrance for them and a curtain is drawn so that whites and Negroes cannot see one another eating. In the long, narrow theater in Southerntown Negroes buy tickets at the same box office (and pay the same admission) but they have a separate entrance and sit on the balcony. Sometimes in larger towns they have theaters of their own where, it is said, whites, by convention, do not go, although the taboo in whites participating in Negro social events is not ordinarily as stringent as in the reverse case. In the county courthouse we see the caste isolation of the Negro externalized in the signs over toilet doors, "For White Men Only," "For White Women Only," "For Colored Men," "For Colored Women." There seem to be no other restrictions in this building, except that the Negroes do not loiter in the corridors and around the doors as do white men. Negroes enter a separate section of the railway station marked "Colored" and ride in separate coaches reserved to them. They sit in separate sections at the back of street cars and busses; sometimes in busses there will be a pathetic drape that marks off the white from the colored section at the back of the bus. Negroes come in at the back doors of houses and are quite strictly forbidden entering and even knocking at the front door. This practice carries the automatic implication that they are servants. Some of the elaborations of the isolation pattern seem to suggest that the Negro is viewed as "unclean" and that contact with him is dangerous. One such is the following: there is one drugstore in Southerntown where both colored and white may drink at the same soda fountain, an unusual state of affairs since most drugstores exclude Negroes from the soda fountain. The caste point, however, is still made since separate sets of glasses are kept for each race, thick glasses for colored, thinner ones for white people. I asked the proprietor of a dress shop whether white and Negro women are allowed to try on the same dresses. He said that occasionally they do, but that in Southerntown they buy dresses in different price classes, so that this does not happen often. Here incidentally is an interesting confirmation of our judgment that we have in Southerntown middle-class white people and lower-class Negroes.

Even in the jail the segregation of Negroes is carried out. Of course, they are confined in separate sections. There are no beds in the Negro cells; it is said that there used to be but that the prisoners would tear them up and destroy them, so they have not been replaced. The Negro cells are absolutely bare. It is equally true to say that the white prisoners are segregated from Negroes, but the whites have beds, sheets, and other trivial amenities of life. The isolation of Negroes is carried out systematically in a great many other situations, in the hospitals, for example. I have already mentioned the mental hospital as a case in point. I was told also, but did not confirm this, that there are separate undertakers, hearses, ambulances, and the like. The fact that the Negro seems "unclean" to white people is frequently stated in reference to personal hygiene, body odor, and the like. The Jim Crow customs seem to add another component to this idea, namely, that the Negro is not only unclean but also dangerous.

Experience is the best teacher in caste matters as in others. I had occasion to feel on my own person the same hostilities which isolate the Negro socially and to see myself in the rôle of a caste traitor, or "nigger-lover." I was as little willing to accept the latter term as southern people are to believe that they are "nigger-haters." The situation in which I was exposed to criticism has already been outlined; I visited a Negro home under the impression that I was to meet a relative at a small family party. Once arrived at the house I discovered a large mixed group engaged in conversation, card playing, and dancing. News of the party was apparently spread through the Negro youngster who brought the ice cream. Criticism by the white caste was intense and centered on the charge that I had played cards with the Negroes, which I had not done; this was "social equality." My defense was the usual one, that I attended the party as a researcher in my scientific rôle and not as a white-caste member. Reprisals, however, were inevitable. First, of course, was the vigorous gossip which tended to make its subject extremely uncomfortable. Threats were made against the Negro host; social invitations by white people were pointedly not given to me. If one lives in Southerntown, "not to be received" is a very serious matter and would be more so if one's family were there; living would be quite intolerable without opportunity for friendly contacts within the white caste. The whole tendency of these manifestations was revengeful and the object was to punish the caste traitor. My most industrious critics did not wish their names to be known to me, so that all the news of the gossip came at second hand; those who told me professed not to share the critical attitudes. Evidently the critics felt that the gossip was very damaging, or else they would not have shot from ambush. By various indirections I discovered two of my chief critics and an interesting fact emerged; both had hostile attitudes toward me on quite other grounds than the one alleged. In the one case it was an economic matter, and in the other a personal conflict that had no relation to race. Once, however, the "incident" had occurred, these people were able to ventilate their full antagonism. On the other hand, genuinely friendly persons tended to make light of the matter as a mistake, as not deliberate, and as negligible in itself. It must be stressed that I received strong support from white persons at the same time that I was being criticized. One friend even went so far as to make an open issue of it and say that the people in Southerntown were too "dumb" to understand what I was doing and should withhold their criticism. This was an overstatement of the case; the people understood all too well that I did not share their basic attitudes and they had appropriate and legitimate hostilities toward me as a result. While I was under the drumfire of gossip, my own tendency was to respond with hostility, to blame the white people instead of myself for the gossip, to be apprehensive about revenge tendencies against me being redirected against my Negro informants. It was a valuable experience from the research standpoint and it made me much more cautious in future actions.

The same incident seemed to touch a match to a number of smoldering complaints that people had about my research, the worst being the persistence with which I referred to Negroes as "Mr." and "Mrs." The end result was an increased silence, lack of response, and blankness in portions of the social horizon where I had formerly met some interest and tolerance. Even so, my research rôle certainly protected me from the full weight of the antagonisms which might have been roused against a Negro breaking the caste code.

It would be an interesting addition to this book if we could describe at what points in the individual lives of the white people the caste code is implanted. But adequate data are not at hand. To the white middle-class child, Negroes must be known mostly in their lower-class, workaday rôles, such as housemaid, cook, nursemaid, houseboy, and laborer. When he thinks then or later of a "Negro," it is the lower class that he has in mind. This fact may explain an incident like the following: I was riding in a car with a white man and his eight-year-old son. The father was telling me that in university towns in the South, Negro faculty members were able to buy Pullman berths when they wished to go north. The father added, a little scandalized, that a white woman whom he knew had seen two of them in a dining car on the train to Washington. The boy said firmly, "Daddy, if niggers really eat on dining cars, I never want to ride in them."

We have already noted that the slavery situation was an important learning situation for the Negro; through pressure at first and soon through desire, he was able to assimilate the main forms of white culture and to build up a conception of his rôle within white society, a conception which nowadays takes account of "constitutional America" as well as caste America. Intimate contact in white homes, especially as house servants, was particularly helpful and doubtless played an important part in preparing Negroes for the middle-class status which many have now achieved. The substitution of caste for slavery, however, has somewhat reversed this tendency and lessened direct informal exchange between Negroes and whites. One result often pointed out is that the Negro's knowledge of white people at the present day is much greater than white people's knowledge of Negroes.[25] If caste segregation be justified on the ground that it prevents race friction, one should

[25] "From these natural causes the white man's knowledge of Negro life is diminishing and the rate is accelerated by the present-day policy of segregation. This operates practically to make an ever widening gulf between the two races which leaves each race more and more ignorant of the other. Without contact there cannot be knowledge; segregation reduces the contacts, and so knowledge and understanding decrease. With decreasing knowledge comes increasing distrust and suspicion, and these in turn engender prejudice and even hatred. So a vicious circle is established whose ultimate effect, unless counteracted, must be a separation of the races into more or less opposing camps, with results as disastrous to the spirit of American institutions as to the genuine progress of both races." Robert R. Moton, *What the Negro Thinks* (Garden City, N. Y., 1932), p. 5; quoted by permission of Doubleday, Doran & Co.

also note the correlated disadvantage, that it prevents knowledge, sympathy, and coöperative attitudes from developing.[26] We must not, of course, suppose that Negroes are outside the sphere of white culture; in place of the old sympathetic accommodation between the races Negroes now have the schools which certainly offer a conception of personal discipline on the American model, the radio, and newspapers which give information; and even the Jim Crow railway cars which teach a technical lesson unknown in Africa. Stated in a formula, Negroes have greater access to the wider American culture, but at the same time a relative withdrawal of favorable notice and sympathetic contact with the white caste in the South. We can surmise, however, that formal access to American social ideals may be cold comfort in lieu of the older warmth and vitality of personal relationships which are rapidly being broken down between the castes. There is no doubt about the necessity of classifying segregation and exclusion of Negroes as aggressive behavior on the part of whites. Individual Negroes object to this categorical treatment which does not distinguish them personally or take account of their achievements or aptitudes. Further, the parallel accommodations provided for them, though supposedly equal, are actually not in most cases equivalent to those provided for whites. Let any traveler who wishes to check this take a quick look ahead into the colored coach on a southern railway train or consider the disadvantage of sitting in a hot balcony in a very small theater. The complaints individual Negroes make invariably include those against Jim Crow practices.[27] The whites in their turn feel that they have a right to choose their own company; and, if they choose exclusively white company,

[26] J. M. Mecklin, *Democracy and Race Friction* (New York, 1914), p. 106.

[27] "In the South the first answer nearly always referred to the Jim Crow cars or the Jim Crow railroad stations; after that, the complaint was of political disfranchisement, the difficulty of getting justice in the courts, the lack of good school facilities, and in some localities, of the danger of actual physical violence." Ray S. Baker, *Following the Color Line* (New York, 1908), p. 130; quoted by permission of Doubleday, Doran & Co.

it is their own affair. The whole behavior of the white-caste members is so routinized that it is only infrequently possible to see the aggression which invests their segregation practices against Negroes. If such practices are violated by Negroes, the supporting aggression comes sharply forward; listen from the window of a southern room and hear what happens to the thoughtless colored delivery boy who knocks on the front door. Not lynching, needless to say, but a competent dressing down on the score of manners.

In the heat of victory and hostility toward the southern states which possessed the postwar Abolitionists' Congress, it was intended to make such exclusion of Negroes impossible. The Civil Rights Act was passed and fortified by amendments to prevent discrimination against Negroes in various public situations.[28] This act was, of course, a blow at the slave and class structure in the South and was intended to make the formation of castes difficult or impossible by preventing the social isolation of Negroes. Its shrift was short, however, since northern enthusiasm for forcible reformation of southern social relationships disappeared and the Supreme Court refused to enforce the act against private citizens. The central point of the legal decisions was that a state might not discriminate against Negroes in the specified ways; but the Court was not prepared to say that a hotel proprietor, theater owner, or railroad executive might not so discriminate if he wished to.[29] Our democratic form of government is, and is evidently intended to be, powerless against massive minority group sentiment, such as that existing in the southern states with reference to Negroes. The prohibition of slave running in 1808 and the later prohibition of manufacture, etc., of alcoholic beverages have demonstrated the same point. Our central government cannot mobilize sufficient systematic ruthlessness to interfere seriously with local custom. To have tried to do so in this instance would have required continuous military rule in the South, a difficult and expensive enterprise and one quite inconsistent with our democratic ideals. People

[28] William J. Robertson, *The Changing South* (New York, 1927), p. 38.

[29] Robertson, *op. cit.*, p. 83.

must consult their own social values to decide whether or not this is for the best.

We cannot leave the subject of white aggression without calling attention to the generally threatening behavior of whites toward Negroes. We have already noted the cases in which punishment of a crime by a Negro is exemplary and symbolic. The posse wants to get the *right* man, of course, but it is not too serious a matter if it does not, since the warning is even more clear when it hangs the wrong one; i.e., the Negro caste is punished through one of its representatives. White people may or may not be very conscious of this threatening atmosphere in which Negroes live, but Negroes are extremely conscious of it and it is one of the major facts in the life of any Negro in Southerntown. I once asked a middle-class Negro how he felt about coming back down south. He said it was like walking into a lion's den; the lions are chained; but if they should become enraged, it is doubtful whether the chains would hold them; hence it is better to walk very carefully. Another Negro thought it was a shame that a Negro man had to shape his behavior so much according to the wishes of the whites and out of fear of what they will do; he has to be careful not only on his own account, but also on account of his family and even of all the Negroes in the community. He said that after the shooting or lynching of a Negro the Negro community is frightened and that the whites act as if to say, "Well, it may be you next." Every Negro in the South knows that he is under a kind of sentence of death; he does not know when his turn will come, it may never come, but it may also be at any time. This fear tends to intimidate the Negro man. If he loves his family, this love itself is a barrier against any open attempt to change his status. Informant said that Negro men are not cowards and do want to defend themselves; but most of the time they just take the easiest way out—accommodation.

This atmosphere of intimidation can be illustrated in another way. With three southern white men I drove out to call on some Negro croppers and see their cabins. The car pulled up in front of a cabin, and the driver called out to a Negro man on the porch, "Hey, Bill, come here." The Negro seemed apprehensive and the driver called back, "Come on, we are not going to hang you," and laughed. We went to three or four cabins and in every place the same little drama occurred. The Negroes were frightened and reluctant. They did not know what might not happen when four white men drove up in a car before their place. Any situation involving unknown white men looks ominous to the Negro. I commented to the driver that "the Negroes seem to be very polite around here," and he answered with a laugh, "They have to be." The Negroes were relieved when they discovered we were on a peaceable errand, and showed us their cabins. Beds, clothing, and furnishings were tattered; the stoves were old; and there were dinky privies outside. Everything in the cabins seemed repulsively mean and squalid, though sometimes clean.

A Negro woman, speaking of the fear that always attends the Negro, told how she and a Negro boy were driving in a car one day. Some white children saw that it was Negroes driving and threatened to throw rocks at them. Such an affair might start an incident, if the Negro fought back. Again, on the same trip, some bicyclists saw them coming and wove back and forth on the road in front of them, as if to dare them to run them down. This vague apprehension of danger, and it is often enough confirmed in fact, is the mental atmosphere in which the Negro must live.[30]

A Negro man reported a similar situation from his own childhood. He used to drive with his father into town on a farm wagon and stay with the horses while his father went into the store. His father was warned against this practice

[30] "Another and more numerous element of the county's white population is determined that the guilty go unpunished for their part in the flogging of Mincey and others. Some Negroes feel more secure after the wholehearted way in which the best white people have denounced Mincey's murderers; others are reminded by Mincey's death that no Negro, regardless of his relation to the leading white citizens, is secure from the mob. It is reported that Mincey's own pastor was afraid to conduct the funeral and that another minister was called." Raper, *op. cit.*, p. 188; quoted by permission of the University of North Carolina Press.

on the ground that some white boys might beat up his son, that this would start a fight between the races, and then all the Negroes would be in danger. He decided it was better to leave the boy at home than to risk this. Informant said it was particularly dangerous for his father to defy the whites because they would revenge themselves, not only on him, but on the whole family; they would want to stamp out a family which manifested such dangerous tendencies.

Very frequently Negroes from the North do not respond immediately with the proper caste behavior to the situation in the South; and, as a result, southern relatives are uniformly alarmed when northern Negroes first come down. There is always the danger that they will "stand up for their rights" and "not make any bones about telling the truth." It amounts to a more or less continuous state of alarm for Negro men and women; the women say of the men, "You never know when they go away from the house what may not happen before they get back." Usually, of course, nothing happens.

Southern white people do not like to believe they have created such an uncomfortable situation for the Negro and are likely to minimize the fact. They tend to rely on the openly ascertained statistics of lynching and violence and to point out that not many Negroes are killed; what the white caste does not take into account is the emotional climate that is established for the Negro by asocial violence and by the many aggressive pressures which are leveled against him whenever he tries to claim his full status as a man in the sense of the wider American conception of a human being. What matters is the fear of extralegal violence, not knowing when or how the danger may appear, not being able to organize oneself with reference to it, uncertainty, and the mist of anxiety raised under such conditions. This threat is all the more pervasive and insidious the higher the class position of the Negro, since the higher positions tend to draw more hostile affect. The northerner, of course, has a somewhat similar experience, especially if he is a researcher on the "nigger question." He too feels an eerie sense of threat when he crosses the caste barrier in any way, such as by signs of courtesy toward Negroes, or when he is seen riding in a car with a Negro where it is not clear that his mission is a professional one.

It has been noted that the Civil War broke up the smooth accommodation relationships that had existed in slavery and substituted a less stable form of social organization in the caste system. It also increased the hostile manifestations toward Negroes, not only in the direct physical sense beginning with the secret orders[31] and continuing through lynching behavior, but also in all the less tangible forms of personal derogation and social exclusion described in this chapter. There was, of course, some fear and hostility before the War, centering particularly around the danger of revolt, but it has obviously enormously increased since then. The intent of the postwar aggression, seen from the sociological standpoint, was to restore and maintain the superior position of the white caste. It was really this superiority which was attacked by the War, the War amendments, the Civil Rights Bill, and the military occupation of the South. It would seem, therefore, that the legitimate hostility of southern white people would be directed against the North, northern armies, the northern theories of social justice, and the leaders who attempted to put them into practice. This was indeed, and still is to some degree, the case. After the military defeat of the South, however, there was no possibility of effective aggression against the North. The defeat was, of course, a great damage to southern pride in addition to being an economic loss. This is probably the context in which increased hostility has been directed at Negroes since the War; the Negroes have been made the butt of the hatred aroused in the South by the interference of the North with its folkways. Hostility against the North, northern people, and their ideas of social justice still exists and is not a negligible factor in American life, present or future; but the military cause, at least, is lost. There remains a passionate insistence on maintaining regional social relations along traditional southern lines. In a larger sense, the War has

---

[31] Robertson, *op. cit.*, pp. 57-58.

been continued by this hostility against Negroes.[32] This is not offered as a single-strand explanation, but merely as one interpretation; it is equally obvious that the threat of Negro competition to the middle-class trustees of southern culture would also arouse, and appear to legitimate, aggression against Negroes.

[32] "It took ten years of misrule and bitter humiliation to create the 'solid South,' but the work was done so thoroughly that it will in all probability persist for years to come. It is a familiar fact that social habits, especially when they become tinged with strong emotion, are the last to change. . . . It was most unfortunate for the Negro whose interests were so intimately connected with those of the white that during this period of crystallization of group feeling he was not only excluded, but was identified from the very start with the outside forces making for the coercion of the white." Mecklin, *op. cit.*, p. 168; quoted by permission of The Macmillan Co.

CHAPTER XVI

Defensive Beliefs of the White Caste

~~~~~~

The function of defensive beliefs is to make the actions of white-caste members toward Negroes seem expedient and in line with current ideals; if this cannot be done satisfactorily, then at least these acts can be made to seem inevitable. But what are the actions which must be barricaded behind distortions and excuses? It seems quite plain from the analysis thus far that they are, first, a method of justifying and perpetuating the gains of the white caste already described, and second, a technique for explaining the various types of aggression directed against Negroes. This aggression, as we have noted, is intended to paralyze pressure from the Negro's side which would tend to alter his fixed status in the lower caste. Now neither of these activities is permissible from the standpoint of democratic theory which stresses, on the contrary, equal opportunity for mobility, fair play, and reward according to social usefulness and individual sacrifice. The very existence of caste is a warrant that the social system in Southerntown is not built along these lines. Instead we find the Negro socially immobile, disadvantaged in economic, sexual, and prestige spheres, and exposed to extralegal violence on the part of white-caste members. This contrast makes a defensive ideology indispensable.

We must recall the general tendency in our society to disavow aggressive activities and intentions toward others; it is a considerable triumph of our early socialization that we have been persuaded to renounce such overt aggression.[1] Another way of saying this is to point out that our

---

[1] See Sigmund Freud, *Civilization and Its Discontents* (New York, 1930), pp. 61-63.

society tries to persuade us to accept frustrations peaceably and to turn the accompanying resentment to socially constructive ends. In simple life situations people do not like to admit that they dislike others or hate others. The same tendency can clearly be observed in Southerntown. If simple denial of hostility, a frequently observed pattern, is not effective, there is always the possibility of putting the blame on the other fellow, of showing that he has tempted us beyond our strength by his exciting acts. This also plays a great rôle among white-caste defensive beliefs in Southerntown. Still other possibilities are to show that the other fellow does not feel our aggression or is himself a scoundrel. Such patterns will also be observed. The study of such beliefs is a considerable part of the work of the psychologist of propaganda[2] and they have been specifically indicated with regard to the Negro.[3]

It is characteristic of the human self, as Sumner has shown it to be of society, that the individual attempts to show a consistent front toward his fellow men; he does not like to be caught in inconsistencies. If he is so caught, as the white southerner is, between his regional mores and our national democratic mores, he attempts to reconcile the discrepancy. The southerner acts according to his imperative regional culture, and rationalizes as best he can. His

[2] See Leonard W. Doob, *Propaganda* (New York, 1935); also H. D. Lasswell, *Propaganda Techniques in the World War* (New York, 1927).

[3] "The evolution of myths concerning Negroes shows a striking resemblance to these mentioned by von Langenhove. In this category would fall the myths concerning Negro mentality, or the closing of the frontal sutures at the age of fourteen; the 'rape myth,' or the belief that some character weakness and inordinate sexual virility in Negroes make them rapists by nature; and the 'insurrection myth,' or the recurrent assertion and belief that Negroes are plotting the downfall of the government. These are general in their acceptance. They illustrate the tendency of authors observed by Langenhove in his study 'to incorporate new ideas with the complex old ones and show that they are not surprising and that all earlier facts tend to prove it.'" The Chicago Commission on Race Relations, *The Negro in Chicago* (Chicago, 1922), pp. 578-579; quoted by permission of the University of Chicago Press.

defensive beliefs form a kind of bridge between the way he must act and the way divergent cultural standards tell him he ought to act. It is of extreme importance to notice that the defensive beliefs here discussed are not senseless. In every case there is some ground and reason for them.[4] What makes the belief defensive rather than a cool reality judgment is that there are concealed reasons for the act as well as ones that are alleged. The concealed reasons lying behind these defensive beliefs are the gains and the aggressions necessary to defend the gains. The defensive beliefs put the stress on partial and inadequate elements in the situation and obscure a clear vision of actual social forces. If Negroes are aggressive only when incited by Yankees, and there is truth in this observation, then the obvious course of action is to eliminate Yankees and not to alter the position of the Negro. In short, the function of the defense is to conceal the disparity between social justice according to our constitutional ideal and the actual caste treatment of the Negro.

It is a great mistake to think that the equalitarian ideal does not function in the South as well as in the North. It does and the proof of this is that among white people it is cherished and applauded in the best northern style. But there is more conflict over the ideal in Southerntown because it is more frequently and flagrantly violated. This is undoubtedly perceived as painful by middle-class white people; they have the same wishes to be fair as other Americans and they do not behave as they do toward the Negro out of innate meanness.[5] Rather they are caught in a culture conflict[6] and must preserve intellectual consistency as

[4] Dr. Hanns Sachs has showed me in a valuable personal way that a rationalization always has a speck of truth in it; otherwise it could not be used. One must never, in individual study or in social analysis, fail to give due credit to this element of truth.

[5] This, by the way, is a strictly northern defensive belief.

[6] "In Jefferson's original draft of the great Declaration there was a paragraph indicting the king for having kept open the African slave trade against colonial efforts to close it, and for having violated thereby the 'most sacred rights of life and liberty of a distant people, who never offended him, captivating

best they can. A possible alternative mode of response would be to recognize flatly the actual situation and attempt to alter it; but the easier path of defense and excuse is taken which follows the fundamental psychic guide of avoiding painful perceptions.

It is, of course, true that southern people are much more exercised over the contradictions in their lives than are northerners. A Negro student bore testimony on this point. He had attended many conferences in the North as a representative of his Negro college and came back with a feeling that northern students are rather cold and indifferent to the Negro's problems. He put it this way: "They will not do anything *to* him, but neither will they do anything *for* him." He thought southern delegates to such conferences are much more interested because they feel the force of the disparity between constitutional statements with regard to equality and actual white-caste behavior toward Negroes; they are wrung by this dilemma and react vigorously to it, while the northern student does not realize the nature of the contradiction in personal terms.

Defensive beliefs in a society, like rationalizations of the individual, make possible the avoidance of the actual situation; they tend to eliminate the problematic, offensive, inconsistent, or hostile facts of life. One clings to the defense and avoids the traumatic perception of social reality.

The master defense against accurate social perception and change is always and in every society the tremendous

---

them into slavery in another hemisphere, or to incur miserable death in their transportation thither.' This passage, according to Jefferson's account, was 'struck out in complaisance to South Carolina and Georgia, who had never attempted to restrain the importation of slaves and who on the contrary still wished to continue it. Our Northern brethren also I believe,' Jefferson continued, 'felt a little tender under these censures, for though their people have a very few slaves themselves, yet they have been pretty considerable carriers of them to others.' By reason of the general stress upon the inherent liberty of all men, however, the question of negro status, despite its omission from the Declaration, was an inevitable corollary to that of American independence." U. B. Phillips, *American Negro Slavery* (New York, 1918), p. 116; quoted by permission of D. Appleton-Century Co.

conviction of rightness about any behavior form which exists. Southern people share this conviction. What is done is *de facto* right and is justified by the consideration that it has not been invented by current culture bearers but comes to them through sacred tradition; exercising independent perception against it is unwise and even impious. So compelling is the traditional order that each and every sharer in it acts *as if* he had a mass of impartially seen experience to support his view. The negative cases and contradictions are overlooked, often without even realizing that an exception to the general view is being stated. Southerners will say, for example, that all "niggers" are worthless and lazy, but that "Spade" is really the manager of the place; he has never been given any responsibility which he did not carry out. The ancestors are right and "Spade" is an insignificant exception. Since any new perception requires energy and courage, rare human qualities, this persistence of tradition probably is based on a fundamental human indolence and timorousness which prefer the historical routine of behavior to an active and independent perception of social fact. If inertia of habit and fixity of complex play a rôle on the pleasure side, social fear and wishes for security are equally important in stabilizing the ancestral routine. Realistic social perception is specifically *not* cultivated; rather every precaution seems taken that it will not occur, and that the folkways and mores will persist. Only acute crisis in a group, such as the defeat of the southern armies, forces a re-canvass of the situation and the gradual stylization of new social perception. This impotence in the grip of custom, always tangible in persons and personal relations, is the primary defense.

There are, of course, other defenses and many of them. Many of the incidents already cited confirm this view, and it would be necessary only to consider them under a new heading to prove the point. Every specific incident reported on previous pages is complex and has been utilized for some one purpose; not every bit of meaning can be squeezed out of a given case under any one heading. Some of the incidents reported in this chapter will obviously make points in addition to the concept of defensive belief. This type of repetition is inevitable since any incident tends to have leading lines to all the major social configurations; what varies is the standpoint of the observer and classifier who moves in cautious circles around the complex event.

A common pattern used to obscure the actual functioning of the caste situation is the idea that the Negro is a mere animal. The defensive value of this belief is obvious. It lies in the fact that our cultural assumptions apply only to human beings, not to species other than man. No one protests because a horse cannot vote and no one fights a bitter war to give civil rights to the army mule. If Negroes are classified with such animals, it becomes plainly ridiculous to apply our democratic assumptions to them. This dehumanization of the Negro is attempted through the belief in his animal characteristics. It was easier to hold this notion in slavery days than it is now;[7] it was also more easily held when there were cultural as well as physical differences to support the idea. It becomes more difficult to retain when only physical differences remain to mark the Negro off from white people. The picture of the Negro as a beast, albeit an amiable one, has been extremely serviceable to the white caste, as is evidenced by its remarkable persistence.[8] In an animal we do not posit feelings similar

[7] "Most apologists for lynching, like the lynchers themselves, seemed to assume that the Negro is irredeemably inferior by reason of his race—that it is a plan of God that the Negro and his children shall forever be 'hewers of wood and drawers of water.' With this weighty emphasis upon the essential racial inferiority of the Negro, it is not surprising to find the mass of whites ready to justify any and all means used to 'keep the Negro in his place.'" Arthur F. Raper, *The Tragedy of Lynching* (Chapel Hill, 1933), p. 19; quoted by permission of the University of North Carolina Press.

[8] "Down to the latter part of the seventeenth century the belief was prevalent in America that the Negro was merely a beast, and even as late as 1902, from a Bible House in St. Louis was published *The Negro a Beast, or In the Image of God*—a book which had an enormous circulation among the poorer whites of the South. Burnaby, writing in 1759, mentions the fact that the Virginians scarcely considered the Negro as being of the human species, and Evans, while visiting in North Carolina, was startled to be asked concerning the sup-

to our own; or if we do, we take them to be unimportant from the human standpoint. One can shield oneself from having to admit aggression against Negroes in at least two ways; one can say either "I am not doing it" and thus deny it altogether, or, what comes to the same thing, "He doesn't feel it." We make the latter assertion when we refer to the Negro as an animal.

Southerntowners were not lacking who were prepared to make this assertion. One white informant said, "They are just like bird dogs. If you have a good bird dog, you do everything you can for it to take care of it; you are kind to it and make it as comfortable as you can. But if you have a mean bird dog, you just get rid of it. Niggers are just the same. You have no more personal relations with them than you do with bird dogs, except to buy their cotton and have suchlike business dealings with them." We do not believe that southern white people really act on this assumption or fully believe it, but they say it and use it as a justification for their treatment of the Negro.

People can show as well by their actions as by their words how they feel about Negroes. Some white people evidently consider Negroes incredibly stupid, lacking in normal social perception, and incapable of knowing when they are misused. The following incident exemplifies this view. A white informant bought a quantity of ice cream for a picnic, much of which was not used but was returned to him. He hailed me one day on the street and said he wanted to show me something interesting; behind his house a group of his tenants were eating the ice cream which had soured by now. The assumption seemed to be that they could not tell sweet from sour ice cream and that they would feel that they were getting a wholehearted treat. A white man would

---

posed presence of a tail and absence of a soul with the African Negroes. While I have heard similar queries advanced regarding the human qualities of the Southern Negro, they are, of course, passing into decay. In the earlier days, however, they doubtless exerted a considerable influence in inhibiting the soul-saving efforts of the whites where they thought no soul existed." N. N. Puckett, *Folk Beliefs of the Southern Negro* (Chapel Hill, 1926), p. 528; quoted by permission of the University of North Carolina Press.

be ashamed to admit having done this sort of thing to a group of white people; but this individual had a certain self-righteous glow about his generosity. It could only be based on the assumption that the Negroes were so stupid they did not know the difference.

White informants frequently state that the Negro is a "savage," which for them is another way of saying "brute." One man thought that Eugene O'Neill's *Emperor Jones* was a true representation of the nature of the Negro; he will revert to type if given the chance. Right under the veneer of American culture is the African savage. As proof, he said that there is a church near his town where voodoo rites are practiced, and where no white man is allowed to come. Sentinels are posted, and, as soon as a white man approaches, the rites are stopped. It is plainly felt to be a very damaging assertion that the Negro is a savage.[9] No distinction is made between a man from another society and a brutalized person. To call the Negro a savage is, from the standpoint of these informants, to put him outside the reach of the American mores. Actually this would be a most effective defense if it were true.

Another aspect of the belief in the animal nature of Negroes is that they are more or less, in theory, denied a per-

---

[9] "Leaving out of the question the anthropometric tests which correspond closely to those of the native African, we find a number of qualities indicative of the relationship. The precocity of the children, the early onset of puberty, the failure to grasp subjective ideas, the strong sexual and herd instincts with the few inhibitions, the simple dream life, the easy reversion to savagery when deprived of the restraining influence of the whites (as in Haiti and Liberia), the tendency to seek expression in such rhythmic means as music and dancing, the low resistance to such toxins as syphilis and alcohol, the sway of superstition, all these and many other things betray the savage heart beneath the civilized exterior. Because he wears a Palm Beach suit instead of a string of cowries, carries a gold-headed cane instead of a spear, uses the telephone instead of beating the drum from hill to hill and for the jungle path has substituted the pay-as-you-enter street car his psychology is no less that of the African." J. E. Lind, "Phylogenetic Elements in the Psychoses of the Negro," *Psychoanal. Rev.* (1917), IV, 303-304.

sonality. This gives them the anonymous character that they often have in the reports of white-caste members. It is not effectively understood that Negroes are enmeshed in a system of personal relationships, that they have friends, write and receive letters, have memories over years, hold grudges, have personal preferences, pain, exultation, immediate objectives, and urgent needs. This depersonalizing technique represents them not in this way but as robots who react only to immediate stimuli.[10] If one has this view, it is a shock to come into sympathetic contact with a Negro personality and to notice its many similarities to white people's. The advantage of this argument is very simple. If the Negroes are not fully human, they do not have to be humanly used, in our current sense of the word. Democracy does not apply to nonhuman or inanimate things, but only to objects with full human qualities. It is perhaps the perennial sin of the northerner that, in theory, at least, he posits a full American personality for the Negro and identifies himself with this type of Negro. In designating this belief as a defense I do not make the contrary assertion that Negro personalities are identical in form with those of white people; it will be the purpose of the next chapter to show some of the important differences, especially in the case of lower-class Negroes.

Another defense, which is perhaps a specialization of the above, is the idea that it is the Negro's own fault that he is a lower-caste, and for the most part, a lower-class man. He is there because he belongs there, and the present-day social structure represents the outcome of an honest competition with a fair start all around. The racially inferior men have lost out; so what of it? The present social position of the Negro in American society is accepted as a proof of permanent inferiority and inaccessibility to high civilization. Because he is lower caste now he must ever be that

---

[10] "Niggers out there were no better than brutes. Here they were given the hardest work, the worst cells, and subjected to the most brutal punishment. Everybody, especially the guards, are prejudiced against them." Clifford Shaw, *The Jack-Roller* (Chicago, 1930), p. 157; quoted by permission of the University of Chicago Press.

way. This is a direct inversion of the facts of the case as they have been laboriously built up by cultural research. Such research exhibits men in any one generation as the product of their historical social life with biological forces shaped in the mold of the culture. It cannot be absolutely stated that there is no truth in the assertion of the biological inferiority of Negroes, but one can say with certainty that it has never been established beyond doubt. The argument that the socially disadvantaged deserve their low status because they are so stupid seems too obvious a way of conserving the advantages of those who, for the time being, are on top in the social structure. The argument, however, is invariably made wherever there is a class or caste structure to defend and where defense is needed.

Another argument concerns certain behavior items frequently observed in Negroes. It is asserted that they lack initiative, are shiftless, have no sense of time, or do not wish to better themselves; and it is implied, if not asserted, that these characteristics are permanent features of Negro personality under all circumstances. One may be able to confirm the observation without accepting the theory derived from it. In life-history work where daily interviewing was involved I noticed that the lower-class Negroes were least reliable on the score of time. Frequently they would miss appointments and presented the weakest of excuses when they came back; some simply solved the dilemma by not coming back at all after a first interview. One man said that he had "sort of" been out of town, whereas I had actually seen him in town. Shiftlessness and lack of initiative are frequently reported by white informants with many circumstantial details. In view of the preceding information on methods of discouraging status advancement in Negroes, one would expect just such characteristics. Who will continue to show thrift and initiative in the face of a social situation which makes these difficult actions seem futile? Who will forever be on time for a date he did not make? This defense, which puts the blame on the Negro, at the same time conceals the provocative social situation in which the supine lower-class character is developed.

It is difficult to disentangle observed fact from stereotype in many of the beliefs about the Negro. There is invariably fact; the question always is, how much? A very common idea is that Negroes are emotionally unstable, capricious, untrustworthy, and some say, definitely unaccountable and mysterious. The question of emotional instability has been discussed at length under the theme of Negro aggression. It was urged there, and is repeated, that because of the caste situation, which prohibits any aggression at all, self-assertion in Negroes is disproportionately felt by white people. It was further charged that the white expectation of Negro aggression is in part fear of retaliation, the feeling that the Negroes ought to be, if they are not, very hostile. The charge of emotional instability should also be confined to lower-class Negroes since its best factual basis is there. When the researcher makes known his interest in Negroes, he receives a great deal of unsolicited information about them which may in the end become boring; the reason is that the communications tend to follow stereotyped lines and to stress the same points over and over again. One of these charges is that Negroes are unreliable and irrational. A hostess may tell you about the devotion of Negro servants to her and explain that she would do anything for them, and in the same breath recite a tale of their inefficiency and unreliability. Of course, she has had servants who were very reliable, but she does not detail this part of the story. On the contrary, one hears constantly of how they do not show up for work, what lame excuses they make, how stupid they often are in household affairs, and how much they have to be policed to get them to do a decent job. Emotional instability is noted very frequently, as is also the childlike character of Negroes. A white informant told how an officer in his town had challenged a Negro on the street and drew a bullet which killed him. He believed that Negroes go off "half-cocked," do not reflect, and have little remorse. Another informant stressed this lack of remorse, saying that he had seen many Negro prisoners, even murderers, and that they do not appear to repent of their crimes; he remarked on how calmly they go to death by execution, but, as it happened, in the case he cited the executed Negro had had religious consolation, had revealed a firm belief in future life, and had exhorted his executioners to prepare themselves for death. In reference to the Negro who shot the officer, I offered the argument that, since many Negroes are taken away from peace officers by mobs, they are perhaps afraid to fall into the hands of "the law." My informant indignantly denied this, said they had no reason to fear lynching in his county, and thought the true explanation was that they were childlike and unstable. There is truth in this statement but it is exaggerated; and this very exaggeration conceals the atmosphere of intimidation in which Negroes live. This informant was especially anxious to deny this aspect of the Negro's world.

The motility of Negroes from plantation to plantation is relevant here. It is set down to "bad character" on the part of the Negro, and we have affirmed that there is truth in this, but we must stress again that the assumption conceals the terrific insecurity of the Negro and his relative lack of opportunity. The "bad character" is itself grown by the situation and not responsible for it, just as reliability and responsibility are features of character when the society puts a premium on them.

Another line of belief about Negroes is that they are immoral, liars, and thieves, which is the equivalent of saying that they do not follow our mores on one point and therefore cannot claim their benefits at any other, i.e., such as voting. We must remember the crime of rape in this connection and the defensive belief that lynchings are mainly done as a result of sexual attacks on white women. There is some truth in all these assertions; the poor are more likely to be thieves and the threatened can turn out to be liars. The fact of the matter would seem to be, however, that, if the Negroes do not follow our mores, it is not because they do not wish to, but rather because they are not allowed, encouraged, or compelled to follow them as the rest of us are.

The assumption of immoral intentions on the part of the Negro is quite widespread. A Negro girl told me the following story about the white people in whose house she worked. One night her aunt's house burned down; her white employers knew there had been a fire and asked her, as she

was serving breakfast, whose house it was. She told them.
They joked about it and said the aunt had probably burned
it down herself in order to get the insurance. Informant
stated that this was not the case because her aunt was not
even present at the time of the fire. She thought the family
made this defensive statement because they were afraid she
might make a request for help.

I was early warned that Negroes will steal anything, but
more especially money, liquor, and tobacco. There was
some confirmation of this assertion; at least tobacco and
minor articles of clothing unaccountably disappeared. It
was not true, however, in the case of every servant and
seemed to be anything but true in the case of various middle-class Negroes; but it was vigorously believed and frequently alleged in reports of informants. Opportunity for
swindling frequently occurs through advancing wages to
servants; often they run away instead of paying back. A
white woman informant told about a colored houseboy she
once had who borrowed fifteen dollars to pay for a suit;
he owed it a long time and never did pay it back. Finally
she fired him rather than have him borrow more. The same
informant remarked that it is hard to get a good Negro
cook; they will not follow recipes, even when they can
read, but will go by "pinches and dabs" and general guess.
She said their "native" cooking is very greasy.

The lying of Negroes—usually lower-class Negroes—is frequently described. "You can't believe a thing a Negro
says," "They will tell you just what they think you want to
hear"—these arguments were frequently brought up in the
wish to discredit my research and my contacts with informants; there was doubtless a great deal of truth in them,
but one might add that Negroes had jolly well better tell
the southern white people the things they want to hear; it
is part of the rôle of a lower-caste man to do this. A surprising number of white informants commented on the mysterious character of the Negro: "The more I see of him, the less
I understand him." This seems to be the opposite of the
notion that southern white people "know their Negroes";
perhaps it represents the white reaction to the secretiveness
and withdrawal of sincere affect on the part of Negroes as

well as tangible differences in Negro character. Certainly all of these beliefs are overstressed and acquire a defensive function since they serve to discredit theoretical claims of the Negro for social justice and fair treatment.

A belief of the same type is the designation of the Negro as superstitious. The effect of this defense is to put the Negro outside of the circle of persons to whom American democratic practices should apply. There is no doubt that it was formerly true, and even today some evidences of superstition can be shown.[11] Some informants believed, for example, that the hoot of the screech owl is the sign of death. One Negro stated that she has fully confirmed the connection through experience. For example, an owl screeched just before her father died and before the son of a neighboring woman was killed in an automobile accident. More recently while working in Southerntown she heard an owl screech, and sure enough, the next week a woman next door died. This informant, a teacher, felt guilty about believing in this "superstition" and said she cannot understand how owls could possibly foresee such events. She thought that it is something more appropriate to the "older generation," but still cannot throw off this particular belief. She hastened to add that she rejected many of the beliefs which uneducated Negroes adhere to.

A white informant gave an example of the inveterate superstition of Negroes; her Negro cook had persistently taken down a screen that covered a window in the kitchen. Informant wanted to keep out the flies; so she protested, threatened, and finally asked for a reason. The cook said that she just could not breathe that "strained air" any more. After all, southern people say, how can you expect us to

[11] "These cases, which could be multiplied almost indefinitely, show clearly the grip of superstition upon the Southern Negroes. Conjuration is constantly having a hand in the practical affairs of life. Reserving further analysis for a later connection, we merely call attention to the fact that the African influence greatly predominates over the European, a fact quite in keeping with our earlier conclusion that dissimilar beliefs either remain intact or are entirely eliminated." Puckett, *op. cit.*, p. 310; quoted by permission of the University of North Carolina Press.

grant social equality to individuals who hold such superstitions? It is not recognized, perhaps not known, by people who use this defense that the outmoding of such superstitions is a very recent affair with white people and that the Negroes are only a little behind in freeing themselves. A rather short life can be predicted for this particular excuse since schools in which Negroes share more and more are steadily decreasing these notions in favor of the rational, materialistic world view.

A number of the beliefs just cited might have been summarized under the complaint that Negroes are culturally inferior and therefore cannot expect to be allowed to share on an equal basis the privileges of our society. To be sure, social inferiority, *at the moment,* is often mistaken for a permanent biological inferiority tending to make Negroes insusceptible to our culture. The fact of inferiority may be granted without drawing the conclusion that it will endure indefinitely. The existence of a group of middle-class Negroes of all shades disposes completely of the biological argument that Negroes are incapable of acculturation in our society.

With Negroes, as with our children, the inexpert use of language is a mark of actual social inferiority. One of the most prized of southern sadistic patterns consists in pointing this out. White informants comment particularly that lower-class Negroes have trouble with past participles. They say "riz" for "rose," "fotched" for "fetched," "retch" for "reached," and "swang" for "swung." It is felt to be a particularly telling blow at Negroes to say that they do not talk correctly. Their mistakes are the subject of many jokes; I remind the reader of the "fornuopulating" case already described. The grandiose coining of words and inaccurate use of long words by Negroes is also specified frequently and with amusement; it is sometimes said that, even though the Negro does not get the right word, he can always make himself understood. The northerner who does not know the limits of the vocabulary and terms of speech of Negro dialect is frequently ridiculed for his pompous assumption that the Negro talks correct and grammatical English—another evidence that the northerner thinks of the Negro as a dark white man. The southerner, however, makes no such mistake, but stresses at many points the inadequacy of the Negro's assimilation into our society and adds the implication that the culture from which he comes is markedly and categorically inferior to our own; yet at least one competent observer views the native civilizations from which our Negroes come as considerable achievements.[12] It is certainly true that the West Coast African cultures did not generate the destructive efficiency of Western European civilization, but they are not for this reason to be denied a claim to high relative status as forms of social life. The fact is that we added the most rather than the least talented of aborigines to our society when we enslaved the African Negro.

Among beliefs which profess to show that Negro and white people cannot intimately participate in the same civi-

[12] "In West Africa, the development of techniques of all kinds is the greatest on the continent. The Benin bronzes, the brass-work of Dahomey, the weaving of the Ashanti, or the wood-carving of the Ivory Coast, Dahomey, and Nigeria are famous, while pottery of a high grade, basketry, and iron-work are found everywhere. The social and political organization also has great complexity, and this region may be distinguished from the Congo area proper in this regard. It was here that some of the great kingdoms of Africa existed from medieval times or earlier to the dates of their downfall before the advance of European colonial expansion; among these were the kingdoms of Benin, Dahomey, and Ashanti, to name only three. In this area we find a well-developed sib organization which, like those of East Africa and the Congo, is totemic in character, and a highly developed ancestral cult which validates and stabilizes these relationship groups. The religions of West Africa are similarly highly developed. . . . It is this forested belt which lies along the Guinea Coast that is the locale of the high cultures of Africa, cultures that in view of their complexity of structure are to be termed 'primitive' only because of the technical definition of the word which makes it applicable to people who have non-written languages. Yet even in this connection it is to be remarked that in West Africa an independent discovery of writing was made, that is to say the syllabary system of the Vai, who are found in Liberia and Sierra Leone." Melville J. Herskovits, "Social History of the Negro," *Handbook of Social Psychology* (edited by C. Murchison, 1935), pp. 221-224; quoted by permission of Clark University Press.

lization is the perennial one that Negroes have a smell extremely disagreeable to white people. This belief is very
widely held both in the South and in the North. A local
white informant said that Negroes smell, even the cleanest
of them. It might not be worse than other human smells,
but it was certainly different. It was asserted to be as true
of middle-class Negroes as of others, at least upon occasion.
Another informant swore that Negroes have such a strong
odor that sometimes white people can hardly stand it. He
described it as a "rusty" smell. This odor was said to be
present even though they bathe, but to be somewhat worse
in summer. Another white informant described the smell as
"acrid." White people generally regard this argument as a
crushing final proof of the impossibility of close association
between the races. I can give only my own testimony on
this point. What I smell mostly among Negroes is perfume,
although, to be sure, I have not made a special research
on the subject. It may be that the perfume is an effort to
avoid the odious stigma of being ill-smelling which Negroes
know to be one of the beliefs of white people about them.
While Negroes, especially sweating Negroes and manual laborers, do have a strong odor, I cannot detect a categorical
difference between it and body odors of white people.[13]
Among middle-class Negroes I have not been able to detect
any identifiable body odors at all.[14] We may remember
that most of the supporting evidence for this belief must
be based on Negro cooks, maids, houseboys, field laborers,

[13] Though I am forced in fairness to confess a personal detail, namely, that I had bad hay fever during a large part of
my research residence in Southerntown.

[14] "At times, I encountered churlishness. Once a man rose
and said, 'I wish to ask you a frank question. Isn't the chief
objection to the Negro due to the fact that he has a bad odor?'
In reply, I agreed that there were lots of bad-smelling Negroes;
but in turn, I asked my questioner if he thought the expensive
magazine advertisements about 'B.O.' were designed to attract
an exclusive Negro patronage. I remarked that I did not think
so, since they were generally illustrated with pictures of rather
nice-looking white girls." J. W. Johnson, *Along This Way*
(New York, 1933), p. 387; quoted by permission of the Viking
Press.

and other lower-class Negroes who do not have either adequate bathing habits or facilities, who do not have in the hot southern climate very adequate wardrobes, and who have little time for washing either themselves or their clothes.

Another consideration appears from quite a different angle. We know that from childhood on one of the most deadly reproaches indicating social inferiority is that a person is unclean or smells bad. Older children give evidence of pride in having established cleanliness training and do not overlook the opportunity to point out that while baby may be mama's darling, he does not, for all that, smell very good. Furthermore, there must be a considerable segment of the white population who do, or believe they do, have a secret bad odor, if one can judge by the advertising and sale of deodorants. They cannot, however, easily be classified by such a trait as color, and there is no reason for classifying them. All of our evidence points to the fact that Negroes are labeled as an inferior caste, and it seems not improbable, under these circumstances, that any shred of fact with regard to bad odor would be utilized to the utmost as a defensive belief. This issue must be left unsettled; but my conviction is that the odor point is greatly overworked and I consider it even possible that the widespread existence of the belief itself may induce a hyperfastidious sensitivity toward Negro odor which is not displayed toward the body odors of white people. It seems quite possible that if the belief were absent, the Negro odors would not rise above the discrimination threshold. In any case it is, for the moment, extremely serviceable as a way of fixing on the Negro an undesirable lower-caste mark and, by inference, justifying white-caste superiority behavior.

Among the defensive beliefs we can refer again to the fear of revolt which exists among white-caste members. The fact that there is little basis in reality for this fear makes us question why the belief exists at all. Negro revolt, although always potential in the long perspective of history, is improbable under present circumstances; we have shown that Negroes are unable to designate the white caste as an out-group and must find other paths for their direct aggressions. The occasional rapes of white women and shootings of white men appear to stir fears of mass action among Negroes and often the conviction is quite alive that such action is about to occur.[15] There is a marked delusional element in this belief and we must search for the unseen sources from which it springs. One such source we have already indicated; it is an inversion of the "Do unto others" principle and has the form "Others will do unto you as you do unto them." This we have called a fear of retaliation based on the knowledge that retaliation by Negroes would in fact be justified. We have also noted that the white-caste men correctly interpret the unconscious wishes of Negroes toward white women and the disavowed excitation of their own women toward Negro men. It is impossible to posit any other situation in view of the well-known attraction of white men and Negro women for one another. What is not taken into account, however, is the barrier to overt social expression of sexuality both in the Negro men and white women; instead the revenge tendencies are directed against the mere existence of such wishes regardless of how unlikely they are ever to find expression. This permits us to say also that the behavior of white women toward Negro men is probably as blameless as the southern stereotype of the white woman demands. Behind the actual or posited desires of Negro men for white women is seen also the status motive, the wish to advance in social rank, to be as good as anyone else, and to have available whatever anyone else has, that is, free sexual access to women, within the mores and without undemocratic distinctions. The race-conscious white man has a proprietary

[15] "The most direct and immediate result of the Emelle outbreak was that the mass of whites were fearful that the Negroes would retaliate. On every hand they said that the Negroes were arming themselves and going by pairs or threes or fours. The Emelle trouble merely aggravated an already insecure feeling on the part of the white people in the plantation area. They told with alarm of a recent case where two Negroes went to the home of a sawmill operator, and in the face of his wife's pleadings for mercy, robbed and murdered him." Raper, *op. cit.*, p. 72; quoted by permission of the University of North Carolina Press.

interest in every white woman; he also acts as if an attack upon or an approach to the white woman were an attack on himself. The horror generated by the rape idea resembles closely the dread which individuals show concerning brutal and sadistic operations on their own bodies. Perhaps the path of this unconscious process is something like the following: the question is asked, "Would you want your sister to marry a nigger?" This amounts to asking whether an individual would defend his sister against an attack by a Negro in case of a pitched battle; and the further question is raised, "What harm could come to you if you did thus defend her?" It is a matter of fact that the approaches of white men to Negro women are interpreted as assaults on the dignity of the Negro man, and no fight occurs because the Negro is categorically prohibited from fighting at all. Out of such considerations arises the conviction of guilt of Negroes and the assumption of the wish to attack white women. This belief has the great value of concealing the actual sexual gains of the white caste which are still accessible to those who are disposed to take advantage of them; that this gain is real is shown by the number of mixed-blood Negroes. Behind the fears of retaliation and revolt lie the social facts of exploitation of Negroes; fear of revolt conceals the true state of affairs.

Yet another defense is the idealization of the "old-timy" Negroes. This is especially characteristic of upper-class people who have enjoyed full accommodation relationships with their Negro slaves and servants. To some degree it has also been adopted by middle-class people. By idealizing the old-time Negro type and wishing for its return, the present-day realities of southern life are avoided and it is not necessary to take account of the actual change in Negro status. It is, in addition, part of the worship of the past which includes an idealization of the agricultural labor unit based on slavery, the cheerful "darkey," the Black Mammy, and the like.[16] From another standpoint it is a demand that the

16 "We must face the future, not the past. Yet scores of thousands of Southern folk, seriously and kindly considering the Negro problem, will insist upon the South's friendliness to the Negroes, and offer as proof, not efforts being made to meet

present-day Negro fit into the old stereotype and accept the limitations to personal maturation and status advancement which were characteristic of "old-timy" Negroes. Doubtless the ideal serves other purposes as well, since it is part of the legendary material of the white caste, promotes its solidarity, and bulwarks its superiority.

Closely connected with this is the idea that Negroes are a naturally happy, carefree people; that they are comical, amusing, and, when they are very small, cute. The argument seems to run: "If the Negroes are so happy, why, after all, should we do anything for them? They like their inferior position, we like what we have, and everything would be fine if it were not for the damn Yankees." There is a good deal of truth in these affirmations, but certainly they are defensively exaggerated by white people. Informant after white informant said that the Negroes are a happy folk, that they never have a worry in the world. Even the troubles they think they have really do not amount to anything.[17] The assumption is that, if they are so happy with little, it would be a shame to change them, and that anyone

---

their present needs, but the touching and universal cult of the Old Black Mammy!

"She deserves a funeral, bless her; and she certainly needs one—a competent, permanent funeral that will not have to be done over again every few days. Her removal will clear the atmosphere and enable us to see the old soul's grand-daughters, to whom we must in justice pay something of the debt we so freely acknowledge to her. We must lay aside the mental attitude of the past—the attitude of a people toward a slave race—and face the present with a forward look. To accomplish this is the task of women, and by all the tokens they are accepting it as theirs." L. H. Hammond, *Southern Women and Racial Adjustment,* Trustees of the John F. Slater Fund, Occasional Papers (1917), No. 19, p. 32.

[17] "Naturally, the negro lacks initiative; takes no thought for the immediate future, living only in the present, without recalling with any degree of concern the experiences of the past and profiting by the same; does not worry about poverty or failure; distrusts members of his own race, and shows little or no sympathy for each other when in trouble; is jolly, careless, and easily amused, but sadness and depression have little part in his psychic make-up." W. M. Bevis, "Psychological Traits of the Southern Negro," *Amer. J. Psychiat.* (1921), I, 71.

who tries to do so is not a true friend of the Negro. This belief again makes the most of one element of truth in order to avoid consideration of the actual status relations existing between Negroes and whites. If a great many Negroes suffer, it is because they have been corrupted by alien ideas and not because of any defects in current social arrangements. White people often seem to show a definite envy of the carefree, cheerful, and charming Negro person. The belief in Negro happiness systematically excludes from consideration the troubles of Negroes, such as poverty, hunger, disease, social humiliation, debauched characters, and lack of opportunity for advancement. These conditions are facts with all Negroes some of the time, and with particular Negroes all are true at the same time. From the stereotype of the happy Negro no one can appreciate the actual amount of individual frustration and social turmoil which Negroes really endure.

People who impose an inferior status on other people, as the whites have done to Negroes, notice that eventually resistance dies down and the inferior group accepts its status, or at least gets used to it and regards it as one of the conditions of life. This acceptance is then used defensively by the superior group in the following way. It is alleged that the people not only accept the status but actually are completely satisfied with it and do not desire anything else. When discontent is to be accounted for, it is then done, not by asking what conditions are actually imposed on the inferior with which he might legitimately be discontented, but rather by asserting that someone has "put ideas into his head." This is the familiar picture of the "outside agitator" who is always responsible for discontent in patriarchal industrial enterprises in the North. Southerners have had a compelling example of this "meddling" and interference with their social relations in the Civil War. At that time the North was their out-group, hated as an out-group always is; since then an accommodation with the North has been forced on the white South, and in the meantime, as we have seen, the Negro caste has become more or less of an out-group. It is probably true that certain current attitudes are derived from the former status of the North as an out-group; this is evidenced in the present day by an overestimation of Yankee hostility and an underestimation of the solidarity and sympathy that is felt with the white South. One white man, for example, assured me with great emotion, as if I could not possibly believe it, that there were honest, ethical white men in Southerntown who strive to be fair and just in all their relationships with Negroes. He said that these white men do not carry guns, are not shot at from the bush; their word is law on their plantations and the worst punishment one of their Negroes can be threatened with is to be "put off the place." It seemed to be assumed that I could not come to such a conclusion on my own part as a result of observing behavior. The meddling Yankee, however, still plays a great rôle as one who has an upsetting effect on Negroes otherwise contented with their lot. Since the Yankee represents formally the "constitutional" definition of individual dignity, it must be said that there is much truth in this stereotype; under this symbol he stands in automatic opposition to caste relations of whatever kind.

We have already given a number of illustrations of the belief that southerners love Negroes individually, are kind to them, and take care of them. This belief is undoubtedly used to allay the anxiety which inevitably arises over the invidious distinctions maintained against Negroes as a caste. Incidentally, we have here the "angel" viewed from the white side; the Negroes are seen as dependent children, and it is said that true parental care is exercised in their behalf. This point is stated frankly by white informants; one man indicated that southern white people recognize their responsibility to "their" Negroes. If a Negro gets sick, a white patron will get him a doctor; if he is hungry, he is given food; if he is in trouble, his white patron will intercede for him (we have already noticed the effect of this practice on dealing out legal justice to Negroes). Informants stated that these relationships between whites and Negroes do not exist in the North and offered them as an offset to the "equality" and "freedom" of the northern Negro. It is true that this paternal rôle is often assumed, especially among those with gentle traditions; but one must note also that it is not a very secure type of help. The "social parent" is all too free to retract his help if the conditions become hard; it is a feudal type of aid and a direct substitute for putting the Negro in the position where he can do the same things for himself. If he is able to, the Negro can hire his own doctor and buy his own food, as well as the service of a lawyer who will do all the interceding in court that is permissible. Another angle on the same problem is the fact that middle-class white people do not share these traditions of caring for the Negro and that their behavior is much more exploitive. Unbound by this obligation, they are able to treat the Negro as a direct economic competitor and to "gain" all the more from him. The social vigor of this tradition is breaking down, and it is not as important a means of meliorating the lot of the Negro as it was formerly.

A very remarkable type of defense is the assertion that Negroes expect aggression and mastery from the white man and are not content unless they get it; further, that they are so used to being gained from that they force any given white man to conform and carry on the traditional white-caste practice. This assertion results in the conviction that Negroes enjoy being put at a social disadvantage and refuse to alter this relationship. It is useless to deny that there is some truth in this, but, according to Negro informants, not very much. A local white man who owned land told me that many white men openly cheat their tenants at the time of the settlement. He said he did it himself. He was proud of the fact and stated that the Negroes liked it, expected it of him, and would not be satisfied if he did not do it; as proof of this he pointed to the fact that his tenants stay with him with extraordinary fidelity. He asserted flatly that Negroes detest a weak white man, and on the contrary, like to be cheated and go out of their way to find a hard task-master. He felt that his harshness was an asset in his dealings with Negroes. This belief is very widespread among white informants and is held by many as a prescription governing relations between employer and worker. The truth of the matter probably is that the lower-class Negroes have developed a strong masochistic streak in respect to white people and really do get positive satisfaction from being bellowed at, cursed, and exploited. I could not help thinking, while talking to the above informant, that he was trying to reconcile himself to the commandment, "Thou shalt not steal," and was giving the curious excuse that his victim insisted on his doing it, which, if true, would be a means of allaying his own guilt feelings about his predatory rôle.

In discussing the same point later with Negroes, I found that they do not accept this statement as a general principle, although they admit that there are many Negroes who seem to act as if it were true. With regard to not moving from plantation to plantation, which is the chief form of proof offered, Negro informants have a different explanation as to why tenants remain with a dishonest employer. One of the reasons is that the unscrupulous employer may rake up some supposed back debt, and they will not even get the ten or fifteen dollars already promised to them. A second reason is that, if they happen to have any tangible property, like mules, a wagon, or household goods, they may lose it too. It would simply be taken away from them and they would have no redress. A third reason is that it is sometimes hard to get a new place in times like these, so that tenants remain even under obnoxious conditions and not because they like to be mistreated. A fourth reason offered is that most of the planters "do them" the same way, and so it does not help much to change. In view of the testimony of Negro informants, the notion that Negroes like to be cheated stands as one of the most transparent of defensive beliefs.

It is not urged that all white-caste members in the South hold all of these defensive beliefs or that they are held with equal intensity by all white people. Many southerners do treat Negroes with a human sympathy, objectivity, and fairness that is quite democratic, and they do this despite the formal cultural evaluation of the Negro. As a result they do not need to cultivate defensive beliefs because their actual behavior is morally defensible in the light of the master American ethical notions. In reality these people act more democratically and realistically than their regional culture specifies. It should be noted that democratic dealings with others do not mean idealization or mushy sympathy for them, but a freehand way of taking them as they come and judging them by their actual behavior, with perhaps the tinge of sympathy that one always wishes in being judged oneself. There exist other southerners who react against the formal evaluation of Negroes, identify with them, and over-protest on their behalf. This attitude has been chronic in the North and has served as a powerful support to the use of force against the South in times past. It would be desirable, but it is impossible, to give a statistical delineation of the degree to which various attitudes are held; for the moment we can only isolate the most heavily patterned beliefs held by those who are actually engaged in administering the caste system from the white side. One thing is certain; where defense is needed as a result of actions unethical in the light of a personally accepted standard, defensive beliefs will arise.

CHAPTER XVII

Gains of the Lower-Class Negroes

∞∞∞∞∞∞∞∞∞∞∞∞∞∞∞∞∞∞∞∞∞∞∞∞∞∞∞∞∞∞∞∞∞∞

Some phrase lingering in the mind will often give the clue to a new way of seeing a problem. The following is uttered by white people with haunting insistency, "The Negroes have all the best of it down here." Of course we now know that this sort of idea can be used as a defensive belief, but we must also ask whether or not it has deeper significance. How could it be that the apparently disadvantaged Negroes have the best of it? Advantage or disadvantage is usually defined in terms of possession, or lack of it, of the values standardized as desirable by a society. From the standpoint of what is prized in American society, the Negroes are certainly disadvantaged. There is another quite different and peculiar perspective which we may take. We can see the behavior forms of a group, like the Negro caste, as nearer to or more remote from the primitive pleasure tendencies of the organism itself. Judged by this criterion, prestige, which may involve much work and renunciation, may be a dearly bought value that hardly compensates for the renunciation its attainment imposes. Conventional social morality may be valuable as a warrant of high social status, but again the individual, in his heart of hearts, may think the game is not worth the candle. We can say that the primary biological measure of what is valuable to the organism is freedom to express impulse without let or hindrance; if it can be shown that in some groups such expression is permitted to a larger degree than in others, we may view such a group as also making gains; but this time gains are defined in reference to the pleasure orientation of the organism. What the well-socialized perceive as disadvantageous or even degrading characteristics may appear from the organic standpoint as valuable behavior forms. For example, in order to perceive how freedom to be aggressive can be of value, we must abandon for the moment the social and moral standpoint of our middle-class-ified American white society. It has not gone without notice that slaves have methods of recouping themselves for their inferior status.[1] One accustomed to the satisfactions of mastery over others may find it difficult to see that crude impulse gratification is a compensating factor to those who must submit to being mastered. Such a man evaluates the problem only from the angle of his social group and will be determined to come out with the answer that the solution forced upon him by his society is the only desirable one.

We have listed the gains of the white middle-class group and until now they have seemed unconditional advantages. For the time being, we have been accepting the American social schema as it is. From the standpoint of this schema it is obvious that there is more fun in being boss than in being lazy. However, we must challenge these valuations if we are to understand in what sense the Negro may be found to "have the best of it."

Northerners will have much more difficulty in grasping this point than southerners, since northerners carry an idealized stereotype of the Negro and accept whatever behavior, like that of the middle-class Negro, tends to confirm it. There is little understanding of the Negro problem as it is experienced in the South and still less of the character structure of lower-class Negroes.[2] Although middle-class Negroes with their numerous mulattoes are more conspicuous and expressive,[3] it is vital to secure an understanding

[1] "The slave acted only under two motives, fear and sensuality. Both made him cowardly, cringing, cunning, and false, and at the same time fond of good eating and drinking and of sensual indulgence. As he was subject to the orders of others, he lacked character, and this suited his master all the better." W. G. Sumner, *Folkways* (Boston, 1906), p. 285; quoted by permission of Ginn & Co.

[2] Newbell N. Puckett, "Negro Character as Revealed in Folk Lore," *Pub. of Amer. Sociol. Soc.* (1934), Vol. 27, No. 2, p. 12.

[3] Alfred H. Stone, *Studies in the American Race Problem*

of the Negro folk. It is this folk, this mass of lower-class Negroes, which may be said to gain in the sense suggested by this chapter. This lower-class group is abundantly represented in Southerntown and no discussion of the situation would be complete without reference to it. It would be a crude form of bias to assume that one's own class, the middle class, was actually representative of the whole Negro caste. This lower-class group is nearest in culture-modeled impulse to the former slave status of the Negro.[4] The "gains" of the Negro are the compensations of the slave who has become a caste man.

In discussing the reaction of the Negro to caste as a constant frustration situation we have pointed out that one course of action is to abandon aggression as a mode of changing the reality situation and to accept substitutive gratification. That is the theme of this chapter: the relatively indulgent behavior permitted to Negroes in lieu of the struggle to achieve higher social status. The Negro makes the best of his situation and exploits his freedom from onerous responsibility and renunciation; as a realist there is nothing else he can do. This does not mean, however, that he is biologically anchored to the gains which we shall discuss. It does mean that he has accessible pleasure possibilities which are abandoned in large degree by the better socialized, in particular by middle-class white people. His

(New York, 1908), p. 40; Edward B. Reuter, *The Mulatto in the United States* (Boston, 1918), p. 397.

[4] "The essential observation of this study is that the Negro population of this section of Macon County has its own social heritage which, in a relatively complete isolation, has had little chance for modification from without or within. Patterns of life, social codes, as well as social attitudes, were set in the economy of slavery. The political and economic revolution through which they have passed has affected only slightly the social relationships of the community or the mores upon which these relations have been based. The strength and apparent permanence of this early cultural set have made it virtually impossible for newer generations to escape the influence of the patterns of work and general social behavior transmitted by their elders." C. S. Johnson, *Shadow of the Plantation* (Chicago, 1934), p. 16; quoted by permission of the University of Chicago Press.

impulse expression is less burdened by guilt and less threatened by his immediate social group; the essence of the gain lies in the fact that he is more free to enjoy, not merely free to act in an external physical sense, but actually freer to embrace important gratifying experiences.

We shall discuss three gains of the lower-class Negro: first, greater ability to enjoy the sexual freedom possible in his own group; second, greater freedom of aggression and resentment within his own group; and third, the luxury of his dependence relationship to the white caste. All these types of freedom represent primitive biological values and none of them is constrained to the degree customary in white middle-class society. If it is confusing to shift the point of view so suddenly, let us remember that it is impossible to present all relevant perspectives at the same time.

It must be clear from data already presented that the white sex mores are not deeply riveted in Negroes so far as behavior within their own caste is concerned. Not only are more sexual objects available to any given person, but the inner barriers against sexual enjoyment are not set up within the lower-class Negro personality to the same degree. The latter fact is crucial. For Negro women there is, in addition, the possibility of gratification without, as well as within, the caste.

This idea of the Negroes also making a sexual gain may seem puzzling; hence the contrast between it and the white sexual gain must immediately be discussed. It is true that white men have a wider range of sexual objects available, but my observation is that they also have inner taboos operating which tend to lessen their enjoyment of these objects; what at first seems like a great gain may be, again from the primitive pleasure standpoint, a relatively minor one. It is argued that inner control of drive expression has progressed to such a point in the white group that genuine sexual satisfaction is greatly limited. It seems likely that the whites repair this damage by adding a sadistic component to their sexual enjoyment. If the sexual pleasure itself is lessened by inner prohibition, it is possible to humiliate and despise the Negro and have the satisfactions of mastery and superiority. Lower-class Negroes, on the other hand, seem to have a sexuality much less checked by the mores and therefore capable of more complete actual expression. The gain from the Negro standpoint would then consist simply in not being so highly acculturated to impulse renunciation. The gain from the white standpoint would consist in adding the pleasures of mastery and control in the sex act to the diminished actual sexual gratification. We are talking here about the type of personality developed by the social forms as they exist; there may, of course, be individual exceptions to the freedom of the Negroes and the relative intimidation of the whites; it is apparently impossible to standardize a culture in any absolute sense.

It seems that already in slavery days there was a kind of intuitive balance operating in the minds of the masters of the white caste, and there is evidence for thinking that impulse freedom was allowed to Negroes and even encouraged as a compensation for deprivation on other scores.[5] If so, this informalized substitution is still operating in the present caste situation. Not only that, it is now often used as a proof that Negroes are innately inferior and incapable of accepting the white mores as guides to conduct. What was once a concession has become a means of rebuke.

Middle-class Negro people, as will be shown, are trying to differentiate themselves from lower-class Negroes, and they are able to point out what characteristics of the lower-class Negroes they do not like. One woman told of a young

---

[5] "To enslave men successfully and safely it is necessary to keep their minds occupied with thoughts and aspirations short of the liberty of which they are deprived. . . . The license allowed appeared to have no other object than to disgust the slaves with their temporary freedom, and to make them as glad to return to their work as they were to leave it. I have known slave-holders to resort to cunning tricks, with a view of getting their slaves deplorably drunk. The usual plan was to make bets on a slave that he could drink more whisky than any other, and so induce a rivalry among them for the mastery of this degradation. The scenes brought about in this way were often scandalous and loathsome in the extreme. Whole multitudes might be found stretched out in brutal drunkenness, at once helpless and disgusting." Frederick Douglass, *Life and Times* (Hartford, Conn., 1882), pp. 166-167.

people's party she gave at which there was dancing. The next day one of the "sisters" from her church remonstrated with her for allowing dancing in her house. Informant asked the sister what boys she had recognized at the party. The sister named half a dozen. "Do you know," informant asked, "that all of these boys have been going to prostitutes down in the slums?" The sister had to admit that she did. Informant told her to go and reform this situation and, when she had done so, to come back and talk again; she might then think of forbidding them to dance. This woman, herself governed by middle-class standards, was pointing out the lower-class patterns she deplored and at the same time ridiculing the contradictory prohibitions of the church.

It is hard to be balanced in describing Negroes' sexuality. One can err, for instance, in two ways: by making it seem too enviable and discounting the misery often associated with it, or by positing the restraints which are automatic in the middle group of the white caste. Southerners are more likely to do the former[6] and northerners the latter. Actually, a much easier temper is observable among Negroes than among whites. The following is one of those uncensored incidents which offers the very best proof. It is a joke which was told repeatedly at meetings of Negroes and which was said invariably to "bring down the house." Informant, who himself used the story, said that it always warmed up the meeting and that the people sometimes laughed at it for twenty minutes. For the sake of contrast, consider how it would be received by a middle-class white group. There was an old brother who was going down to a frolic one evening with his "gittar" under his arm. As he went along, he noticed that there was a service going on in the church. He was a little early; so he tucked his "gittar" under the church steps, went in, and sat down in the back seat. As he entered, the preacher said, "The judgment of the Lord is beginning in the house of God one of these mornings." He understood the preacher to say, "The judgment of the Lord is beginning *tomorrow* morning in the house of God." This disturbed the old fellow and he slipped

[6] T. N. Page, *The Negro: The Southerner's Problem* (New York, 1904), p. 82.

out of the church at once. He did not go to the frolic because he figured that his house was right close to the church and, if the judgment of the Lord was beginning at the house of God in the morning, it would not be long before it got to his house too. So he decided to go home and straighten things out with his "ole 'oman." He went home and said, "Ole 'oman, the judgment of the Lord is beginning in the morning and I want to make my peace with you. You know that ham I said was stolen from the back porch? Well, it wasn't stolen, I gave that to sister Jane. You know that money I said I lost? Well, I didn't lose it, I gave it to sister Lize." And he went on telling his wife about various of his doings with the sisters. "Well," said his wife, "if the judgment of the Lord is beginning in the morning, I have something to tell you too. You see these little chaps running around here? Well, they ain't none of 'em yours." "Well," said the man, "the judgment of the Lord ain't goin' to wait until morning." The frankness with which infidelity is treated in this story must represent a low level of social denunciation of it; the double standard, though, does seem to be indicated as a Negro ideal, if not a fact.

On another occasion I hazarded an opinion to a Negro about the reasons why tenants move so frequently; I guessed that in many cases they get into sexual entanglements and then find some other man or woman hating them, so that they become uncomfortable where they are. He agreed, with some surprise that I should have suspected it, and added a point of his own, that in some cases tenants may move to another plantation to get a new field for erotic operations.

The confirmation given by Negro informants of the large degree of sexual freedom among lower-class Negroes is most convincing, although, to be sure, whenever it comes from a middle-class Negro it is accompanied by a derogatory valuation. A Negro teacher complained about the "disorganization" in the Negro home. The Negro man does not seem to care how many women he has relations with; the woman does not care whether she has relations with various men. Informant said that he did not see how a race could advance in the face of this kind of behavior. He was despondent about his school children. In his grade school he has had dozens of girls passing through and being graduated from the eighth grade in the last four years. He thought that hardly one of them had escaped sexual contact and a great number of them were now on the streets as prostitutes. He complained that he did not seem to be able to do anything for them in school that would help them to maintain personal restraint; probably, he thought, the trouble was that the parents at home either encouraged the children or winked at deviant behavior. The same situation has been reported by other observers of lower-class Negroes.[7] This informant, however, was distinctly valuational in his judgment and did not take into account the different historical circumstances and present social position of his Negro families; actually they seem to be sexually expressive in a manner very similar to, but to a greater degree than, peasant white communities in other parts of the world.[8]

[7] "The active passions of youth and late adolescence are present but without the usual formal social restraints. Social behavior rooted in this situation, even when its consequences are understood, is lightly censured or excused entirely. Conditions are favorable to a great amount of sex experimentation. It cannot always be determined whether this experimentation is a phase of courtship, or love-making without the immediate intention of marriage, or recreation and diversion. Whether or not sexual intercourse is accepted as a part of courtship it is certain no one is surprised when it occurs. When pregnancy follows, pressure is not strong enough to compel the father either to marry the mother or to support the child. The girl does not lose status, perceptibly, nor are her chances for marrying seriously threatened. An incidental compensation for this lack of a censuring public opinion is the freedom for children thus born from warping social condemnation. There is, in a sense, no such thing as illegitimacy in this community." Johnson, *op. cit.*, p. 49; quoted by permission of the University of Chicago Press.

[8] "In this respect they are characteristic of all peasant merry-making, a reaction to, and escape from, the other extreme of their life-cycle. The frolics and 'parties,' held on Saturday nights, were mentioned by practically all the younger members of the community. The churches inveighed against them as an incident of the evil of dancing. They are held from house to house; there is usually an abundance of corn whiskey available, and they not infrequently end in violence. The

Another Negro man, in talking about his family life, said that his wife was quite strict with him; whenever he went downtown she warned him against drinking and to keep away from the girls. He admitted that he was greatly tempted because the Negroes "raise Cain" every Saturday night, Sunday, and Sunday night; and they are all up to some kind of "corrupt" behavior. He added that a Negro man, or woman, did not think well of himself unless he had three or four sex partners on the string. His wife bullied him a good deal on this score; he conceded that he was not strong enough always to meet her higher standards.

It is difficult to get the truth about the lower-class patterns from middle-class Negro people since they are anxious to deny that they themselves share the freer attitudes toward sexuality and would prefer also to exclude the fact that lower-class Negroes have such attitudes. Lower-class Negroes, on the contrary, if they can be made to talk, are much franker. I have already mentioned a conversation I once overheard, by chance, between two Negro girls who were discussing men. One of them complained that Negro men lack consideration for their women and often come to them "for pleasure" all sweaty from the day's work. The other said that a Negro man always has about ten women beside his wife on the string—one never satisfies him. One of the girls said that a friend of hers was a "sporting lady" but that there was nothing in this business any more; the market is glutted and customers so impudent as to offer fifty cents for sexual favors. The difference between this moral atmosphere and the conventional middle-class attitudes is quite striking.[9] In any case it is clear that social patterns

---

houses are small and ill-lighted and couples make little secret of the character and intensity of their love-making under the wide-flung blanket of darkness." Johnson, *op. cit.*, p. 182; quoted by permission of the University of Chicago Press.

[9] It has shocked many northern Negroes of middle-class standards who have become acquainted with lower-class Negro patterns. Thomas, for example, has made an intemperate evaluation of the situation as follows: "So lacking in moral rectitude are the men of the negro race that we have known them to take strange women into their homes and cohabit with them with the knowledge, but without protest, from their wives and

governing sexual behavior are much less restrictive than they are among middle-class people and that as a consequence actual impulse freedom for Negroes is much greater. It is, of course, especially among poor rural Negroes that these differing mores prevail.[10]

If there are "gains" on the part of Negroes, there should be a sense of such gains by whites; and occasionally we should note the envy which accompanies a perception that others have something that they have not. Such envy is an unquestioned fact with many white people. One evidence of it is that there is a continuous interest in Negro sexuality and a certain nostalgic longing for such inner freedom to enjoy as the lower-class Negroes have. White people, in the South, and North, show a marked interest in the sexual behavior of Negroes and there is huge enjoyment of the many jokes which show the lack of moral discrimination among them.[11] These jokes also illustrate very frequently the potency of Negroes and their unbounded, unfettered sexuality. The truth is that by telling and enjoying these jokes white people get an imaginative measure of the freedom from inner limitation which Negroes enjoy. There is even more direct evidence of envy which crops up occasionally.

---

children. So great is their moral putridity that it is no uncommon thing for stepfathers to have children by their stepdaughters with the consent of the wife and mother of the girl. Nor do other ties of relationship interpose moral barriers, for fathers and daughters, brothers and sisters, oblivious of decent social restrictions, abandon themselves without attempt at self-restraint to sexual gratification whenever desire and opportunity arises. That such licentiousness is prevalent is not surprising, when we reflect that animal impulse is the sole master, to which both sexes yield unquestioned obedience." William H. Thomas, *The American Negro* (New York, 1901), pp. 179-180; quoted by permission of The Macmillan Co.

[10] Carl Kelsey, *The Negro Farmer* (Chicago, 1903), p. 65.

[11] A case in point, and one of a long series, is the famous rape joke. A Negro woman brings a Negro man into court on the serious charge of rape. The judge questions her as to various circumstances of the crime and finally asks her *when* it occurred. "Well, jedge," she answers, "I don't rightly remember but it seems like it was jes rape, rape, rape all during June, July, and August."

On one of the man hunts referred to earlier, the posse had to go through a cotton field and came upon a Negro couple having intercourse. As soon as the Negroes saw them coming, they jumped up and ran in opposite directions. When the men came back, they were laughing at this and one of them said, "That is another good reason for being a nigger!"

To be sure, it is only in unusual circumstances that this envy is made clear, but undoubtedly it exists. Northerners, for example, are quite prone to think of the Negro section in a town as one where the social barriers against impulse expression are less and where the example of the freer Negroes has a vivifying effect. New Yorkers undoubtedly have this sense about Harlem cabarets. Interpreters of the caste system in the South often indicate very directly their sense of the correlation between sexual freedom and low status, and sexual limitation and higher status.[12] The future of the Negro is then said to be bound up with the acquisition of personal restraint on the white model and the rejection of impulse freedom.[13] It is clear that an envious attitude is displayed here, and the claim of the Negro to have both high status and impulse freedom is rejected. We shall pass for the moment the question as to whether it is a necessity of our social structure that this sacrifice be made to attain high social usefulness.

A very important claim is made by Evarts[14] in respect to the behavior of Negro dementia praecox patients. Sexual perversions are said to be less frequent among Negroes, masturbation rarer, and smearing and self-mutilations less common than among white patients. The reason alleged is that the direct genital expression of Negro sexuality is less prohibited and the inner pressures which might drive Negroes to substitutive forms of sexual gratification do not exist. This is only an hypothesis, but it is one which should

[12] Howard W. Odum, "Social and Mental Traits of the Negro," *Studies in History, Economics and Public Law* (1910), Vol. 37, No. 3, p. 479.

[13] Stone, *op. cit.*, p. 205.

[14] A. B. Evarts, "The Ontogenetic against the Phylogenetic in the Insane of the Colored Race," *Psychoanal. Rev.* (1916), III, 397.

be carefully checked in mental hospitals. Against it stands the fact that mental disease among Negroes is more common than among white people when the proper qualifications are made.[15] The reconciliation of this paradox, if the first statement of fact is correct, might add much to our theory of psychosis. We might find, for example, that the type of strain precipitating psychosis among Negroes is different from the type found to be effective among white patients; or our conviction about constitutional factors might be strengthened. Our analysis permits us to see the problem with some degree of clarity; we know that a psychosis must be a different kind of fact in a middle-class Negro from what it would be in a lower-class Negro, since the social pressure on individuals in the two classes is not the same.

It hardly needs arguing that there is much greater aggressive freedom within the Negro caste than within the white caste. The whites are "solid," that is, they are an in-group and have made an out-group of the Negro caste; Negroes, on the contrary, are split within themselves and accommodated to the whites. The material on aggression within the Negro caste has already been given and will not be repeated here. We shall note only two things, that such freedom is a luxury in social life and that those who lack it must do something else with their renounced aggression. Very often the result is that it hangs like a noxious mist in the personality and cripples the expressiveness and spontaneity of the individual. To give up the freedom of open resentment is no small price to pay for civilized life.[16] Negroes are the gainers, in that it is not socially advantageous or necessary for them to renounce this freedom, nor does it seem that the persistent attempts of the white caste to prohibit such aggression, at least against whites, have been effective in extirpating it.[17] A second consideration is that

[15] Horatio M. Pollock, "Mental Disease Among Negroes in the United States," *State Hospital Quarterly* (1925-26), VI, 66; also E. B. Winston, *A Statistical Study of Mental Disease* (Chicago, 1930), p. 121.

[16] Sigmund Freud, *Civilization and Its Discontents* (New York, 1930), p. 91.

[17] Douglass, *op. cit.*, pp. 127-128.

sexual freedom and aggressive freedom are not unconnected but, on the contrary, seem to have a close relationship, at least in the Negro caste. Lower-class Negroes are known to be notably aggressive, both in family and other types of relationships, and this aggression frequently centers around sexual rivalry. It is usually the function of the family to stamp into the growing child the inhibitory structure which limits freedom in this respect. Apparently the Negro family in the lower-class group does not achieve this end, very likely because it is not able to set the indispensable good example of renunciation. Further, since it is sexual rivalry that calls out hostility in its strongest forms, we would expect to find more aggression accompanying the greater sexual freedom of the Negroes. If we ask why it is that the Negroes enjoy greater freedom in these respects, we can answer confidently that this is so because their institutional controls are defective and not because they are abandoned or intemperate through extraordinary biological excitation. The proof lies in the fact that middle-class Negroes, more fully within the restraining set of white American society, achieve the necessary renunciation.

When white people say that Negroes get the best of it, they usually refer consciously to the economic dependence of the Negro tenant on his white boss, and they imply that the white man has to do the organizational work and to endure the worry attendant upon long-range planning and financing. They mean that the Negro lives from day to day, or at worst year to year; whereas the white man has to "live" by longer time spans, sustain attention over indefinite periods, and forego thoughtlessness and irresponsible living. The foresight of the white owner, manager, and businessman is admitted to be a costly virtue from the standpoint of individual comfort, and the Negroes who do not have to pay this price are recognized as the gainers. It is sometimes even alleged with a groan, when the cares of life are heavy and the cotton business precarious, that the cost is too high and that it would be preferable to be a Negro without responsibility than a white man with responsibility for Negroes.

Responsible individuals will inevitably sympathize with this state of mind and recognize justice in the white-caste claim. It can be said, of course, that the Negroes have not elected their mode of life but have been adequately trained to irresponsibility through the slavery system and its lineal descendant, the plantation-share-crop system. The bountiful commissary and the Santa Claus planter offer all that is needed to live until the next year. The human organism is such a thing that under these circumstances it will accept the immediate pleasure gain and avoid the rigors of impulse renunciation. It must be noted that this dependence of Negroes is not regressive, but seems, on the contrary, a straight gratification of an infantile wish, a gratification continuing without break from childhood on. Culture, operating like an inclined plane, ordinarily forces people away from such gratification in our society and demands that they assume an independent competitive status. With the Negro the plane is but little inclined and he does not have to take the burden of internalizing restrictions on impulse in anything like the degree that is demanded of his white-caste superior. It seems very likely that the share-crop system imposes more responsibility on the Negro than slavery did and that the reluctance to assume it is the source of some of the longing that older Negroes have for slavery days.[18] There are, however, advantages to the white caste in Negro dependence; one of them, as we have already indicated, is that it guarantees a secure labor supply, one of the prime considerations in cotton farming.

[18] "The older Negro families are, indeed, divided rather sharply in their memories of slavery, and both groups have in turn passed them along in both practice and philosophy to their own offspring. Zack Ivey, for example, is one of the older heads and strong spirits of the community. He was more frank than is the custom of Negroes to be in contrasting his present condition with that of slavery. He complained: 'I done had a harder time since I been free than when I was a slave. I never had such a hard time in my life as I'm having now.' . . . For Zack Ivey life was a simple, elemental process of love-making, child-breeding, frolics, and religion, very much as it is now in the community." Johnson, *op. cit.*, pp. 19-20; quoted by permission of the University of Chicago Press.

Middle-class Negro informants uniformly deplored the passivity of lower-class Negroes and often reproached them with it. One said he believed that many tenant farmers do not care much whether they make money out of a crop or not. They are satisfied with a secure furnish, take it easy, and let the white man worry. Another stated that an owner who tried to encourage thrift by cutting down the furnish or the Christmas money so that the tenant would get more money in the fall might even get along less well with his tenants than the dishonest one who allowed a larger furnish and cheated the Negro mercilessly in the settlement. A bird in the hand is worth two in the bush to lower-class Negroes. Informant believed that habits which might lead to advancement are especially weakened by the security of the furnish. So long as they have a living, however meagre, and the indefinite guarantee of this living, Negroes are not forced to save; they always know that they will be furnished a house the year around and food for six or seven months while the crop is growing. Under these circumstances the Negro cropper experiences none of that institutional pressure which produces an ambitious and aggressive attitude toward economic life.[19] Another educated Negro with intimate plantation experience had a clear perception of the cultivation of dependence among lower-class Negroes; he was trying to explain to me why tenants do not

[19] "Procuring the means of a simple existence is too easy to make necessary the full employment of strength and time. Domestic servants seldom live on the premises, and demand the right to leave when the evening meal is over. Generally they consider all broken or left-over victuals their perquisite. A white family with a negro cook often supports from one to five colored persons, besides feeding any friend who comes to the kitchen on an errand or to visit. This fact helps to explain the number of loafers seen upon the streets of any Southern town. They are supported by the pilferings of a mother or sister, wife or sweetheart, and a few cents gained by holding a horse, carrying a note or a package, furnish tobacco and whisky. The white men for whom they do some little services turn over their discarded clothing, and too many desire little more." Holland Thompson, *From the Cotton Field to the Cotton Mill* (New York, 1906), pp. 266-267; quoted by permission of The Macmillan Co.

move off a place where they receive bad treatment. He said that the landlord who uses them badly is generally the kind who is willing to advance money, say, at Christmas. This point is important.[20] Christmas money makes Negroes feel they are well taken care of; often the landlord who settles honestly will not advance amounts at times outside the regular furnish season. He expects his tenants to save their money and use it during the months when they are not furnished. The dishonest landlord will settle for "twenty-five dollars" and never give a statement. The croppers will not know how much they are charged with, or how much cotton is sold for; they just receive the news that they have earned a specified amount. Because of their caste position they dare not press for details for fear of getting into "trouble." At the same time the dishonest landlord will say, "You know I have always taken care of you; so come around if you need anything." Actually the tenant gets as a loan the money he should have received as a settlement. Informants said, however, that the lower-class Negroes are very ignorant and careless and do not figure things out any too clearly. Most of them are illiterate and believe what they hear rather than what they read. The landlord's paternalistic assurances have more meaning for them than their own actual experience.[21] If they are attached to him personally, they may continue to remain as a result of this attachment, even though they can see that they fare less well than their neighbors. A tenant of this sort will simply charge up a

[20] It seems almost as if the Negroes regard the money as a gift, quite overlooking that they have to pay it back later. The planter who gives Christmas money would then fall into the category of the generous parent; the one who doesn't, into the rôle of a niggardly person.

[21] "In things economic there is everywhere now this dull, sometimes fatalistic, and unquestioning dependence upon the landowners and the soil, both of which are at times capricious. Toward this situation with its uncertainties the Negro families have adopted an attitude of easy-going trustfulness, reinforced by religion and adjustable in an amazing degree to the frequent discouragements of crop failures." Johnson, *op. cit.*, p. 4; quoted by permission of the University of Chicago Press.

better settlement to the fact that his neighbor has had "luck."

The furnish system is a kind of permanent dole which appeals to the pleasure principle and relieves the Negro of responsibility and the necessity of forethought. Very important in the above account are the personal dependence and attitude of passive expectation of the tenant toward his landlord, and, quite in line with this attitude, the interpretation of the furnish and Christmas money as a kind of gift. The analogy between this attitude and that of the child in the family is clear; it is not realistic, of course, because the Negro actually works hard for his money, but this seems to be one of the cases where the illusion of having a loving parent is more valuable than an effective analysis of the actual situation which would serve to discredit this belief. One can think of the lower-class Negroes as bribed and drugged by this system. The effect of the social set-up seems to be to keep Negroes infantile, to grant them infantile types of freedom from responsibility, and also to exercise the autocratic control over them which is the prerogative of the patriarchal father. The shift from a clinging, dependent adjustment to parents over to an independent attitude toward the world is always perceived as slightly traumatic by children. Parents at least are careful to enjoin the child to "act like a big boy," and so on, as a means of persuading him to abandon infantile adjustments. The southern caste set-up, on the other hand, encourages the lower-class Negro to "act like a little boy"; and this in fact he does.

A concomitant feature of the dependence of the lower-class Negro is the fact that he works only under compulsion. The furnish, while secure, is given in consideration of the Negro's labor, soon to be performed, or actually being performed, while the furnish is forthcoming. The compulsion is direct and bears on the Negro's wishes for shelter, food, and security in his dependence. In exchange for these values he offers his work. The historical reference to the slave milieu is obvious, and the form of compulsion has indeed changed very little. This arrangement does not, however, especially suit the lower-class Negro for types of work other than that in the plantation system to which he is adjusted.[22] The evidence is unmistakable that the moral indolence allowed to Negroes is perceived by them and by their white caste masters as a compensating value and gain.

The matter of gains is often summed up in a single statement: Negroes are a happy people. This belief has indeed become part of the romantic image of the Negro. We have already considered its use in the chapter on white defensive reactions; we can afford to examine more in detail the truth in it. The Negro gains already discussed ought to result in personalities freer of conflict, less bound by inner restrictions, and capable of operating at low tensional levels. Freedom to express impulse is generally felt to be one of the basic conditions of happy human life. Most middle-class informants, in describing the happy lot of the Negro, stressed the dependence and lack of grinding responsibility as fundamental. A middle-class Negro said ironically that the Negro seems to be happy whether he has anything or not, while the white is not happy unless he does have "something." The formula is that the local Negro is cheaply supplied with minimal necessities, protected, cheated, and given a bit of money to spend at Christmas—and this seems to satisfy him. Informant seemed to feel that many Negroes are really happy and carefree and he ventured the explanation that this is because they have nothing to lose. A white informant believed equally sincerely that Negroes are happy, but ascribed it to their greater nearness to "savagery" and their lack of social restraints. Still another Negro said that Negroes are carefree and cheerful as alleged by whites, but not through innate causes. They are happy because they have no responsibility, nothing to lose, and are taken care of by the white plantation owner. They will not

[22] "The chief failings of all negro labor are temperamental and moral. The negroes as a class do not work except under direct compulsion. They do not like monotonous labor. They do not like to be alone nor to engage in any employment where they cannot communicate with their fellows. In the small Southern tobacco factories, the negroes talk and sing at their work as there is little machinery and no tension." Thompson, *op. cit.*, p. 264; quoted by permission of The Macmillan Co.

take initiative for themselves, they have to be told everything to do, where to "put the plow" and when to pick the
cotton. It is implied that the lower-class Negroes live in a
luxurious state of irresponsibility and indolence, acting only
under external pressure to achieve subsistence. They are
said to live now pretty much as they did in slavery days.[23]

A Negro girl observed that many people wonder why the
Negroes are happy, and she thinks they are, though of
course they have some troubles. She said that they have
never had anything and never expect to have anything, so
they might as well be happy. For example, her mother wor-
ries some, but in the main is cheerful, although she works
desperately hard and is very poor. Her father seems to be
content in spite of the fact that he recently has had his
house confiscated by the county because he was unable to
pay the taxes. Implied in all these statements is the idea
that possessions are a burden and that there are some compensations for being without them; the conclusion is drawn
that the Negroes have great impulse freedom without the
noxious barriers of conscience and restrictive social patterns.
What poisons life for so many people in Western European
society is internalized taboos which make it impossible for
them ever to enjoy a spontaneously expressive biological
life. Sexual acts, for example, may be performed but without gratifying abandon and release. Many people are torn
between personal ideals and wishes, such as those for dependence, which must be rejected if feelings of adequacy
are to be achieved. But in the case of lower-class Negroes no

---

[23] "Take men of any original character of mind, and use
them as mere animal machines, to be operated only by the
motive-power of fear; provide for the necessities of their animal life in such a way that the cravings of their body shall
afford no stimulus to contrivance, labor, and providence; work
them mechanically, under a task-master, so that they shall have
no occasion to use discretion, except to avoid the imposition of
additional labor, or other punishment; deny them, as much as
possible, the means of enlarged information, and high mental
culture—and what can be expected of them, but continued, if
not continually increasing stupidity, indolence, wastefulness,
and treachery?" F. L. Olmsted, *A Journey in the Seaboard
Slave States* (New York, 1904), II, 112-113; quoted by permission of G. P. Putnam's Sons.

such extraordinary demands are made on the body, and it is theoretically quite intelligible that such Negroes should be more comfortable, cheerful, and positive than the more culturally battered whites.

One aspect of this "happiness" is easily discerned. In social groups of their own, Negroes appear to have a kind of naturalness and lack of tension in personal relationships that is not characteristic of whites; they seem to fall easily into conversation and to get in touch with one another with a kind of charming directness. There are a blithe chatter and lack of constraint which I can phrase only as a general ease and immediacy of "libido outflow." At a picnic, for example, the older women seemed very motherly, natural, and warm toward the babies present. There was nothing effusive about it either, but a general, simple enthusiasm. Three or four babies were being handed around from woman to woman, heaved over shoulders, and patted on their little backs. The children seemed to be well behaved, though very much alive; they sat in straight rows, were silent and very good; but there was nothing tense and strained about their goodness. It seemed the result of satisfaction in life rather than mere suppression by the parents. I can only state these as impressions, but they were exceedingly striking and consistent throughout my experience.

For any one keyed to our wider culture patterns there are many irritating aspects of this comfort and happiness of Negroes. For example, a Negro professional man cannot afford to play the indulgent parent rôle to his fellow caste members because he has to live from his bill collections. One such man told me that he does not dare to deal with his clients except on a cash basis, or at least with 95 percent of them. If he did credit work, most of them would say to him later, "Well, I told you I did not have any money; we will have to look toward the future." "Looking toward the future," as he quite well understood, means no pay at all. Again the white person is frequently irritated by a lack of "time sense" among lower-class Negroes. Unless some immediate, tangible satisfaction is to be achieved by the contact, the Negro often does not come. I have had repeated opportunity to observe my own annoyance at such broken appointments. I was invited for example, to meet a Negro minister at the house of one of his parishioners. The minister did not come although I waited a reasonable length of time. I was informed later that he came "just after I left." The parishioner said that he would call me the next day and make another appointment, but he did not reach me until two days later; we made a second appointment and this time when I arrived neither of them was there. Finally I managed to meet the minister, but it was by an indirection rather than by plan. Negroes do not seem to be particularly annoyed if others are late for appointments; they readily understand how those things go. One concludes at last that they simply lack the vigorous prodding of a conscience tender on the score of punctuality. Among middle-class Negroes there is the same tendency with regard to time, but they quickly respond to insistence on this score; they have, of course, the school pattern to guide them. Lack of time sense and other irresponsible traits have often made the behavior of Negroes seem inscrutable to white people who claim never to know what is going on in Negro heads.[24]

A qualification on the score of "happiness" is made by local Negroes; they say that the people are happy if they stay around Southerntown, but not so if they have been away and know other modes of life. If they have been away they lose their dependence on white people and at the same time identify with northern Negroes who are more aggressive; then, when they come back, they find it hard to accept local conditions and regain their old attitudes. For example, they get out of the habit of standing aside in a store when a white person comes in and insist on going on with their purchases; they do not take a cursing out so easily, and the like. What has happened is that the northern conception of personal dignity has become clear and concrete,

---

[24] "I mean simply to give expression to the conviction, speaking of the average, of course, and not of the rare exception, that their actions have no logical or reasonable basis, that they are notional and whimsical, and that they are controlled far more by their fancies than by their common sense." Stone, *op. cit.*, p. 144; quoted by permission of Doubleday, Doran & Co.

aggression is mobilized against white-caste members, and the smooth character of the older accommodation is lost. On the other hand, training in orderly work habits, forethought, and foresight is forced upon the Negro in the northern situation and his older dependence attitude must be modified. Naturally when he returns to Southerntown he finds that he is less happy, that his adjustive efforts are more laborious and disquieting. This follows the general culture-personality principle, viz., that new aspects of the personality are elicited with every major change in the overt social situation of the person. It would be a rewarding research to follow the "happy" Negro from his caste adjustment in the southern cotton field to the new situation which is imposed on him by northern technology, northern ideals, urban life, and different responses from white people.

Corresponding to the directness of impulse expression one would expect to observe also a relative lack of sublimated expressive patterns among lower-class Negroes. My data are not secure or definitive on this point, but I will state my impression that this is the case. Lower-class Negroes do not have the need or the training to adopt some of the most prized of middle-class sublimations. For example, they do not have to *read* romantic novels or adventure stories; to a very high degree they *live* them in the course of their more expressive daily lives.[25] Sublimated behavior is always substitutive and its forms are built up at the expense of more direct media of gratification. We have already noticed gambling and attendant quarrels as a prevalent form. Perhaps seducing and love-making should be listed as unsublimated patterns. Boasting and ragging have already been noted as direct aggressive forms. Religious behavior in the rural Negro churches can hardly be described as a sub-

[25] Odum has shown in fact that the state is in the lowest quartile for expenditures for public libraries and for the public registered as library borrowers. We do not know what representation lower-class Negroes have in this group, but it must be very large. Again Odum shows that the state is low on the list of states in matters of cultural advance. "Cultural advance" usually implies sublimated expressive patterns of one kind or another. Odum, *Southern Regions of the United States* (Chapel Hill, 1936).

limated pattern; rather it is emotionally vitalized to the last degree and highly expressive even in a physical sense. There is much behavior that is sheer gratification of indolence tendencies, the mark of a relaxed and aimless existence in exact contrast to the intense "time is money" attitude of the mobile middle-class people.[26] Gossip and "visiting" play a considerable rôle among lower-class Negroes, as they do with rural folk everywhere. A number of informants stressed the value of hunting and fishing as recreational behavior among Negroes around Southerntown. It is clear that both of these patterns, which also serve in the food quest, have a strong element of sadistic and destructive pleasure in them; in proof of this let us note that many a modern man feels troubled at using the poke-hook, watching the butcher, or skinning the game after the kill. In such a case defenses have been built up in the individual against these sadistic satisfactions. They seem, however, to be widely valued and practiced by Negroes.

One of my Negro informants told me some hunting lore which will in its detail illustrate the amount of time and attention given to hunting. He said that he thought the ways of animals are interesting and that men could learn much from them. For example, a rabbit chased by a dog will always try to find a hill and run up it. It knows it can outdistance a dog on a hill because of its stiff and powerful hind legs. It will not, however, want to run down the other side of the hill very fast because it knows it is likely to topple over and get caught. The dog, on the other hand, will not chase a rabbit up the hill, but will run around. When the rabbit has outdistanced a dog, it will stop and lick its paws;

---

[26] "Aside from the conventional outlets there are other means of using leisure time which, while perhaps less harmful than the frolics and parties, yet contributed little to the cultural development of the community. There is practically no reading and no concerts or lectures, apart from those offered in connection with church programs. Those who do not like what is offered by the community may 'piddle around the house,' 'set on the porch and rock,' 'lay down and sleep,' 'wallow around the house,' 'play with the cat,' 'walk about and visit,' or 'jest set down.'" Johnson, *op. cit.*, pp. 182-183; quoted by permission of the University of Chicago Press.

this is to kill or change the scent. Then it will turn around and backtrack along the same way, so that if the dog comes on the trail he will follow it in the wrong direction. The same informant gave me some interesting information about coons and dogs. When a dog chases a coon, the coon will often do what they call "cutting" a tree. It will run up the trunk a few feet and then jump from the far side, apparently to make the dog think it is up the tree and to break the trail of its scent. A young dog will be fooled by this, but an old, trained dog will run around the tree to the other side and smell to see if the coon has jumped. Sometimes after a long chase a coon will run up a tree and its mate will run down, "cutting" and running on. The dog may be fooled into taking up the new scent, in which case he is following a fresh coon which has a good chance of outrunning him. Young coons do not know how to "cut" and they just run up the tree. A coon's mate will only come down and "cut" when it is dark, never when it is light. Sometimes the coon will turn and fight the dog, and it is a good fighter with a chance to win. If it can get the dog to chase it into the water, its chances are much better. It knows how to push the dog's head under water and drown it. There is a technique for following coons with a flashlight or a head lamp. The young coon will stare straight at the lamp and by its glistening eyes direct the hunter's shot; an old coon will turn its head aside so that its eyes cannot be seen; or close one eye. Such detailed observation and knowledge of tradition, compounded with I do not know what accuracy, bespeak a great amount of attention to hunting and tracking. The same informant said that one of the few things that Negro and white men do together is to hunt; apparently here the issue of social equality does not come up and perhaps the Negroes serve as good guides and comrades.

Discussion of control of the impulse life and character formation leads inevitably to the family. Personality formation must be intelligible in terms of patterns in the family. The study of the family as a formal unit has been slighted in this research, but some things are known. One is that the lower-class Negro family differs from the middle-class white family and seems by comparison to be "disorganized." This is undoubtedly a result of the fact that during slavery days it was impossible for Negroes to approximate white family structure.[27] It has already been indicated that in the lower-class Negro family the woman plays a more important rôle than in the usual American family. This is due both to historical factors and to the economic position of the Negro woman.[28] Her economic independence puts her in a position to challenge the assumption of the strict patriarchal position by the Negro man. The family among lower-class Negroes seems, by and large, to be a much less stable unit than in the white group, to exercise less coercive control over children, and to liberate them earlier for productive activity. Children liberated for work and economic independence shortly after adolescence are also liberated from parental control in other respects, even though, as is usually the case, they thereupon assume a dependence relationship to the white planter in place of that to their own parents.[29] The patriarchal family form is much more nearly approximated in the middle-class Negro group where the man tends to be the chief wage earner and the woman the custodian of the home; even here, however, there are cultural features similar to the lower-class family—a greater independence of women and a more casual relationship of the man to his family. In both middle- and lower-class Negro groups will be found stricter strains of middle-class culture where the family is unified around paternal authority and the children are strongly disciplined. In the lower-class group these tend to be socially mobile families. One middle-class Negro in-

[27] Booker T. Washington, *The Future of the American Negro* (Boston, 1899), pp. 47-48.

[28] "The position of the Negro woman always gave her greater advantage in dealing with their white masters than the Negro men. Historically she has been the controlling influence over the children. Moreover, in the present economic arrangement, her earning power is only a fraction less than that of the male, and as a rule more sustained and dependable. She, thus, in large part escapes one of the most powerful factors influencing adversely the status of women generally in the American society." Johnson, *op. cit.*, p. 29; quoted by permission of the University of Chicago Press.

[29] Johnson, *op. cit.*, p. 62.

formant spoke of his own lower-class background, said his family was very strict with its members; none of the children drank alcoholic beverages or coffee and only one of them smoked. The parents were able to keep up a good disciplinary front before the children, and the father was particularly severe in his physical punishments. In the main, however, lower-class parents do not set restrictive examples and, as a result, their children perpetuate the parental character form; children model themselves primarily on what their parents do and how they truly act rather than according to verbal admonitions. The schools, as we have observed them, do not play a great rôle with lower-class children since they attend them for only a few years and therefore are not influenced in a great degree by the school regimen.

We shall digress for a moment to consider the problem of impulse management as it is related to various social formations. It differs in America in at least four systematic ways. First, membership in a social class is undoubtedly a differentiating factor. Middle-class white people prepare their children for a different rôle in life than do lower-class white people. Second, it differs by nationality, as can be seen in any town where there is a large first generation Italian population; it will be found that young girls in the Italian group are more strictly watched than are similar girls in the native American group. Third, there seem to be definite differences as between rural and urban areas within native American society. For example, boys growing up on frontier areas may be called upon to put forth much more aggression than urban boys going to experimental schools. Fourth, and most germane to our problem, there are important cultural differences attendant upon race and caste and especially the lower class of the Negro race. It may be true that the family form in each case above is crudely similar and that the differences may be viewed as small, if contrast is made with a widely variant type of family organization; though small, the differences in impulse patterning in these various culture forms are significant in discussing personality formation among Negroes. The social milieu, including the restrictions as well as the permissive outlets for organic forces, provides the ground plan for impulse patterning. The rough structure of this ground plan is firmly set in the little family unit into which the new child comes, and it is stamped into each new individual. The child always sees, hears, and feels a concrete father and mother; but this concreteness is an illusion since the parent is actually an agent transmitting unwittingly the features of the historical life of the group. Parents do not invent culture, they just act. This is true of Negro parents today, and it was true of the parents of the ancestors of our Negroes when the racial stock lived in Africa. The aggressive fact of induction into the American slave system broke up the transmission of the African culture forms and substituted for it a slowly developing adjustment to American social life.

It is important to remember that however pleasure-ridden the lower-class Negro may seem to be at the present time, this character form was developed in the American milieu. It seems a fair inference from the anthropological evidence that every Negro who landed in America had a well-organized personality keyed to operate in *some* culture.[30] He was not merely an unformed thing awaiting American molding; indeed the native personality form had to be destroyed before the new form could be substituted, and very often the native was destroyed in attempting to alter his conception of himself. The "native" personalities with which Negroes landed in America[31] were fitted to control impulse according to the prescriptions of a native society; when operating in its cultural matrix this personality form defined when and how aggressive activity was permitted, toward whom dependence reactions might legitimately be shown, under what circumstances sexual excitations might be ventilated, how the food quest should be

[30] "The conclusion, still held by many students, that the Negro slave came to this country a savage child with or without his loin cloth, and as naked culturally as he was sartorially, is one which cannot today be accepted." M. J. and F. S. Herskovits, *Rebel Destiny* (New York, 1934), p. ix; quoted by permission of McGraw-Hill Book Co., Inc.

[31] Though, to be sure, America was not always the first point of landing and therefore personality modifications had frequently supervened before the Negroes arrived on our soil.

conducted, and so on. The Negro was taken by force out of this native culture to which he was adjusted, compelled forcefully to alter his personality and adjust himself to slavery conditions. Those who could not perform this feat pined away and died, got sick, or were exterminated in hopeless revolt. In the course of time routine, affection, example, and even reward were substituted for the initial force as agents in aiding Negro acculturation, an acculturation very different from that of the white immigrant to America who remodels his own personality under the stress of ambition and hope of status advancement. The immediate goal of the slave system was to teach the Negro labor routines and to make effective aggression from his side impossible. Aggressions against whites were severely put down, as were also those against Negroes, though perhaps not so violently. The slavery system was not a benign device for inducting the Negro into full participation in American life, but obviously a device for getting work done without regard to its effect on Negro personality.[32] "Breaking in" was the term used for the first forcible acculturation of Negroes, and it was recognized as a separate and difficult process. It could not be conducted by sheer force or brutality since there are limitations apparently to the amount of hostility that humans can endure and still continue to live and work.[33] It was not necessary to transmit rigorously the American family form to Negroes in order that they should serve as slaves; so they were left a considerable sphere of freedom on the score of sexual life, religion, play, and the like, while at the same time their African adjustments were destroyed by the change in their basic economic orientation to society. The cultivation of dependence reactions by the slavery system, it should be noted, is quite extreme and probably stood in marked contrast to the African personality structure of many of the Negroes; this must have been true because no culture can maintain itself and tolerate a great number of dependent and infantile adults. In brief, for African control

[32] Johnson, *op. cit.*, p. 127.

[33] U. B. Phillips, *American Negro Slavery* (New York, 1918), p. 53.

by native mores there was substituted American control by labor routine and force with considerable possibility of unpatterned impulse expression, especially in the sexual sphere. This is equivalent to saying that for the individual conscience, certainly characteristic of every well-socialized African native, there was substituted the slave accommodation to outside direction and external pressure. The divergencies in behavior exhibited by present-day lower-class Negroes seem best accounted for in this way. They are still responsive to external coercion rather than to internalized conscience pressures.

In addition to the conscience of the adult individual as a determinant of ethical conduct, there is always the "social pressure" exercised by the community and applied by good example from others, gossip, and expectations of ethical behavior. Since lower-class Negroes have developed a collective moral life appropriate to their caste position and different from that of the middle-class white group, their culture operates in different ways and permits the types of gains we have been referring to. From the standpoint of the slave-owner and caste master of the present day there is probably an advantage in these differing standards and the substitutive freedom possessed by the Negro; this advantage lies in the fact that it is easier to manage and get physical labor from a man who lives on the plane of emotional freedom on which Negroes do. Negro informants in Southerntown recognize this. One of them said that a good deal of the "disorganization" in Negro life on plantations is due to the fact that the laws are not enforced against the tenants. Plantation owners permit polygamy, bigamy, adultery, and assaultive behavior and sometimes even prevent community peace officers from interfering under the threat of electoral retaliation. Whether planned or not, it seems that direct and instinctual gratification is offered to lower-class Negroes in exchange for the money and mastery which are the chief cultural values of the whites. It is not difficult to see how a different kind of collective conscience has been standardized in the Negro group and how the person trying to act according to wider American standards would lack support from his social environment.[34] Negro individuals, accustomed to external control, dependent on their bosses, and not habituated to renunciation of impulse, are seen from the white valuational standpoint as instinct-driven, and, as such, easy to use as slave or caste laborers. For the sake of contrast one need think only of the enslavement of Rotary Club members by some alien culture and try to picture the modifications that would have to take place in their personalities in order to tolerate a slave or caste adjustment; they would certainly be ill-disposed, at least at first, to accept the compensations of impulse freedom which appear to make the lot of the lower-class Negro tolerable. They would be much more inclined toward revolt, ambition, and high self-evaluation and would hardly cherish a permanent dependence relationship to their owners. Something parallel to this adjustment must have been made by the Negroes who were brought to America and who had to reorganize personality in terms of the slave adjustment.

The question of the American Indian has frequently been raised in this connection and it is sometimes assumed that he was biologically inaccessible to a slave accommodation, whereas the Negro was organically predisposed to it. A different and much more tenable hypothesis has been offered;[35] it is that the Negroes faced white culture alone, one by one, each against the whole force of white society; whereas in the case of the Indian it was a conflict between societies. The Indian always had his organized society supporting him, and the memories of it were strong in the familiar physical features of the land. Either his culture was actually present to support him or its interpretation of life was vital in his physical milieu. Under these circumstances and with such support the Indian could face extermination

[34] "Lower the tone of the environment, and it becomes a very easy matter to take a 'moral holiday.' It is hard for the individual conscience to hold its own where the community is indifferent or equivocates on moral issues." J. M. Mecklin, *Democracy and Race Friction* (New York, 1914), p. 109; quoted by permission of The Macmillan Co.

[35] By Dr. Robert A. Warner. Dr. Warner has not yet put his hypothesis forward because it is still in tentative form.

rather than yield to slave status. This support was, in the main, lacking for Negroes; their own culture and geography were remote, as proved by the long sea journey. There were few who could continue to speak their own tongues or carry on the traditional types of African life. They must have despaired of recreating the native mode in America or returning to the appropriate native society. The other possible alternatives were an isolated death—which had no significance in the eyes of others, as did the death of an Indian fighting with his own group—flight, or accommodation. Flight was in the main impossible until Negroes were actively and illegally aided by northern white people. It is suggested that these were the circumstances under which African Negroes accepted the inevitable and submitted to personality reorganization and accommodation to slave status in America.

African patterns of sex control were abandoned probably because of their futility in the new slave milieu. It was rather to the interest of the planters during most of the slavery regime to have large numbers of Negro children born; and, as a result, the new sexual patterns were markedly permissive and remarkably disorganized by comparison with those of any other culture. Another feature of this permissiveness of the planter caste was undoubtedly the belief that a satisfied Negro is easier to work than a restricted one, less apt to be aggressive against the regime, and less jealous of his woman or women.[36] It need not be that any of these arrangements were part of the formal planning or philosophy of the planter caste; they were quite as effective if done without conscious intent or the benefit of moral and theoretical justification. From our standpoint the "disproportionate" sex impulse of the Negro would then be a feature of his permissive slave culture rather than a result of his disproportionate biological desire, as is so often alleged.[37] Other differences, such as those in the drill and

[36] This point has been suggested in discussion by Mr. Earl F. Zinn, of the Institute of Human Relations.

[37] Odum, "Social and Mental Traits of the Negro," *Studies in History, Economics and Public Law* (1910), Vol. 37, No. 3, p. 563.

efficiency of the lower-class Negro conscience, would be attributed rather to the permissiveness of the milieu than to any defect in his capacity for socialization.[38] It is particularly important to have a correct theory of the type and nature of the original socialization of the American Negro, since there are about him so many curbstone theories rooting in naïve biologism; biological differences there may be, but they cannot be posited until maximum weight is allowed to the historical social explanations.

The permissive character form of the Negro unfits him in one sense for widespread *immediate* participation in our society. To run a society at our technical level we must have a trained, responsible lower-class group. Negroes are capable of this training, but, as seen in their southern plantation adjustment, they do not exhibit it. An efficient lower-class group, however, means a constant danger to the class system because pressures toward social mobility operate to evacuate members from this class and even to challenge the principle of social reward proportionate to class status. As we have seen, in Southerntown and county, it is the aim of the caste system to maintain the Negro labor supply immobile in its lower-caste, lower-class status; and, as a result, the system provides the Negro with the reward of impulse freedom in exchange for the possibility of higher status and increased income.

We have agreed that still another alternative exists in the frustrating situation of the Negro caste; it is to direct aggression toward the real world and compete at any cost with the white middle-class group. This way out has been chosen by those Negroes who achieve middle-class status within the Negro caste. They compete for the dominant white values, mastery through skill, prestige, high income, and pride in high personal standards. That their behavior is viewed as aggressive is clearly shown by the white-caste response to it. They have adopted the most realistic solution and are following the dominant American ideal; they achieve high recognition within their own caste and some

[38] Thomas, *op. cit.*, p. 207.

informal and grudging cognizance of their value from the white caste. We will now discuss the dilemma of this group.

It is essential to understand the gains of lower-class Negroes and the life situation in which these gains appear if the situation of the Negro middle class is to be clearly seen. White people tend to lump all Negroes together and to characterize the caste by its lower-class members. This behavior on the part of the whites is probably a form of resistance against status advancement on the part of *any* Negroes. The fact is, however, that middle-class Negroes are sharply differentiated in their behavior from their lower-caste mates. We have already noticed the different family form, the pride in home, morality, and independence, and their orderly behavior. All of these items have a special value to middle-class people. Since it is not taken for granted that Negroes can behave according to our best social ideals, the middle-class Negro must underline his conformity. His moral qualities are asserted not only as marks of acceptance of American ethical ideals, but also as a negation of the low opinion of Negro morals held by white people. This contrast with the middle-class Negro group shows up clearly the gains of lower-class Negroes; it is just these gains which are condemned by middle-class Negroes, as they are allowed and derided by the white caste. If we had no other way of characterizing lower-class Negroes, we could do it very effectively by noting the characteristics which the middle class has itself renounced and condemns in the lower-class group. From the sociological standpoint it may be all well and good to say that the training which gives status to each middle-class Negro has been achieved at someone else's expense, that he has been reserved from workaday life and trained while others were working for him, and that his training represents a precipitation of capital. From the point of view of the middle-class person it looks quite different. He feels that he has earned his training and that renunciation was involved in it; he has renounced pleasure he could have had while being trained; and he has worked at tasks that were not always enticing. There is personal punch to middle-class mobility as well as the socio-automatic feature.[39] This element of sacrifice is important and gives the middle-class person a different perspective on social life; it is especially true of middle-class Negroes who have so clearly before them the example of lax, pleasure-dominated personalities among their own lower-class group.

In the behavior of Negro teachers one sees clearly the effort to spread middle-class ideals and behavior standards. One teacher told me of a lower-class girl who was boarding at his school. Her mother was dead and her father had recently intrusted her to informant's care. The father had gone away and written only infrequently; this increased informant's feeling of responsibility for the girl. It appeared that she had stolen a number of things around the school, especially money and food, and informant distrusted her and felt that she was not very reliable; if she would steal money, what might she not do? She asked his permission to visit her sister, and he refused because he had not been directly in touch with the sister. He was afraid the girl might fall into the hands of some man, have intercourse, and become pregnant. He considered the care of lower-class students of this type one of his most perplexing problems.

Another informant showed the typical middle-class moral reactions. In the course of life-history interviewing she said that she was a very intolerant person and that her friends had occasionally reproached her on this score. She had recently criticized the behavior of certain people in the town and a friend had said that she should not condemn them because if she had been brought up under the same circumstances she would be doing the same things. The bad Negroes, in this case lower-class Negroes, did not have the advantage of being reared in a good Christian home. What is seen by us from the organic standpoint as a gain in impulse freedom is viewed from the middle-class valuational standpoint as "bad behavior."

Another middle-class informant was suffering severely from sexual privation, incredible as this may seem by con-

---

[39] Harold D. Lasswell, "The Moral Vocation of the Middle-Income Skill Group," *Internat. J. Ethics* (1935), Vol. 55, p. 130.

trast with the white-caste stereotype of Negroes. He said that he would not break his code because he knew that white people were always reproaching Negroes for immorality and he did not want to let his group down; he resented the charge of the whites especially bitterly because he knew what they do among themselves, as well as with Negroes. Furthermore he realized that in his middle-class position immorality was an accusation that would readily be used against him and with more than usual damage, both by lower-class people in his own group and by all of the white people. There is a not inconsiderable pressure within the middle-class group to keep its members in line from the side of sexual conformity, and it seems to be realized that status advancement is practically possible only when it is accompanied step by step with renunciation of sexual freedom. A professional man stated, for example, in evidence of this that there was a good opportunity for him to work in another town if he could be sociable with other people and keep from being immoral. He cited several instances where Negro professionals had lost their clientele by not following the code. Among middle-class Negroes immorality has come to be felt as a kind of betrayal of the group to the scorn and derogation of the white caste.

We must refer to school training for Negroes again at this point. It is, of course, the wide-open American door to social mobility and the one frequently used by Negroes. The white caste cannot completely withhold these opportunities from Negroes due to the momentum of the mass education pattern in America. Nevertheless the school training of Negroes makes them more skilful in dealing with whites, arouses latent wishes for advancement and personal dignity, and increases their demands on the caste system. Really, from the standpoint of maintaining the feudal system, it is against the interests of the whites to educate Negroes. Our type of education stands against the ideas of luck, chance, and magic which help to distort the reality picture of the lower-class Negro; it insists instead on effective recognition of social reality and genuine material efforts to change it. By the same token, the schools carry the pattern of impulse renunciation along with them and in this way they prepare

Negroes for middle-class status. Schools insist upon order, punctuality, suppression of urgent aggressive behavior, and conformity to the master American sexual code. These requirements, if sustained over time, can considerably alter the lower-class Negro personality and prepare it for middle-class status. With such ideals, for example, the daughter of the family is not permitted to have an illegitimate child.[40] The sustained effect of the training is especially important. Lower-class Negroes who go to school for a short time, for only a few years in a group of their own kind, may be relatively little affected; those Negroes, however, who continue in high school, and especially those in the college period, may be deeply and permanently changed. Many of them may later revert to lower-class freedom in personal behavior, thereby giving evidence of a lack of proper family training; but many also attain and maintain middle-class levels of renunciation. It may indeed be that sexual and aggressive renunciation is indispensable to mobilizing the energy necessary to follow through our labyrinthine school training. Lower-class children do not, in the main, have to make such renunciation, as is evidenced by the fact that the state is high in the list of states for percentage of children between ten and seventeen years old who are gainfully occupied.[41] Negroes must have more than their share of such children. It might be said that lower-class children gain in being free of the discipline of our onerous school patterns; far from perceiving the work they do as a tedious alternative, they may well think of it as the door to possibilities of gratification which are long denied to those who continue school. Middle-class Negro people, of course, take the schooling of their children for granted, as do middle-class people in the rest of our society, and tend therefore to perpetuate their social kind.

It can be assumed that human beings never give up possibilities for gratification just for fun; self-restraint is difficult and there must be an adequate social premium on it. The general formula seems to be that the middle-class Ne-

---

[40] Johnson, *op. cit.*, p. 68.

[41] Odum, *Southern Regions of the United States* (Chapel Hill, 1936).

groes sacrifice the direct impulse gains of the lower-class group and expect to have in return the gratifications of prestige and mastery.[42] They *expect* to get them, but the fact is that they are not always paid out according to our cultural model. One evidence of this is the tendency to group Negroes together regardless of class position and personal sacrifice. As a result, all Negroes are subjected to the same social isolation and personal derogation which only lower-class Negroes, by their nonconformity, are felt to deserve. The middle-class Negro tries to maintain allegiance to the dominant American standards and then experiences the bitter fact that this allegiance is not rewarded as it is in the white caste; instead he is ignominiously lumped with persons in his own caste whose behavior standards are inferior to his own.

It seems to be a fact in our society that superior control of the impulse life accompanies the higher status positions and that it is maintained on condition of a return in the form of social appreciation and encouragement. The failure of this adjustment in the case of the middle-class Negroes is particularly discouraging. The Negroes are offered little by the white caste in the way of social premiums for impulse renunciation; granted that the task is not easy, it can only be successful when society offers some kind of bonus for its initial accomplishment and perpetuation. Even then, not all individuals so advantaged can succeed in it. The Negro caste, enduring the hardest conditions of life and categorically excluded from desirable status ranks which they can see other persons with similar standards occupying, have less reason to impose thwarting restrictions on themselves. Lower-class Negroes, as we know, solve the dilemma by indulging more freely in direct impulse gratifications; middle-class Negroes renounce this freedom to a degree, but do not feel justly recompensed in social recognition. This fact was repeatedly hammered home in the life-history materials and it is crucial to an understanding of the often-observed discontent of the "mulattoes" and "marginal men."[43]

[42] Franz Alexander and William Healy, *Roots of Crime* (New York, 1935), pp. 276-277.

[43] Robert E. Park, "Human Migration and the Marginal

The above explanation is not in conflict with the idea that the culture of the lower-class Negro is different and therefore permissive of more direct gratification, or with the idea that the failure to coagulate the Negro family is responsible for laxity. Lower-class culture cannot be changed in a more restrictive direction, nor can the family be consolidated until the social situation is changed and the economic and status rewards for labor and self-discipline are increased.

A life-history informant made this point very plainly in reference to her own life. In the succession of dutiful routines by which she has attained middle-class status she felt that she has somehow missed the chance to be a natural woman; the freedom she sees others having has not been hers, and her restrictive life has left its imprint on her character. She felt that there is no longer any chance to beat her way back to a more gratifying form of life than she now has. In an attempt at consolation I pointed out that in exchange for this renunciation she has secured two types of satisfaction; one, that of living up to her personal standards and doing her duty; and the other, the satisfaction that comes from being a responsible woman, one on whom others lean and rely. It proved to be, in fact, a consolation to the informant, but still one in which there was also regret for the lack of the gratification and freedom she has always desired. This informant shows the dilemma of her group; she has a "white" conscience, lives up to white standards, limits her personal life according to middle-class conventions, and has some of the managerial satisfactions that go with the substitution. On the other hand, she misses the emotional freedom of the field Negroes who are not required to maintain a level of consistent behavior and to renounce immediate personal satisfactions for remote impersonal ends. Status rise and unwelcome self-limitation seem to go hand in hand.[44] The question is, however, whether middle-class Negroes are not being forced to accept renunciation without the countervailing rewards of deference, ec-

---

Man," *Amer. J. Sociol.* (1928), Vol. 33, p. 893.

[44] E. T. Kreuger, "Negro Religious Expression," *Amer. J. Sociol.* (1932-33), Vol. 38, p. 31.

onomic security, prestige, and mastery being provided; certainly, as compared with middle-class people in the white caste, they are unduly deprived in this respect. This disproportion is another way of stating the dilemma of the "marginal man."

The foregoing informant has illustrated another aspect of the dilemma of middle-class Negroes and perhaps of all middle-class people in our society. The personal renunciation by which they buy status advancement reduces joy in life and makes a spontaneous happy adjustment very difficult. The bodies of middle-class people, as well as those of lower-class people, are daily producing excitations which demand expression through social patterns; if the patterns are sufficiently permissive, painful tensions may be kept at that minimum which means happiness. If they are unduly restrictive, each individual will carry a burden of ungratified longing which makes contented, day-to-day living impossible. It may well be that this discontent is the price of middle-class status. In any case, under the stigma of caste inferiority, even lower-class Negroes seem willing to give up "happiness" and seek status, as the slow but progressive emergence of Negroes into the middle-class group demonstrates. Certainly, if middle-class Negroes are denied adequate status recognition from the white caste, they are accorded it by their own group, and this is an important portion of their reward. It is true, in fact, if not in theory, that they are recognized by the white people as different from and superior to local lower-class Negroes and are treated accordingly. The question is not whether they are recognized at all, but whether they are recognized enough to consolidate them in middle-class status. So far as the social perspective of Southerntown is prophetic, middle-class Negroes have no reason to be unduly optimistic about either the economic or the status advancement of their children; and they are not so. They know very well how limited are the opportunities and how much less the comparable rewards will be than those the children of white middle-class members may expect.

It is a common error in judging lower-class Negroes to compare them unfavorably with foreign immigrants, stressing the lackadaisical Negro work habits and referring to the energy and zeal for advancement of a foreign peasantry.[45] Without proper historical perspective it can be made to seem that the Negro is biologically defective and has a low position in the social structure because it is all that he is capable of filling. It so happens that in the neighborhood of Southerntown there is a considerable Italian colony which was recruited some years ago when the big landowners feared the loss of Negro labor by migration to the North. A white man who knows them well stated that many of them now own land, that very few are on relief, and that they are responsible and ambitious citizens. Since immigrants play the role of "temporary Negroes" in northern economy, it will be well to understand how their behavior is differentiated from that of the lower-class Negro. Apparently the Italians near Southerntown come from a hard-bitten peasantry and represent by no means the lowest social class in their native society. They came here under the spur of ambition and with the intention to take every advantage of American opportunities. They have held their own for centuries in an economy which was none too generous in its rewards, and occasionally one of them has advanced from peasant to a higher status. They know America as the "land

---

[45] "To state it bluntly and coldly, it is for the Negro a recital of conditions as old as his freedom: too much time spent out of his crop, and away from his work; too much waiting for the weather to improve; too much putting off to a more convenient season; a too constant and too successful besieging of those in authority for money accommodations and supplies; too little reckoning against the future day of settlement; too much 'leaning on the Lord,' and too little upon himself, in things not spiritual; too much living for today and not enough for tomorrow. With the Italian it seems to be simply a grim determination to have more at the end of this year than he had at the end of last, regardless of weather or price; to wrest from every square foot of the soil he rents all that nature can be forced to yield; to get a visible, tangible return for every dime and hour he spends; to live on less than he makes, whether the latter be much or little; to hire nothing done that he can do himself; to keep the future ever in mind, and to lay by a store against age and a rainy day." Stone, *op. cit.*, p. 184; quoted by permission of Doubleday, Doran & Co.

of opportunity,"—the land of rapid rise in economic position
and social status—and their anticipations are organized
around this conception. Once here, there are no categorical
barriers put in their way and they are able to continue their
frugal, determined fight for social advancement. They have
brought with them what the Negroes have never had a
chance to develop, namely, good working habits and capacity for foresight and abstemious behavior. Their women
may work at the outset, but they are withdrawn from field
labor as rapidly as possible. While the ladder of status advancement is freely open before them, it is closed, as we
have seen, to the Negro by virtue of his caste position. The
southern jealousy of the Negro who "rises" or threatens to
rise in a socio-economic sense tends to discourage him from
acquiring the social treasure of good habits. It is mildly
dangerous for a Negro to be too prosperous, to have too
fine a house, too good a car, or any other sign of social advancement. He meets at once the possibility that whites will
think he has a position that should be held only by whites.
During the time of my research there was a county super-
visor in a neighboring area who while campaigning for
election, signed a sworn statement that Negroes had only
been given common laboring jobs under his administration
and that they had *not*, as slanderously alleged, had the
chance to drive road machines, that is to occupy white
men's jobs. The Italian is free from caste limitations of this
sort and his freedom consolidates the valuable adjustive
habits which he brings from his Italian society. Lower-class
Negroes, on the other hand, are virtually excluded from
hope of status change and, as a result, they see no reason
for accepting the personal and familial order and the discipline of the whites. It is my impression that much the
same state of affairs prevails among the poorest of lower-
class white people. By long social frustration they have been
robbed of the orderly social habits which make for status
advance. The Negroes, at least, compensate by accepting
lower-order forms of gratification which we have here designated as gains. This sociological impoverishment of the
lower-class Negro is of the utmost importance since it is no
easy matter to alter such "bad" habits and to supplant them

by habit formations adjusted to our wider culture. At least in all its important posts our technology demands independent and responsible individuals who are capable of a high degree of foresight and renunciation; it will take much time under the best conditions to drill Negroes in the social attitudes required for full participation in American society. Yet our technology is steadily pressing against the existence of such a social fact as caste; our techniques demand that individuals be able to replace one another without consideration of matters irrelevant from the technical standpoint, matters such as caste and color.

Of course the slack work habits of Negroes are irritating to their caste masters. We have already noticed the complaints on this score in the chapter on the economic gain. From the standpoint of the white middle class, the immobile Negroes have one great advantage over the Italians; however inefficient they may be, they do stay in their places and are not able to squeeze out of their laborious duties into higher class and caste status. Italian peasants would be much better as cotton-field workers provided they could be kept there. The relative fixity of the lower-class Negro is the compensation for his relative inefficiency and lack of personal drive to work.

To compare the varying gains made by whites and Negroes the following formula will be serviceable. The white caste have the satisfactions that go with mastery, superiority, control, maturity, and duty well-fulfilled. They have the pleasure also of despising the Negroes who are inferior in self-renunciation and self-esteem. The Negroes, on the other hand, get much more and much freer direct impulse satisfaction. The internal checks on gratification are less, and the social organization among lower-class Negroes does not put a great strain on its members. For example, the sexuality of white men is superior since they have access to two classes of women, but it is internally checked by prohibitions set up in developing this personality for the masterful rôle. The Negro man, as we have seen, is limited to sexual choices within his own caste, but there they may be more numerous and less burdened with inner or outer restraints. Whites must organize action with respect to remote goals;

Negroes may live from day to day and make the most of passing opportunities for gratification. Still we must note that the whites feel they are doing the Negroes out of something. The evidence for this is the defensive beliefs which we have already discussed. It is, of course, against democratic mores not to let other people grow up. There is much less protest from lower-class Negroes on this score than northern white people are likely to realize. The lower-class Negro is comfortable after a fashion in the South and recognizes that life there has some attractions. One informant said that "up there" in the North the Negro is likely to be handled objectively, held to an account of what he does, expected to be punctual, orderly, rational, etc., according to northern efficiency standards. Around Southerntown, on the other hand, the white people have a special tolerance for Negro vagaries, rather expect them, in fact. This is the accommodation, often slothful accommodation, to the southern system which Negroes exhibit. There is some pressure for status change, but not at all to the degree that a northerner would imagine when he tries to put himself in the broken shoes of the field Negro. The wearer of these shoes has his own compensations, and there is some evidence that he is not a little envied by white people.[46] The fact of white envy makes all the clearer the equivalence between mastery satisfactions and direct impulse satisfactions which we have been discussing.

Of course, the behavior patterns of lower-class Negroes could not be standardized as an independent culture; it is very doubtful if any culture could survive when its members were permitted so much direct and dependent gratifi-

---

[46] "On occasions, I have been amazed and amused watching white people dancing to a Negro band in a Harlem cabaret; attempting to throw off the crusts and layers of inhibitions laid on by sophisticated civilization; striving to yield to the feel and experience of abandon; seeking to recapture a taste of primitive joy in life and living; trying to work their way back into that jungle which was the original Garden of Eden; in a word, doing their best to pass for colored." J. W. Johnson, *Along This Way* (New York, 1933), p. 328; quoted by permission of the Viking Press.

cation. A reader of these pages[47] has suggested that the American Negro has much more personal freedom than is possible in a primitive society and that at the same time he gets some benefit from our modern technology. It is in this sense that one may speak of the lower-class Negro culture as parasitic; the Negro is able to indulge extraordinary impulse freedom at the expense of the nervous energy and moral renunciation of the white upper classes. Negro habits of life could not survive in an independent competing society.

It remains to be stressed that the dominant aim of our society seems to be to middle-class-ify all of its members. Negroes, including lower-class Negroes, are no exceptions. Eventually they must all enter the competition for higher status which is so basic and compulsive an element in our way of life. This will mean giving up their "gains" and approximating more nearly the ideal of restraint, independence, and personal maturity which is implicitly attached to our demands for individual competition and mobility.

[47] Professor Maurice R. Davie, of Yale University.

CHAPTER XVIII

Caste Symbolism: Race Prejudice

〰〰〰〰〰〰〰〰〰〰〰〰〰〰〰〰〰〰〰〰〰

It is useful to assume that the institutions of a given society are related. One is often deceived on this score by a technique of cultural analysis which separates patterns and institutions according to conventional methods. Although convenient, and sometimes indispensable, this technical device does a certain violence to the realities of the social life. However far apart on the pages of a research monograph the descriptions of the "family" and "caste" may appear, in the personalities and lives of the Negroes they are intimately related. The individual Negro is not a social analyst, but a person living his culture with all possible unity and consistency. Since we are concerned here with the way in which affects are patterned by social organization, we will be interested to see how attitudes generated in the family situation are carried over to caste. It is not a question of historical analysis, but rather of how the child coming into the group relates various social forms from the emotional standpoint.

The idea of the paternal rôle of the king and noble class is familiar even in recent modern history, and it is equally striking how regularly terms drawn from family discourse appear in reference to wider social institutions; some such terms are the "Little Father" of all the Russians, "the family of nations," "the Holy Father," and the democratic notion of "brotherhood of man." It seems an inevitable assumption that such figures of speech are intended to evoke for the wider institutions the potent responses and attitudes which have existed toward family members in childhood. They are the simplest and most accessible of images and are intended to make the impersonal institutions seem familiar and eternal as the parents do to the child. Since the monogamous patriarchal family is the prime character-forming agent in our society, it is from this unit that symbolisms are derived rather than from the sib, clan, or other type of grouping.

These considerations cast a new light on the very common statement of southern white people that Negroes are "like children." The observation has often been recorded.[1] It is said that like children they are irresponsible, pleasure-loving, and easily distracted.[2] We have already considered these statements both from the standpoints of their defensive value for the white caste and of their significance as character manifestations in Negroes. It is often said that like children Negroes do not own anything and do not have the surging acquisitiveness of middle-class adults. We may note also that they are expected to be obedient without question and to omit all defiant reactions; as in the case of children, their elders and betters know what is good for them. Negroes are called by their first names without respect to their wishes, as are children. They are patronized and much ir-

---

[1] "The mind of the Negro can best be understood by likening it to that of a child. For instance, the Negro lives in the present, his interests are objective, and his actions are governed by his emotions." Jerome Dowd, *The Negro in American Life* (New York, 1926), p. 401; quoted by permission of the D. Appleton-Century Co.

[2] "It appears that the negro mind does not dwell upon unpleasant subjects; he is irresponsible, unthinking, easily aroused to happiness, and his unhappiness is transitory, disappearing as a child's when other interests attract his attention. He is happy-go-lucky not philosophical. His peculiar mental attitude is not the result of a knowledge that his poverty, his social position, his unhealthy and cheerless surroundings cannot be bettered, therefore are to be borne cheerfully; but that of a simple nature which gives little thought to the future and desires only the gratification of the present. Responsibility is accepted thoughtlessly and as readily laid aside, its weight is not felt nor does it occasion any anxiety. The simplest amusements distract him, and he gains pleasure from occasions which should rather give rise to sadness. Depression is rarely encountered even under circumstances in which a white person would be overwhelmed by it." E. M. Green, "Psychoses Among Negroes: A Comparative Study," *J. Nerv. and Ment. Dis.* (1914), Vol. 41, p. 703.

rational behavior is tolerated from them (remember the lenient attitude of the courts) which would be vigorously suppressed in white adults. A childlike deference of the "Honor Thy Father and Thy Mother" type is required.[3] Negroes, like children, are said to have no care for the future and, were the parental solicitude of adults withdrawn, they would be helpless. Children are looked upon as amoral and not fully responsive to adult moral standards; the same view is frequently taken of the Negro. Many jokes are told about both children and Negroes because they do not speak correctly or understand adult limitations on impulse; in both cases the superiors get obvious pleasure from identifying themselves with their less acculturated "children." In both cases again the parents or parental caste exhibit a marked sense of possession and superiority toward the inferiors, children or Negroes, and corresponding responsibilities toward them are assumed. It may also be said that a "full humanity" or "full personality" is denied to Negroes and children; both are expected to reconcile themselves to a smaller portion because they are not yet grown-up. These correspondences are too pat to be accidental, and it may be fairly stated that the white caste feels itself in a symbolic parental relationship to Negroes. There is, however, one major difference between Negroes and children, viz., Negroes have adult rather than child bodies. The parental caste, therefore, though it attempts to handle and treat them like children, also fears them because with their grown-up bodies they are thought to have the lack of discipline characteristic of young children. It is one thing to treat an actual child as parents do and quite another to treat an adult in the same way. In response to this difference there arises the vigorous aggressive control by the white caste which has already been discussed, a feature unnecessary in dealing with the relatively impotent child. Parents seem to react quite correctly with punishment to the hostile fantasies of children, fantasies which would be

[3] Obviously I am not thinking here of the "experimental" parents of the advanced middle-class white group who are making various modifications of traditional practice.

so dangerous to the grownups if the children could put them into effect. We cannot fail to notice also that in many cases the mulattoes are actual children or relatives of their white-caste superiors and in some cases they know of this relationship.

It is, of course, characteristic of the parental status that the elders have prerogatives denied to the child, but that along with these prerogatives they have duties and responsibilities absent in child life. The middle-class white people recognize these responsibilities and describe them as "taking care of" their Negroes. From the lower-class Negro side the same relationship is seen as having a white patron.[4] It is well known from the study of family relations that aggressive responses are suppressed within the family group for the sake of unity and peace. We have observed a similar process at work between the castes, i.e., suppression of Negro hostility toward the white caste and the taking up of accommodation attitudes. Very likely we have too little emphasized the strength of such attitudes among lower-class Negroes. Negro informants stress that lower-class Negroes often idolize the planters and their power and take much the attitude of the weak, small boy who claims, "My father can whip your father." The Negroes feel satisfaction in the size of the plantation and the wealth of the planter; one informant described their attitudes toward a particular planter as close to worship. These are powerful bindings in the family and between the castes, because through them the less competent and efficient, Negro or child, gains a sense of power which he cannot achieve in his own person. As we have pointed out, the Negro often sees "the furnish"

---

[4] "For those still living in the county there is, it would appear, one unfailing rule of life. If they would get along with least difficulty, they should get for themselves a protecting white family. 'We have mighty good white folks friends, and ef you have white folks for your friends, dey can't do you no harm.' . . . Nor should it be supposed that all of this dependence upon the whites is based upon fear. There is a solid and sympathetic paternalism among some of the white planters toward their Negro dependents which is felt by them." C. S. Johnson, *Shadow of the Plantation* (Chicago, 1934), p. 27; quoted by permission of the University of Chicago Press.

symbolically as a parental gift, while his work afterward is the binding duty of support to the providing parent. The analogy between this and the actual child-parent relationship is obvious. This parent-child symbol between the castes is one of the strongest barriers which a real economic democracy in the South would have to face. Very probably the caste institution could only be broken up when "brother" identifications with other Negroes, and perhaps whites, were substituted for the passive idealization of the "father"-planter and boss.

This aristocratic paternal relationship is, of course, not confined to relations between the castes, although it is most clear-cut and conspicuous there. It has also been observed in the white mill towns of the South,[5] at least in the developmental phase of the cotton industry. The pattern seems to have been transferred entire from the patriarchal plantation to the field of factory labor.[6] Such bindings are of enormous force in maintaining the social order and continuing it without change.

A speculation which might be of considerable interest is the nature of the taboo placed on sexual contact between Negro men and white women. Even the thought of such a relationship evokes so much horror in the white man that one suspects that it must be deeply supported emotionally in his own life history. It is the unutterable crime and is

[5] Harriett L. Herring, _Welfare Work in Mill Villages_ (Chapel Hill, 1929), p. 217.

[6] "The employers in the cotton-mill South come by their superiority complex quite as naturally. Historically, they are aristocrats. The first mill builders, who rescued the post-Civil War South from the poverty of a disrupted agricultural system, were men of family or position, often of both. The fact that they alone had plans and the contrivance to carry them out, would in itself have marked them as figures of distinction. They supplied the essential boon for a broken people—the opportunity to work. The reward they reaped was adoration. If anything were needed to clinch their position, it was furnished in the response of the common people to their complete paternalism. I use the word in its pure sense. It was fatherhood." Broadus Mitchell and G. S. Mitchell, _The Industrial Revolution in the South_ (Baltimore, 1930), pp. 147-148; quoted by permission of the Johns Hopkins Press.

felt fully to justify even the unprintable mutilations occasionally wrought on its Negro perpetrator. The only serviceable analogy that comes to mind is that such a relationship is perceived as a violation of the incest taboo, that the white woman occupies toward the Negro the same utterly inaccessible rôle that the white mother does to her white son. As a result of the intimacy of family bindings the most bitter revengeful tendencies can be generated around the incestuous affections. Is it not likely that the antagonism of the white boy against his mother-profaning male parent is directed toward the Negro man who dares to approach a white woman? From this standpoint every sexual contact is a rape and every woman in need of defense from such contact. Certainly every effort is made to place the white woman before the Negro in the same "holy" light in which the mother appears to the son.[7] In venturing this explanation we must remember what a peculiar state of affairs is to be explained and how bizarre the white attitude toward the rape problem seems; and we grant that some potent, but not very obvious, explanation is required. The comparison with the incest taboo corresponds to the rest of the paternal-filial symbolism just described.

These considerations throw a new light on "whiteness." It becomes the symbol of personal maturity and dignity. The white man is the one who has really grown up and is himself capable of taking the parental rôle. Aspects of the rôle of the grown-up person are prestige, privilege, and responsibility, as compared with the rôles of children. While the whites often say that the Negroes are like children,

[7] "I answer that our freedom from this curse is merely incidental to the general relations obtaining between the races, and properly ascribable to the general station and character of the white population, to the persistence of the same relative status between the masses of the two races that existed when the one was master and the other slave. Then the Negro was bred to absolute obedience, made to respect the white race because it was white, taught that the person, even the name, of the humblest white woman was something not to be profaned by touch or word or thought." A. H. Stone, *Studies in the American Race Problem* (New York, 1908), pp. 94-95; quoted by permission of Doubleday, Doran & Co.

they do not say that they themselves are like parents, stern and loving parents who claim the prerogatives of that status. A caste system, as compared with a true democracy, is a categorical barrier on growing up; an equivalent statement from the sociological point of view is that a caste system is a categorical barrier to social mobility. There is one very important difference between the Negro and the child. The inferior status of the white child is temporary and the hope of personal maturity is present, sure and strong; with the Negro the status of the child is confirmed and chronic, and there is no hope of escaping it. One might say, good-naturedly, that, if the lower-class Negroes are "like children," the middle-class and mulatto Negroes are like adolescents, halfway to the adult status. Power, prestige, and mastery are the prime values of our society, and they are therefore automatically the goals of the completely mature person. Control of money is the conventional route to such status advancement.

Lower-class Negroes are not always so childlike, in fact, as their social rôle would make them out to be. A statement of his social rôle always indicates what is desired of the individual, but not always what is delivered by him. The deference, subservience, and dependence of the lower-class Negro are often a social mask which he wears because he must and which conceals a well-fibered character capable of assuming adult status, did the social organization permit.[8] Some children are like that too, formed and hard-

[8] "The patience of the Negro, his persistent good humour under the most trying circumstances, his meekness in contrast to the fierce resentment of the Indian, his apparent passivity under the white man's abuse and domineering, have led many to think the Negro to be careless, indifferent, and spiritless, incapable of any serious reflection upon the issues of life, and habitually of that state of mind described by the phrase 'happy-go-lucky.' In this they are deceived, not by any intention of the Negro, but by their ignorance of the Negro's psychology and the Negro's wholly intentional secretiveness. In so far as the Negro has revealed himself to the average white man there is sufficient justification for thinking him indifferent and passive, even spiritless; but closer acquaintance soon discloses that the Negro is thoroughly alert to all that goes on around him." R. R. Moton, *What the Negro Thinks* (Garden City, N. Y.,

ened with a mature psychic structure, while to all intents and purposes they play the social rôles of children.

We turn now to the mysterious but much discussed theme of race prejudice. In describing caste distinctions we have already indicated the factual material related to prejudice against Negroes. The major consideration seems to be that it is a defensive attitude intended to preserve white prerogatives in the caste situation and aggressively to resist any pressure from the Negro side to change his inferior position. There has been much consideration of the problem by various writers. Young[9] lists "visibility" of the Negro, either physical or cultural, competition between whites and Negroes, and the traditional low position of minority groups as factors in such prejudice. Others stress what might be called the narcissistic theory of race prejudice, i.e., that it is a reaction of hostility toward persons unlike us in feature or culture.[10] Still another emphasizes the idea that "blackness" has a bad name in Western European society and tends to be associated with the devil or witchcraft.[11] Many students emphasize that race prejudice is widespread and inevitable[12] and that very often disclaimers are merely conscious rationalizations of the commonly felt attitudes.

From the standpoint of personality study, race prejudice seems to be a denial of complete humanity to some person or group. It is easy to surmise hostile or negative attitudes in the out-group and to overlook the fact that it too is bound by moral feelings and restrictions. The person against whom we are prejudiced never has complete human status

---

1932), pp. 63-64; quoted by permission of Doubleday, Doran & Co.

[9] Donald Young, *American Minority Peoples* (New York, 1932), p. 589.

[10] Edwin R. Embree, *Brown America* (New York, 1931), p. 199; also E. B. Reuter, *The Mulatto in the United States* (Boston, 1918), p. 168.

[11] Owen Berkeley-Hill, "The 'Color Question' from a Psychoanalytic Standpoint," *Psychoanal. Rev.* (1924), XI, 249.

[12] Reuter, *op. cit.*, p. 319.

in our eyes and is always felt in some manner to be a brute, trickster, or an enemy. It is, of course, well known that such feelings are not pinned alone to physical characteristics, but may also be attached to cultural differences,[13] although it is questionable whether the term "race" prejudice should be used in this case.

In the case of the Negro such prejudice centers around the physical features which permit him to be marked off as a caste man. Its function is to keep the Negro in his caste position and it is therefore to be viewed as a defensive-aggressive measure on the part of the white caste. White prejudice is said constantly to be incited by "outrages" committed by the lower-caste group. These "outrages" usually consist of some claim for equality which is perceived as aggressive by the upper caste. Behavior which would be unobjectionable in an upper-caste member is often perceived as outrageously contumacious when done by a lower-caste man. In sum, the fact seems to be that aggression from those against whom we are prejudiced (hostile) is disproportionately felt. Race prejudice is sometimes said to be "caught" out of the social atmosphere; but the tendency to derogate others must be present from the outset and it is merely systematized and given an object and a social excuse when the person comes into the formal circle of race prejudice attitudes. Persons with little need to prop self-esteem through the pain and humiliation of others may participate in formal prejudice patterns, but they will participate without much affect and as a mere convention.

It seems again, in the case of race prejudice, that our formal cultural explanations do not really satisfy, although they account for the event well enough in their own terms. Race prejudice is an emotional fact and must be connected with the rest of the emotional life of each individual who experiences it. In the attempt to add something to the perception of our problem, several factors must be considered. The first is the life history of the individual. We must re-

---

[13] Van Buren exhibits a characteristically prejudiced attitude toward the Irishmen he saw in the South. *See* A. de Puy Van Buren, *Jottings of a Year's Sojourn in the South* (Battle Creek, Mich., 1859), p. 318.

member that the taking on of culture forms is not such a smooth process as it often seems. Culture means renunciation of impulse freedom as well as expression and this renunciation is uniformly perceived as a frustration. Frustration is experienced in connection with all the simplest limitations placed on the freedom of the child, in such matters, for example, as weaning or cleanliness training, and in the prohibitions placed on running or walking, on talking, on revenge, and on the hopeless love aspirations of the child. The character of the grown-up person is a record of these frustrations and the reactions to them. We know also that, when frustration is experienced, there is uniformly called into action an aggressive tendency whose object is to restore the gratifying state of affairs or master the gratifying object. For the most part, however, this aggression is useless since the small child faces the bulwarked might of the society which is immune to his attacks. The result is that probably every mature person carries some generalized hostility toward the milieu, a hostility which cannot find a legitimate object on which it may be vented. It is suggested that, when society does indicate an object, like the Negro whom one may detest with a good conscience, much of this irrational affect is drained off. Something like this has apparently been suspected by other researchers.[14]

The above is a generalized factor which will be present in all individuals on the basis of life experience, although by no means with equal strength since different individuals are frustrated in different degrees and are therefore aggressive in different degrees. A further explanation which would account for the reasonless aggression manifested in race prejudice derives from the daily life of adult people. It runs as follows: we all tend to overestimate the sympathy and comity present in personal relationships and we are all

[14]"Undoubtedly the facts of profoundest significance for the understanding of the phenomena of race friction in American democracy are those connected with the genesis and growth of personality." J. M. Mecklin, *Democracy and Race Friction* (New York, 1914), p. 10; quoted by permission of The Macmillan Co.

taught to disavow so far as possible hostile motives toward those we love. As a result, the amount of hostility engendered by daily life experience is altogether underestimated. For example, professional and business rivalries may give rise to intense resentment against colleagues which one dare not express. The daily humiliations of an insurance agent may leave a psyche boiling with unsuitable hostility. The normal routine of life is limiting to all and exceedingly irritating to many. Monogamous institutions are certainly perceived by large numbers of individuals as a chronic frustration situation. Changes of a national character, like defeat in war or attacks on one's social class, may be felt as frustrations by great numbers of persons. Here again are the sources of considerable hostility which may not be expressed against the actually exciting objects. When a particular group such as Negroes are designated by our society as objects who may legitimately be despised, the fact is very likely to be welcome to many hard-pressed individuals; social disapproval on aggression is so common and the loopholes so few that it is a case of any target in a storm. This is plainly only a more detailed account of the value of the out-group in helping to maintain sympathy and coöperation within the "we-group". Just because we underestimate the frustrating character of daily life and the annoyance we experience at these frustrations do we find race prejudice so mysterious. Our hypothesis is that in the case of race prejudice these vague aggressions are centered on the target of prejudice and are there expressively released. If this be true, one may say that a lower caste is of particular value to a society in case a suitable target for out-group hostility is either not available or too dangerous to attack. Our puzzlement about race prejudice is an aspect of our unrealistic perception of the nature of our immediate social relationships; we deny appropriate aggression in them and experience it spurtling out through the socially permitted derogation of the inferior group. The "visibility" of the Negro in this case is the sign that tells the prejudiced person whom to hate and makes easy and consistent discrimination possible. Real competition gives an added reason for hostility and exploitation of the group against which one is prejudiced and adds a fear of retaliation to the picture.[15]

The matter could be summarized somewhat as follows: cultural restrictions in childhood and the limitations of daily life in adulthood provide numerous frustrations for every individual; hostility is aroused in response to these frustrations. If expressed, this hostility would tend to break up in-group solidarity; so it is systematically discouraged and suppressed. One of the methods of discouragement is to pretend that such hostility does not exist. Though repressed it is not extirpated but utilizes such permissive social formations as race prejudice traditions to vent itself safely on an object. Race prejudice is mysterious because no real occasion is required for its expression; the object does not necessarily have to offend or frustrate. On the contrary there are deflected to the object against which one is prejudiced the hostilities that should be directed toward nearer and dearer persons. Our conception works with three key concepts. First a generalized or "free-floating" aggression which is derived from reactions to frustration and suppression within the "we-group." It can be thought of as a tendency to kick, hit, scorn, or derogate someone or something if one could only find out what. A second necessity is that of a permissive social pattern. This must exist in order to lift the in-group taboos on hostility. The permissive pattern iso-

---

[15] The discriminating research of Horowitz provides an important confirmation of our theory since he shows it is not actual contact, i.e., real reason for hating the Negro, which is efficient, but rather contact with the tradition of race prejudice which is effective in producing the phenomenon. It is clear that there is a strong emotional disposition, in this case, hostility, which makes use of the permissive tradition. Horowitz writes: "Young children were found to be not devoid of prejudice; contact with a 'nice' Negro is not a universal panacea; living as neighbors, going to a common school, were found to be insufficient; Northern children were found to differ very, very slightly from Southern children. It seems that attitudes toward Negroes are now chiefly determined not by contact with Negroes, but by contact with the prevalent attitude toward Negroes." Eugene L. Horowitz, "The Development of Attitude toward the Negro," *Arch. Psychol.* (Jan., 1936), No. 194, pp. 34-35.

lates a group within the society which may be disliked. Usually it is a defenseless group. In the South the caste rôle of the Negro is the pattern which permits white people systematically to derogate him. The permissive pattern often comes down from earlier days, although it can also be invented on the spot or by analogy with a group against which one is already prejudiced. The third essential in race prejudice is that the object must be uniformly identifiable. We have to be able to recognize those whom we may dislike. This stipulation is met by the physical or cultural marks which make the object of race prejudice "visible." In our sense race prejudice is always irrational; if antagonism can be sufficiently explained by real, personal, or social rivalry we do not talk of "prejudice." There are, of course, other ways of utilizing or managing the aggression which can be expressed in prejudice against a minority group; they include, for example, using it for constructive alteration of real life conditions, through the war pattern, or by turning it on the self as in neurosis.

APPENDIX

Life History of Middle-Class Negroes[1]

It is most important to attempt to view the caste and class structure of Southerntown from the angle of a human being born in the town and gradually assimilating the culture and finding his rôle in the social scheme. This perspective is possible only in the life history. A complete research will require life histories for Negroes and white people of both lower and middle classes. Without such materials, indeed, the research as it stands must be confessed incomplete. It was possible to do only one part of this task during the time available. A number of histories, as has been indicated, were secured from middle-class Negroes, and these have served to vitalize all of the material gained by less intensive methods. It is because of these life histories that we have any insight at all into the dynamics of the class and caste structure. Unfortunately they cannot be presented in full for reasons already given, but it seems fair to suggest some of the findings which emerge upon surveying the documents, even though the linear material is not given.

One methodological point became quite clear. The use of the daily interview provided a wide-open window on the social life of Southerntown, although its alleged purpose was to study the mental life of the subject. One could not avoid hearing from each coöperator a report of the events and attitudes toward them which were shared by other people. This informal report was particularly valuable since the subject was not acting as a conscious informant but was merely talking about himself and what interested

[1] This material has been placed in an appendix because it is really a separate theme which does not follow the main logical outline of the book. It should be expanded into a volume of its own; perhaps in the future this may be possible.

him; the result was that community processes could be seen with more intimacy and naturalness than if a method of formal questioning had been used. The most useful material in the foregoing discussion has been excerpted from the life histories. It was also true that in daily interviewing, using a greatly modified psychoanalytic technique, the subject's bias in reporting on other people and their actions could be observed; in this way I could learn to evaluate the social data much more accurately than if the interview relationship had been superficial or defensive. It was also possible by the same method to see the institutional forces at work in the informant and to observe with clarity the impulse life of the subject operating against and through the conventional action patterns. The socialized person gives a picture in miniature of his society and possesses in some degree or other all of its main features; his language, fears, fantasy, ambitions, dreams, and frustrations are records of interaction with his society. A skewed outline of the culture derived from any one person can be corrected by studies of others; there will doubtless be found main patterns for the total society and subpatterns for the subgrouping to which an individual belongs.

One sees clearly in the life-history material how class and caste position set limits for the personal development of the individual Negro or white person; they do not determine it absolutely in detail since the culture is never the mechanically perfect instrument which our concepts make it seem. As will be shown later, different personality types among Negroes will "take" the caste situation in different ways, although the limits of difference are narrow. For example, one Negro man may resist the caste pattern quite effectually; another, as an adult, may be well suited to it psychically and will find it just the type of social form which is most expressive for him. Heretofore we have tried to give a more or less standardized description of the kinds of reactions that class and caste positions *tend* to elicit from Negro and white individuals in these positions; now we will take up the question of differences in those reactions to a stereotyped social rôle.

Life-history materials on middle-class Negroes show, if

any showing be needed, how completely false is the de-humanized conception of the Negro.[2] Negro personalities are fully implemented with all recognizable human reactions; to list a few of them, courage, cunning, slyness, humor, pity, loyalty, guilt, jealousy, and vengefulness. Negroes have memories of their ancestors, have friends, hopes for their children, write letters, and, in the case of the middle-class group, plan for the future. The interviewing situation and the trusting relationship that can develop where there is an exchange of information and sympathy reveal much that is not normally known to white people at all.

There is a particular advantage in studying middle-class Negroes first in getting a view of the Negro caste. From them one can see both ways, back to the lower-class position they have come from and forward to the full human status they aspire to but cannot reach. A number of my best informants began life in plantation Negro families and knew firsthand the behavior of the lower-class group; they bore within themselves the record of their social mobility and there was clear evidence of the setting up of middle-class limitations on the impulse freedom which they had seen around themselves as children. These Negroes stand, in effect, beating at the caste barrier, competent and disciplined in the sense desired by our society but categorically debarred from full status. They see very clearly what the white people have that they want but do not have. We already know that it is erroneous to attribute middle-class characteristics to lower-class Negroes;[3] but, when properly

---

[2] "In a general sort of way the Southerner does understand the Negro, but this understanding is limited almost completely to the practical affairs of life, and consists chiefly in knowing how to make the Negro work. Regarding the feelings, emotions, and the spiritual life of the Negro the average white man knows little." N. N. Puckett, *Folk Beliefs of the Southern Negro* (Chapel Hill, 1926), p. vii; quoted by permission of the University of North Carolina Press.

[3] "It would of course be committing the psychologist's fallacy upon a gigantic scale to read the ideas of *The Souls of Black Folk* into the minds of the masses of the negroes of the South, and yet it doubtless voices the feelings of a cultured few largely of the mulatto class." J. M. Mecklin, *Democracy*

understood, the studies of middle-class persons can be most instructive with regard to the lower-class culture.

It is unmistakable that middle-class Negroes have different conceptions of their rôles from lower-class Negroes, and that these conceptions are nearer to the dominant American middle-class pattern. It would require the actual life-history material itself to show that there are unconscious as well as conscious elements in this "conception" of the rôle, though perhaps the term should be limited to the person's conscious understanding of what others expect from him. If it is so limited, however, it becomes a quite partial instrument of analysis. We might ask if any person conceives of himself as he really is or responds to others as they expect him to.

There were both middle- and lower-class Negro informants who accepted the interviewing situation. The middle-class Negroes were interested from a professional standpoint in what they might learn about their own personalities and those of others. Interviewer and informant sat in chairs beside a table, looked where they would, or out the window, but not necessarily at one another, unless a direct response was desired. The interviewer put the burden of the conversation on the informant, allowed him to pursue the discussion of his own life in any way that he would, and made little attempt to interpret or organize the material of the subject's life; it was about the same sort of experience one would have in the exploratory period of an analysis. There was no effort to arouse resistance or interpret unconscious material, as would necessarily be the case in an analysis. It was a somewhat freer conversation than one would ordinarily have and was as little guided as possible. In all my informants the Negro blood was vastly predominant over a white strain, although there was evidence of white blood in all the middle-class Negroes; it was, however, in no case nearer than a grandfather and entered in most cases in the great-grandparents' generation.[4] Class membership, how-

---

and Race Friction (New York, 1914), p. 155; quoted by permission of The Macmillan Co.

[4] "In any study and discussion of the race problem, scientific accuracy as well as a decent regard for simple truth requires

ever, rather than attitudes toward white blood, seemed to
be dominant in determining character.

However it may be among lower-class Negroes, in the
life histories of the middle-class group the father plays a
considerable rôle and the mother does not seem to play a
disproportionately important rôle, although her influence is
always great in our family type. The father seems to appear
regularly as disciplinarian and as one who stresses restrictive aspects of the culture. It is very likely that families
whose children emerge into the middle class have already
a tradition and discipline which is superior to the mine run
of lower-class Negroes, and, further, that the family form
tends to approximate the white patriarchal type. If extensive histories of lower-class Negroes were gathered in
Southerntown and county, it seems very likely that the rôle
of the mother would emerge much more strongly and that
of the father less strongly than in the middle-class group.
This would be consonant with the discussion of family type
among Negroes made by Frazier, to whom reference has
already been made.

It surprised me a little, though it should not have, to
note that the racial attitudes of adult Negroes are derived
from the basic character-forming process in the Negro
family. They tend to "take" the racial situation as adults
according to the personality structure they have developed
within family life. Without reflection, it had seemed that it
might be otherwise; that, for example, a Negro child would
react directly to the caste situation and to his adult experience with the race problem. This did not seem to be the
case; the discussion of adult racial attitudes always ended
in a discussion of attitudes toward parents and siblings.
The Negro child, like the white child, sees at first only
"parents," and the caste or color point is not an important

---

that the writer indicate whether his discussion has to do with
full-blooded Negroes or with the men of mixed blood. The
failure to make this simple and elementary distinction, more
than any other one thing, has made the vast bulk of the literature relating to the Negro in America either worthless or
vicious." E. B. Reuter, *The Mulatto in the United States* (Boston, 1918), p. 397; quoted by permission of Richard G. Badger.

differentiating issue. What the parents do and how the child reacts to them determine the basic attitudes, and these are later transposed to the racial situation. The passive Negro in adult interracial contacts is the one who has developed this technique for getting along with his own Negro parents; it is his way of reacting to deprivation by authority. In the life-history material the first memories of color seemed to center around overhearing the gossip and talk of adults. This talk usually related to racial "incidents," the bad lot of the Negro, and so on. Sometimes the presence of lighter children in the family would call attention in a preliminary way to the color problem and the darker ones would watch them carefully for signs of snobbishness. But even here the problem seemed to be a special case of sibling jealousy over parental favoritism and really not the caste issue as the adult Negro must face it. The race issue can be faced only after the more fundamental family problems have been solved.[5]

It would seem from our histories that Negro children are likely to be exposed vigorously to a knowledge of death, birth, parental sexual relations, and violence. This was especially true of those informants who came from the lower class. Such children are also more likely to have the responsibility for younger siblings, especially in the case of girls. It seems probable that the process of social sophistication is speeded up in these children as a result of their exposure to important life events.

Another finding which could easily be anticipated is the fact that my Negro informants seemed to face the racial situation in accordance with their character types; that is,

---

[5] "Neither my father nor mother had taught me directly anything about race. Naturally, I gained some impressions and picked up some information. Many things I would have learned much sooner had I not been restricted in play. My vague, early impressions constituted what might be called an unconscious race-superiority complex. All the most interesting things that came under my observation were being done by colored men. They drove the horse and mule teams, they built the houses, they laid the bricks, they painted the buildings and fences, they loaded and unloaded the ships." J. W. Johnson, *Along This Way* (New York, 1933), p. 31; quoted by permission of the Viking Press.

their character traits as judged by other Negroes seemed to be consistent with those they exhibited in the interracial situation. One informant, for example, was a leader among Negroes, stout-hearted, righteous, determined, and honest. He was constantly relied upon among Negroes for just these qualities. At the same time he was the informant who presented the boldest face against white-caste intimidation and who pressed the situation to its limit. He never yielded a step short of the threat of serious danger to himself or others; he refused to anticipate intimidations; he had actually to see them. A second informant was recessive and retiring in relations with other Negroes, an amiable person, but with very few friends or contacts. He preferred to work by himself and secured a position which gave him this opportunity. He was not frightened by others but rather made it a habit to avoid contact with them. His behavior in the caste situation was exactly the same. Whenever possible, he avoided white people, wrote letters instead of seeing them personally, was not disproportionately frightened in the case of real danger, but always avoided the occasions of danger. It would take the full life-history material to reveal the character of this man sufficiently to show how consistent his behavior actually was in the racial situation. Another informant had a character much suspected by fellow Negroes. He was boastful and arrogant with them, but at the same time not a dependable person. In cases of actual conflict with other Negroes he would show fear after a preliminary threatening or arrogant attitude. Needless to say, he was not trusted. In his behavior with whites his attitude was submissive and dependent; if given a little rope and relieved of his fear, he might become arrogant, but he would speedily retreat in the face of pressure from the white side. His overdocility was welcomed by his white friends; but it did not increase their trust of him and it seemed that he was actually despised by many of the people for whom he played the sycophant. A fourth informant was characterized by a very formal personality, affectless and compulsive. She was well liked by other Negroes, but no one appeared to be really close to her and she tended to have acquaintances rather than warm friends. In dealing with white people she appeared inert and managed to thin out her reactions, so that she was neither very much injured by white condescension nor very resentful. She went her own way in dealing with whites as in her life within her caste. In spite of the more or less uniform front of accommodation which Negroes have to put up to the white caste, they are individuated and distinguishable from one another; and these rôles, their true personalities, are the ones also recognized among their Negro friends.

Life-history material from middle-class Negroes is little different from the similar reports of middle-class white people in the North. This is what one would expect since the social ideals which beckon to the two groups are so similar. Frustrations, aggression, compensations for these in the form of substitute gratification, and the whole host of psychological dynamisms can be illustrated as well from Negro as from white. There does not seem to be anything new in principle to be learned from middle-class Negroes. Their dilemmas are the ones which individuals face over our whole Western European culture area. One might say that middle-class Negroes, at least, are "white" in their life histories.

It would be very remarkable, however, if there were not some traces of lower-class Negro culture in middle-class people, and these indeed can be found. They are not important distinguishing marks but rather incidentally interesting ones. One of these attitudes is a widespread belief in the predictive character of dreams, a very obvious pattern in lower-class Negroes. My informants tended also to have some modern sophistication on the subject of dreams gained from the popular magazines treating psychological subjects; this knowledge usually amounted to the assumption that dreams were more important than people ordinarily thought and served rather as a confirmation of the lower-class belief than as an acceptance of Freud's dream theory. A few dreams will be reported here, but only the most obvious characteristics of them will be discussed because it would require the actual context of the life history to interpret the unconscious forces operating in these dreams. We cannot agree with Lind[6] that middle-class Negro dreams represent simple wish fulfilments; they seem, on the contrary, to be quite as elaborated and disguised as dreams of white middle-class adults. Repeatedly illustrated in the material was the conviction that dreams have a diagnostic character with regard to the future of the dreamer. For example, a woman reported a dream that she had in 1916, just before America entered the War. She saw in the sky a great solid band of blood, then a sea with ships on it and on the ships Negro soldier boys dressed in khaki. One of her brothers was on a ship. A volley of bullets was moving toward the ships and struck them and as the bullets hit, the ships began to sink. The subject then woke up. Informant believed that this dream did have a predictive significance; and actually the brother in question got into an army camp during the War, although he did not go to France. It was not until after the War that she recalled the dream. This "remembering after the event" is quite frequent in these dreams. Repeatedly also aggressive wishes come to the fore as they do in this dream.

Another informant told me that about a year before the death of her father she had a dream about it, which predicted some things pretty exactly, such as the place where he was to be buried and the little tree standing at the foot of his grave. This dream was also remembered with increased vividness after the actual death of the father.

Another informant told me that he dreamed repeatedly about eating meat and said it was a common belief among his people that to dream of eating meat meant death or bad luck.[7] This man seemed to have an ominous sense that evil

[6] "If we accept unreservedly Freud's dream theory, especially the essence of it, that a dream represents a wish fulfilment and that wherever it is not immediately recognized as such, the activities of the censor are responsible, we must admit that the colored race fails to show this distorting activity; consequently their psychological activities are analogous with those of the child, and investigation of them might prove of considerable value in studying the genesis of the psychoses." J. E. Lind, "The Dream as a Simple Wish Fulfilment in the Negro," *Psychoanal. Rev.* (1913-14), I, 300.

[7] "A dream of fresh meat signalizes death. This is especially

was hanging over him, and he was anything but the image of the cheerful, happy-go-lucky Negro. One can see how "eating meat" would have an indirect reference to death since the animal must be killed before it is eaten.

Another informant told me how he dreamed about his brother. He and this brother, who had died in recent years, were going out to a peach orchard. They appeared in the dream walking toward the peach trees. He commented that to dream of the dead usually means bad luck and he wondered what would happen. Ominous anticipation of this kind connected with death seemed quite frequent among middle-class informants, perhaps an evidence of the aggression which is so plainly not to be expressed in the actually frustrating caste situation of daily life.

There are, of course, other types of predictive dreams than those relating to death. One informant said that once when he was out of a job he kept dreaming of traveling. Shortly after this he secured a position as a traveling speaker and did actually move about a great deal. The same informant had an often-repeated dream with a possible erotic meaning. He saw a snake that looked like a rag, kind of floppy; when he would look away from it, it would come to life and move. He said that the people in his group believed that snakes meant enemies and it was dangerous to dream of them.[8]

In another case a dream actually served to prevent an

---

true if it is pork that you dream of; a dream of killing hogs indicates a death." Puckett, *op. cit.*, p. 500; quoted by permission of the University of North Carolina Press.

[8] "Without doubt the most widespread dream-sign is that a vision of snakes indicates the presence of an enemy, a fact which might have some significance to that school of psychology which interprets dreams largely as sex symbols. If you fail to kill the dream-snake your enemies are very powerful, but if you kill the serpent you will conquer. The color of the snake, indicates the color of your enemy, though some say that a black snake always represents the devil. In England a nightmare of fighting with and conquering serpents denotes victory over your enemies, but among the Ibos of Africa a dream of snakes also indicates enemies." Puckett, *op. cit.*, pp. 497-498; quoted by permission of the University of North Carolina Press.

elopement. Without the knowledge of any of her family, informant's sister was planning to elope. The night before, her father dreamed that she was going to get married. He asked her mother about it in the morning and the mother said she did not think so. An older sister also had the same dream on the same night. They all watched the suspected sister and she did in fact try to escape from the house to meet the young man. So they made the youth go and ask the father for permission to marry her. When the father saw him coming down the road, he told the young fellow that he already knew about it from the dream. The same informant had a dream in which he anticipated meeting his wife. The dream occurred about a year before he actually met the girl, but he pictured her so clearly that when he first noticed her he knew at once that she was the girl in the dream and the one he wanted to marry. All of these dreams seem to be explicable on the ground either of chance or of retrospective alteration of the dream material. Of course, they all have contextual elements in the present-day mental and social life of the dreamer, as well as in the life history.[9]

The predictive dream is certainly more obvious in the life histories of middle-class Negroes than it is in histories of white persons in the same social class; these beliefs have of course existed in times past among white people but they are not now strikingly in evidence.

There is some evidence also for survivals of superstitious ideas among middle-class Negroes, although again they are not a major element. Superstitious beliefs are steadily disappearing in Southerntown as the rational views put forward by the schools and by our literature become more prevalent. The fear of screens as dangerous because they block out the good air is steadily decreasing according to health officials; but traces of older irrational views of the world are still alive. One informant made a good deal of a "predictive sense" of future events that she had. She told the following incident to illustrate: it was New Year's Eve of her twentieth year and the other students were frolicking and ringing bells, the

[9] Sigmund Freud, *The Interpretation of Dreams* (New York, 1913), pp. 138-259.

boys were serenading the girls, and so on. While all this was going on, it seemed as if a voice spoke to informant and said that someone who was alive now would not be alive next New Year's Eve. This voice seemed to come from outside herself and she turned to see who was speaking. Then she knew instantly that it was an inner voice. About four months later informant was shocked on going home for a visit to find her mother sick in bed. They embraced and laughed and cried, they were so happy to see one another. Four months later the mother died. This kind of a report is intelligible from the cultural standpoint and undoubtedly represents a real psychic experience. To explain it one would obviously need the life-history material.

Another informant illustrated the "Jonah" belief in the following way: he said he had had a lot of family trouble in the last years. Only recently all four of his grandparents had died within a short time. In the spring a younger brother had died. A year ago his sister died in childbirth. He wondered why this flood of troubles had come, if there was a "Jonah," and if he had done something to bring them on. He had asked his father about it and tried to find out what had "jinxed" him. This belief obviously leads over to the theme of witchcraft and would probably be related to other magical beliefs if this informant were a lower-class man. It is clear that he was using the Jonah idea to try to make reasonable the series of frustrations which had been imposed on him and his family through death; instead of reconciling himself to helplessness he took advantage of the Jonah idea that the frustrations were a punishment or that someone else had brought them about. These magical beliefs can be called upon at psychological need and used to make life seem reasonable and tolerable again. Puckett gives a rich store of information on magical beliefs and practices;[10] but in reading it one always has the feeling that the magical acts would be more intelligible if seen in the actual sequence of the individual's life history; one would then see clearly when magical beliefs are invoked and when not, and what psychic needs they serve. In the case above, the

[10] Puckett, *op. cit.*, p. 125.

Jonah idea was obviously used as a defense against a series of painful realities in the life of this informant.

The belief in lucky and unlucky days was noticed in the case of an informant who had to borrow some money and was careful to search out a favorable day on which to do it. In another case Negro carpenters were needed to work on a Negro community house and the committee tried to persuade them to begin work on a particular day which happened to be Friday. All the carpenters refused to begin on Friday, saying it was bad luck.

Apart from these beliefs in predictive dreams, a predictive sense of the future, and some other superstitious hangovers which do not play a great rôle with middle-class Negroes, the materials offered by their life histories are remarkably similar to those of white persons in the North. There was no opportunity during this research to get systematic life-history materials from southern white people of any class, but such materials would be invaluable for testing our dynamic theories of the social structure and for defining the socialization of the individual. It is one of the urgent needs of social psychology to see the life-history problem against the background of class structure and to get life records from persons who are also described from the sociological standpoint.